# Judaism, Race, and Ethics

# DIMYONOT דמיונות

## Jews and the Cultural Imagination

**Samantha Baskind, General Editor**



Volumes in the Dimyonot series explore the intersections, and interstices, of Jewish experience and culture. These projects emerge from many disciplines—including art, history, language, literature, music, religion, philosophy, and cultural studies—and diverse chronological and geographical locations. Each volume, however, interrogates the multiple and evolving representations of Judaism and Jewishness, by both Jews and non-Jews, over time and place.

OTHER TITLES IN THE SERIES:

David Stern, Christoph Markschies, and Sarit Shalev-Eyni, eds., *The Monk's Haggadah: A Fifteenth-Century Illuminated Codex from the Monastery of Tegernsee, with a prologue by Friar Erhard von Pappenheim*

Ranen Omer-Sherman, *Imagining the Kibbutz: Visions of Utopia in Literature and Film*

Jordan D. Finkin, *An Inch or Two of Time: Time and Space in Jewish Modernisms*

Ilan Stavans and Marcelo Brodsky, *Once@9:53am: Terror in Buenos Aires*

Ben Schachter, *Image, Action, and Idea in Contemporary Jewish Art*

Heinrich Heine, *Hebrew Melodies*, trans. Stephen Mitchell and Jack Prelutsky, illus. Mark Podwal

Irene Eber, *Jews in China: Cultural Conversations, Changing Perceptions*

# Judaism, Race, and Ethics

## Conversations and Questions

Edited by Jonathan K. Crane

The Pennsylvania State University Press
University Park, Pennsylvania

Library of Congress Cataloging-in-Publication Data

Names: Crane, Jonathan K. (Jonathan Kadane), editor.
Title: Judaism, race, and ethics : conversations and questions / edited by Jonathan K. Crane.
Other titles: Dimyonot (University Park, Pa.)
Description: University Park, Pennsylvania : The Pennsylvania State University Press, [2020] | Series: Dimyonot: Jews and the cultural imagination series | Includes bibliographical references and index.
Summary: "A collection of essays examining the contentious, dynamic, and ethically complicated relationship between race and religion in Judaism. Includes perspectives from the fields of history, philosophy, sociology, ethics, religious studies, law, psychology, literary studies, and theology"—Provided by publisher.
Identifiers: LCCN 2019058367 | ISBN 9780271085807 (cloth)
Subjects: LCSH: Race—Religious aspects—Judaism. | Racism—Religious aspects—Judaism. | Jewish ethics.
Classification: LCC BM645.R3 J83 2020 | DDC 296.3/8—dc23
LC record available at https://lccn.loc.gov/2019058367


Printed in the United States of America
Published by The Pennsylvania State University Press,
University Park, PA 16802-1003

The Pennsylvania State University Press is a member of the Association of University Presses.

It is the policy of The Pennsylvania State University Press to use acid-free paper. Publications on uncoated stock satisfy the minimum requirements of American National Standard for Information Sciences—Permanence of Paper for Printed Library Material, ANSI Z39.48–1992.

# Contents

# Preface

JONATHAN K. CRANE

In his opening address to the National Conference on Religion and Race in Chicago on January 14, 1963, Abraham Joshua Heschel provocatively challenged the very title of the meeting.

> Religion and race. How can the two be uttered together? To act in the spirit of religion is to unite what lies apart, to remember that humanity as a whole is God's beloved child. To act in the spirit of race is to sunder, to slash, to dismember the flesh of living humanity. Is this the way to honor a father: to torture his child? How can we hear the word "race" and feel no self-reproach? . . .
>
> Perhaps this Conference should have been called "Religion *or* Race." You cannot worship God and at the same time look at man as if he were a horse.[1]

Since they have diametrically opposed impacts on society, it is virtually unintelligible to link religion and race. However much this may be so, it would be ill advised to consider them radically disconnected or as always operating as opposing forces. Indeed, there are as many ways in which religion divides society and race unites as there are ways they mix and mingle categories and communities. Considering race and religion in exclusively disjunctive terms—as either/or—does both a disservice.

To do well by both, then, requires that we consider them simultaneously. It does not mean giving preferential treatment to either one, or putting one before the other sequentially or logically. By examining each in relation with the other, we find that they have a long, complicated, and dynamic relationship. We also realize that they are not perfectly distinct; they overlap in odd and perhaps surprising ways. Theirs is an ethically complex relationship, knotted by long-standing associations, assumptions, and theologies. Disentangling them needs to be done carefully.

The Society of Jewish Ethics hosted its first deliberation on these concerns at its 2014 conference. A panel examined their complex intersection by drawing from fields as diverse as history, philosophy, anthropology, law, and bioethics, as well as from classic and modern Judaic sources, Jewish theology, and Jewish ethics. The original papers presented at the conference stimulated conversations that went well beyond the confines of the panel and keynote lecture. Participants noted the pressing need to better understand Judaism's many conceptualizations of race, the ethical dimensions of constructing concepts of race in the first place, the ways in which race has affected Judaism and (especially) modern American Jewish identity, and the pragmatic issues of relations between Jews and other minority communities.



The Society welcomed the opportunity to continue the conversation. The Tam Institute for Jewish Studies at Emory University offered to host a symposium in the fall of 2015 on the topic of race and Jewish ethics. It brought together the original panelists and added other scholars to the conversation, along with the public. This dynamic two-day symposium increased our appreciation of the complexity of the relationship between race, racism, and religion, and generated enthusiasm about publishing these deliberations.

Few foresaw that the ideas and realities of race, racism, and religion would soon become so emotionally fraught and so hotly debated on a national scale. They became touchstones for political candidates, parties, and communities during the presidential campaign of 2015–16. In those political arenas, however, both religion and race suffered vast oversimplification. Nuance was stripped away in favor of generalization. Charged epithets and verbal abuse replaced civil discussion. The first years of the Trump administration have witnessed a veritable explosion of tension and vitriol about color and religion, racism and anti-Semitism, sometimes degenerating into violence and even fatalities. Such divisiveness demonstrates the pressing necessity that we better understand these complicated topics and lived experiences. The urgent need for the kind of conversation presented in this volume became, it seemed to us, undeniable.

Many institutions and individuals helped make this volume possible. The officers of the Society of Jewish Ethics were prescient in hosting the original panel, and I am grateful for their confidence in the project. The Tam Institute for Jewish Studies at Emory University deserves huge applause for both providing generous funding for the follow-up symposium and generating broad institutional support for, and community participation in, that event. I am indebted in particular to Eric Goldstein for his insightful leadership and to Mary Jo Duncanson for her diligent attention to detail. They helped ensure generous support for the symposium from the Rabbi Jacob M. Rothschild Memorial Endowment Fund and from Emory's Robert E. Hightower Fund, Laney Graduate School, Graduate Division of Religion, and Departments of Anthropology, Religion, and Sociology. The faculty and staff at Emory's Center for Ethics have been unflagging supporters and thoughtful interlocutors throughout this process. I am also thankful for the enthusiasm with which Patrick Alexander at Pennsylvania State University Press received the manuscript. He has guided it to publication with the utmost care.

I thank the contributors to this volume as well. Stellar scholars from many corners of the academy, all have brought unique skills to understanding the intricate ways in which religion and race intersect. Their probity, concern about these issues, and perseverance are unmatched.

For years now, I have explored issues of race and religion with my in-laws, Charles and Nola Miller, who grew up as Jews in apartheid-era South Africa. They readily shared stories about the insidiousness of chauvinism, bigotry, and xenophobia in that society, stories that illustrated how relations between religion and race are anything but simple. Their unwillingness to be complicit in a racist regime and their outspoken solidarity with vulnerable populations inspire me. For all their insight, wisdom, and love, I dedicate this volume to them.

## Note

1. Abraham Joshua Heschel, *The Insecurity of Freedom: Essays on Human Existence* (New York: Schocken Books, 1966), 85–86.

1

# A Colorful, Complicated Conversation

## An Introduction

JONATHAN K. CRANE

Imagine a course on color that appreciates color from different disciplines and perspectives. Physics displays the broad array of wavelengths constituting the visible spectrum. Botany demonstrates how plants transform many kinds of light into usable energy and in the process burst with colors. Physiology dissects how eyes receive colors, and neurobiology unpacks how brains perceive them. Art history exhibits how certain colors are differently revered and used across human time and space. Literature similarly unspools colorful stories. Such conversations dig into aesthetics, considerations of what people think is beautiful and what not. History, sociology, and anthropology observe and describe how communities enact those notions of beauty and value. Economics, political science, and law operationalize and legislate color preferences. Philosophy and theology explain and justify those biases.

This multidimensional course would, if nothing else, uncover the fact that colors are hardly flat, superficial, or static. Especially in the human arena, colors are multifaceted and dynamic. Because we ascribe values to them, and especially because one group may value a particular color while another community may not, colors are ethically fraught. To compound matters, their values often shift over time.

Consider, for example, how two colors—say, white and black—are spoken of in religion and specifically in the Bible. According to biblical sources, neither color is used to describe people's congenital skin. If they are linked to skin at all, biblical texts invariably refer to some temporary condition. Skin color is contingent and superficial rather than an inherent quality.

For example, white is most often associated in the Bible with disease and infection (e.g., Leviticus 13). Though white indicates ritual impurity, it does not mean that a person whose infection has white in it is eternally impure and thus forever excluded from religious practices or the community at large. Miriam, sister of Moses and Aaron, can illustrate this (Numbers 12). Maybe for talking disparagingly about Moses's choice of wife, Miriam became afflicted with a skin condition that was white like snow (מצרעת כשלג). Aaron turned to Moses and begged him to intercede on her behalf. Moses uttered perhaps the oldest and most concise prayer for healing in the Bible: "Please, God, please heal her." After being quarantined for seven days outside the camp, she was fully healed and reintegrated. White human skin is but a temporary condition. Other biblical instances of white refer to clothes, animals, and hair.

Black similarly describes animals, hair, and certain cloud formations. Black is also used to refer to human ailments and conditions. When Job describes his skin as growing black and peeling (שחר in 30:30), he is speaking about his boils and fever. Jeremiah describes himself as darkened (קדרתי) because his people have been crushed politically (8:21). Elsewhere, a song proclaims, "I am black [שחורה] and beautiful, O daughters of Jerusalem, like the tents of Kedar and the curtains of Solomon" (Song of Songs 1:6). This beautiful dark skin is not congenital but conditional: "Do not stare at me because I am darkened [שחרחרת] from the sun burning me; my mother's sons were angry with me and made me tend the vineyards, my own vineyard I could not tend" (1:7). Skin darkened from exposed forced labor is nonetheless to be considered beautiful.

In a different biblical song, white and black are used simultaneously to describe people's appearances. Here, the author laments the desecration of the city of Jerusalem and Zion generally, saying that their princes were once "brighter than snow, more dazzling than milk" but are now "darker than coal and unrecognizable in public" (Lamentations 4:7–8). Even as this verse may demonstrate a social hierarchy of colors, its comparisons upend that very ranking. On the one hand, royalty, easily recognizable figures in society, are likened to white objects, but only when their regimes are intact. Once those regimes have been dismantled, the leaders become so dark that they are no longer known. This dichotomy suggests that whiteness is the color of singular leaders and blackness the color of anonymous masses. The objects to which they are compared suggest a different set of values, however. Elites are compared to snow and milk—fickle things vulnerable to even slight changes in the environment; they easily melt or rot. The masses, by contrast, are like coal, a durable and potent object that can power civilization. Whereas a society can do without either frozen water or dairy, none can survive for long without fuel. White and black are thus simultaneously lauded and disparaged in this source. When it comes to black and white, symbolism and values inextricably intertwine and creatively upend each other.

Significantly, the two colors are best perceived when they are juxtaposed. On this point, the rabbis repeat many times this teaching about revelation itself. "The Torah: how was it written? Upon white fire, in black fire."[1] We may read the Torah's black-inked letters and words, yet we can see them precisely only because they rest upon the comparatively pale parchment. The two colors more than coexist; they dynamically illumine each other. When they intertwine, black and white reveal revelation itself.



**Complicating Color**

While black and white complement each other, theirs is also a complicated relationship, especially when religion is taken into consideration.[2] This is particularly evident in the social arena, as people came to see skin color as signaling something other than a superficial or temporary condition of illness or overexposure to the elements and rather as a marker of internal, if not eternal, quality and corollary status. The story of how and why this shift occurred is, of course, anything but straightforward. The burgeoning field of race studies, the development of critical race theory, and the increasing attention given to race in popular culture indicate the depth, complexity, and urgency of appreciating this story.[3]

To be sure, no single treatment of these topics could ever be comprehensive, much less exhaustive. However truthful a project on color and race may be, none can claim a monopoly on truth. The immensity and intensity of these matters do not deter us, however, from the need to engage them from multiple, overlapping perspectives, because these many vantage points, in scholarship as in parallax view, sharpen perception, add depth, and highlight detail.

One issue seems particularly thorny: the relationship between perceived racial differences and actual practices of oppression. While untangling the relationship between perception and practice is tricky enough, a middle term muddles it all the more. Evaluation or assessment of superiority and inferiority links perceived racial differences to oppressive practices. Though perception, evaluation, and practice are distinct and can be examined individually, they nevertheless implicate one another in powerful and sometimes insidious ways.[4]

Recent studies of race and racism, for example, challenge the common idea that oppressive practices like slavery resulted from a hierarchical evaluation of skin color.[5] Among other things, they discuss the reverse observation put forward by the eighteenth-century Quaker abolitionist and preacher John Woolman, who realized that oppressive policies spurred racist ideas and ideologies. He found that *slavery caused racism*, not the other way around.



In his 1762 treatise *Considerations on keeping negroes*, Woolman wrote, "Placing on men the ignominious title of slave, dressing them in uncomely garments, keeping them to servile labour, in which they are often dirty, *tends gradually to fix a notion in the mind*, that they are a sort of people below us in nature, and leads us to consider them as such in all our conclusions about them" (emphasis added).[6] If, as Woolman attests, prejudices spring from practices, then consistently treating people cruelly gives rise, over time, to certain ideas that explain and even justify such treatment. Over the course of generations, oppressive practices like slavery fix in people's minds the notion that the enslaved are meant for that position and owners are meant for theirs.

That such a rationale would grow out of practice sounds almost organic. Woolman's stress on gradualism suggests that the cognitive aspects of oppression are late, unnecessary, and not even inevitable.

In a certain way, Woolman contradicts himself. When discussing slavery in the Bible, he claims that it is unconscionable to deny liberty and justice to innocent people. "To suppose it right, that an innocent man shall at this day be excluded from the common rules of justice, be deprived of that liberty, which is the natural right of human creatures, and be a slave to others during life, on account of a sin committed by his immediate parents, or a sin committed by Ham, the son of Noah, is a supposition too gross to be admitted into the mind of any person, who sincerely desires to be governed by solid principles" (12). "Too gross" suggests that any justification for oppression is unseemly, ugly, distasteful—especially for those yearning to abide by the solid biblical principles of love and equity. It is not that such justifications are inherently unintelligible; they are just undignified. Woolman thus leaves open the possibility of a more dignified justification for oppression, one that in fact upholds the Bible's "solid principles." Woolman cites biblical verses in support of this possibility: "But for men, with private views, to assume an absolute power over the persons and properties of others, and continue it from age to age in the line of natural generation, without regard to the virtues and vices of their successors, as it is manifestly contrary to true universal love, and attended with great evils, there requires the clearest evidence to beget a belief in us, that Moses intended that the strangers should as such be slaves to the Jews" (16–17). The practice of transgenerational enslavement required that slave owners see slavery as God's will. The brilliance of Woolman's argument lies in his showing that the justification for this oppressive practice was not God's will but a manufactured perversion of it. As Woolman shows through a careful reading of the Bible, it was Moses, not God, who purposely constructed explanations and theologies to justify the inhumane practice of slavery.



Twelve years earlier, in 1754, Woolman opened his first treatise, *Some considerations on the keeping of Negroes*, with this observation: "Customs generally approved, and Opinions received by Youth from their Superiors, become like the natural Produce of a Soil, especially when they are suited to favorite Inclinations."[7] In other words, those who benefit from customs and ideas rarely question their provenance. Like plants that become accustomed to growing in unusual soil, people also become inured or habituated to unusual circumstances.

Habituation thus has at least two aspects: becoming accustomed to certain practices or behaviors, and not questioning the reasons used to justify them. Woolman, of course, was not the first to acknowledge the power of habituation. Much earlier, in the twelfth century, Moses Maimonides, a great Jewish physician, legal sage, and theologian, also spoke about habituation as an obstacle to apprehending truths about the world.

To support his position, Maimonides cited the ancient peripatetic philosopher Alexander of Aphrodisias, an expounder of Aristotelian works, who identified three reasons for disagreement about truths: "arrogance and vainglory; secondly, the subtlety, depth, and difficulty of any subject which is being examined; [and] thirdly, ignorance and want of capacity to comprehend what might be comprehended."[8] In short, attitude, the complexity of the subject, and personal incapacity often cause people to disagree about the truth. Maimonides adds a fourth reason: habit and upbringing. "For man has in his nature a love of, and an inclination for, that to which he is habituated." He refers to desert dwellers to illustrate this point.

> [They] dislike the towns, do not hanker after their pleasures, and prefer the bad circumstances to which they are accustomed to good ones to which they are not accustomed. Their souls accordingly would find no repose in living in palaces, in wearing silk clothes, and in the enjoyment of baths, ointments, and perfumes. In a similar way, man has love for, and the wish to defend, opinions to which he

> is habituated and in which he has been brought up and has a feeling of repulsion for opinions other than those. For this reason also *man is blind to the apprehension of the true realities and inclines toward the things to which he is habituated.*[9] (emphasis added)



In his view, people not only become accustomed to certain patterns of existence and behavior, but they also lose sight of the peculiarity of their own opinions and convictions.[10] They hold fast to their beliefs even when they are contradicted by facts. Maimonides contends that such conservativism operates in theology as well. "Such is, e.g., the case with the vulgar notions with respect to the corporeality of God, and many other metaphysical questions, as we shall explain. It is the result of long familiarity with passages of the Bible, which they are accustomed to respect and to receive as true, and the literal sense of which implies the corporeality of God and other false notions; in truth, however, these words were employed as figures and metaphors for reasons to be mentioned below."[11] People become inured to stories told and retold, including religiously grounded ones.[12] In time, individuals and society generally take for granted as given and unquestionable what were once fabricated metaphors and theories.

Religious beliefs come belatedly to justify existence, particularly unfair existence. This claim echoes Max Weber, the great nineteenth-century German sociologist and philosopher of religion, who writes, "in short, religion provides the theodicy of good fortune for those who are fortunate." The term *fortunate* means, for Weber, "all the 'good' of honor, power, possession, and pleasure," and he adds that "it is the most general formula for the service of legitimation, which religion has had to accomplish for the external and the inner interests of all ruling men, the propertied, the victorious, and the healthy."[13] The elite, those who have benefited in some way from existence, will embrace those features of a religion that "provide the theodicy" for their good fortune.

Theological justification is necessary because the elite are unsatisfied with being merely fortunate. They cannot abide the idea that their fortune is temporary or the result of happenstance. They want to know that they are genuinely entitled to their bounty. As Weber puts it, "The fortunate [person] is seldom satisfied with the fact of being fortunate. Beyond this, he needs to know that he has a right to his good fortune. He wants to be convinced that he 'deserves' it, and above all, that he deserves it in comparison with others. He wishes to be allowed the belief that the less fortunate also merely experience his due. Good fortune thus wants to be 'legitimate' fortune."[14] The American historian of race Nell Irvin Painter interprets Weber this way: "innate qualities are needed to prove the justice—the naturalness and inalterability—of the status quo."[15] One wants to be on top because one is inherently better, not just lucky. Such qualities, however, are only supposedly innate. While religions, political theories, sociology, philosophy, and other schools of thought proclaim that those innate qualities exist, they have no empirically verifiable existence beyond those socially constructed claims. 

The fortunate thus build belief systems to justify the disproportionate and unequal distribution of goods, honor, power, etc. As society becomes habituated to both inequities and their justifications, it becomes harder to disentangle them. Dismantling long-held privileges is difficult—but not impossible. Some might call for an immediate overturning of the whole system justifying oppressive practices. Such calls for a complete overhaul of society often lead to revolution. Think of Marx, for example.

Others—among them Maimonides—call for piecemeal, incremental adjustments to the social and economic order. After discussing gradations in the biological makeup of the human nervous system in which soft sections slowly shift into harder ones, Maimonides makes this psychological claim: "It is, namely, impossible to go suddenly from one extreme to the other: it is therefore according to the nature of man impossible for him suddenly to discontinue everything to which he has been accustomed."[16] Thus he concludes that "God refrained from prescribing what the people by their natural disposition would be incapable of obeying, and gave the above-mentioned commandments as a means of securing His chief object, viz., to spread a knowledge of Him [among the people], and to cause them to reject idolatry. It is contrary to man's nature that he should suddenly abandon all the different kinds of Divine service and the different customs in which he has been brought up, and which have been so general, that they were considered as a matter of course."[17] In his view, religious innovations cannot be revolutionary if they are to garner public support; only incremental reforms will work. This is particularly true if those reforms require that the fortunate shed some of their power, prestige, or property.

That elites would resist relinquishing their wealth, power, and advantage is hardly surprising. What about the people at the other end of the spectrum—how would the oppressed react to change? According to Maimonides, "it would be just as if a person trained to work as a slave with mortar and bricks, or similar things, should interrupt his work, clean his hands, and at once fight with real giants." That would be both unintelligible and unreasonable to expect. In his view, every person, regardless of position in society, is conservative: everyone, including the enslaved, favors incremental change over revolution. Does this perspective reflect Maimonides's own experience of sudden rupture, of being pushed out of Spain by the Almohad Caliphate during his youth, and of the difficulties of living in exile, possibly as a feigned convert to Islam? Perhaps. Whatever its roots, it is a call for the oppressed to seek relief through gradual reform rather than full-scale revolution. This modest proposal for change reflects and reinforces the institutions of slavery practiced in the contexts in which Maimonides lived and traveled. Critics might accuse Maimonides of reluctance, even fear, about advocating immediate liberty for the enslaved. Others might defend him, pointing out that he was upholding an earlier biblical perspective that slavery is a divinely sanctioned institution. But Maimonides did not endorse other practices that were allegedly approved by God, among them genocide and the murder of rebellious teenagers at the city gates. Even if, in his *Guide of the Perplexed*, Maimonides fails to be a liberator of the oppressed, his point remains: change is difficult for society as a whole, for both the fortunate and the unfortunate, the elite and the oppressed. Even if more is needed, sometimes incremental change is the most that can be expected.



### Contemplating Color

Since changing society is difficult, even thinking about changing it is daunting. Yet that is precisely what intellectuals can and must do, at least according to the controversial public intellectual Edward Said. In his view, the intellectual "is neither a pacifier nor a consensus-builder, but someone whose whole being is staked on a critical sense, a sense of being unwilling to accept easy formulas, or ready-made clichés, or the smooth, ever-so-accommodating confirmations of what the powerful or conventional have to say, and what they do."[18] The scholars who have contributed to this volume demonstrably resist the commonplace. They search for trouble, problems, cracks, and opportunities through critical race theory, the impulse to medicalize race and racism, Yiddish literature's consideration of lynching and blackness, how law works to impose collective identity, how memory inspires both silence and screams, and, ultimately, the ways in which Jewish ethical agency is variously constructed.

By not settling for rehashing popular analyses, well-worn theories, or comforting narratives, these contributors go beyond articulating their own community's suffering to the exclusion of all others'. Much as Said anticipates, they accept the challenge to "universalize the crisis, to give greater human scope to what a particular race or nation suffered, to associate that experience with the suffering of others."[19] This expansion of concern often robs thinkers of happy complacency and sets them adrift, as if in exile. Since Said views himself as an intellectual in exile (his autobiography is titled *Out of Place*), he frequently champions displaced thinking, especially in ethics. He considers it vital to reject the kind of certainty exhibited by those who think within circumscribed and often self-imposed horizons. Certainty marks the sort of professionalism in which deference to authority and reinscription of power structures are common. Instead of worshipping at the feet of certainty, Said encourages scholars to be more secular and amateur.[20]



Many of the essays in this volume take up Said's challenge. They problematize assumptions, unpack popular narratives, and uncover insidious agendas. Others are more ambivalent about a radical intellectual secularism that jettisons all forms of certainty; they resist being cast adrift in some postmodern, postracial, postracist, postreligious worldview. Being so unrooted is too otherworldly for them, putting them in a nonplace rather than in a good one from which to consider the complexities of color in modern society.[21] Whatever tack they take, these essays demonstrate the many ways in which color, when considered seriously, undermines complacency.

The role of the intellectual in unsettling complacency should not be understated. As Said himself shows in his magnum opus, *Orientalism*, intellectuals shape how society both thinks about the world and acts upon it. For better and for worse, whether intentional or not, scholars influence both popular discourse and public policy. Discounting their impact would be a mistake.

This is particularly so when considering race, racism, anti-Semitism, and their colorful cognates and oppressive practices. Consider, for example, some observations made by one Nahum Wolf in 1912. In a lament about a recent spate of anti-Jewish publications across both Europe and the United States, Wolf warned against embracing the ideas put forward by really smart people. "Genius is no warrant against prejudice and a great mind no bar against false presumptions," he said. Once exposed to the insidiousness of prejudice of any sort, "the would-be genius imbues them from his very childhood and remains thereafter slave to anti-Semitism just as the ordinary man. Moreover, the great man, who is bent to carry everything to its extreme, furthers national prejudices to their utmost as well." Such intellectuals erect out of these anti-Jewish ideas "a theory as cardinal and extreme as might be any theory of his on the riddle of the universe."[22]

Wolf examined German views of Jews to demonstrate his point. On the one hand, "the average German ascribed whatever qualities he found in the Jews—bad or good, if any—to a certain *superiority*." From a commoner's perspective, Jews appeared admirable, and they were thus to be welcomed, in part or in whole, into German society. German intellectuals, on the other hand, "construed a theory diametrically opposed to this. To them, it is the *inferiority* and not the superiority that is accountable for all the qualities of the Jews." It was this latter perspective "that lent the anti-Semitic movement in Europe all its vitality and gave birth to a literature as copious and profuse as any."[23] Wolf worried presciently that it would be the intellectual's perspective that ultimately would shape both public opinion and public policy. Perception, evaluation, and practice commingle in pernicious ways.

Such deference to chauvinist genius proved devastating. The twentieth century was littered with the bodies—in Europe, the United States, and beyond—that intellectual elites deemed not only unworthy of protection but deserving of outright annihilation. As Abraham Joshua Heschel said at midcentury, "Few of us realize that racism is man's gravest threat to man, the maximum of hatred for a minimum of reason, the maximum of cruelty for a minimum of thinking." In their innermost essences, chauvinist and racist theories are not founded on true humanist—that is, universalizable—thinking, nor can they be. As if anticipating Said, Heschel challenged his peers: "We have attained a high standard of living. We must seek to attain a high standard of thinking."[24] Three decades later, Said proclaimed, "If you wish to uphold basic human justice you must do so for everyone, not just selectively for the people that your side, your culture, your nation designates as okay. The fundamental problem is therefore how to reconcile one's identity and the actualities of one's own culture, society, and history to the reality of other identities, cultures, peoples."[25] However countercultural Heschel's and Said's calls for (Jewish, Islamic, and secular) intellectuals to dismantle narrow, self-interested thinking may have been, they were hardly new.

Centuries earlier, Woolman challenged (Christian) intellectual leaders to acknowledge their own hypocritical small-mindedness when it came to color and oppression. "Selfishness being indulged, clouds the understanding; and where selfish men, for a long time, proceed on their way, without opposition, the deceivableness of unrighteousness gets so rooted in their intellects, that a candid examination of things relating to self-interest is prevented. And in this circumstance, some who would not agree to make a slave of a person whose color is like their own, appear easy [that is, unperturbed] in making slaves of others of a different color, though their understandings and morals are equal to the generality of men of their own color" (30). Unsurprisingly, elites who benefit from structures built upon disproportionate distribution of goods are reluctant to critically examine their assumptions and bounty. Such complacency is inadequate, especially for people who claim to be members of a tradition that espouses universal equality. "Whence is it that men, who believe in a righteous omnipotent being, to whom all nations stand equally related, and are equally accountable, remain so easy in it; but for that the ideas of Negroes and slaves are so interwoven in the mind, that they do not discuss this matter with that candor and freedom of thought, which the case justly calls for?" (31). For Woolman as for Heschel and Said, members of the Abrahamic traditions should examine, with candor and courage, their own prejudices and oppressive practices, especially those founded on color differences. They call on intellectuals to challenge willful ignorance about their own, perhaps unwitting, participation in racist systems.



### Not Ignoring Color

The task of this volume is manifold. Its first goal is to produce knowledge about Judaism and race and racism. We construe Judaism broadly; it includes classic and contemporary literature, laws, history, popular culture, theology, ethics and philosophy, rituals and practices. How Judaism acknowledges and attends to race and racism is thus a central question for the essays collected here.

We also examine the ways in which Judaism dismisses race and racism. Just as fields of knowledge are socially constructed, so too are fields of ignorance. Like scientific research, religions consider certain questions and labor to provide meaningful answers. In the process, however, other issues fall by the wayside. These unaddressed questions demarcate a field of unknowing or ignorance.[26] In order to acknowledge the ways in which Judaism ignores race and racism, it is also necessary that we examine hate and oppression.

We do not assume that Judaism is monolithic. Judaism has never been a single concept or corpus of texts, structures or strictures, or set of practices. Nor do Jews cohere in a uniform group, today or in any age. It is not possible to speak of a single concept of Judaism, or of "the" Jewish view on race. Charles Mills makes a similar argument when speaking about white ignorance: "this is, of course, true for all sociological generalizations, which has never been a reason for abandoning them, but of employing them cautiously." For Mills, "white ignorance as a cognitive phenomenon has to be clearly historicized."[27] Jewish racial ignorance also needs historicizing. For example, with few exceptions, the biblical selections surveyed at the start of this chapter demonstrate that skin color was acknowledged more as a contingent artifact (of injury or exposure to sun) than as some inherent quality bespeaking divinely established social status and treatment. Over time and place, however, the relationship between phenomena, values, and practices shifted. Cautiously tracking these shifts is a third goal of this volume.



In this enterprise, caution and care are as important as courage. Letting bad ideas, ignorance, and oppression go unchecked is dangerous. Woolman warned against allowing faulty assumptions and ignorance to go unexamined. "It is a happy case to set out right, and persevere in the same way. A wrong beginning leads into many difficulties; for to support one evil, another becomes customary. Two produces more, and the further men proceed in this way, the greater their dangers, their doubts and fears and the more painful and perplexing are their circumstances. So that such who are true friends to the real and lasting interest of our country, and candidly consider the tendency of things, cannot but feel some concern on this account" (25). Those who care about the "real and lasting interest" of society should investigate with candor how color, religion, and oppression interact. The authors of this volume concur.

Of course, no investigation of these topics can be exhaustive or conclusive; it is perforce ongoing. Heschel once described the meeting between Moses and Pharaoh as the original conference on race. That conversation has not ended, according to Heschel. As it continues, it should "dedicate itself not only to the problem of the Negro but also to the problem of the white man, not only to the plight of the colored but also to the situation of the white people, to the cure of a disease affecting the spiritual substance and condition of every one of us."[28] Whiteness, no less than blackness, needs critical reassessment. We ignore these and related issues at our peril.[29]

#### Jewish Ethics

This volume aims to unpack color in the realm of Judaism, Jewish thought and ethics, Jewish communities and individuals. This is not an exhaustive catalog of history, intellectual or otherwise. More like that imagined course on color, this is a dynamic, multidisciplinary—even multisensory—collection of investigations of color, religion, and oppression. Our contributors investigate color through the lenses of biology, philosophy, ethics, theology, law, medicine, literature, psychology, and sociology. Whiteness, white fragility, and white racial frames are as problematic as blackness, not to mention as Jewishness itself.[30] Racism is investigated alongside anti-Semitism. Oppression is questioned and liberation inspired. Personal anecdotes intermingle with scripture, philosophical meditations with critical race theory. This project does not pretend to present a single position. Nor does it provide a coherent, overarching argument in which the chapters speak with one another, though a few of them do. Rather, these stand-alone chapters approach questions of color, race, and religion from the perspectives of many genres and fields. Each has its own reference list, and each ends with a classic text from the Bible or rabbinic literature, along with questions intended to amplify themes raised therein.



Still, as we readily admit, all of this is insufficient. Many ideas, values, and practices are intertwined here, and teasing them apart is not so easy. It is a Herculean task, perhaps a Sisyphean one. Woolman anticipated as much.

> Through the force of long custom, it appears needful to speak in relation to color. Suppose a white child, born of parents of the meanest [poorest] sort, who died and left him an infant, falls into the hands of a person, who endeavors to keep him a slave. Some men would account him an unjust man in doing so, who yet appear easy [unperturbed] while many black people, of honest lives, and good abilities, are enslaved, in a manner more shocking than the case here supposed. This is owing chiefly to the idea of slavery being connected with the black color, and liberty with the white. *And where false ideas are twisted into our minds, it is with difficulty we get fairly disentangled.* (29; emphasis added)

The task may be daunting, but it is not impossible. The very act of asking tough questions, of highlighting what has been underappreciated, of coloring from different angles the issues of race and Judaism—all of these things demonstrate some of the higher kinds of thinking Heschel, Said, and Woolman advocate.

**Notes**

1. Midrash Tanhuma, *Bereshit* 1. See also Jerusalem Talmud *Shekalim* 6/49d; Jerusalem Talmud *Sotah* 8/22d; *Devarim Rabbah* 3 (*Ekev*); *Shir HaShirim Rabbah* 5; *Midrash Tehillim* (Buber) 90.

2. To give just one example, Hoberman traces the complicated relationship between Jews and African Americans in the nineteenth century, and the residue of that tense and complicated relationship in the twentieth century, to the story of Exodus; see Hoberman, "'God Loves the Hebrews.'" Also consider listening to the 2017 podcast "Seeing White" by John Biewen at the Center for Documentary Studies at Duke University, http://podcast.cdsporch.org/seeing-white.

3. As an illustration of race's pervasive penetration of culture, *National Geographic* devoted its April 2018 edition, which coincided with the fiftieth anniversary of Martin Luther King Jr.'s assassination, to

the complex issue of race. It did so with eyes wide open, conscientiously examining its own history, attitudes, presumptions, and presentations about race.

4. In *The Insecurity of Freedom*, Heschel underscores the importance of paying attention to facts, values, and practices. "Efforts must be exerted on two levels; on the level of principles and attitudes as well as on the level of practical application. We must continue to dedicate ourselves not only to the problem of the Negro, but also to the problem of the white man" (103).

5. See, for example, Kendi, *Stamped from the Beginning*; Painter, *History of White People*.

6. Woolman, *Considerations on keeping negroes*, 24 (hereafter cited parenthetically in the text).

7. Woolman, *Some considerations on the keeping of Negroes*, opening sentence.

8. Maimonides, *Guide of the Perplexed*, 1:31.

9. Ibid.

10. Maimonides also addresses becoming accustomed to the superfluous and excessive. "The soul," he contends, "when accustomed to superfluous things, acquires a strong habit of desiring things which are neither necessary for the preservation of the individual nor for that of the species." Holding on to both unnecessary oppressive practices and their justifications affects the whole person negatively. Ibid., 3:12.

11. Ibid., 1:31 (trans. Pines, 67; trans. Friedländer, 41–42).

12. For example, Hoberman, in "'God Loves the Hebrews,'" shows that some nineteenth-century Jews viewed slaveholding as biblically sanctioned and abolitionism as lacking biblical warrant.

13. Weber, *Essays in Sociology*, 271.

14. Ibid.

15. Painter, *History of White People*, 194.

16. Maimonides, *Guide of the Perplexed*, 3:32.

17. Ibid.

18. Said, *Representations of the Intellectual*, 23.

19. Ibid., 44.

20. Ibid., 120.

21. See Sargisson, *Contemporary Feminist Utopianism*, 41.

22. Wolf, "Are the Jews an Inferior Race," 492.

23. Ibid., 493.

24. Heschel, *Insecurity of Freedom*, 86, 104.

25. Said, *Representations of the Intellectual*, 93–94.

26. See Proctor, "Agnotology."

27. Mills, "White Ignorance," 235, 233.

28. Heschel, *Insecurity of Freedom*, 87.

29. As noted earlier, Heschel makes a similar argument. Ibid., 103.

30. See DiAngelo, *White Fragility*; Feagin, *White Racial Frame*.

31. Mishnah ʿEduyot 1:13; see also Mishnah *Gittin* 4:5, Babylonian Talmud *Pesaḥim* 88a–b; Babylonian Talmud *Baba Batra* 13a.

### References

Appiah, Kwame Anthony. *In My Father's House: Africa in the Philosophy of Culture*. Oxford: Oxford University Press, 1992.

DiAngelo, Robin. *White Fragility: Why It's So Hard for White People to Talk About Racism*. Boston: Beacon Press, 2018.

Efron, John M. *Defenders of the Race: Jewish Doctors and Race Science in Fin-de-Siècle Europe*. New Haven: Yale University Press, 1994.

Feagin, Joe R. *The White Racial Frame: Centuries of Racial Framing and Counter-Framing*. 2nd ed. New York: Routledge, 2013.

Feliciano, Cynthia. "Shades of Race: How Phenotype and Observer Characteristics Shape Racial Classification." *American Behavioral Scientist* 60, no. 4 (2016): 390–419.

Goldstein, David B. *Jacob's Legacy: A Genetic View of Jewish History*. New Haven: Yale University Press, 2008.

Goldstein, Eric L. *The Price of Whiteness: Jews, Race, and American Identity*. Princeton: Princeton University Press, 2006.

Heschel, Abraham Joshua. *The Insecurity of Freedom: Essays on Human Existence*. New York: Schocken Books, 1966.

Hoberman, Michael. "'God Loves the Hebrews': Exodus Typologies, Jewish Slaveholding, and Black Peoplehood in Antebellum America." *American Jewish Archives Journal* 67, no. 2 (2015): 47–69.

Idelson-Shein, Iris. *Difference of a Different Kind: Jewish Constructions of Race During the Long Eighteenth Century*. Philadelphia: University of Pennsylvania Press, 2014.

Kautsky, Karl. *Are the Jews a Race?* Translated from the 2nd German ed. (1926). Westport, Conn.: Greenwood Press, 1972.

Kay, Judith W. "The Exodus and Racism: Paradoxes for Jewish Liberation." *Journal of the Society of Christian Ethics* 28, no. 2 (2008): 23–50.

Kendi, Ibram X. *Stamped from the Beginning: The Definitive History of Racist Ideas in America*. New York: Nation Books, 2016.

Maimonides, Moses. *The Guide of the Perplexed*. Translated by Shlomo Pines. Chicago: University of Chicago Press, 1963. Also translated by M. Friedländer, 2 vols. (London: Routledge and Kegan Paul, 1903), available at http://www.sacred-texts.com/jud/gfp/gfp000.htm. Citations are to part and chapter.

Marcus, Kenneth L. *Jewish Identity and Civil Rights in America*. New York: Cambridge University Press, 2010.

Mills, Charles W. "White Ignorance." In Proctor and Schiebinger, *Agnotology*, 230–49.

Ostrer, Harry. *Legacy: A Genetic History of the Jewish People*. New York: Oxford University Press, 2012.

Painter, Nell Irvin. *The History of White People*. New York: W. W. Norton, 2011.

Proctor, Robert N. "Agnotology: A Missing Term to Describe the Cultural Production of Ignorance (and Its Study)." In Proctor and Schiebinger, *Agnotology*, 1–33.

Proctor, Robert N., and Londa Schiebinger, eds. *Agnotology: The Making and Unmaking of Ignorance*. Stanford: Stanford University Press, 2008.

Pryde, Thomas. "Characteristics of the Jewish Race." *Old and New Testament Student* 14, no. 4 (1892): 206–12.

Rosenzweig, Franz. *The Star of Redemption*. Translated by Barbara E. Galli. Madison: University of Wisconsin Press, 2005.

Said, Edward. *Orientalism*. New York: Vintage Books, 1978.

———. *Representations of the Intellectual*. New York: Pantheon Books, 1994.

Sargisson, Lucy. *Contemporary Feminist Utopianism*. London: Routledge, 1996.

Sicher, Efraim, ed. *Race, Color, Identity: Rethinking Discourses About "Jews" in the Twenty-First Century*. New York: Bergahn, 2013.

Weber, Max. *From Max Weber: Essays in Sociology*. Translated and edited by H. H. Gerth and C. Wright Mills. New York: Oxford University Press, 1946. Available at https://archive.org/stream/frommaxweberessa00webe/frommaxweberessa00webe_djvu.txt.

Wolf, Nahum. "Are the Jews an Inferior Race?" *North American Review* 195, no. 677 (1912): 492–95.

Woolman, John. *Considerations on keeping negroes; recommended to the professors of Christianity, of every denomination. Part second.* Philadelphia: B. Franklin and D. Hall, 1762. https://quod.lib.umich.edu/e/evans/N07291.0001.001.

———. *Some considerations on the keeping of Negroes. Recommended to the professors of Christianity of every denomination.* Philadelphia: James Chattin, 1754. http://downloads.it.ox.ac.uk/ota-public/tcp/Texts-HTML/free/N05/N05781.html#index.xml-body.1_div.2.

## Classic Text and Questions to Ponder

Perceiving differences, evaluating those differences, and developing and reinforcing practices based on those evaluations are ancient habits. Among other things, they have been applied to gender, class, and, of course, race. Appreciating their dynamics is a first step to acknowledging dangerous assumptions and pernicious practices. The following Mishnah (a Jewish law) (ca. 200 C.E.) highlights the importance of such work. On the one hand is Beit Hillel (the school of Hillel), whose position is rather dogmatic. The other position is held by Beit Shammai (the school of Shammai), which typically does not win when disputing Beit Hillel on a matter of law or practice.

> One who is half a slave and half a free man should work one day for his master and one day for himself, [according to] the words of Beit Hillel. Beit Shammai said to them: You have fixed [the problem] for his master, but you have not fixed [the problem] for himself. He is not able to marry a slave-woman, nor is he able [to marry] a free woman. Is he to refrain [from marrying]? But wasn't the world created for people to be fruitful and to multiply? For it is said, "He did not create it to be an empty place; but established it to be inhabited" (Isaiah 45:18). But for the rightful ordering of the world they force his master to free him, and he writes out a document for half his value. [Then] Beit Hillel went back and taught according to Beit Shammai.[31]

Beit Shammai urges thinking afresh about long-standing practices regarding the partially indentured. It models a way of looking at the situation from a different vantage point, from the perspective of the underling or disempowered, rather than from the viewpoint of the elite. Larger concerns, like the biblical injunction to procreate, should override long-standing practices that benefit the already privileged. The novelty of this perspective is so powerful that it inspires Beit Hillel to retract its position.

- For Maimonides, habituation complicates analyzing, and ultimately changing, social relations and structures. He also promotes incrementalism instead of outright revolution. Do you agree or disagree? Why?
- Beit Shammai challenges the assumption that this rule regarding half slaves should benefit the elite. Remember, it was the elite (educated, powerful men) who composed and codified such rules in the first place. Beit Hillel ultimately changed its position and hence the law. What do you make of this?
- How is thinking about color, race, racism, and religion an ethical enterprise? How can the failure to think about them be defended on ethical grounds?

2

# In the Color Line

## The Tenacity of Racism and Its Challenge to Ethicists

**SUSANNAH HESCHEL**

W. E. B. Du Bois famously wrote in 1903 that "the problem of the twentieth century is the problem of the colour line."[1] Race continues to be the problem of the twenty-first century, extending to numerous other issues of social justice, including gender, sexuality, religion, ethnicity, and economics. The tenacity of racism remains a puzzle to scholars and social activists alike, and a great deal of scholarship is devoted to demonstrating its pervasiveness, especially in ways that are often implicit or covert. In that way, scholarly analyses of racism carry the valence of revelatory knowledge rather than of simply supplying information. The implication is that once we have been made aware of subtle, unrecognized expressions of racism, we will be inspired to make radical social change.

What has changed is the theological discourse. My interest here is in the religious aspects of the civil rights movement that were effective in changing understandings of the Bible and American society, and that were produced by a remarkably productive collaboration between Jewish and Christian theologians. This chapter briefly examines the role Jews played in the civil rights movement and the role of mythic "Jews" in the debates over racism in the 1960s, and then examines the efforts of theorists in the humanities and social sciences to delineate the multifaceted nature of racism. I conclude by arguing that a particular theological ethic was expressed in the spirit of the movement that understood the nature of God and the human person by drawing on little-known but important Jewish and Christian teachings, articulated in the writings of Abraham Joshua Heschel and Martin Luther King Jr.

### Jews and "Jews"



For Jews, race begins with historical experiences of antisemitism. Theological polemics against Judaism, formulated by pagans, Christians, and Muslims, inevitably attacked Jewish bodies and lives. As targets of hatred in these Christian and Muslim theological tracts, which were fueled by Christian and Muslim resentment over Jews' refusal to convert, Jews have a keen sense of the nuances of religious and racial antisemitism, especially when resentment has fueled the demonization of Jews. Jewish responses have varied. Before the rise of Hitler, many German Jews, for instance, thought greater assimilation into German society would overcome hatred of Jews, only to discover that a new wave of antisemitism was targeting assimilated Jews precisely because they were not visibly marked as Jewish. Zionists responded to antisemitism by calling upon Jews to leave Europe altogether and establish their own state in Israel. Yet Zionism has failed to bring an end to antisemitism and has been accused of racism itself for creating a state based on Jewish nationality and for harboring racist hostility toward Palestinian Arabs.

What does race mean to Jews in the United States? Our narrative of American Jewish history is a narrative of joy, of American exceptionalism that has welcomed us and given us, as Jews, an unprecedented freedom, and we have risen to the top. On issues of race, we think of Jewish symbols: Joachim Prinz speaking at the 1963 March on Washington on the steps of the Lincoln Memorial; Mickey Schwerner and Andrew Goodman registering voters in the South, murdered together with James Chaney in Mississippi; Abraham Joshua Heschel and other rabbis who marched in Selma for voting rights in 1965. We think of the uncounted Jews who participated in Freedom Summer, at lunch counter sit-ins, and as Freedom Riders who integrated interstate buses, and we remember the Jewish refugee scholars from Nazi Europe who went to teach at historically black American colleges and universities.

At the same time, some Jews opposed Jewish involvement in the civil rights movement, just as some African Americans opposed the politics of nonviolence and civil disobedience promoted by Dr. King and his followers, insisting that violence was necessary to overthrow white supremacy and oppression. Arguing for a separatist black community, the black power movement stimulated rage and resentment. The Black Panthers also helped inspire a Jewish movement led by Meir Kahane, the Jewish Defense League, both in the United States and in Israel, to which I return below.

Where do Jews stand in the conversation about race? As prime targets of racist hatred that resulted in mass murder, Jews have been particularly attuned to expressions of antisemitism, and the Holocaust has become an important element in any discussion of race and the dangers of racism. African American Jews experience a double dose of racial targeting, and also have the task, when they choose, of "explaining" racism to Jews and Jewish identity to blacks.



As much as Jews have been targets of antisemitism, they have also been disproportionately engaged in efforts to overcome racism, particularly in the United States. Jewish immigrants who fled pogroms in Russia were shocked to learn of lynching in the United States, and the headlines of the Yiddish press at the turn of the twentieth century screamed against the "pogroms" targeting black Americans.[2] The rise of the civil rights movement in the late 1950s and '60s had significant Jewish support, especially from Jewish students and rabbis, both Reform and Orthodox, even as some Jews argued that the civil rights movement was not relevant to Jewish concerns. Jewish intellectuals also played a prominent role in post–World War II American discussions of racism, particularly during the 1960s.

The centrality of Moses and the Hebrew prophets in the discourse of the civil rights movement, rather than of Jesus and Christian imagery, fostered Jewish support and encouraged Jews to view the movement as an expression of biblical values. On the other hand, as Michael Staub has demonstrated, some Jewish leaders spoke out against Jewish involvement in the movement on the grounds that Jews should devote their energies to Jewish affairs, or by arguing that some black leaders were interested not in integration but in black power, which they portrayed as a threat to American Jews.[3]

In addition to their physical presence among the Freedom Riders, at the 1963 March on Washington, in the march in Selma, and at many other civil rights events, Jews were also invoked metaphorically in discussions of race. Neither white nor black, both victims of racism and successful despite it, Jews appeared in ways that were both sympathetic and reviled, invoked by disparate figures from Malcolm X and James Baldwin to William F. Buckley and Norman Podhoretz.

Telling his father that his best friend in high school was a Jew earned James Baldwin a slap across the face that sparked in him "all the hatred and all the fear, and the depth of a merciless resolve to kill my father rather than allow my father to kill me." The fate of the Jews at the hands of the Nazis, and the world's general indifference to it, haunted Baldwin and felt like a warning of what might happen if "the United States decided to murder its Negroes systematically instead of little by little and catch-as-catch-can."[4] If Baldwin identified with Jews as victims, Malcolm X expressed a kind of envy. He observed that when Jews spoke at length about the crimes of the Holocaust, they were not accused of teaching hatred toward Germans, whereas blacks were accused of spreading hate and fomenting violence when they spoke of the crimes that whites committed against them.[5]

Jews were also invoked at the other end of the political spectrum, but as part of the larger goal of refusing to acknowledge racism when discussing race. During a debate with James Baldwin, for example, sponsored by the Cambridge Union at Cambridge University in England in 1965, William F. Buckley began by declaring that "the fact that your skin is black is utterly irrelevant to the argument that you raise"; that is, Buckley said, Baldwin should not speak *as a black man* about race in America. Buckley went on to challenge black Americans to be more like Jews and become physicians and lawyers.[6] His denial of white racism, and of any distinctive experience of African Americans, also established Jews as the racial model of American success that anyone supposedly might imitate, thus also denying Jewish particular experience. In one of the most bizarre yet widely read essays to appear in the journal *Commentary*, Norman Podhoretz, its editor, published an essay titled "My Negro Problem—and Ours" in 1963. Podhoretz wrote at length about *his* problem, saying nothing of substance about racism or the experience of being black in the United States, or acknowledging the existence of African American Jews. Whites hate blacks, he argued, because black men are "free, independent, reckless, brave, masculine, erotic" and thus whites envy them—but Podhoretz made no attempt to consider the politics underlying his fantasies. In citing Baldwin's work, Podhoretz at most saw "the Negro's disaffection with the white world." Love does not overcome hate, he insisted; only political action can bring change. Yet Podhoretz's essay revealed that he was stuck in a narcissistic male fantasy about his own white male Jewish identity, projecting his obsession with his Jewish masculinity as if it were of any consequence in understanding racism.

Paul Berman borrows Freud's felicitous expression "the narcissism of small differences" to explain why Jews play such a prominent role in debates over race. Despite important differences, Berman argued in a 1994 volume of essays about black-Jewish relations, African Americans and Jewish Americans share the experiences of racism, catastrophe, and constantly endeavoring to preserve a unique culture even while assimilating into the larger white, Christian society.[7] The claim that antisemitism and racism differ only in marginal ways is generally made by Jews; African Americans emphasize the differences. Cornel West, for example, sees the assault on Native Americans as the original sin of the United States, while the enslavement of Africans "served as the linchpin of American democracy; that is, the much-heralded stability and continuity of American democracy was predicated upon black oppression and degradation."[8] Indeed, it is thanks to racism against black people that European ethnic minorities in the United States, including Jews, came to be classified as "white" in the first place.



Berman's book is founded on a binary opposition between Jews and blacks that acknowledges neither the existence of African American Jews nor the racism that Ethiopian and other African Jews face within the State of Israel, although that racism had reached a crisis point precisely when Berman was editing his book. According to Berman's analysis, blacks and Jews have so much in common that they inevitably must feud in order to differentiate themselves from each other.[9] However plausible that explanation may have seemed to Berman, it utterly fails to explain the widely different political views and personal experiences of the two groups. The "narcissism of small differences" seems reductionist in light of the tensions that have increased between the two groups since the 1970s, and the assumption of shared experience collapses when we consider the degree of violence and murder directed against African Americans today, often by police and other state authorities, and the enormous economic discrepancies between the two groups. Just as European liberalism failed to protect Jews from the rise of antisemitism, Nazism, and the Holocaust, Jewish liberalism failed to eradicate racism from Jews, as black Jews in Israel (and the United States) will quickly note. Nor did the alliances between black civil rights leaders and Jewish supporters prevent the rise of suspicion and hostility between the two groups, whether over affirmative action or Zionism, giving rise to a tension that continues to this day.

### The Tenacity of Racism

Du Bois was right that we live in an era of race, what theorist Roberto Esposito calls the era of "biopolitics" in his book *Bios: Biopolitics and Philosophy*, or the power of the state over our bodies and lives. Certain regimes regulate life and death by deliberately manipulating the distribution of necessities and by fomenting racial conflict, the Nazi death camps being the prime example of race's determining death. Despite the debunking of racial theory, the repudiation of slavery, and the horrors of the Holocaust, racism continues to dominate global conflicts. Precisely its ability to conceal itself, or to seduce onlookers into distracting formulations, is one of the key markers of racism. Another is its tenacity: long after scholars proved that racial theory was based on hot air, it stubbornly persists. Yet another factor in racism's endurance is its intertwining with religion—or, as Vincent Lloyd argues, the way that racism becomes a form of "secularized" religion.[10]



The tenacity of racism mirrors the central claim made about race: its immutability. One of the puzzling features of racial theory is the context of its development in nineteenth-century Europe. During the era that saw the rise of historicism—the claim that human beliefs, cultures, and institutions are determined by changing historical contexts over time—as a dominant intellectual force, racial theory came to power in the academic disciplines, claiming a static timelessness for human attributes. Where historicism sees development over time, racism insists on timeless, immutable qualities. Whether racial theory arose as a rebellion against historicism, or as a distorted effort to assert absolutes in an era that was losing theological certainty, the outcome was the mobilization of the idea of race in political and economic systems of conquest on a global scale. Racial theory was essential to European imperialism around the globe.

The rise of two such contradictory ways of thinking, historicism and racial theory, during the same era resulted in conflicting analyses. For example, the quest for the historical Jesus rejected doctrinal claims and instead contextualized Jesus and his teachings within first-century Palestinian Judaism. Yet even scholars who presented a historical Jesus claimed that he also possessed an ahistorical identity—a unique spiritual consciousness or racial distinctiveness—that transcended his context and could not be subjected to historical analysis.[11] Another example is Orientalism, which encompassed both a historicist approach to the religious texts and practices of Islam yet relied on racist images of Muslims as primitive, cunning, and sexually corrupt. The initial nineteenth-century scholarly attempts to demonstrate the chronology of the suras of the Qur'an, contextualizing Muhammad's revelations within the differing social and political atmospheres of Mecca and Medina, often retained negative images of Muhammad as fraudulent, overexcited, confused about the authenticity of his own religious experiences, and so forth—images that were not employed in studies of other religious leaders who received a divine message, such as Jesus, Paul, or Moses.[12]

Racism itself is subject to historical change, and yet it often seems to retain an unchanging, static element at its heart. The lynching of African

American men, women, and children reached a peak in the United States in the period from the late 1800s to the 1960s. Lynchings usually occurred in the presence of large gatherings of white men, women, and children, often on Sundays following a church service, and were photographed. Though we no longer pass around postcards of lynchings as souvenirs, as we did in Du Bois's day, we now have cell-phone videos of police killing African Americans, videos available for the world to watch, indicating that racism has become impervious to historical and technological change. One purpose of early photographic representation was to catalog bodily difference; with photographs of lynchings and videotaped shootings, we are brought as witnesses into the actual moment in which murder is taking place. Scholars of Holocaust photographs have argued that the photographs reproduce the gaze of the Nazi killers, so that we view the images through the perpetrator's eye, making the camera a surrogate weapon.[13] If photographs of racially charged murder turn our gaze into that of the murderer, what do they do to the racial fabric of our society? The brutality of racism is, for better and worse, part of our social interactions; the question is whether we can turn witnessing into actual change. Discussions of race are supposed to take us forward, to bring about an end to racism, but racism remains a stubborn and tenacious force in our society, with murderous consequences. Michelle Alexander notes that there are more black men in prison today than were enslaved in the antebellum years.[14]



White Americans say that we repudiate racism as a society. We declare that we shall overcome, and we pass legislation, alter school curricula, elect an African American president, and immediately after that we elect a president endorsed by the KKK. Racism persists despite historical and social change. Our situation may seem hopeless, but perhaps the problem of racism is far more complex than we have recognized. Scholarship on racism has unveiled its many subtle expressions, the countless microaggressions that continue to accumulate every day, and has shown that though the expression of racism has become more covert, its impact is no less damaging. The abundant evidence that racism is far more tenacious than we realized undermines our sense of American exceptionalism and optimism. White people's growing awareness of racism and its impact has generated deep despair and gloom, as Michelle Alexander suggests in her comparison of James Baldwin and Ta-Nehisi Coates.[15] Baldwin's letter to his nephew, written in 1962, Alexander points out, ended with hope for the future; Coates, writing some fifty years later, ends with pessimism.

### Scholarly Analyses of Racism

Studies of racism have proliferated in many academic disciplines, and the scholarship has become theoretically sophisticated. The larger social and economic consequences of racism are made clear, and subtle expressions of racism are brought to light. Yet the scholarship does not simply provide *information*—for instance, the outrageous number of African Americans under the jurisdiction of the prison system, which has surpassed two million, or the even larger number of families and communities that are consequently affected.[16] Thinking about racism brings what we might call "revelatory knowledge," an expansion of the mind, a new way of seeing, thinking, and understanding. Once we become aware that something is racist, we can't forget it, but we too often attempt to conceal or distract ourselves from that revealed knowledge. Analyses of racism arrive like the medieval theological notion of divine accommodation, only a little bit at a time, accommodating what we are capable of grasping when we are willing to let down our defenses and truly listen and think. More studies are always needed. In whatever way this revelatory knowledge comes to us and however piecemeal it may be, overcoming racism requires that white people think with a new mind and dismantle the institutions that structure our society. Each new examination of racism does not bring an end to racism, but it leads us to the next step of analysis, and to new proposals for social change. There is always more to recognize, analyze, and unpack, because racism is tenacious and also quite slippery, elusive, chameleonlike.

Recent discussions of racism have shown unmistakably that liberalism, both political and intellectual, has failed to deliver the degree of change that we had hoped for. Great passions united blacks and whites, Christians and Jews, in the civil rights movement, yet some of its most important accomplishments, such as school desegregation and voting rights, have been challenged and even undermined in recent years. The philosopher Tommie Shelby has argued that attempts to repair pockets of institutionalized racism cannot succeed unless we recognize the fundamental, pervasive injustice in the United States.[17]

Judith Butler writes of "frames" that regulate not only our discourse but also our emotions and ethical commitments according to certain power relations.[18] Some frames view African American experience only as a story of victimhood and then keep our attention focused on white oppression. That binary of oppressor and victim has been challenged in many contexts. Shelby calls for a reorientation of ethics, for transforming our view of "victims" of economic and social injustice by recognizing that these "victims" are actually moral agents struggling against injustice.[19] Moreover, Shelby writes, the "fundamental normative question for the members of historically oppressed groups still living in the midst of societal injustice" should be "what kind of society would merit our allegiance and is therefore worth fighting for?"[20] Other African American philosophers, artists, and theologians are grappling with the problem of overcoming Afro-pessimism. What resources are there for optimism? Andrew Prevot responds to Afro-pessimism by advocating a new theological paradigm that is rooted in black experience; his theology strives for divine transcendence and emphasizes the significance of our humanity, drawing its inspiration from Catholic mysticism.[21]



Our discussion of race is paradoxical. We agree that there is no such thing as race, yet race still carries multiple meanings.[22] Ta-Nehisi Coates observes astutely that "race is the child of racism, not the father."[23] That is, racism spawned the very idea of race and the now discredited "field" of racial theory. And, as we shall see, racism's disavowal of its historicity is essential to its power. Racism tries to deny its responsibility for race, and this very denial bespeaks its insidious potency. The radical nature of racism—a belief system that claims to define the radical root of humanity in fixed, static taxonomies and hierarchies of human beings—is matched by the need for radical opposition. Coates himself is a son of the Black Panthers, the son of a movement that was feared and despised in its day and that demanded a confrontation of racism with radical opposition.

Is racism a secularized form of religion, as Lloyd argues? Racial theory was employed in the nineteenth century as part and parcel of imperialism and colonialism, and it played an extraordinary role in nearly every academic discipline, including theology. Studies of race tend to ignore religion, which is unfortunate. The result is a neglect of the intimate relationship between body and soul that stands at the heart of racist claims. Already in the Middle Ages, as Suzanne Akbari has demonstrated, disdain for Muslims and Jews was linked to their bodies—their alleged ugliness and odor.[24] Those qualities were alleged in order to evoke disgust, a tenacious emotion that fuels us in dangerous ways. The real danger, however, was believed to lie in the spiritual beliefs and character traits of Jews and Muslims—their baneful moral influence on good Christians. Corruption, greed, and carnality were claimed to be dangerous because they could poison all of society. This is an important point because it demonstrates an underlying, unacknowledged premise of racists: their own vulnerability, the danger posed to them that they are unable to defend against. Race was not only static and immutable but also fluid and contagious—racists feared that white people could become black, that Christians could become Jews. Shakespeare captured this fear in *The Merchant of Venice*: "The Hebrew will turn Christian. He grows kind," says Antonio after receiving a loan from Shylock, a loan he will soon regret having taken, since he also agreed to forfeit a pound of his flesh if he could not repay it (1.3). Initially, there seemed to be no danger in the bond Antonio made with Shylock; only later did the danger become apparent, when Shylock tried to claim his bond—and Antonio's death. The danger Shylock posed lay in his insistence on claiming the bond and his refusal to show mercy; this is not a physical threat per se but a moral one—Shylock's immorality turned him into a physical threat to Antonio's life. Not his body, but what was inherent in it, was the danger.[25] Race is defined by moral and spiritual qualities—kindness marks the Christian—and can change through social intimacy. Shylock's servant worries, "I am a Jew if I serve the Jew any longer" (2.2). The ultimate fear is not of skin color or other bodily attributes but of what the body contains: moral and spiritual degeneracy. Moral qualities were inherent in the body, so that race was conceptualized as a form of incarnational theology.[26]

Yet skin is not always dark or appearance different. Racism requires training in how to read the body and know what is incarnate in it; racism is a form of hermeneutics, a way to read the world. The philosopher Charles Mills, in his groundbreaking book *The Racial Contract*, writes, "on matters related to race, the Racial Contract prescribes for its signatories an inverted epistemology, an epistemology of ignorance, a particular pattern of localized and global cognitive dysfunctions (which are psychologically and socially functional), producing the ironic outcome that whites will in general be unable to understand the world they themselves have made."[27] Demolishing the pseudoscholarship of racial theory, however, puts us in the peculiar position of examining a phenomenon, race, that was the construct of racists who have since been discredited. Racial theory has long since been revealed as rubbish, so why has racism not gone away?

## Racism's Self-Concealment

Racism eisegetically and insidiously reads degeneracy into human beings, but it often does so by concealing its intentions. Indeed, one of its most successful tactics is to conceal itself in subtle ways. Racism continues to dominate the globe, sometimes disguised as "law and order," mandatory prison sentences, protection against voter fraud, the birther movement's attacks on President Obama, or as a tool to make a political conflict intractable, as in the racialization of the Israel-Palestine conflict or the Sunni-Shiite wars, or in the legitimation of servitude in what is called the caste system of India. "What makes Western racism so autonomous and conspicuous in world history," George Fredrickson points out, "has been that it developed in a context that presumed human equality of some kind."[28] No wonder this way of reading the world produces confusion and increased feelings of vulnerability.



Racism is frequently implicit. Nancy Harrowitz has elucidated the origins of the "criminal man" described by late nineteenth-century founders of the field of criminology, including Cesare Lombroso, within anti-Semitic racism concerning Jews.[29] The image of the "criminal" was drawn from antisemitic cartoons of Jews, but that connection was never made explicit. If overcoming racism requires revelation, deploying racism requires concealment.

Concealing racism brings its own kind of trauma. The psychoanalyst Kimberlyn Leary observes, "Passing always occurs in the context of a relationship: it requires, on the one side, a subject who does not tell, and on the other, an audience who fails to ask."[30] In response to racism we are often told to become "colorblind"; the slogan, we are told, should not be "black lives matter" but "all lives matter." No need for a feminist movement to protect women's rights; it's human rights that matter—a clever strategy for supporting the status quo and its injustices. As Sara Ahmed notes, "It has become commonplace for whiteness to be represented as invisible, as the unseen or the unmarked, as a non-colour, the absent presence or hidden referent, against which all other colours are measured as forms of deviance. . . . But of course whiteness is only invisible for those who inhabit it."[31] But whiteness is indeed marked as a specific historical and ideological configuration, as a power within the context of material forces. What is needed is a black countergaze, black voices that speak about whiteness from a nonwhite location, the philosopher George Yancy writes.[32] What does whiteness mean to those who are not white? The Afro-Caribbean psychiatrist, philosopher, and political theorist Frantz Fanon once described the fantasy of the white child: "Mama, the Negro is going to eat me!" Who is afraid of whom? Fanon asks.[33] The white fear is rooted in the fantasies that invent racism. In reality, an African American has far more reason to be frightened by a white person, especially one wearing a suit of governmental representation, such as a police uniform.

In the United States, one problem that besets the study of race is the overwhelming focus on the black-white binary to the neglect of other racial, ethnic, and diasporic categories. Privileging antiblack racism and white supremacy, the black-white binary keeps us from examining race beyond the binary—that is, how racism exists in situations in which we are intertwined—in biracial and mestizo identities, and in the outsider racializations that construct Asians, Latinos, Muslims, Native Americans, or, in earlier generations, Irish, Italian, and Jewish citizens as alien—or as "exemplary models for their people." Moreover, the binary fails to acknowledge the nature of the oppression experienced by black Africans at the hands of black African dictators, and the internalized oppression of self-hatred.

Lisa Lowe points to the ways in which legislative acts (such as the Chinese Exclusion Act of 1882 and Alien Land Laws of 1913, 1920, and 1923) constructed Asian immigrants to the United States as "illegal aliens." She calls attention to the "acts of labor, resistance, memory, and survival" of those "alienated" subjects who produce "politicized cultural work that emerges from dislocation and disidentification."[34] From the legal definition of illegal aliens there emerged a racialized cultural depiction of Asian Americans. Aimee Bahng has examined the ways in which Asian Americans appear in American horror films as monster aliens with distorted bodies from foreign planets—as enormous or as able to maneuver through tactics of martial arts or by developing technological advances against the hegemony of white people.[35] Science fiction novels of conquest, imperialism, and aliens are often displaced metaphors for despised racial groups. Fears evoked by narratives of, say, Asian technological advances are expressed in the title of the economist Yoshi Tsurumi's book about Japanese economic prowess, *The Japanese Are Coming*. American imperialism and capitalism shaped migration to this country, yet the migrants, essential to the economy, became sites for promoting racialized hatred. Donald Trump has called for building a wall on the U.S. border with Mexico, claiming, without proof, that Mexicans are "rapists," despite the fact that border cities generally report the lowest crime rates in their respective states. Racism is concealed under the guise of protection against a nonexistent criminal threat. Antiliberalism flourishes under the guise of "protecting" the United States. Lowe points out that the experience of Asian Americans can lend a critical perspective to a national memory forged in narratives of liberal democracy and citizenship that actively forgets acts of exclusion and disavows U.S. imperialism.[36] That is, race conceals itself even—or especially—in the general narrative of this country's history.

How do we explain the persistence and tenacity of racism? Perhaps the most salient feature of studies of race is that it never exists on its own. It is fed and empowered by money, politics, and power, but also by producing pleasure, arousal, and comfort. The social scientists Andrew Penner and Aliya Saperstein have demonstrated that gender and financial cues shape race: "status cues, such as living in the suburbs, make both women and men more likely to be seen as white," whereas "receiving welfare makes women (but not men) more likely to subsequently be seen as Black and incarceration makes men (but not women) less likely to subsequently be seen as white." Studies of hiring practices demonstrate that a résumé with a typically white name will result in a job interview, whereas a résumé with a typically black name will not.[37]



Such social scientific research on racism reveals the tenacious ways in which racism functions, often concealed beneath other kinds of structures, such as gender or economic status. Yet revealing the power of race does not necessarily explain its tenacity, nor does it necessarily lead to its repudiation. Perhaps race remains so tenacious because it has ingrained itself in unconscious processes. The psychoanalyst Henry F. Smith describes intrapsychic processes that produce and maintain the logic of race, processes that emerge from our earliest primitive defenses, which "split our objects . . . into the feared and the safe, the loved and the hated . . . the envied and the denigrated," and then become "projected and introjected in endless repetitions."[38] Smith's explanation clarifies why, even though we may repudiate racism, it still coils around our minds at deep levels. Of course, the functions of race do not operate only at the unconscious level, nor is it inevitable that racism becomes part of our mechanisms of projection and introjection. The social production of racist structures and attitudes returns us to the question, Why is racism so tenacious?

Conventional measures of economic footing, social status, and educational level fail to explain the tenacity of racism and why its political importance so often overrides issues of great personal relevance, such as jobs, health care, and education. This exemplifies what Elizabeth Freeman, in a different context, calls "erotohistoriography," which examines "a politics of unpredictable, deeply embodied pleasures that counters the logic of development."[39] The tenacity enjoyed by racism points us to the recognition that "racism has its own life," as Sharon Patricia Holland writes in her book *The Erotic Life of Racism*. Holland notes that race functions in much the same way as incest. Both work to bind us: the taboo of incest defines the boundaries of the family without forming barriers among its members; race, too, preserves "our sense of separateness and belonging," thus keeping us from "the project of universal belonging, against the findings, if you will, of the human genome project." Why would people want to be kept from universal belonging? Holland proposes that the answer, and the key to racism's tenacity, is its emotional valence: "Racism can also be described as the emotional lifeblood of race; it is the 'feeling' that articulates and keeps the flawed logic of race in its place."[40] The appeal of racism lies in its sense of transgression and the excitement that it generates, which may produce feelings of empowerment that seem to overcome, at least temporarily, self-denigration. The cruelty embedded in racism delivers a feeling of domination: the racially targeted object is denigrated and the racist is elevated, at least within that racial context. A racially ordered society is hierarchical and opens its upper ranks to the favored group, regardless of economic or social status. Acts of racial cruelty elevate one's social status; racism turns masochism into sadism.

In her study of slavery, Saidiya Hartman asks why regimes of slavery are infused with what she calls the "erotics of terror." She points to the legal transposition of the definition of rape, an act of violence, into an act of forced sexual intercourse. As intercourse, this definition of rape shrouds the violence of racial domination with the suggestion of sexual complicity.[41] Rape is not a sexual act, but an act of violence.

Studies of racism that focus on mental and emotional constructs—the erotics of race—must also keep in mind the materiality of the racialized body. Consider George Yancy's description of an encounter in an elevator: a white woman clutches her purse when he walks in. "After all, within the social space of the elevator, which has become a hermeneutic transactional space within which all of my intended meanings get falsified, it is as if I am no longer in charge of what I mean/intend. What she 'sees' or 'hears' is governed by a racist epistemology of certitude that places me under erasure." The erasure to which Yancy refers is erasure of the fact that he is, among other things, a Yale-educated professor of philosophy; racism turns an intellectual into a "Negro [who] *is* the genital and *is* the incarnation of evil."[42] In this way, erasure has a double effect: it eliminates facts and replaces them with fictions and fantasies. Again, this way of seeing the world and remaking it in such unreal ways destabilizes both those who are viewed through such a lens and those who do the viewing. Subject and object become other than what they understand themselves to be. Racist epistemology unmakes the world.

### Religion

How has religion, and especially Judaism, responded to racism? The rise of racial theory in the nineteenth century during the same era as the rise of historicism raises unresolved questions about the intellectual history of that era. The search for timeless, immutable principles in the face of historicism's claims of mutability and instability appears as a contradiction.

For theologians in particular, historicism seemed to undermine religious certainties. At the same time, the racist logic of timeless, immutable principles recapitulates the logic of classical theology, the central principles of which claim to transcend time and history.

If racial theory arose so as to appropriate the immutability previously held by religious principles, it found in religion both its strongest support and its greatest foe. Bruce Duthu, a colleague of mine on the faculty at Dartmouth College and a member of the Houma Nation of Louisiana who is also a legal scholar of tribal sovereignty, told me about a Catholic church in southeastern Louisiana, where he grew up, in which wooden bars were nailed to the top of the pews to designate the Indian section of the church. In the early 1960s, a newly arrived priest immediately tore down those bars and delivered them to the local bishop, who had for too long permitted them. The priest informed the bishop that if anyone wanted to know why the bars had been removed, he would tell them to ask the bishop to explain why they had been permitted in God's church in the first place. The Catholic Church had installed the bars, but a Catholic priest also removed them. During the civil rights movement, as David Chappell has demonstrated, the Bible that had been used for so long to justify segregation in the American South became the source of inspiration for those who fought to end segregation and dismantle Jim Crow. The oppressors were defeated when their own weapon was turned against them.[43]

Significant social change takes place in the name of religion only in settings in which religion plays a significant role, such as the civil rights movement in the United States and the nonviolent resistance to British colonial rule led by Mahatma Gandhi in India. By contrast, for some German Protestant theologians, concerned about the contextualization of the historical Jesus, racial theory arrived as a gift: apparent historical similarities between Jesus and other rabbis of first-century Palestine, which threatened to undermine his originality and uniqueness, could be overcome by claiming Jesus's racial identity as an Aryan. Race trumped historicism in that context.

Within contemporary American religious thought, historicism is secondary to social ethics: what matters most is not whether Jesus's message was original but its usefulness in creating a more just society today. Yet religion in the United States operates under restraints, argues Vincent Lloyd. Religion and race are both "managed" in contemporary America, Lloyd writes, regulated by secular forces that he identifies as white. The inscription at the Martin Luther King Jr. Memorial in Washington, D.C., Lloyd notes, does not mention religion, although King was a Christian minister, and it invokes race only as something to be overcome: "Our loyalties must transcend our race."[44] The object of those "loyalties" is not specified—it might be religion, justice, equality, humanity—but can race be "transcended"? Or is race the "transcendent" element that is not specified or addressed because it seems to transcend and survive our many efforts at eradication? The pronoun "our" in the admonition can carry a different nuance depending on whether we read it as referring to whites or blacks. If religion is the power that can best eviscerate racism, racists will turn to secularism to manage and constrain religious power, Lloyd suggests.



### Theological Directions

In the 1970s, the national coalition of blacks and Jews broke down and seemed doomed. Yet the memory of that coalition continues to be evoked and debated. Of those Jews who opposed Jewish involvement in the civil rights movement, some followed Meir Kahane, founder of the Jewish Defense League and of the Israeli political party Kach, which was subsequently outlawed by the Knesset as fascist. Kahane drew inspiration from the Black Panthers to develop a Jewish movement of power and violence, similarly nourished by resentment.

American Jews of that era were essentially divided between two poles, one represented by Abraham Joshua Heschel, a theologian who embodied religious Judaism and a commitment to social justice and ecumenism, and the other symbolized by Kahane, who tried to create a Jewish version of the Black Panthers, a group he admired greatly. Heschel, born in 1907 in Poland to a distinguished family of Hasidic *rebbes*, escaped Nazi Europe at the last moment. He had a close personal bond with King and spoke of the failures of human beings who had produced "Auschwitz and Hiroshima." Kahane, born in 1932 in the United States, advocated an extreme form of Jewish nationalism, including violence, arguing that "Jewish existence [is] the highest moral imperative."[45] His slogan "Never Again!" was applied to Jews, whereas the phrase for Heschel applied to all human beings.

While racial theory argues that certain attributes are fixed in particular "races," Kahane turned the argument around. It is not Jews who have fixed attributes, but racists whose antisemitism is fixed and immutable. Jewish behavior was irrelevant to Kahane; Esau will forever hate Jacob; Gentiles will forever hate Jews. Zionism and the State of Israel will not bring an end to antisemitism, nor will Zionism allow Jews to escape antisemitism, which is doomed to prevail forever in Kahane's scenario. Kahane thus affirms the claims of racial theory but in reverse, applying them to racists rather than to their targets.

For Heschel, by contrast, racism is anathema; he called it "Satanism, unmitigated evil," and "an eye disease." Rather than the outgrowth of Christian anti-Judaism, Heschel argued that Nazi antisemitism was a "pagan" attack on both Christianity and Judaism. As such, racism cannot coexist with religion because it contradicts fundamental theological assumptions, such as the biblical claim that God is the creator of all human beings, not just of one people or a hierarchy of peoples. Precisely the immutability of such biblical teachings provides Heschel with the claim that historical manifestations of racism are contrary to true religious belief.



Kahane often wrote with admiration of the Black Panthers for their social services within the African American community and their affirmation of black identity, and especially for their militarism and fearless advocacy of violence. He invoked the Black Panthers frequently in his writings, calling for an equivalent in the Jewish Defense League that he created in 1968 and in his earlier activities in the movement to free Soviet Jewry.[46] As Shaul Magid points out, Kahane's goal was not simply "defense" of Jewish interests but the active use of violence as "a requisite instrument of Jewish subject formation and a battle against American Jewish liberalism" and against Gentile antisemitism.[47] Though he wrote in an era, the 1960s, that was not marked by attacks on Jews, Kahane's politics of Jewish resentment helped fuel a nascent Jewish nationalism that ultimately became dangerous in Israel; indeed, Kahane's political party, Kach, was ultimately outlawed in 1988 by the Israeli parliament as racist and antidemocratic.

Heschel, by contrast, did not believe in nourishing resentment but in promoting optimism. Although he was not a pacifist, he opposed the war in Vietnam as a pointless war that had deteriorated into atrocities against civilians. Heschel's alliance was with King and the Southern Christian Leadership Conference. His reading of scripture and Jewish tradition was entirely different from Kahane's; the prophets and Hasidism were two of the most important sources for his political engagement. Indeed, Heschel's book *The Prophets*, a study of prophetic consciousness, was one of the key texts for King and his colleagues.

Numerous philosophers and theologians have proposed paths to reconciliation between perpetrators and victims of horrific crimes in an effort to bring about a radical change in relations and also a massive shift in the course of history. Efforts to acknowledge the suffering of others and achieve coexistence and even forgiveness have occurred in the wake of several major and deeply traumatic events, including South African apartheid and the genocide in Rwanda. In the United States, however, we have commemorations of the civil rights movement but little effort at recognizing the effects of racism, including slavery, largely because racism is ongoing: the crime has not yet come to an end.



King and Heschel had similar theological sensibilities, despite the enormous differences in their backgrounds and religious commitments. King made the Hebrew Bible central to the civil rights movement, emphasizing the role of Moses and the teachings of the prophets, and Heschel provided an understanding of prophecy that went beyond demands for social justice. Drawing on classical Jewish sources, Heschel wrote of the pathos of God, that God responds to human deeds and is affected by the way we treat each other. Rather than remote and transcendent, God is immanent and deeply involved in human life. Further, Heschel wrote that the prophets were in sympathy with God, profoundly disturbed by injustice and by the treatment of those who stand at the margins of society—widows and orphans. To injure a human being, he wrote, is to injure God, a position that does not endorse incarnation but rather an exquisite attunement of God and human beings. For Heschel, it is not simply that human beings are sacred images of God; holiness is not given to us but created by us.

For King, too, suffering was neither private nor inconsequential; by merging with the biblical narrative, his movement took on cosmic proportions. During the Montgomery bus boycott, King declared, "God is using Montgomery as His proving ground," assuring his followers, "Remember, if I am stopped, this movement will not stop because God is with the movement." Later, in 1968, he said, "It is possible for me to falter, but I am profoundly secure in my knowledge that God loves us; He has not worked out a design for our failure." In Memphis, the night before he was assassinated, King described civil rights activists as the biblical bush that held the presence of God: the bush burned but was not consumed. From that bush came the voice of God, speaking to Moses. King declared, "Bull Connor would say, 'Turn the firehoses on.' And as I said to you the other night, Bull Connor didn't know history. He knew a kind of physics that somehow didn't relate to the transphysics that we knew about, and that was the fact that there was a certain kind of fire that no water could put out."[48] Divine immanence meant not only God's presence within the civil rights movement but also the transcendent nature of those who participated in the movement.

## Conclusion

Writing in the midst of the racism that has been aroused in the United States during Donald Trump's presidency, with its daily headlines broadcasting Trump's racist slurs against Mexicans, Muslims, and African Americans, not to mention his misogyny, it is difficult to hope that racism will ever be overcome. Reading the pessimism that infuses Ta-Nehisi Coates's best-seller makes the hope of the civil rights movement seem defeated. Much remains on the agenda for Jewish thinkers. Analyses of antisemitism continue, but perhaps it is now time to refocus our attention. Few studies of antisemitism incorporate the newer methods of analyzing racism, such as those of Freeman or Holland, and few place antisemitism within the larger context of social prejudice and racism. Antisemitism is too often presented as a unique phenomenon, "the longest hatred," not to be compared with other examples of hate.



A central question today for the African American community is: how can we overcome Afro-pessimism? What tools are available, whether political or spiritual, and what alliances can be forged? Jews are beset with pessimism, too, though they may not always recognize it. The anger and resentment that Kahane fostered, and that continues to circulate its poison throughout the world today, is mired in assumptions of racial theory that attempt to defy historicism. The claim that Esau will forever hate Jacob and that antisemitism is immutable should be rejected just as racial theory was repudiated. Racism and antisemitism are historical phenomena, produced in particular contexts, often supported by psychic processes or erotic desires that can be regulated, refocused, and, hopefully, renounced. Jews, too, may be beset by a pessimism that needs to be confronted and recognized as misguided. The ethical imperative today requires a change of focus: studies revealing the extent of racism are insufficient. Once racism is revealed to us, what will motivate us to undertake concrete social transformation and changes in our own personal, often deeply held and even unconscious, racist desires? What we require from our ethicists are resources for the hope that racism will indeed be overcome.[49]

When Jesse Jackson addressed the country on live television at the 1984 Democratic National Convention to ask forgiveness for having made an anti-Jewish comment a few months earlier, he invoked the friendship that has become an American icon: "We are bound by Dr. Martin Luther King Jr. and Rabbi Abraham Heschel, crying out from their graves for us to reach common ground."[50] The King-Heschel friendship has had an extraordinary afterlife as a source of profound inspiration for reconciliation across immense gulfs, and especially as a source of hope to transcend the fraught political map of black-Jewish relations. Their friendship is a reminder of a great moment in which these two men of radically different backgrounds crossed immense gulfs of color, religion, gender, and political orientation. Photographs of them standing side by side are reprinted in publications about black-Jewish relations, and their friendship stands as a call for vision, hope, and transcendence of political conflict. The United States may not yet be ready for reconciliation, let alone forgiveness, given the extent and depth of the racism that disfigures our past and our present. Yet small acts of symbolic meaning may at least stimulate our desire to create change.



## Notes

1. Du Bois, *Souls of Black Folk*, 9.
2. Diner, *In the Almost Promised Land*.
3. Staub, *Torn at the Roots*.
4. Baldwin, *Fire Next Time*, 51, 67.
5. See the recording of an interview with Malcolm X at the University of California, Berkeley, on October 11, 1963, at https://www.youtube.com/watch?v=FZMrti8QcPA.
6. The debate question was "Has the American Dream Been Achieved at the Expense of the American Negro?" The debate can be viewed at https://www.youtube.com/watch?v=oFeoS41xe7w.
7. Berman, "Introduction."
8. West, *Race Matters*, 107.
9. Berman, "Introduction," 4–6.
10. Lloyd, "Introduction."
11. I discuss this in chapter 5 of my book *Abraham Geiger and the Jewish Jesus*.
12. Heschel, *Jüdischer Islam*.
13. Metz, "Photography and Fetish."
14. Alexander, *New Jim Crow*.
15. Alexander, "Coates's *Between the World and Me*."
16. Alexander, *New Jim Crow*, 6.
17. Shelby, "Racial Realities and Corrective Justice."
18. See Butler, *Frames of War*.
19. Shelby, *Dark Ghettos*.
20. Shelby, "Racial Realities and Corrective Justice," 160.
21. Prevot, "Divine Opacity."
22. Lee, "Introduction."
23. Coates, *Between the World and Me*, 7.
24. Akbari, *Idols in the East*.
25. Heschel, "From Jesus to Shylock."
26. See Heschel, "Race as Incarnational Theology."
27. Mills, *Racial Contract*, 18.
28. Fredrickson, *Racism*, 11.
29. See Harrowitz's study *Antisemitism, Misogyny*.
30. Leary, "Passing, Posing, and 'Keeping It Real,'" 85.
31. Ahmed, "Declarations of Whiteness."
32. Yancy, "White Gazes."
33. Fanon, *Black Skin, White Masks*, 112.
34. Lowe, *Immigrant Acts*, 9.
35. Bahng, "Extrapolating Transnational Arcs."
36. Lowe, *Immigrant Acts*, 21.
37. Penner and Saperstein, "Engendering Racial Perceptions," 320.
38. Smith, "Invisible Racism," 11.
39. Freeman, "Time Binds," quoted in Holland, *Erotic Life of Racism*, 43.
40. Holland, *Erotic Life of Racism*, 107, 110, 3, 6.
41. Hartman, *Scenes of Subjection*, 85.
42. Yancy, "White Gazes," 56.
43. See Chappell's *Stone of Hope*.
44. Lloyd, "Introduction," 1.
45. Kahane, *Never Again*, 191.
46. Beckerman, *When They Come for Us*.
47. Magid, "Anti-Semitism as Colonialism," 251–52.
48. Quoted in Osborn, "Last Mountaintop of Martin Luther King, Jr.," 153.
49. I would like to express my thanks to Jonathan K. Crane for inviting me to present a paper at the conference "Race with Jewish Ethics," held at Emory University in October 2015. My thanks, too, for the

excellent comments from colleagues who were present, and my particular appreciation to Robert Erlewine for a thoughtful reading of that paper. As always, I am grateful to the Dartmouth College faculty seminar on race for many stimulating discussions.

50. Jackson, "Speech to the Democratic National Convention," 385.

## References


Ahmed, Sara. "Declarations of Whiteness: The Non-Performativity of Anti-Racism." *borderlands* 3, no. 2 (2004). http://www.borderlands.net.au/vol3no2_2004/ahmed_declarations.htm.

Akbari, Suzanne Conklin. *Idols in the East: European Representations of Islam and the Orient, 1100–1450*. Ithaca: Cornell University Press, 2009.

Alexander, Michelle. *The New Jim Crow: Mass Incarceration in the Age of Colorblindness*. New York: New Press, 2010.

———. "Ta-Nehisi Coates's *Between the World and Me*." *New York Times*, August 17, 2015.

Bahng, Aimee. "Extrapolating Transnational Arcs, Excavating Imperial Legacies: The Speculative Acts of Karen Tei Yamashita's *Through the Arc of the Rain Forest*." "Alien/Asian," edited by Stephen H. Sohn, special issue, *MELUS* 33, no. 4 (2008): 123–44.

Baldwin, James. *The Fire Next Time*. New York: Dial Press, 1963.

Beckerman, Gal. *When They Come for Us, We'll Be Gone: The Epic Struggle to Save Soviet Jewry*. New York: First Mariner Books, 2011.

Berman, Paul. "Introduction." In *Blacks and Jews: Alliances and Arguments*, edited by Paul Berman, 1–28. New York: Delacorte Press, 1994.

Butler, Judith. *Frames of War: When Is Life Grievable?* New York: Verso, 2009.

Chappell, David L. *A Stone of Hope: Prophetic Religion and the Death of Jim Crow*. Chapel Hill: University of North Carolina Press, 2004.

Coates, Ta-Nehisi. *Between the World and Me*. New York: Spiegel and Grau, 2015.

Diner, Hasia. *In the Almost Promised Land: American Jews and Blacks, 1915–1935*. Baltimore: Johns Hopkins University Press, 1977.

Du Bois, W. E. B. *The Souls of Black Folk*. Rockville, Md.: Arc Manor Press, 2008.

Esposito, Roberto. *Bios: Biopolitics and Philosophy*. Translated by Timothy Campbell. Minneapolis: University of Minnesota Press, 2008.

Fanon, Frantz. *Black Skin, White Masks*. Translated by Charles Lam Markmann. New York: Grove Press, 1967.

Fredrickson, George M. *Racism: A Short History*. Princeton: Princeton University Press, 2002.

Freeman, Elizabeth. "Time Binds, or, Erotohistoriography." *Social Text* 23, nos. 3–4 (2005): 57–68.

Harrowitz, Nancy. *Antisemitism, Misogyny, and the Logic of Cultural Difference: Cesare Lombroso and Matilde Serao*. Lincoln: University of Nebraska Press, 1994.

Hartman, Saidiya V. *Scenes of Subjection: Terror, Slavery, and Self-Making in Nineteenth-Century America*. New York: Oxford University Press, 1997.

Heschel, Abraham Joshua. "Kaddish for Our Souls." In *Abraham Joshua Heschel: Essential Writings*, edited by Susannah Heschel, 78–79. Maryknoll, N.Y.: Orbis Books, 2011.

———. "Religion and Race." In *The Insecurity of Freedom: Essays on Human Existence*, 85–100. New York: Farrar, Straus and Giroux, 1966.

Heschel, Susannah. *Abraham Geiger and the Jewish Jesus*. Chicago: University of Chicago Press, 1998.

———. "From Jesus to Shylock: Christian Supersessionism and *The Merchant of Venice*." *Harvard Theological Review* 99, no. 4 (2006): 381–405.

———. *Jüdischer Islam: Islam und jüdisch-deutsche Selbstbestimmung*. Translated by Dirk Hartwig, Moritz Buchner, and Georges Khalil. Berlin: Matthes und Seitz, 2018.

———. "Race as Incarnational Theology: Affinities Between German Protestantism and Racial Theory." In *Prejudice and Christian Beginnings: Race, Gender, and Ethnicity in Early Christian Studies*, edited by Laura Nasrallah and Elisabeth Schüssler Fiorenza, 211–34. Minneapolis: Fortress Press, 2009.

Holland, Sharon Patricia. *The Erotic Life of Racism*. Durham: Duke University Press, 2012.

Jackson, Jesse Louis. "Speech to the Democratic National Convention (1984)." In *The Will of a People: A Critical Anthology of Great African American Speeches*, edited by Richard W. Leeman and Bernard K. Duffy, 372–93. Carbondale: Southern Illinois University Press, 2012.

Kahane, Meir. *Never Again!* New York: Pyramid Books, 1971.

Leary, Kimberlyn. "Passing, Posing, and 'Keeping it Real.'" *Constellations* 6, no. 1 (1999): 85–96.

Lee, Emily S. "Introduction." In *Living Alterities: Phenomenology, Embodiment, and Race*, edited by Emily S. Lee, 1–18. Albany: State University of New York Press, 2014.

Lloyd, Vincent W. "Introduction: Managing Race, Managing Religion." In *Race and Secularism in America*, edited by Jonathon S. Kahn and Vincent W. Lloyd, 1–19. New York: Columbia University Press, 2016.

Lowe, Lisa. *Immigrant Acts: On Asian American Cultural Politics*. Durham: Duke University Press, 1996.

Magid, Shaul. "Anti-Semitism as Colonialism: Meir Kahane's 'Ethics of Violence.'" *Journal of Jewish Ethics* 1, no. 2 (2015): 203–32.

Metz, Christian. "Photography and Fetish." *October* 34 (Autumn 1985): 81–90.

Mills, Charles W. *The Racial Contract*. Ithaca: Cornell University Press, 1999.

Osborn, Michael. "The Last Mountaintop of Martin Luther King, Jr." In *Martin Luther King Jr. and the Sermonic Power of Public Discourse*, edited by Carolyn Calloway-Thomas and John Louis Lucaites, 147–61. Tuscaloosa: University of Alabama Press, 1993.

Penner, Andrew M., and Aliya Saperstein. "Engendering Racial Perceptions: An Intersectional Analysis of How Social Status Shapes Race." *Gender and Society* 27 (June 2013): 319–44.

Podhoretz, Norman. "My Negro Problem—And Ours." *Commentary*, February 1963. https://www.commentarymagazine.com/articles/my-negro-problem-and-ours.

Prevot, Andrew L. "Divine Opacity: Mystical Theology, Black Theology, and the Problem of Light-Dark Aesthetics." *Spiritus: A Journal of Christian Spirituality* 16, no. 2 (2016): 166–88.

Shelby, Tommie. *Dark Ghettos: Injustice, Dissent, and Reform*. Cambridge, Mass.: Harvard University Press, 2016.

———. "Racial Realities and Corrective Justice: A Reply to Charles Mills." *Critical Philosophy of Race* 1, no. 2 (2013): 145–62.

Smith, Henry F. "Invisible Racism." *Psychoanalytic Quarterly* 75 (2006): 3–19.

Staub, Michael E. *Torn at the Roots: The Crisis of Jewish Liberalism in Postwar America*. New York: Columbia University Press, 2002.

Tsurumi, Yoshi. *The Japanese Are Coming: A Multinational Interaction of Firms and Politics*. Cambridge, Mass.: Ballinger, 1976.

West, Cornel. *Race Matters*. 25th anniversary ed. Boston: Beacon Press, 2017.

Yancy, George. "White Gazes: What It Feels Like to Be an Essence." In *Living Alterities: Phenomenology, Embodiment, and Race*, edited by Emily S. Lee, 43–64. Albany: State University of New York Press, 2014.

## Classic Text and Questions to Ponder

In Heschel's view, racism is a tenacious and slippery feature of society. Insofar as racists think race is immutable, racism itself is also immutable. Racism conceals and reinscribes itself in tenacious ways, coloring how people think and behave in their personal daily lives. When aggregated, such negative assumptions spoil civilization to the point of complete destruction. Just before unleashing the flood, "Adonai saw how great was man's wickedness on earth, and how every plan devised by his mind was nothing but evil each day. And Adonai regretted that [God] had made man on earth, and [God's] heart was saddened" (Genesis 6:5-6). So in sorrow, God embarked on blotting people from the earth.

- How is racism like religion, "insist[ing] on timeless, immutable qualities"?
- If racism (and its various notions of race) does in fact change or mutate, in what ways do those alterations go unnoticed? Why are those changes virtually invisible?
- Do you agree that racism is an indelible feature of society? Why or why not? What could be done to blot it out?

# 3

# When Our Legs Utter Songs

## Toward an Antiracist Ethic Based on Amos 1–6

WILLA M. JOHNSON

The church, scholars, policymakers, and legislators have all used the Hebrew Bible to socially construct, bolster, and maintain structural racism in the United States. Antiracist voices have countered these appropriations of the text. For example, during the civil rights era, some black theologians used the Hebrew Bible to argue that God was on the side of the oppressed. But this argument has been characterized as banal and unrealistic. In 1903, the eminent W. E. B. Du Bois refuted the notion that a loving, omnipotent God controlled human affairs. He saw this idea as incongruent with the plight of African people in the United States and elsewhere. "Who today actually believes that this world is ruled and directed by a benevolent person of great power who, on humble appeal, will change the course of events at our request?" Du Bois asked. "Who believes in miracles? Many folk follow religious ceremonies and services and allow their children to learn fairy tales and so-called religious truth, which in time children come to recognize as conventional lies told by their parents and teachers for the children's good. One can hardly exaggerate the moral disaster of this custom."[1] Du Bois, the first American sociologist of religion, understood the social problems faced by Africans and African Americans, certainly within the context of slavery and other historical inequalities, and perhaps from a perspective that black theologians and other religionists may not have appreciated.

In this chapter I argue that the prophetic texts in the Hebrew Bible, particularly the book of Amos, provide a framework for an antiracist ethic. This is distinctly different from claims that have historically maintained that the Bible is directly applicable to the American context, as if God had ordained the United States as a substitute for ancient Israel.[2] If these American exceptionalists and apologists for racism had understood the biblical text in its own historical and social contexts, then they would neither have attempted to substitute the United States for Israel, nor ignored Amos and other prophetic voices. These texts are clear about "God's" absolute intolerance of oppression and the incongruity between oppression and worship. Here I pause and place "God" in quotation marks. The whole notion of a sociology of religion linked to a social constructivist perspective presupposes that religions with "God" and texts such as the Hebrew Bible are part of a socially fabricated "conceptual machinery" that is necessary to communicate the community's knowledge and most cherished values.[3] These were mechanisms for socialization processes that shaped the kind of communities and world in which ancient Israelites wished to participate. Thus the Hebrew Bible's notion of a God who calls a prophet to deliver messages about social justice is itself an artifact of ancient Israelites' beliefs about how people should treat one another in order to live up to their highest human good. Reckoning with these factors translates biblical texts from an otherworldliness to a this-world relevance. In this respect, Amos argues simply and eloquently for us to *live worship*. He recasts worship as social justice, exemplified in numerous ways. It is how we conduct everyday tasks and how we transact business. It is precisely this aspect of the book of Amos that makes it suitable as a beginning ground for an antiracist ethic. I build this argument by employing the works of Rabbi Abraham Joshua Heschel and Dr. Martin Luther King Jr. Before I discuss Amos, it is necessary to define racism and discuss the meaning and relevance of *whiteness*, *white privilege* or *power*, and *white religiosity* or *Christianity*. These concepts are key to understanding the hierarchical strata established by structural racism. I then connect the historical use of stories from the Hebrew Bible to racist or white supremacist uses of the Bible in the United States. Finally, I briefly outline King's and Heschel's use of religion and the Bible before suggesting how prophetic texts can become a foundation for an antiracist ethic.



### Racism and Uses of the Hebrew Bible in American Culture

I use the term *structural racism* to mean something more than antilocution (hate speech) or discrimination (unequal access) directed against individual persons, or myriad insults hurled, intentionally or not, against nonwhites on a daily basis.[4] Although these incidents—*microaggressions*, *microinvalidations*, and *microassaults*—are one form of racism, racism is a by-product of power differences incorporated into structures of privilege and supported by social, economic, and political factors.[5] Eduardo Bonilla-Silva explains,



> When race emerged in human history, it formed a social structure (a racialized social system) that awarded systemic privileges to Europeans (peoples who became "white") over non-Europeans (the peoples who became "nonwhite"). Racialized social systems, or white supremacy for short, became global and affected all societies where Europeans extended their reach. I therefore conceive a society's racial structure *as the totality of the social relations and practices that reinforce white privilege*. Accordingly, the task of analysts interested in studying racial structures is to uncover the particular social, economic, political, social control, and ideological mechanisms responsible for the reproduction of racial privilege in society.[6]

Thus racism extends far beyond mere prejudice—that is, thinking ill of people because of their group membership. The nature of racism is pervasive rather than episodic. To quote Joe Feagin and Louwanda Evans, racism "appears as a *vampire-like system*" that for more than two centuries has extracted from the racially targeted their emotional, cognitive, and other energies in most social institutions.[7]

### Whiteness: A Shifting yet Stable and Enduring Concept

One key to grasping Bonilla-Silva's notion of racial structures is understanding whiteness and white privilege. In everyday life we use certain physical biological features, such as hair texture or skin color, that are passed generationally as the basis for determining a person's race. But this idea is too facile, because the label "white" and the power associated with whiteness have not always been extended to all light-skinned people. During the nineteenth century, white Anglo-Saxon Protestants in the United States considered Irish immigrants nonwhite. Indeed, into the early twentieth century, immigrants from southern and eastern Europe were deemed nonwhite as well.[8] In 1923, in *United States v. Bhagat Singh Thind*, the U.S. Supreme Court ruled that "although a high-caste Hindu [was] of the Caucasian or Aryan race, s/he is not white within the meaning of the naturalization laws." However, sometime during the early twentieth century, views changed. According to Allan J.

Lichtman, the court reasoned that "'immigrants from Eastern, Southern and Middle Europe, among them the Slavs and the dark-eyed, swarthy people of Alpine and Mediterranean stock' would merge into the white population 'and lose the distinctive hallmarks of their European origin,'" whereas Asians would not. Consequently, the court ruled that children of Chinese descent in Mississippi were "colored," and therefore relegated to black schools.[9]



Moreover, historically, race has been and continues to be conflated with religion. As late as the mid-nineteenth century, Judaism was openly denigrated as an unviable relic that had been replaced by Christianity, and portions of the Hebrew Bible, excluding prophetic texts, were scorned.[10] Accordingly, for many years, Jewish people were not considered white in the United States and Europe. Accused of being a "stiff-necked people" responsible for the crucifixion of Christ, Jews were widely reviled, discredited, and stigmatized throughout the Western world.[11] The most extreme example of the racialized treatment of Jews came at the hands of the Third Reich and its collaborators. Similarly, the trend has been to racialize Muslims and Islam, despite the fact that many Muslims, like Jews, have fair skin and European features.[12]

The concept of whiteness is therefore a fluid category that has evolved over time. Nevertheless, one element of the whiteness paradigm remains constant in the minds of most white Christians: however construed, whiteness is always viewed as more meritorious than blackness. As Du Bois wrote, "Everything great, good, efficient, fair, and honorable is 'white'; everything mean, bad, blundering, cheating, and dishonorable is 'yellow'; a bad taste is 'brown'; and the devil is 'black.' The changes of the theme are continually rung in picture and story, in newspaper heading and moving-picture, in sermon and school book, until, of course, the King can do no wrong,—a White Man is always right and a Black Man has no rights which a white man is bound to respect."[13] Thus who is white may change, but the superiority of whiteness is divinely ordained, an eternal truth.

What scholars have until recently called white privilege is better described as white power, as my sociologist colleague James Thomas has noted, and white power is hierarchical.[14] For example, white males are more highly valued than white females, and white heterosexuals are more valued than white gays, lesbians, or transgender individuals, just as able-bodied whites are more esteemed than disabled whites. Erving Goffman's stigma theory is useful for understanding the hierarchy. According to Goffman, the more stigmatized one's identity, the more discredited the individual is within society.[15] On such a scale, African Americans and other people of color are necessarily more stigmatized than whites. In the Western world, white Christians deemed themselves as having superseded Israel as God's chosen people. White Christians appropriated stories from the Hebrew Bible as applicable to them. But this is in contradistinction to the ways in which African Americans have, for example, historically understood the Exodus story as liberative. Thus, in the United States, these stories have been used to justify slavery, antimiscegenation laws, and other forms of institutionalized racism against people of African descent and others.[16] Ironically, Christians, who bear substantial responsibility for these abuses of the Hebrew Bible (and of Judaism), have also diminished the Hebrew Bible itself when it suited their purposes and denied the link between Jews and the creation of the Hebrew Bible.[17]

Western Christianity has asserted a religious foundation for white superiority by connecting the Hebrew Bible stories of the curse of Ham, the mark of Cain, and the Tower of Babel in the book of Genesis; the story of Moses and his Cushite wife in Numbers 12; and the banning of foreign women and their children in Ezra 9–10 and Nehemiah 13, among other passages. From the New Testament, Christians have used 2 Corinthians 6:14–18 to warn against miscegenation.[18] These laws gave an otherworldly, divinely authorized power to racist laws and practices. This presumed authority is evident in Virginia Circuit Court judge Leon Bazile's 1965 refusal to vacate the 1959 felony convictions of Mildred Jeter and Richard Loving, an African American woman and white man, for the crime of intermarriage. Bazile reasoned:

> Almighty God created the races white, black, yellow, malay and red, and he placed them on separate continents. And but for the interference with his [arrangement] there would be no cause for such marriages. The fact that he separated the races shows that he did not intend for the races to mix.
>
> The awfulness of the offense is shown by Section 20–57 which declares: "All marriages between a white person and a colored person shall be absolutely void without any decree of divorce or any other legal process."
>
> Then section 20–59 of the Code makes the contracting of a marriage between a white person and any colored person a felony.[19]

The association of biblical stories with racism, in a country where many Americans continue to believe in the Bible's literal truth and inerrancy, has made racism nearly untouchable. Professor of journalism Curtis Wilkie, who was born and raised in Jim Crow Mississippi, explains,

God remained a powerful force across the South into the next century. I imagined Him a stern, older white male, Christian in His choice of religion and segregationist in His philosophy. It was simple to rationalize segregation: if God had wanted us all to be equal and alike, He would not have created a white race and a black race. There were ample biblical citations. Dr. G. T. Gillespie, president of Belhaven College, a Presbyterian school in Jackson, invoked passages ranging from chapter 4 in Genesis, dealing with the mark on Cain, to chapter 9 in the Book of Ezra, which described sorrow among the Jewish people after men from their community took heathen wives. ("For they have taken some of their daughters to be wives for themselves and for their sons; so that the holy race has mixed itself with the peoples of the lands.")[20]



A dean of Harvard's Lawrence Scientific School, Nathaniel Shaler viewed himself as uniquely qualified to articulate nineteenth-century religious and scientific views about the Negro, the immigrant, and the *so-called* inferior races.[21] During his tenure at Harvard, he educated many of the most influential people of his day, including Charles Davenport, the American eugenicist.[22] Among other theories, Shaler's notions about the role of *racial instincts* and the ability of African Americans loom large.[23] In "The Negro Problem," Shaler assessed slavery and the relationship between the races in the antebellum period and afterward as an amicable, mutually beneficial experiment:

> Although this experiment of making a citizen of the negro grew out of a civil war, and necessarily led to the awakening of much hatred among the people where it was undertaken, there is no reason to doubt that is [*sic*] being very fairly tried, and that if ever such changes are possible they will be here. There was no deep antagonism between these two diverse peoples, such as would have existed if either had been the conqueror of the other; on the contrary, a century or two of close relations had served to develop a curious bond of mutual likings and dependencies between the two races. It was only through slavery that it could have been possible to make the trial at all. American slavery, though it had the faults inherent in any system of subjugation and mastery among men, was infinitely the mildest and most decent system of slavery that ever existed. When the bonds of the slave were broken, master and servant stayed beside

> each other, without much sign of fear or any very wide sundering of the old relation of service and support. As soon as the old order of the relations was at an end, the two races settled into a new accord, not differing in most regards from the old.[24]



After denouncing generations of greedy Europeans for introducing Africans to North America, Shaler maintained, "There can be no sort of doubt that judged by the light of all experience *these people are a danger to America* greater and more insuperable than any of those that menace the other great civilized states of the world. . . . The chance evils of Ireland and Sicily are all light burdens compared with this load of African negro [*sic*] blood that an evil past has imposed on us" (emphasis added). Shaler argued that slavery fostered a friendly, if unequal, relationship between the races, as demonstrated in the roles of master and slave. He also claimed that a fundamental difference existed in the nature of blacks and whites. Not only were Africans dangerous, but they were as different in motives as blacks are visually distinct from whites.[25] Shaler used scripture to bolster these claims: "The Hebrew Bible and all similar harvests of knowledge is full of these ideas as to the fixedness of racial attributes. Investigators have only extended the conception by showing that the varieties of men, following a common original law, hold fast to the ways of their forefathers, and that the moral as well as physical characteristics of race are to a greater or lesser degree indelible, whether the given kind belong to the human or to a lower creature."[26] Shaler's stature and influence make his writings on race, the Bible, and theology an exemplar of how influential people used the Bible to promote racialized and white supremacist ways of thinking.

### Reading the Bible Differently

During the 1960s and 1970s, by contrast, the black theologians James Cone, Gayraud S. Wilmore, and others used biblical religion and philosophy to address the many social problems that ensnared African Americans. They associated racial oppression and the plight of African peoples with theodicy, the concept that tried to square the existence of a just and benevolent God with the evident fact of suffering and evil in the world.[27] William R. Jones, in *Is God a White Racist? A Preamble to Black Theology*, also saw social problems as linked to theodicy, but his concept of *divine racism* diverged from those of other scholars. Jones, interestingly, began his exploration with questions raised by W. E. B. Du Bois in the early twentieth century, during the height of

Jim Crow. Ultimately, Jones rejected Christian models for explaining black suffering, just as Du Bois had.

But beyond the biblical models proffered by Cone and others, Rabbi Heschel and Dr. King both developed sound alternative bases for attacking racism. Historically, rabbis and other Jewish thinkers, along with Christian and Muslim religious scholars, have (re)interpreted sacred texts in light of social circumstances and found in them relevant meanings for contemporary social conditions. It could be argued, for example, that the Catholic Church's 1965 *Nostra aetate*, which repositioned the church's relationship to Judaism, as did the 2002 apology by the Presbyterian Church in America for its involvement and complicity in slavery, are reassessments of doctrinal and scriptural understandings about historical wrongs.[28] In both instances, the Catholic and Protestant churches addressed some aspects of racism.



To be clear, I am not arguing, as literalists do, that prophetic texts were originally intended to prevent racism. Rather, I maintain that the biblical text, as a socially constructed document, contains within it materials that may be used to model an antiracist ethical framework. In the history of scholarship and interpretation, whether in Judaism, Christianity, or Islam, there is strong evidence for reading biblical texts as I propose here.[29] I also base my argument on recent interpretations of prophetic texts and on broader objections to the church's complicity in racism.

The way I propose reading Amos is not entirely new; it draws on the work of Heschel and King.[30] Their arguments resembled those made by the church and justice-minded lawmakers and policymakers in the United States during slavery and Jim Crow in that they were associated with certain epistemological positions. The church, policymakers, and lawmakers linked the Hebrew Bible to eugenics, ideas about social evolution, and a hierarchy of humankind. All of these ideas have long since been discredited. But Heschel and King did not use religion and religious texts as apologists for racism did, but instead found in these texts different values. I employ here what Kristina Rolin identifies as the *thesis of epistemic advantage*, which "invites us to explore whether marginal or underprivileged social locations give us epistemic benefits vis-à-vis particular research projects." The question that emerges, then, is whether my social location as an African American woman who was raised as a Christian adds to the epistemic value of understanding historically racist uses of the Hebrew Bible in the United States. If by *epistemic value* we mean "values which promote the attainment of truth either intrinsically or extrinsically," then I suggest that my social location provides a rich vantage point—as Heschel's and King's did—for critiquing

Christianity's role in the white racial frame and likewise for constructing a biblical interpretation that advances an antiracist argument.[31]

Diana Lipton identified Heschel's two-volume work *The Prophets* as his main contribution to biblical scholarship, in part because the work has been influential for decades among Jewish and, I would add, other social activists and scholars.[32] Armed with the Hebrew Bible, Heschel proclaimed an alliance between freedom and responsibility and extolled the merits of righteous rebellion over resignation to the status quo. For Heschel, there was no distinction between prayer and protest when the aim was to remedy injustice. "Judaism is forever engaged," he wrote, "in a bitter battle against man's deeply rooted belief in fatalism and its ensuing inertia in social, moral, and spiritual conditions. Abraham started in rebellion against his father and the gods of his time. His great distinction was not in being loyal and conforming, but in defying and initiating. He was loved by the Lord not for ancestral worship but because he taught his descendants to 'keep the way of the Lord by doing what is just and right' (Gen. 18:19)."[33] Addressing racism at the height of Jim Crow, Heschel, a contemporary of King's and a fellow foot soldier in the civil rights movement, considered racism and religion antithetical to each other:

> Religion and race. How can the two be uttered together? To act in the spirit of religion is to unite what lies apart, to remember that humanity as a whole is God's beloved child. To act in the spirit of race is to sunder, to slash, to dismember the flesh of living humanity. Is this the way to honor a father: to torture his child? How can we hear the word "race" and feel no self-reproach?
>
> Race as a *normative* legal or political concept is capable of expanding to formidable dimensions. A mere thought, it extends to become a way of thinking, a highway of insolence, as well as a standard of values, overriding truth, justice, beauty. *As a standard of values and behavior, race operates as a comprehensive doctrine, as racism. And racism is worse than idolatry. Racism is satanic, unmitigated evil.*[34] (emphasis added)

Heschel pressed the issue further by asserting that racism is "a treacherous denial" of God's existence.[35] This suggests that humans are either antiracist and in harmony with God or proracist and practicing idolatry. The two polarities—fellowship with God and the embrace of racism (or any injustice)—cannot coexist. Instead, Heschel, who lived an *embodied*

*Judaism*—the nexus at which inner devotional life finds expression in daily life—calls attention to this dual responsibility.[36] In a section in *The Prophets* devoted to the book of Amos, Heschel declares that for the living God, justice is not merely a notion but a divine preoccupation. He explains that God demands right doing for those in a covenant with God. Mutual obligation to God carries with it concomitant concern.[37] With actions to establish justice, God anticipates *pathos*—"emotional involvement, passionate participation, is a part of religious existence."[38]



Similarly, in his April 16, 1963, "Letter from Birmingham Jail," Dr. King characterized the prophet Amos as "an extremist for justice." In that letter to clergymen, King answered criticism from some ministers and pastors who called his course "unwise and unjust." King replied, "I am in Birmingham, because *injustice is here*." Four months later, in his "I Have a Dream" speech, King again called upon the book of Amos to underscore his plea for racial equity and justice for African Americans. "We cannot be satisfied," King said, "so long as a Negro in Mississippi cannot vote and a Negro in New York believes he has nothing for which to vote. No, no, we are not satisfied, and we will not be satisfied until justice rolls down like waters and righteousness like a mighty stream." Both Heschel and King refused to view the prophetic texts as separate from contemporary social contexts—or to consider prayer and worship as disconnected from actions for social justice in the world. Amos's point is not that social justice is religious but that religion must necessarily embody social justice. King and Heschel viewed the prophetic call for social justice as viable in the here and now and as requiring commensurate action on behalf of the oppressed. Frederick Douglass said, "I prayed for twenty years but received no answers until I prayed with my legs."[39] Heschel offered a similar characterization of his participation in the historic 1965 voting rights march from Selma to Montgomery: "For many of us the march from Selma to Montgomery was about *protest and prayer*. Legs are not lips and walking is not kneeling. And yet our legs uttered songs. Even without words, our march was worship. I felt my legs were praying" (emphasis added).[40] Partly from their understanding of prophetic literature, Heschel and King provide a cogent and compelling path from a biblical text to an antiracist ethic that applies as much to today's world as it did in antiquity and in the tumultuous 1960s.

Over the past decade, scholars have begun to recognize the racist uses of the Hebrew Bible texts and to reread these texts with different understandings. For example, Jennifer Knust's reparative reading of the curse of Ham in Genesis 9:18–29 begins by acknowledging the historical misreadings of the texts that once argued for slavery and other forms of institutional racism. She not only addresses the uses of the Hebrew Bible that I mentioned above but also argues against readings of this text that blame "Jews for foisting racist theories of Ham's blackness on a willing Euro-American public." Noting our collective ignorance of the precise historical circumstances that yielded the story, Knust concludes that a "xenophobic impulse lies at the heart of the passage" in its present form.[41] If Knust is correct, then it bears pointing out that from the perspective of sociology, racism and xenophobia are vastly different from each other. The first requires and appropriates power, as I pointed out above; the second does not, as I have argued elsewhere.[42] It is also important to note how differently Genesis 9:18–29 (and other texts) may have functioned in the ancient world and in modern contexts. While ancient Israel experienced alternating moments of power and subjugation to more powerful neighbors, it possessed little authority during the vast majority of its history, except during the United Monarchy. In fact, Israel suffered declining power from the era following the dissolution of the United Monarchy until the Babylonian exile of 586 B.C.E. Thus, for most of its history, ancient Israel did not possess the requisite power and privilege to impose institutional racism.[43] By the time ancient Judahites (or Yehudites) returned from exile under the Persians circa 539 B.C.E., they lacked autonomy over the land that had formerly been theirs. The social conditions that convert prejudicial or xenophobic views into racism did not exist. The same texts, however, in the hands of modern European nations or the United States in the late seventeenth century would yield quite a different effect. Rather than experience diminished status, for example, the United States gained political and economic prestige as a world power.



### Amos 1–6: A Paradigm for Social Justice

Biblical scholars have written for centuries about the content, form, functions, and roles of the book of Amos.[44] They have considered its authorship, its association with the corpus of Wisdom literature, and whether it was initially the work of one or more poets who wished to record theological and social commentary rather than prophecy.[45] My reading examines chapters 1–6 in order to identify the causes of divine agitation in the text. Below, I discuss the salient themes that emerged from the book of Amos by using a discourse analysis, a method of examining the language that ancient Israelite communities employed to frame arguments and discussions about specific topics related to social justice.[46] I examine the prophetic oracles against Israel and foreign nations with special attention to the riddles posed in Amos 3:3–8, which, wittingly or not, underscore an important link between social justice and worship raised throughout the book of Amos. From these offenses and the riddles, I infer a definition of social justice and begin to articulate a framework for an antiracist ethic.

The book of Amos as a whole has three important recurring themes that fit together with the prophet's emphasis on the theme of social justice in unexpected ways. Our years of conditioning or expectation concerning the book and social justice obscure or render ineffective related dimensions of the text. A discourse analysis by definition forces us to consider not only the most apparent or dominant theme(s), like social justice, but the themes and their relationship(s) to one another and to the entirety of the book. The prophet details Judah's, Israel's, and even foreign nations' injustices, the first of which is oddly connected to land and exile. Some iteration of the Hebrew root גלה appears throughout the book. As a verb, גלה means "to uncover, reveal"; as a noun, the root takes on two related but different meanings: גלות, to denote "the state of exile"; and the third iteration of the root גולה, which refers to people who have fled their homeland or, in the case of Amos 1:6, people who have been removed from the land. It is the use of this tri-consonantal root in its different functions that helps us understand the fuller case that Amos is making within its historical context, namely, the loss of the northern kingdom over which Jeroboam presided. Sandwiched between the first and last uses of this tri-consonantal root, including in the first and last chapters, the prophet exposes Israel and Judah for their hypocrisy and unwillingness to obey the Torah, and thus explains why the northern kingdom will be overtaken. The mention of exile within this context is doubly significant. Israel's and Judah's wrongdoing signified not simply disobedience and injustice to and against God but a breach of the ברית עולם ("everlasting covenant") with God.

Amos 5:1 beckons the listeners: "Hear this which I lift up to you, a dirge, O House of Israel." The cause for lamentation is the people's recalcitrance. This time, rather than the clever repetition of a singular root, the author utilizes a refrain at the end of each stanza in Amos 4:6, 8, 9, 10, and 11 to highlight God's sorrow at the unrepentant attitude: ולא־שבתם עדי נאם יהוה ("and you did not *turn back, even to Me*, declares God"). This phrase, which is used five times in Amos 4, expresses a great deal more than regret; it conveys a deep sense of sadness about the breached covenant and trust, symbolized by the land gift from which the people of Israel would be exiled.

The third significant finding of the discourse analysis is summarized in Amos 3:2, where God reminds Israel of the reason for the grave disenchantment expressed in the book of Amos. The phrase reads אתכם רק ידעתי מכל משפחות האדמה ("*I knew only* you of all of the families of the earth") (emphasis added). At the heart of God's grievance is the fact that God had selected Israel, of all the earth's peoples, for an exclusive relationship that held unique responsibilities. Living social justice was the lifeblood of the everlasting covenant. While repetition and other poetic devices are used throughout the oracles in the book of Amos, Amos 3:2 signals the sole intimacy that God shares with Israel through the use of two familiar and simple words, the verb "to know," ידע and the adverb רק, "only." Brown, Driver, and Briggs suggest that the use of רק carries "restrictive force."[47] This underscores the privileged nature of God's intimacy with Israel. Therefore, for Israel to substitute offerings in lieu of right doing, as if God would be none the wiser, explains the need for lamentation and professional mourners.

In Amos 1, God's accusations of wrongdoing against foreign nations are interspersed between the chastisements of Israel for abusing its population. The oracles condemning foreign nations share a common thread, but are otherwise vastly different from the pronouncements made against Israel. Foreign nations are judged for causing their populations to be exiled, for ignoring the "covenant of brotherhood," and for ruthlessly and violently pursuing neighboring nations (1:4–13). Accused of being deluded, Judah is said to have "spurn[ed] the Teachings of the Lord" and to have failed to observe the law (2:4). Against Israel, however, Amos cites a litany of specific crimes committed by the elite against the poor and powerless. These "oppressions" (3:9) include elites accepting monetary and material bribes that result in injustice against the poor and needy (2:6), the powerful trampling the heads of the poor and convoluting the path of the humble (2:7), and fathers and sons committing indiscretions by having sex with the same women and thereby defiling God's name (2:7). Moreover, the rich and powerful sat by every altar on cloaks they had taken in pledge, and they drank wine in God's house with the funds gained by assessing fines (2:8). Not only did they sin, Amos argues, but they caused others to do likewise—Nazarites to drink wine and prophets not to prophesy (2:12). Having sinned by enriching themselves at the expense of the less powerful, they then brought their sacrifices the next day and their tithes on the third day (4:4). In short, they made a show of bringing offerings (4:5).

In sum, the wrongdoings charged against Israel constitute abuses of power associated with robbing impoverished people of justice and giving them no recourse for resolution. These wrongdoings were then compounded when the elites appeared at the altars with offerings, singing songs and hymns, attending festivals, and bringing tithes. Worship acts performed *without* concomitant acts of justice in daily life yielded God's wrath.

There is an interdependence between worship and daily behaviors—two kinds of activity identified in Amos 1–6—which for Amos involved decorum in business transactions and the role of money and greed. The prophet not only lists sin as resulting in *oppressions*, but he also rejects worship and offerings. The prophet asks, "Can two walk together if they have not met? Does a lion roar in the forest when he has no prey?" (3:3–4). The obvious answer to both questions is no, but Israel missed the obvious. Thus the prophet says, "I loathe, I spurn your festivals, I am not appeased by your solemn assemblies. If you offer Me burnt offerings—or your meal offerings; I will not accept them; I will pay no heed to your gifts of fatlings. Spare Me the sound of your hymns and let Me not hear the music of your lutes. *But let justice well up like water, Righteousness like an unfailing stream*" (5:21–24; emphasis added). God rejects Israel's worship because it lacks just and equitable practices on behalf of the poor, needy, and humble—the community's most powerless members. While Amos does not address racism per se, victims of racism are among the powerless. Thus, based on Amos 1–6, pursuing *social justice* may be defined as *guarding the welfare of society's most vulnerable and oppressed members*. Social justice is not optional, according to Amos, but it is a prerequisite of worship. Without social justice, there can be no worship that is acceptable to God.



### Why Amos?

If several other prophets delivered stronger, arguably more powerful messages than Amos, why utilize Amos 1–6 as the basis for an antiracist ethic? Simply put, Amos eloquently articulates a basic formula for social justice that cuts to the heart of the problem. Sociologist Joe Feagin argues that the white racial frame in the United States includes the notion of the virtuous white American. This frame both shapes the ways in which white Americans view themselves but also how they view African Americans and other nonwhites. Feagin notes:

> In assessing the pro-white material that is central to contemporary racial framing, one finds much that has persisted over centuries. Many of these elements accent the virtues, privileges, and power of whites and whiteness. The great-chain-of-being idea did not

> disappear from this white perspective as the country moved from being predominantly agricultural to its advanced urban-industrial period today. That old hierarchical notion has continued over the centuries as a more or less unconscious cultural model essential to the way most people orient themselves in society. Whites as a group remain at the top of the racial hierarchy, and a majority view that as still appropriate. Important white views, values, and framing remain normative, the societal standards to be adopted by children of all backgrounds as they grow up and by new immigrants. Numerous studies today offer much evidence that the word "American" is often synonymous with "white." In several psychological studies researchers examined how strongly three major racial groups were associated with the catgory "American." In all the studies their subjects saw African Americans and Asian Americans as less associated with the category "American" than white Americans.[48]

I see broader implications for Feagin's notion of *white virtuosity*. In fact, both W. E. B. Du Bois and Feagin make the case for Christianity's role in establishing what Feagin calls *the white racial frame*—the shared set of emotional and cognitive perspectives held by whites toward any nonwhites in the United States but historically against African Americans and Native Americans. Du Bois and Feagin provide a nuanced account of how racism against people of African descent and indigenous peoples was codified legally and in allegiance with widespread Christian approval.[49] Du Bois carefully delineates the views of Protestant denominations and leaders concerning slavery. He notes, for example, that Massachusetts judge Samuel Sewall and his fellow Congregationalists Samuel Hopkins and Ezra Stiles attacked slavery by declaring the slave trade wrong, but the denomination took no formal position on slavery. Methodist church founder John Wesley argued that slavery was the "sum of all villanies," "contrary to the laws of God, man, and nature and hurtful to society." Yet the Methodist Church also retreated. Some Baptists, according to Du Bois, even in the Deep South state of Georgia, were initially generally hostile to slavery, while other denominations never found their voice on the issue.[50] For a brief period, it appears, Christian denominations flirted with acknowledging slavery's inhumanity, but almost all of them ended up either pro-slavery or, at best, silent on the matter.[51] The same kinds of conversations occurred during the penning of the Declaration of Independence and the ratification of the U.S. Constitution, with a similar outcome. By the mid-1800s, some denominations, such as the North

Carolina Baptist Convention, had adopted resolutions affirming that teaching slaves biblical passages would "inculcate the relative duties of masters and servants."[52] In other words, Christianity was used to make slaves docile and obedient and to reinforce white supremacy. Even when denominations, such as the Quakers, argued vociferously against slavery, Feagin identifies salient features of the white racial frame in some of their abolitionist rhetoric.[53] Feagin juxtaposes Judge Sewall's utilization of biblical sources and human rights rhetoric to argue against slavery with Sewall's racialized, if not racist, language denigrating how African Americans would use their freedom. "They can seldom use their freedom well; yet their continual aspiring after their forbidden Liberty, renders them Unwilling Servants. And there is such a disparity in their Conditions, Colour & Hair, that they can never embody with us, and grow up into orderly Families, to the Peopling of the Land: but still remain in our Body Politick as a kind of extravasat Blood."[54] Feagin rightly claims that Sewall's notions have a direct connection with the white racial frame.



In contrast to Feagin, however, I see religion as having played a much longer role in the white racial frame. Even now, perceptions about race persist as a part of religious thinking and in thinking about religion. Therefore, we should consider the term *white religiosity*, or more specifically *white Christianity*, as an important, fixed element of Feagin's white racial frame. We have only to look at the writings by White Citizens' Councils during the 1950s for examples of more recent reluctance by denominations to acknowledge candidly their role continuing racism in the United States.[55] In other cases, where notions of whiteness and dominance prevail, Christianity is always a salient feature of the oppression. Therefore, by *white Christianity* I mean a Christian view assumed by people of European descent that privileges those who are deemed white and Christian over nonwhite racial and non-Christian religious social groups.[56]

The central point is how Christianity is and has been racialized and used to rationalize racism. In the United States, white Christianity justified anti-miscegenation laws, slavery, and Jim Crow in addition to a host of policies that socially, politically, and economically disadvantaged African Americans (and other groups). It subordinated the humanity of Africans—counting people of African descent as property and as three-fifths of a person to ensure the establishment of a union that included the southern states.[57] In Europe, a similar appropriation of religion has been common for centuries in writings by Catholics and Protestants against (nonwhite) Jews, as a way to privilege white Christians over Jews and pagans.[58] As in the case of the United

States and people of African descent, Constantine's laws, enacted as early as 315 C.E., began penalizing Jews in myriad economic, social, and political ways.[59] The process of racializing Islam and Muslims in Europe and North America seems to be following a similar path. John Esposito and Ibrahim Kalin maintain that these anti-Muslim sentiments existed well before 9/11.[60] These cases validate the importance of white Christianity not merely to white virtuosity but to the white racial frame.



Why use the book of Amos in this context? Since religion has been employed as justification for racialized oppression in the United States and elsewhere, it is only fitting that a religious text be invited to critique these uses of religion. On the matter of decorum in worship, Amos provides readers with the most elementary ethical guide to social justice and unadulterated worship. The United States, with its rhetoric of American exceptionalism, has claimed the stature of a nation chosen by God to be "*better than, stronger than and more righteous than all others*."[61] Yet the nation has exploited racialized dichotomies to serve the interests of personal wealth for the few, and has through divisiveness made its trade in rousing rather than resolving racial animus.[62] The prophet Amos insists that abandoning idols such as greed is essential to achieving social justice.[63]

The presumption is rife in the United States that the nation is further along concerning racial equity than it is. Unsurprisingly, whites and blacks in the United States are worlds apart in their perceptions about racial inequality, according to a 2016 survey by the Pew Research Center. The survey reveals that 88 percent of blacks—but only 53 percent of whites—believe the country still has work to do to ensure racial equality for blacks. The same study shows that 8 percent of blacks believe the country has done the work necessary for blacks to obtain equality; however, 38 percent of whites think adequate measures have already been taken.[64] The civil rights years successfully erected some legal barriers to racial oppression, but they did not erase centuries-old legacies that laws instituted, such as intergenerational poverty, an education differential, fair access to bank loans and housing, and the right to live free of pervasive threats of ad hoc violence. Abe Markman argues that as a result of the Nixon and Reagan administrations' push for *law and order* in the aftermath of the civil rights movement, a backlash materialized in the form of accelerated rates of incarceration of black men, for example. Yet after the 2008 election of one black man, President Barack Obama, journalists and others declared that the country had entered a postracial period.[65] Instead, I argue, Barack Obama's candidacy and presidency teach us how far the country must travel to resolve its racial history. It is more precise to say that we in the United States are in a *pre-postracial moment*. Moreover, we need to go back to basic concepts of justice and equity—the ideas offered by Amos. The questions raised by the birther movement about Obama's legitimacy to become president recast Obama—and, I would argue, all African Americans—as not legitimately American. Many Americans view the graduate of Columbia University and Harvard Law School as unfit for the presidency based on his race alone.[66] Ironically, during the 2008 election cycle, questions about Senator John McCain's citizenship were insignificant by comparison, despite the fact that Obama's opponent was born on a U.S. military base in Panama. Anti-Obamaism then seized on Obama's father's Muslim identity to double down on the notion that the biracial Obama, who arguably more fully represents the United States' diversity than McCain did, was not merely *foreign* but, as a supposed non-Christian, *not at all one of us real Americans*. Accepting a duly elected African American president was beyond the pale. On the very day that echoes of America's newly proclaimed postracial moment reverberated at Obama's inauguration, Republican legislators met to plot his political demise. Rural yard signs asking passersby to "Pray for America" or "Pray for our country" were emblematic of the ethos in certain corridors of the United States. Insisting that Obama was a foreign-born Muslim reasserted Christianity's key role in the white racial frame.



The election of President Obama was prescient in other ways. Between 2007 and 2008, according to the Southern Poverty Law Center, the number of hate groups rose by 4 percent. Mark Potok remarked, "Barack Obama's election has inflamed racist extremists who see it as another sign that *their* country is under siege by the nonwhites." The Southern Poverty Law Center also noted an increase in racialized violence. "Scores of racially charged incidents—beatings, effigy burnings, racist graffiti, and intimidation were reported after the election."[67] A *Washington Post* report maintained, "During the early days of Obama's initial candidacy and the first year of his presidency, according to several people familiar with the matter, many of the threats against [President Obama] had a frightening racist quality."[68]

If attitudes about President Obama were not indicative of racial animus, then the disproportionate number of blacks killed by police shootings ought to summon our attention. In 2015, blacks, who make up only 12 percent of the American population, represented 27 percent of police killings. These kinds of problems have only worsened under the Trump administration. Forty-nine percent of race-based hate crimes in the United States were committed against African Americans, according to a 2017 report by the Federal Bureau of Investigation. The only group to have suffered more hate crimes was Jewish persons, who experienced 58 percent of religion-based hate crimes.[69] The disproportionate number of police killings of blacks is emblematic of the breadth of social inequality in the United States. If the shootings appear to be the work of individuals, then the stunning proof of a twenty-year legacy of police torture and brutality against African Americans and Latinx citizens by Chicago police, and the U.S. Department of Justice report about the Baltimore Police Department's treatment of black citizens, ought to clarify that these problems are undoubtedly artifacts of institutionalized racism. The Justice Department's report about the BPD reveals scathing criticism of policing tactics in Baltimore, including unconstitutional stops, searches, and arrests, predominantly of black citizens; the use of excessive force against blacks; and the BPD's retaliation against blacks for using their right to free speech. All reveal deeply ingrained patterns of racism.



In a June 16, 1963, telegram to President Kennedy, Rabbi Heschel urged Kennedy to declare a "state of moral emergency." The physical violence in the United States affirmed in the reports about police and other forms of violence against African Americans is similar to the proliferation of violence during Jim Crow and the civil rights years. Factors such as these negate any glimmer of "postracialism" that Obama's election might have seemed to augur for some. Instead, they show that we are closer to the "state of moral emergency" that Rabbi Heschel declared more than half a century ago. Why call on Amos to help us deal with this national burden of racism? We come to the prophet Amos because this "extremist for justice" meets the nation where it is poised, in another hour of national crisis, at a pre-postracial moment.[70]

### Toward a Framework for an Antiracist Ethic

Only great hubris would lead me to think I could articulate a fully formed framework for an antiracist ethic. I can, however, summarize what revisiting Amos 1–6 has taught me, and reach toward an antiracist ethic in view of present circumstances. First, it bears noting that racism could easily be added to a contemporary version of Amos's litany of oppressions, because intrinsic to racism is the same sort of power differential that appears between elites and the masses in Amos. It bears repeating here that racism is *systemic privilege awarded to Europeans (or people who became white) over non-Europeans.* Whites who are disproportionately powerful are by virtue of this privilege responsible for helping to secure racial equity.[71] In the United States, racism is thus not *their problem* or *your problem*—it is not a black problem or a white problem—it is an *American* problem. Heschel eloquently argued as much more than forty years ago. The fact that racism is normalized in large police departments shows vividly that white supremacists' views were never vanquished, but they were forced underground.

Second, racism is human degradation that has myriad ill effects. These outcomes range from emotional and cognitive trauma to physical illness, injury, and even death.[72] An antiracist ethic must recognize the full and constant destructive toll of racism and both its immediate and intergenerational implications.



Third, if we look to oracles against the foreign nations in Amos 1, we learn that an antiracist ethic must value humankind and thus keep a covenant of brotherhood. Violence is impermissible against any Other. With Dr. King we must proclaim, "Injustice anywhere is a threat to justice everywhere."[73] Like King and Heschel, we too must take to the streets in peaceful nonviolent protest against the profound racism that stalks the nation. Given the dominance of Christianity in Western civilizations, I am especially obligated, in ways large and small, to address the church's legacies of antisemitism and Islamophobia. I must overtly combat this racism everywhere it occurs, and dissuade it anywhere it rears its head. When an imam and his companion are gunned down solely because they are Muslim, the nation should be appalled and express its outrage.[74]

Fourth, an antiracist ethic must understand the intergenerational economic, social, and political consequences of racism on the Other. Thus laws that merely extend protections to the Other are not nearly enough to erase the stain that racism has left. Before our eyes, some of the rights won in the 1960s have in recent years eroded and have begun to be rolled back. Consequently, an antiracist ethic must have at its core a *commitment to be vigilant and to do vigilantly*.

In recent years, sociologists have coined the terms "doing sociology" and "doing religion." But Amos implored us centuries ago to *do religion*. In fact, religion is only effective if it is done. The book of Amos offers a chance for citizens in the United States to address the state of emergency and redress racism by *doing* civility and justice for all. It was neither easy nor immediate, but Mayor Rahm Emanuel did what no other mayor in Chicago had done before him.[75] He apologized to the victims of police brutality and torture in Chicago. His public apology marked recognition of racist wrongdoing against African Americans and Latinxs beginning in 1972 and extending through the police shooting death of Chicago teen Laquan McDonald in 2014. Amos asks, "Can two walk together if they have not met? Does a lion roar in the forest when he has no prey?" The mayoral response in Chicago signified the meeting of the two sides that is necessary for dialogue—an acknowledgment of the communal cries, an opportunity for both sides to walk together. The point is not that this was free of struggle, but that the struggle ensued. This is *doing religion*. The protests that led to a Chicago task force investigation opened a space where truth could be told and heard. Therefore, some level of reconciliation could begin in the city of Chicago—a place to learn beyond (mis)perceptions, to repair what Amos calls "the covenant of brotherhood" (1:9). Without such spaces, *difference* will continue to dominate our discourse. And yet, when Chicago's African Americans and others demonstrated, a task force investigated and the mayor apologized. An official at the center of the police abuses of power was fired, and reparations were paid to some of the victims of police torture. This is Amos's brand of *doing civility*, *doing religion*, and *doing justice*. Then only have "our legs uttered songs."

## Notes

1. Du Bois, *Negro Church*, ix.
2. Hartnett, "Folly of Fighting for Providence," 201.
3. Berger and Luckmann, *Social Construction of Reality*, 103–6.
4. Sue et al., "Racial Microaggressions in Everyday Life"; Allport, *Nature of Prejudice*, 14.
5. Bonilla-Silva, *Racism Without Racists*, 9.
6. Ibid.
7. Evans and Feagin, "Cost of Policing Violence," 892. For Allport's definition of prejudice, see Allport, *Nature of Prejudice*, 6–9.
8. Yancy, *Who Is White*, 32.
9. Lichtman, *White Protestant Nation*, 38, 39.
10. For a thorough study of early biblical scholars' views on the Hebrew Bible and Judaism, see Wellhausen, *Prolegomena*.
11. Ibid., 500; see also Connelly, "Catholic Racism and Its Opponents"; Goldstein, *Price of Whiteness*; Hirschfeld, *Racism*; Heschel, *Aryan Jesus*.
12. Moosavi, "Racialization of Muslim Converts"; Hafez, "Shifting Borders"; Esposito and Kalin, *Islamophobia*.
13. Du Bois, *Negro Church*, 25.
14. Sociologist James Thomas made this point in a University of Mississippi Critical Race Studies Group meeting in 2016.
15. Goffman, *Stigma*, esp. 1–19.
16. Kidd, *Forging of Races*; Goldberg, *Curse of Ham*; Haynes, *Noah's Curse*; Du Bois, *Negro Church*.
17. Gregg, *Shared Stories, Rival Tellings*; Wellhausen, *Prolegomena*.
18. Botham, *Almighty God Created the Races*, esp. 69–90. The Catholic Church took a somewhat more inclusive stance on the question of mixed marriage. See *Perez v. Lippold*, the case argued before the California Supreme Court in 1948, in which the court held by a 4–3 majority that the state's ban on interracial marriage violated the Fourteenth Amendment to the U.S. Constitution.
19. Bazile, "Opinion of Leon M. Bazile."
20. Wilkie, *Dixie*, 49.
21. Livingstone, "Science and Society," 182.
22. Sussman, *Myth of Race*, 47.
23. Kerkering, *Poetics of National and Racial Identity*, 161.
24. Shaler, "Negro Problem," 697–98.
25. Ibid., 699, 700.
26. Quoted in Livingstone, "Science and Society," 183.
27. Jones, *Is God a White Racist*, xix–xx.
28. Zylstra, "Should Denominations Apologize?"
29. See esp. Gregg, *Shared Stories, Rival Tellings*.

30. Heschel, *Insecurity of Freedom*; Heschel, *Prophets*; Martin Luther King Jr., "Letter from Birmingham Jail" (April 16, 1963), http://abacus.bates.edu/admin/offices/dos/mlk/letter.html; Martin Luther King Jr., "I Have a Dream" (August 28, 1963), https://www.archives.gov/files/press/exhibits/dream-speech.pdf.

31. Rolin, "Values, Standpoints," 12.

32. Lipton, "Abraham Joshua Heschel," 25.

33. Heschel, *Insecurity of Freedom*, 13–14.

34. Ibid., 85–86.

35. Ibid., 86.

36. Wolf, "Abraham Joshua Heschel," 108.

37. Heschel, *Prophets*, 1:32, 34.

38. Ibid., 2:38.

39. Frederick Douglass, A–Z Quotes, http://www.azquotes.com/quote/81106.

40. See http://blogs.library.duke.edu/rubenstein/2015/01/14/jewish-voices-selma-montgomery-march.

41. Knust, "Who's Afraid of Canaan's Curse," 388, 393.

42. Johnson, *Holy Seed Has Been Defiled*, 109–11.

43. Ibid., 41–55.

44. I translated all of the passages from Hebrew using the Hebrew text in Jewish Publication Society, *Hebrew-English Tanakh* (Philadelphia: Jewish Publication Society, 2000), and Karl Elliger and Wilhelm Rudolph, eds., *Biblia Hebraica Stuttgartensia* (Stuttgart: Gesampt, 1977).

45. Milstein, "'Who Would Not Write,'" 442.

46. See Schneider, "How to Do a Discourse Analysis."

47. Brown, Driver, and Briggs, *Hebrew-English Lexicon*, 956.

48. Feagin, *White Racial Frame*, 93–94.

49. Ibid., 23–57; Du Bois, *Negro Church*, 6–34.

50. Du Bois, *Negro Church*, 21, 22.

51. Ibid., 22; see also Feagin, *White Racial Frame*, 51–55.

52. Du Bois, *Negro Church*, 29.

53. Feagin, *White Racial Frame*, 52–53. Feagin identifies the following important characteristics of the early racial framing, or protoracial framing, of African Americans and Native Americans: (1) references to physical characteristics such as skin color, facial features, and hair texture to differentiate social groups; (2) associating physical characteristics with cultural ones; and (3) regularly employing the linked physical and social distinctions to identify white superiority over the inferior groups in the existing social hierarchy. This framing was then used to justify and rationalize the dominant group's accumulation of material and other resources by dehumanizing African Americans and Native peoples. Ibid., 41–49.

54. Ibid., 52.

55. For examples of White Citizens' Councils' use of Christianity to support racial segregation and the oppression of black people, see the following documents, all at the University of Mississippi, Special Collections, Council Collection, box 1, folder 22: S. E. Rogers, "Christian Love and Segregation" (excerpt from an address delivered before the Manning [S.C.] Lions Club, Summerton, S.C., November 13, 1956); Stuart O. Landry, "Rebuilding the Tower of Babel: A Study of Christianity and Segregation" (New Orleans, 1957); G. T. Gillespie, "A Christian View on Segregation" (Winona, Miss.: Association of Citizens' Councils, 1954); T. Robert Ingram, "Why Integration is Un-Christian!" (Jackson, Miss.: Citizens Councils of America, n.d.).

56. Bonilla-Silva, *Racism Without Racists*, 9.

57. Ghachem, "Slave's Two Bodies," 827.

58. See, for example, Marcus, *Jew in the Medieval World*; Bethencourt, *Racisms*.

59. Marcus, *Jew in the Medieval World*; Erner, "Christian Economic Morality," 469; Weber, *Protestant Ethic*.

60. Esposito and Kalin, *Islamophobia*, xxii.

61. Hartnett, "Folly of Fighting for Providence," 201.

62. Brown, "'Of All the Hardy Sons of Toil.'"

63. See also Heschel, *Prophets*.

64. Pew Research Center, "On Views of Race and Inequality," 4.

65. Weisenfeld, "Post-Racial America?"; Markman, "So Many Unarmed Black Americans," 8.

66. Eilperin, "New Dynamics of Protecting a President."

67. Southern Poverty Law Center, "Hate Group Numbers Up by 54%."

68. Eilperin, "New Dynamics of Protecting a President."

69. FBI, "2017 Hate Crime Statistics."

70. King, "Letter from Birmingham Jail."

71. Heschel, *Insecurity of Freedom*, esp. 85–111.

72. Sue et al., "Racial Microaggressions in Everyday Life"; Mays, Cochran, and Barnes, "Race, Race-Based Discrimination"; Wheeler, Brooks, and Brown, "'Gettin' on My Last Nerve.'"

73. King, "Letter from Birmingham Jail."

74. Rojas, Remnick, and Palmer, "First-Degree Murder Charge Added."

75. Ruthhart, Bryne, and Dardick, "Emanuel Apologizes."

76. Babylonian Talmud *Berakhot* 58b.



## References


Allport, Gordon W. *The Nature of Prejudice*. 25th anniversary ed. New York: Basic Books, 1957.

Bazile, Leon M. "Opinion of Leon M. Bazile (January 22, 1965)." Virginia Humanities, Library of Virginia. https://www.encyclopediavirginia.org/opinion_of_judge_leon_m_bazile_january_22_1965.

Berger, Peter L., and Steven Luckmann. *The Social Construction of Reality: A Treatise in the Sociology of Knowledge*. New York: Anchor Books, 1966.

Bethencourt, Francisco. *Racisms: From the Crusades to the Twentieth Century*. Princeton: Princeton University Press, 2013.

Bonilla-Silva, Eduardo. *Racism Without Racists: Color-Blind Racism and the Persistence of Racial Inequality in America*. 4th ed. Lanham, Md.: Rowman and Littlefield, 2014.

Botham, Fay. *Almighty God Created the Races: Christianity, Interracial Marriage, and American Law*. Chapel Hill: University of North Carolina Press, 2009.

Brown, Tommy. "'Of All the Hardy Sons of Toil': Class and Race in Antebellum Southcentral and Southeastern Alabama." *Alabama Review* 68, no. 3 (2015): 213–50.

Brown, Francis, R. Driver, and Charles Briggs. *The New Brown-Driver-Briggs-Gesenius Hebrew-English Lexicon*. Peabody, Mass.: Hendrickson, 1979.

Connelly, John. "Catholic Racism and Its Opponents." *Journal of Modern History* 79, no. 4 (2007): 813–47.

———. "Eschatology and the Ideology of Anti-Judaism." *Studies in Christian-Jewish Relations* 9 (2014): 1–22.

Du Bois, W. E. B. *Darkwater: Voices from Within the Veil*. New York: Dover, 1999.

———. *The Negro Church*. Introduction by Phil Zuckerman, Sandra L. Barnes, and Daniel Cody. 1903. Reprint, Lanham, Md.: AltaMira, 2003.

———. "Race Prejudice in Germany—Anti-Semitism—The Present Plights of the German Jew." *Pittsburgh Courier*, December 19, 1936.

Eilperin, Juliet. "The New Dynamics of Protecting a President: Most Threats Against Obama Issue Online." *Washington Post*, October 8, 2014.

Erner, Guillaume. "Christian Economic Morality: The Medieval Turning Point." *International Social Science Journal* 57, no. 185 (2005): 469–79.

Esposito, John L., and Ibrahim Kalin. *Islamophobia: The Challenge of Pluralism in the Twenty-First Century*. Oxford: Oxford University Press, 2011.

Evans, Louwanda, and Joe Feagin. "The Costs of Policing Violence: Foregrounding Cognitive and Emotional Labor." *Critical Sociology* 41, no. 6 (2015): 887–95.

Feagin, Joe R. *The White Racial Frame: Centuries of Racial Framing and Counter-Framing*. 2nd ed. New York: Routledge, 2013.

Federal Bureau of Investigation. "2017 Hate Crime Statistics." https://ucr.fbi.gov/hate-crime/2017.

Ghachem, Malick W. "The Slave's Two Bodies: The Life of an American Legal Fiction." *William and Mary Quarterly* 60, no. 4 (2003): 809–42.

Goffman, Erving. *Stigma: Notes on the Management of Spoiled Identity*. New York: Simon and Schuster, 1963.

Goldberg, David M. *The Curse of Ham: Race and Slavery in Early Judaism, Christianity, and Islam*. Princeton: Princeton University Press, 2003.

Goldstein, Eric L. *The Price of Whiteness: Jews, Race, and American Identity*. Princeton: Princeton University Press, 2006.

Gregg, Robert C. *Shared Stories, Rival Tellings: Early Encounters of Jews, Christians, and Muslims*. Oxford: Oxford University Press, 2015.

Hafez, Farid. "Shifting Borders: Islamophobia as Common Ground for Building Pan-European Right-Wing Unity." *Patterns of Prejudice* 48, no. 5 (2014): 479–99.

Hartnett, Stephen John. "The Folly of Fighting for Providence, or, the End of Empire and Exceptionalism." *Cultural Studies, Critical Methodologies* 13, no. 3 (2013): 201–14.

Haynes, Stephen R. *Noah's Curse: The Biblical Justification of American Slavery*. Oxford: Oxford University Press, 2002.

Heschel, Abraham Joshua. *The Insecurity of Freedom: Essays on Human Existence*. New York: Farrar, Straus and Giroux, 1959.

———. *The Prophets*. Two volumes in one. 1962. Reprint, Peabody, Mass.: Hendrickson, 2007.

Heschel, Susannah. *The Aryan Jesus: Christian Theologians and the Bible in Nazi Germany*. Princeton: Princeton University Press, 2008.

Hirschfeld, Magnus. *Racism*. Translated and edited by Eden Paul and Cedar Paul. Port Washington, N.Y.: Kennikat Press, 1938.

Johnson, Willa M. *The Holy Seed Has Been Defiled: The Interethnic Marriage Dilemma in Ezra 9–10*. Sheffield: Sheffield Phoenix Press, 2011.

Jones, William R. *Is God a White Racist? A Preamble to Black Theology*. Boston: Beacon Press, 1973.

Kerkering, John D. *The Poetics of National and Racial Identity in Nineteenth-Century American Literature*. Cambridge: Cambridge University Press, 2003.

Kidd, Colin. *The Forging of Races: Race and Scripture in the Protestant Atlantic World, 1600–2000*. Cambridge: Cambridge University Press, 2006.

Knust, Jennifer. "Who's Afraid of Canaan's Curse? Genesis 9:18–29 and the Challenge of Reparative Reading." *Biblical Interpretation* 22 (2014): 388–413.

Lichtman, Allan J. *White Protestant Nation: The Rise of the American Conservative Movement*. New York: Atlantic Monthly Press, 2008.

Lipton, Diana. "Abraham Joshua Heschel: His Place in a Biblical Chain of Tradition." *European Judaism* 41, no. 1 (2008): 25–35.

Livingstone, David N. "Science and Society: Nathaniel S. Shaler and Racial Ideology." *Transactions of the Institute of British Geography* 9 (1984): 180–210.

Marcus, Jacob Rader. *The Jew in the Medieval World: A Sourcebook, 315–1791*. New York: Jewish Publication Society, 1938.

Markman, Abe. "Why Are So Many Unarmed Black Americans Killed by Police?" *Humanist*, July–August 2015, 8–11.

Mays, V. M., S. D. Cochran, and N. W. Barnes. "Race, Race-Based Discrimination, and Health Outcomes Among African Americans." *Annual Review of Psychology* 58 (2007): 201–25.

Milstein, Sara. "'Who Would Not Write?' The Prophets as YHWH's Prey in Amos 3:3–8." *Catholic Biblical Quarterly* 75 (2013): 429–45.

Moosavi, Leon. "The Racialization of Muslim Converts in Britain and Their Experiences of Islamophobia." *Critical Sociology* 41, no. 1 (2015): 41–56.

Pew Research Center. "On Views of Race and Inequality, Blacks and Whites Are Worlds Apart." June 27, 2016. https://www.pewsocialtrends.org/2016/06/27/on-views-of-race-and-inequality-blacks-and-whites-are-worlds-apart.

Rojas, Rick, Noah Remnick, and Emily Palmer. "First-Degree Murder Charge Added in Killing of Queens Imam and

Aide." *New York Times*, August 16, 2016.

Rolin, Kristina. "Values, Standpoints, and Scientific/Intellectual Movements." *Studies in History and Philosophy of Science* 56 (2015): 11–19.

Ruthhart, Bill, John Bryne, and Hal Dardick. "Emanuel Apologizes for Laquan McDonald Police Shooting." *Chicago Tribune*, December 9, 2015.

Schneider, Florian. "How to Do a Discourse Analysis." Politics EastAsia, May 13, 2013. http://www.politicseastasia.com/studying/how-to-do-a-discourse-analysis.

Shaler, Nathaniel Southgate. "The Negro Problem." *Atlantic Monthly*, November 1884, 696–709.

Southern Poverty Law Center. "Hate Group Numbers Up by 54% Since 2000." February 26, 2009. https://www.splcenter.org/news/2009/02/26/hate-group-numbers-54-2000.

Sue, Derald Wing, Christina M. Capodilupo, Gina C. Torino, Jennifer M. Bucceri, Aisha M. B. Holder, Kevin L. Nadal, and Marta Esquilin. "Racial Microaggressions in Everyday Life: Implications for Clinical Practice." *American Psychologist* 62, no. 4 (2007): 271–86.

Sussman, Robert Wald. *The Myth of Race: The Troubling Persistence of an Unscientific Idea*. Cambridge, Mass.: Harvard University Press, 2014.

Weber, Max. *The Protestant Ethic and the Spirit of Capitalism*. Edited and translated by Peter Baehr and Gordon C. Wells. New York: Penguin Books, 2002.

Weisenfeld, Judith. "Post-Racial America? The Tangle of Race, Religion, and Citizenship." *Religion and Politics*, October 24, 2012. http://religionandpolitics.org/2012/10/24/post-racial-america-the-tangle-of-race-religion-and-citizenship.

Wellhausen, Julius. *Prolegomena to the History of Ancient Israel*. 1885. Translated by Douglas A. Knight. Durham: Duke University Press, 2000.

Wheeler, Evangeline A., Leonie J. Brooks, and Janae C. Brown. "'Gettin' on My Last Nerve': Mental Health, Physiological and Cognitive Implications of Racism for People of African Descent." *Journal of Pan African Studies* 4, no. 5 (2011): 81–101.

Wilkie, Curtis. *Dixie: A Personal Odyssey Through Events That Shaped the Modern South*. New York: Simon and Schuster, 2002.

Wolf, Arnold Jacob. "Abraham Joshua Heschel After Twenty-Five Years." *Judaism* 47, no. 1 (1998): 108–14.

Yancy, George. *Who Is White? Latinos, Asians, and the New Black/Nonblack Divide*. Boulder: Lynne Rienner, 2003.

Zylstra, Sarah Eekhoff. "Should Denominations Apologize for Racial Acts They Didn't Commit?" *Christianity Today*, September 18, 2015, 21.

## Classic Text and Questions to Ponder

Johnson offers an interdisciplinary biblical hermeneutic that honors a sociological analysis of the book of Amos and employs scholarship from the sociology of race and ethnicity. Johnson uncovers in Amos a powerful antiracist ethic that could liberate society from both overt and underground racist attitudes and practices. Prophecy is but one genre of socially powerful words; another is prayer. Prayer can also liberate those trapped by insidious modes of thinking about differences and valuing them preferentially. For example, Talmudic rabbis taught that one should say a particular prayer when encountering people who appear unusual. Upon seeing a black person (*kushi*), a red-skinned person, an albino, a hunchback, a dwarf, or someone afflicted with edema, one should recite the prayer "Blessed is God who varies the forms of creation."[76] A favorable interpretation of this blessing holds that the rabbis acknowledge that congenital differences are no less expressions of God's creative power. It simultaneously asserts God's incredible capacities, which transcend human comprehension, and it preempts the human impulse to stereotype, distance, and demean the apparently different. A less favorable interpretation of this blessing points out that the rabbis construct it precisely because they view such people as abnormal and require liturgical acknowledgment—or, worse because they see such people as less than normal; thus the one uttering the blessing essentially gives thanks for not being so formed. Prayer, like prophecy, can cut multiple ways.

- When does "doing religion," like prophecy or prayer, liberate, and when does it not?
- In regard to the Bible, Johnson assumes both God's "absolute intolerance of oppression and the incongruity between oppression and worship." What is at stake in this assumption?
- A sociology of religion promotes the idea that powerful and influential people socially construct and therefore define a society's knowledge, norms, and values. Thus religion (theology, liturgy, prophecy, rituals, laws, etc.) as a social institution provides a key aspect of human socialization. How might a sociology of religion relate to religious (Jewish) ethics?

4

# Jews as Oppressed and Oppressor

## Doing Ethics at the Intersections of Classism, Racism, and Antisemitism

JUDITH W. KAY

From my office overlooking Commencement Bay, I daily watch three sturdy tugboats, two red and one forest green, guide enormous cargo ships around hidden sandbars. Sometimes the tides shift, leaving the sandbars exposed. At other times, milky water from nearby glaciers obscures them. One day I found myself riveted as two tugs blasted their horns to stop the advance of a giant tanker toward an undetected shoal. The stand-off took some time; the captains turned their tugs and stood side by side to bravely face the tanker head-on. I found their unity and courage profoundly moving. Eventually, the tanker relented and allowed the tugs to guide it safely into port.

Explaining antisemitism is akin to describing submerged dangers that even experienced pilots cannot see. Sometimes antisemitism shows itself in visible conduct—vandalism, verbal threats, physical attack—that most citizens recognize as wrong. But sometimes, for decades at a time, things look pretty good for us Jews. Calm waters keep the sandbar hidden. Yet it lies there, ready to gut a ship at any time. This vulnerability, this deep knowledge that security may be temporary, keeps Jews a little nervous. Even terrified. Jews recall uneasily the assimilation, intermarriage, and professional jobs characteristic of many pre-Holocaust western European Jews. Few Gentile onlookers at the time would have called the Jewish situation precarious or guessed that most Jews would soon find no safe harbor anywhere. A few Jewish leaders grasped that the middle-class security and assimilation brought by a temporary economic high tide would not be enough to propel them over the dangerous reef. Indeed, they saw dimly that this very class position might provide the pretext for exclusion and expulsion. Isolated between Gentile working and owning classes, Jews were blamed by both groups, which prevented all three from challenging the classism that soon roiled the world's economy. Is the situation of Jews in the United States different today? Yes, because a strong democracy encourages leaders to condemn bigotry. And no, because we have not yet excavated our harbors from the interlocking sandbars of antisemitism, classism, and racism.[1]



Most Jews and Gentiles find it difficult to see, name, and confront antisemitism. Even its overt display in the summer of 2017 in Charlottesville, Virginia, with white Gentiles chanting, "Jews will not replace us," did not always bring condemnation of antisemitism per se. Many denounced the racism also on exhibit, but many others could not seem to utter the "A" word. The forces of antisemitism—its structural dynamics and its hooks in people's minds and hearts—can be as elusive as shifting sandbars. I invite you, dear reader, to become like those tugboat captains, to learn the contours of the shoals upon which so many liberation movements have run aground. And to act with like solidarity and fierceness to ensure that social change movements make it ashore.

What is the situation of Jewish ethicists on Gentile campuses today? One day more than two decades ago, all save myself and one colleague in the sciences seemed oblivious to anything amiss. During the semester when I was standing for tenure, I had written an article for the student paper on antisemitism in response to some issues on campus. A white Gentile tenured male colleague responded at length on a progressive faculty listserv. He argued that I had labeled him an antisemite (I had not mentioned him in my article). He positioned himself as the victim of an oppressive Jewish voice who was silencing him, just as Jews were succeeding in shutting down debate on college campuses around the country. In his eyes, I was the oppressor and deserved public blame—and probably not tenure. My Gentile colleagues fell silent. No one noted that perhaps he was in a position of power relative to me; that maybe I—the only female Jewish untenured assistant professor on my campus—was the one being threatened into silence, not him. For several years I had worked with colleagues of African heritage to address racist incidents on campus. Even they fell silent.

As I stood in my office, breathing hard, the wall of silence brought to mind the German professoriate, early Nazi collaborators. "Even before the government-imposed dismissal of Jewish civil servants in the wake of the Law for the Restoration of the Professional Civil Service, passed in April

1933," writes German scholar Robert K. Weninger, "radical student leaders and sympathisers among the professoriate [at Heidelberg University] had begun to harass and boycott their Marxist and 'non-Aryan' colleagues."[2] Peter Drucker, an Austrian-born academic, described a faculty meeting at the liberal Frankfurt University not long after Hitler, on January 30, 1933, had been appointed chancellor of Germany:



> The new Nazi commissar wasted no time on the amenities. He immediately announced that Jews would be forbidden to enter university premises and would be dismissed without salary on March 15. This was something that no one had thought possible despite the Nazis' loud anti-Semitism. Then he launched into a tirade of abuse, filth, and four-letter words such as had rarely been heard even in the barracks and never before in academia. . . . [He] pointed his finger at one department chairman after another and said, "You either do what I tell you or we'll put you into a concentration camp." There was dead silence when he finished; everybody waited for the distinguished biochemist. The great liberal got up, cleared his throat, and said: "Very interesting, Mr. Commissar, and in some respects very illuminating. But one point I didn't get too clearly. Will there be more money for research in physiology?"
>
> The meeting broke up shortly thereafter with the commissar assuring the scholars that indeed there would be plenty of money for "racially pure science." A few of the professors had the courage to walk out with their Jewish colleagues, but most kept a safe distance from these men who, only a few hours earlier, had been their close friends. I went out sick unto death—and I knew that I would leave Germany within forty-eight hours.[3]

According to historian Richard J. Evans, 15 percent of full professors (not all Jewish) had been dismissed by the fall of 1933.[4] My experience was nothing like theirs, except for a faint shiver of isolation.

Mostly barred from Gentile institutions of higher education until after World War II, Jews now grace the halls of academe. Yet my small liberal arts college (founded by a Protestant denomination) houses about ten professed Jewish faculty members among some 245. Jewish students who so identify number about 120 of 2,400 undergraduates. How might we analyze the social location of white Jews in the academy, especially those who wish to form coalitions to challenge racism?

Many coalitions, without sustained attention to antisemitism, have not been able to navigate the harbor. One thinks of early labor associations of Jewish workers who looked to Gentile socialists for solidarity. Yet these socialists did not perceive the unique needs of Jewish workers who eventually came to suffer mightily from pogroms in Russia that intensified in the 1880s. Following the expulsion of the Jews from Moscow, at the congress of the Second International in Brussels in 1891,



> A. Cohen, a representative of the organizations of "Yiddish-speaking workers" in the United States, moved the following question for the agenda: "What shall be the attitude of organized workers in all countries to the Jewish question?" . . . The congress decided to strike the question from the agenda. It did not resolve that it was the duty of the socialist parties to fight against anti-Semitism. . . . Instead, the congress denounced both "anti-Semitism" and "philo-Semitism." The resolution also included the following statement: "The Jewish-speaking workers have no other means of liberation except unity with the Socialist-labor parties in the countries they inhabit."[5]

The choice was clear—abandon the effort to end the oppression of Jews, or organize separately from Gentile workers. In this and other ways, the shoal of antisemitism can prevent potential working-class solidarity.

Antisemitism has surfaced consistently in ways that sidetrack or sink movements to end classism or racism. I argue that classism and racism depend on antisemitism to divide and conquer. These dynamics work effectively when Gentiles are conditioned not to recognize or understand antisemitism and to isolate Jews from their fellow oppressed groups. I aim to expose these dynamics so that we all can do our part, from our social location, to forge alliances and clear our harbors of all oppressions.

A distance of over a century allows us to comprehend how a movement to end classism that sought initially to bring Jews into alliance with fellow workers was diverted by antisemitism. But why isn't there a grassroots movement to end Jewish oppression today? In his *Socialism of Fools: Anti-Semitism on the Left*, activist rabbi Michael Lerner asks why Jews as an oppressed group have not made it into the U.S. dialogue about liberation. The civil rights movement, he suggests, helped move forward the women's and gay liberation movements, but no such comparable movement against antisemitism emerged.[6] Activists have not always sustained efforts to address anti-Jewish oppression among the rank and file.[7] When I was a graduate student, the leftist groups on campus were antisemitic in portraying Jews as oppressors only and as inherently the enemy of liberating forces. Forced out, we progressive Jews aligned with the Radical Jewish Union. We never were able to form a forward-looking coalition with Gentiles.



Without the external pressure of a grassroots movement to compel the study of antisemitism, academic liberationists proceeded to study racism, sexism, and other "isms." The distinctive structural dynamics of anti-Jewish oppression remained largely unexplored by Gentile scholars. Such historical factors, plus the cultural denial of antisemitism, suggest that any deployment of Gentile liberation theories by Jewish ethicists needs to be approached with suspicion.

Liberationists remind us that the liberatory intent of any analytic construct or practice is no guarantee of its accuracy, adequacy, or immunity to the ingress of oppressive ideas.[8] They themselves are not immune to false consciousness given their social location within intersecting oppressions.[9] One method that liberationist scholars use to help expose their own blinders is to strive for insight into how knowledge production is affected by social location. This chapter focuses on the social location of white, Ashkenazi Jews in the United States in predominantly white, Gentile settings who work at the intersections of classism, racism, and antisemitism.

Two analytical tools prove particularly helpful in mapping the structural aspects of antisemitism: oppression and intersectionality. Oppression is understood to be systemic and structured in institutions and social dynamics. Race theorists, for instance, have explicated the linked interdependent practices of racism constituting a structure of white supremacy. They understand racism as the systemic, structured, one-way targeting of groups for mistreatment (using skin color as a pretext) by whites who escape such targeting. I suggest that antisemitism deserves to be studied using this analytical tool of structural oppression, too. Oppression, of course, implants attitudes; both targeted and nontargeted groups internalize attitudes that condition them to accept their roles in the exploitive system. But combatting antisemitism should not only be focused on prejudice and hatred. Liberationists hope to change structures as well as habits of heart and mind. The path forward entails risk, resistance, and a commitment to forming effective coalitions with the shared goal of transformational structural change.

Although the tool of intersectionality needs refining for use by Jewish ethicists, it too will help map the structure of these interlocking sandbars (to continue the nautical metaphor with which I began).[10] Womanist sociologist Patricia Hill Collins views intersectionality as "an emerging field of critical inquiry and practice that examines how social inequalities are organized, endure, and change."[11] I suggest that although intersectionality was intended to prevent our seeing single oppressions in isolation, it has not totally escaped the dualism of treating groups as either oppressed or oppressive. This binary poses perils for Jewish ethicists because it could fail to capture a key structural feature of antisemitism—namely, that Jews are simultaneously oppressed and oppressor. An intersectional analysis, combined with the analytic tool of oppression, will reveal the insufficiency of framing antisemitism as hatred.



First I sketch the intersections of classism and anti-Jewish oppression, and then turn in the second section to mapping how racism and anti-Jewish oppression differ structurally, despite their other similarities. With a map of these differently structured "sandbars" in hand, in the third section I explore how antisemitism anchors the sandbar of racism. Anti-Jewish oppression, it appears, functions today to snag and sidetrack movements against racism.

In the final section, I identify some questions we ethicists find ourselves facing as we ponder how to eliminate these interlocking oppressions. As feminist ethicist Karen Lebacqz argues in a seminal essay, ethics undertaken with a liberatory aim reshapes how ethics ought to be conducted.[12] Rather than assume a mask of neutrality, liberation ethicists argue that unless one is deliberately resisting oppression, one is passively supporting the status quo.[13] Ethicists may contest (as many academics do) the deliberate adoption of a liberatory goal in their scholarship. This essay does not make the case for embracing that aim for one's scholarly pursuits. Instead, it assumes that some ethicists will identify the elimination of oppression as a moral issue and a worthy undertaking; they are interested in understanding how Jewish ethics can open up new lines of moral inquiry and action.

When we reframe antisemitism as a structural oppression, we can understand why it cannot be explicated without studying its intersections with classism. We thus begin our exploration of the harbor by mapping these two interlocking sandbars.

## Mapping Sandbars: Anti-Jewish Oppression's Intersection with Classism

Ethicists today who wish to study antisemitism have access to analytic tools such as intersectionality. The concept of intersectionality emerged from U.S. social movements in the 1960s as an inquiry into social inequalities, power, and politics. Intersectionality, Collins notes, has grounding in "the black feminist politics of the 1960s and 1970s."[14] Womanists specifically argued that liberation could not be won without attention to race, class, and gender. Collins writes that black activism generated the pamphlets, poetry, essays, edited volumes, and art that enabled the Combahee River Collective to produce its powerful position paper "A Black Feminist Statement" in 1977.[15] She notes that Chicanas and other Latinas, indigenous women, and Asian American women were undertaking similar analyses, such as those found in Gloria Anzaldúa's enduring volume *Borderlands/La Frontera: The New Mestiza*. The social movements of the 1960s and 1970s carved out space for "race/class/gender studies" in the academy; by the 1980s, a tiny trickle of Gentiles of color and white women began to legitimate academic programs and departments such as women's studies and African American studies. The umbrella term "intersectionality" emerged in the 1990s "in this border space between social movement and academic politics."[16]



Although some authors define oppression as "prejudice plus power,"[17] scholars of intersectionality argue that power is relative to one's position within intersecting social group memberships.[18] A man of mixed African and Irish heritage became president of the United States, yet he endured mistreatment not aimed at white presidents. He had relative power from class and gender privilege, while remaining subject to mistreatment by being deemed black.

Intersectionality builds upon previous work on the nature of oppression as structural as well as attitudinal. Liberation theorists such as Iris Marion Young argue that the term "oppression" can be deployed to explain the complexities of unjust social structures in ways that counter the pervasive language of liberal individualism in U.S. politics. Moving away from a narrow political meaning of oppression as the subjugation of a group by a tyrant, liberationists expand the term to include individuals' experiences as members of groups that are systematically targeted for mistreatment.[19]

Liberation ethicists aver that it is a fundamental error to define oppression solely in terms of prejudices.[20] Social justice educator Lee Anne Bell emphasizes that "social inequality [is] woven throughout social institutions as well as embedded within individual consciousness. Oppression fuses institutional and systemic discrimination, personal bias, bigotry and social prejudice in a complex web of relationships and structures that saturate most aspects of life in our society."[21] For the remainder of this chapter, I use the term "oppression" to refer to the systemic, structural, and one-way targeting of a group for mistreatment by another group that escapes that targeting, by the exploitive society as a whole, or by its agents. Both targeted and nontargeted groups internalize attitudes that recycle and perpetuate oppression. The term "internalized oppression" refers to how the targeted group has digested the attitudes and mistreatment aimed at it. As the result of sporadic violent attacks over the centuries, Jews internalized a posture of distrust toward Gentiles, which fuels a need to be in control. Internalized domination, for its part, consists of the oppressor group's formation of dispositions, such as the mindset that regards some groups as second class.[22] Whites are conditioned to act on their presumed superiority to people of color; Gentiles are conditioned to blame Jews.[23]



By regarding oppression as structural, this internalization of social constructs can be seen to require the underlying material structure of the sandbar.[24] For example, the process of becoming white in the United States involves more than a disembodied acquisition of prejudice: it embodies such things as becoming painfully disconnected from whites in one's primary group or being physically segregated from people of color in white suburbs. Ethicists can study such material realities rather than rely for insight solely on the emotions of either the oppressor or the oppressed. An absence of feeling oppressed (or oppressive) is not a reliable guide to understanding one's multiple positions within an oppressive society. (Although the presence or absence of such feelings may lead to analysis about how oppressive dynamics affect the moral psyche.)[25] Nor is one's identity necessarily a clue to one's intersectional social location. Liberationists examine structures rather than identities alone. White Jews might claim different identities (atheist, cultural, anti-Zionist) that do not exempt them from anti-Jewish oppression, internalized Jewish oppression, and internalized white domination.

The phrase *structural dynamics* refers to how forms of mistreatment are woven into an exploitive system that forms a complex of practices that leave no one unscathed. Various forms of mistreatment rise to the level of oppression when they become institutionalized and structured within a society (as well as implanted into individual hearts and minds). Any individual might mistreat another individual, but unless that mistreatment is enacted by a member of a group that has the institutional backing to enforce it, it does not constitute oppression. As Beverly Tatum observes, oppression creates inequalities between groups; some have the power to enforce their stereotypes throughout the fabric of society, while other groups do not.[26] A Jewish student who demeans a Christian classmate is not enacting oppression, because Jews as a group lack the power to organize such conduct systemically in ways that harm Christians. Similarly, a student of African heritage who calls a white classmate a derogatory racial term is not enacting racial oppression, because African Americans as a group lack the power to make such attitudes systemic in ways that harm whites as a group. Such disrespect and conduct are morally wrong, but they do not amount to structural oppression.

Intersectionality's emergence within scholarship by people of color makes it particularly useful to Jewish ethicists who seek to navigate the waters ahead. But if we are to rise to the challenges of coalition building, Jewish ethicists will need to refine this concept. An analysis of antisemitism will reveal how intersectionality might easily miss that sandbar's structure. Specifically, the concept of intersectionality presumes a solid grasp of the dynamics and functions of each of the various oppressions that intersect. Feminists who write about the intersection of sexism and racism, for instance, assume that solid groundwork has been done elsewhere on the fundamentals of sexism; the notion of its intersectionality with racism is used to complicate, interrogate, and enrich that existing work. For example, indigenous activist Andrea Smith specifically presents prior analyses of sexism and of the genocide of Native Americans—which had both been studied separately—and seeks to demonstrate how intersectionality challenges prior understandings.[27]

The assumption in womanist writings that we have a sufficient grasp of the dynamics of sexism to see how it has been limited by our studying it in isolation from racism may or may not be in error. But any assumption of the sufficiency of accounts of antisemitism is questionable. Studies of the intersections of racism and anti-Jewish oppression have not always begun with an adequate conception of antisemitism.

Furthermore, an uncritical use of intersectionality could prevent a well-drawn map of antisemitism's structure. Sometimes intersectionality implies a binary analysis—I am oppressed as a female but am an oppressor as a white person. These binaries are then thought to intersect. As a white female, my experience of sexism is different from that of a Latina owing to the intersections of sexism and racism. In this way, intersectionality can, ironically, remain binary. One notes intersections, but they are of singular groups classified as either oppressed or oppressor. Intersectionality does not appear to identify oppressions whose dynamics set up the oppressed group to play an oppressive role. That is, it could lead one to fail to notice how a group, such as Jews, could be simultaneously oppressed and oppressor.

Our tugboat captains want us to understand why the binary of oppressed or oppressor is not sufficient to map the sandbar of antisemitism. They also want us to see how this sandbar divides Jews from other oppressed groups.

A corrective begins by reconceiving antisemitism as a form of oppression—that is, as the systemic, structural, one-way mistreatment of Jews by non-Jews. This oppression cannot be understood apart from its intersections with classism. Let's attend to this intersectionality that has shaped anti-Jewish oppression from the early modern period to the present.

Anti-Jewish oppression has involved a particular dynamic of classism, which means that anti-Jewish oppression is difficult to map without an analysis of class oppression. Classism is the division of society into different groups hierarchically stratified on the basis of their relation to production. Slavery is one form of class society in which the enslavers own the bodies of those who work, their offspring, and the profits of their labor. Capitalism is a form of classism in which those involved in the direct production of goods and services constitute the working class. The small owning class consists of those who exploit workers by taking "the surplus produced . . . and us[ing] it for their own material well-being"—in Karl Marx's terms, those who either own the means of production or live off the inheritance of previous owners (unearned income). Within this conception of capitalism, the middle class is part of the working class—its members work for a living and provide services as social workers, doctors, lawyers, bankers, teachers, and managers—but these roles have the added function of funneling profits from the working class to the owning class.[28]

Jews have often been channeled by both classism and anti-Jewish oppression (and Jews' own subsequent internalized oppression) to occupy visibly exploitive roles between lower-class workers and the ruling elites.[29] Rabbi Robert J. Marx calls Jews "the people in between" who occupy an "interstitial role."[30] This chapter calls this position "middle agency." Although this occupational pattern was evident sporadically in early Jewish history (Joseph could be seen as a middle agent between Pharaoh and slaves), it did not become a systemic structural dynamic until the early modern period. As economic historian Arcadius Kahan has detailed, at that time, stateless European Jews were prohibited from owning land or working it, and were thereby prevented from becoming either peasants or landed gentry. Owning-class elites might admit Jews into their kingdoms on the condition that a few Jews perform visibly exploitive kinds of work. Thus Jews were initially forced into lending money or collecting taxes—highly visible, overtly exploitive jobs of transferring wealth from the lower to the upper class. As Kahan observes, "The Jews served the gentry as middlemen. . . . Like the nobility, the gentry preferred in many cases to have the Jews act as a buffer between them and the peasantry, so that for the opportunity of employment and income the

Jews assumed the role of the gentry's agent in the economic exploitation of the peasantry and in effect became the scapegoat of the righteous wrath of the peasants."[31] Although most Jews in Poland were impoverished before World War II,[32] the image of the Jew by then had become hardened—all Jews possessed bags of gold acquired by using their class position and wits to outsmart and exploit poor Gentiles. Anti-Jewish oppression and classism combined to isolate Jews from peasants and, later, the working class (despite the fact that most Jews worked for a living). In the early modern period, ruling elites may have acted intentionally to allow the isolation and scapegoating of Jews. Once this structural dynamic was embedded in systems, institutions, and the minds of both Gentiles and Jews, the oppression took on a life of its own. It no longer required intentionality.[33] Dominant elites benefited by obfuscating how Jews were oppressed and encouraged recognition only of Jews' exploitive role. Both this external oppression and Jews' consequent internalized oppression propelled many to seek temporary security as agents of Gentile elites.[34] The oppression set up Jews simultaneously as both oppressed and oppressor.



This structural dynamic of maneuvering Jews into becoming agents of the Gentile owning class was not confined to Europe; it can be seen in the United States as well.[35] Many impoverished Jewish immigrants to the United States entered the working class by peddling scrap metal, rags, or candy. Barred from setting up shop in white Gentile neighborhoods and from getting a college education, many white Jews opened small stores in neighborhoods that served poor people, especially poor people of color. Jews could find jobs teaching in the inner cities, which white Gentiles tended to avoid.[36] Some of the wealthier Jews became landlords, but in poor places such as Harlem. After World War II, ruling Gentiles allowed Jews to enter higher education and the professions. Jews fled into middle-agent roles for many reasons. The Holocaust had targeted Jews as communists. McCarthyism and the execution of accused communist spies Julius and Ethel Rosenberg scared U.S. Jews away from overt solidarity with the working class. Terrified, they sought security in a practice that centuries of antisemitism had instilled in them—aligning with ruling elites. The Nazis and their collaborators had murdered Jews as racially inferior. Terror from genocide made assimilation into whiteness look promising. Their internalized oppression—"Maybe I'll be safe if I can gain economic security and racial acceptance"—is understandable, and it demonstrates how both external circumstance and internalized oppression can propel Jews to become agents of the oppressive society. Although there are always individual exceptions, most Jews did not become owners of the means of production, as they were prohibited from taking hold of the reins of economic power, which were reserved for what today we call the 1 percent.[37] Oppression sets Jews up as middle agents whom non-Jews can then exploit. In the movie *Blinded by the Light* (2019), a father and teenage son are targeted by vicious anti-immigrant racism. The father tells the son to avoid girls at school. Instead, he should hang out with Jews—he'll be successful then. The father, perhaps owing to his experiences of racism, urges his son to exploit Jews. The son calls his dad a racist.



Today, middle-class Jews, like middle-class Gentiles, function as conduits of classism. Middle agents transmit class control downward by exercising authority over the poor, the uneducated, and the working class (many of whom are people of color) through jobs such as social workers, professors, and middle managers.[38] Again, Gentiles do the same kind of work but are not targeted, the way Jews are, for being pernicious. Most of these exploitive behaviors are not intentional by either Jews or Gentiles. Instead, structural dynamics, internalized oppression, and internalized domination are reproduced without awareness (unless identified and resisted).[39]

Gentiles have been conditioned for centuries to blame Jews for economic downturns. When the marchers in Charlottesville, Virginia, chanted, "Jews will not replace us," they were enacting their internalized domination. The Pew Research Center estimates that in 2013 there were about 5.3 million Jews in America, roughly 2.2 percent of the adult population: Jews are not about to take over.[40] Unfortunately, blaming Jews rather than capitalist Gentile rulers means that efforts to protest classism will run aground on the shoals of antisemitism. By deflecting their anger onto Jews as their oppressors, Gentile workers fail to unite with Jews to challenge classism directly.[41] Jewish oppression is denied, leaving Jews to be attacked for being privileged and allegedly dangerous.

To summarize, anti-Jewish oppression intersects with classism to set up some Jews to be targeted as middle agents of the oppressive society. Jews escape certain kinds of mistreatment, but their isolation and interstitial position keep them vulnerable to blame and isolation from potential allies. Lerner captures the implications of these dynamics: "No matter how much economic security or political influence individual Jews may achieve, they can never be sure that they will not once again become the targets of popular attack should the society in which they live enter periods of severe economic strain or political conflict. It is precisely this hidden vulnerability that constitutes the uniqueness of Jewish oppression."[42] Antiracism scholars Gerald Weinstein and Donna Mellen call this a "convoluted dynamic: the systematic creation of vulnerability, followed by the effort of Jews to overcome that vulnerability by accommodating to oppressive forces, which are, in turn, only too willing to let Jews become the more visible 'agent' of and scapegoat for the oppression of others."[43] This oppression sets Jews up as simultaneously oppressed and oppressor.



I have shown how the knowledge project of intersectionality can be useful to ethicists, if refined to avoid the binary that regards groups as either oppressed or oppressor. That binary portrays white Jews *solely* as oppressors because of their white privilege. This picture misses the key intersecting structural dynamics of antisemitism and classism—middle agency. Jewish flight into middle-agent roles after World War II is a function of anti-Jewish oppression as well as of white privilege. It is futile to ponder how much Jewish privilege is due to middle agency, how much is due to whiteness, and how much is due to internalized Jewish oppression. The important conclusion here is that a nonbinary intersectional analysis of structural dynamics reveals the inherent vulnerability of Jews' class position.

This analysis of intersecting structural dynamics further reveals why hatred is insufficient to characterize anti-Jewish oppression. A brief review of definitions of antisemitism by scholars from a variety of disciplines reveals their focus not on these structural dynamics but on forms of mistreatment (social exclusion) and/or content (hatred, prejudice, belief, ideology).

Antisemitism has been seen primarily as a disposition, as expressed in the title of the movie *The Longest Hatred: The History of Anti-Semitism* (1993).[44] Historian Bernard Lewis contends that "normal prejudice" creates conflicts between groups, but that antisemitism is characterized by "the special and peculiar hatred of the Jews." Although he differentiates the oppression of blacks from the oppression of Jews by noting the differences in their mistreatment (exploitation versus extermination), he concludes that both are "manifestations of racism" involving hatred.[45] Essayist Cynthia Ozick regards antisemitism as hatred: "We thought that the cannibal hatred, once quenched, would not soon wake again." Referring to the antisemitism on full display at the United Nations conference called to condemn "racism, discrimination, xenophobia and related intolerance," Ozick refers to "virulent hatred under the auspices of anti-hatred."[46] She quotes the German-Jewish philosopher Franz Rosenzweig, who affirms that the issue is one of hatred. In writing of "*hatred of the Jews*" (his emphasis), he remarked, "You know as well as I do that all its realistic arguments are only fashionable cloaks."[47]

It is also presented as a belief: "Antisemitism, in its overt form, is the belief that Jews are a pernicious influence in the entire structure of modern life and hence must be effectively removed."[48] Studies of antisemitism have focused on the emotions and needs of Gentiles. Philosopher Jean-Paul Sartre writes, "[The anti-Semite] is a man who is afraid. Not of the Jews, to be sure, but of himself, of his own consciousness, of his liberty, of his instincts . . . of everything except the Jews. He is a coward who does not want to admit his cowardice to himself. . . . The Jew only serves him as a pretext; elsewhere his counterpart will make use of the Negro or the man of yellow skin."[49] Emotions, beliefs, and psychological needs do not speak to structural dynamics.



Sociologist of religion J. Milton Yinger is an interesting example of a scholar who analyzes the social structures of antisemitism quite well but persists in referring to it as a prejudice.[50] This reductionism could of course be a feature of sociological discourse at the time (the 1960s), but it has led more recently to narrow treatments of antisemitism as a prejudice, an approach that discourages fuller studies of its structural dynamics. It is as if Yinger himself does not recognize the significance of his own analysis. "The Jews," he writes, "who occupy places on almost every status level of society, are more apt scapegoats for more diverse groups than is a minority that is concentrated primarily in lower status levels. Jews are importantly involved in most of the sharply conflicting developments of modern life." But then he concludes that moderns "dare not admit . . . that their hostility to Jews is a categorical prejudice."[51] The challenge today perhaps is the reverse—people might understand antisemitism as a prejudice but fail to comprehend its complex structural dynamics, which in part explains how white Jews are recognized as oppressors of, for example, people of African heritage and Arabs (which overlooks the existence of African-heritage and Arab Jews), while anti-Jewish oppression is denied.

Scholar Paul E. Grosser and activist Edwin G. Halperin continue the focus on ideology and mistreatment with their definition: "Anti-Semitism: Attitudes and actions against Jews based on the belief that Jews are uniquely inferior, evil or deserving of condemnation by their very nature or by historical or supernatural dictates." They note that this definition may not account for "attacks against Jews apparently motivated by considerations such as philosophical differences, power struggles and political maneuverings."[52] Noting as well how stereotypes accumulate and mutate over time, they do not focus on the continuity of structural dynamics despite changes at the ideological level.

Historian Israel Gutman, in the *Encyclopedia of the Holocaust*, suggests that the "causes of antisemitism . . . are based primarily on the religious and spiritual creed of Judaism and on the role played by Jews in the economy and other spheres of life in the Western world," as well as enduring stereotypes and "calumnies" that accumulated over centuries. This nuanced view appears at first to elevate the analysis of antisemitism beyond Jew-hatred. He studies the advocates of a "new antisemitism," who emerged following the emancipation of European Jews in the 1870s. They tried to present antisemitism as rational and objective, not emotional, such as with the allegedly scientific claim that "Jews by nature turn to business, capital, and the stock market." Gutman exposes how German Jews became "concentrated in certain professions" due to material forces such as Germany's extension of citizenship to Jews if and only if they gave up "many elements of their tradition and organizational pattern." Their coerced assimilation was accompanied by simultaneous prohibition from positions of Gentile leadership "such as the officers' corps, and higher posts in the academic field and in the government administration." This exclusion led to "their disproportionate numbers in some professions . . . [which] made them conspicuous and exposed them to suspicion and hatred," from which conversion to Christianity did not protect them. Despite such excellent analysis of the structural dynamics that resulted in middle agency, Gutman's main point is to show how the "new antisemitism" eventually became just as irrational and hateful as its pre-Enlightenment forms. By the end of his essay, he does not advocate transformation of structural dynamics, only excision of hatred.[53]

Recent analyses by historian Robert Wistrich and journalist Ron Rosenbaum perpetuate this almost exclusive focus on the attitudes, stereotypes, and emotions of Gentiles at the expense of intersecting structural dynamics. Wistrich's monograph, *A Lethal Obsession: Anti-Semitism from Antiquity to the Global Jihad*, documents centuries of "the longest hatred." He cites many recent and present-day defamations of Jews, Israel, and Zionism whose "tone and content . . . along with the manifest will to exterminate the Jews," he suggests, "are virtually identical to German Nazism."[54] He compares surveys of anti-Jewish sentiment in countries around the world and documents what he calls a "culture of hatred" in socialist, leftist, and intellectual circles, "in the contemporary Arab-Muslim world," and in anti-Zionist discourse surrounding the Israeli-Palestinian conflict.[55] Wistrich argues that antisemitism is "much more than mere prejudice about or discrimination against Jews," but he is referring here to its "paranoid and hysterical" quality, not to its structural dynamics. Regarding Jews "as a despised 'other,'" he writes, "has over centuries produced an almost unfathomable abyss of dehumanization of the Jews." Without offering an analysis of antisemitism beyond "ancient myths, dark hatreds, and irrational fantasies," he addresses its latest forms in "Holocaust inversion, 'anti-Zionist' anti-Semitism, conspiracy theory, 'antiracist' racism, the legacy of Third Worldism, anti-Westernism, and self-destructive Islamist ideologies."[56] These do little more than catalogue justifications for antisemitism.



*Those Who Forget the Past*, the volume of essays on antisemitism collected by Ron Rosenbaum, does not disrupt this pattern of analysis. Instead, it shows how antisemitic attitudes and beliefs build on past images and accusations while morphing to fit the present. For instance, Rosenbaum notes how antisemitic websites "lurched from the false announcement" that Israel possessed advance knowledge of the attacks on New York's World Trade Center in September 2001 "to a defense of the ancient 'blood libel' charges that Jewish ritual called for using the blood of murdered Christian children to make pastry for religious feasts." "After nearly two decades of reading the literature of anti-Semitism," Rosenbaum confesses, "—both the thing itself and the analysis of the thing itself—I have yet to find a satisfactory explanation for its persistence."[57] His volume studies culture and ideology—indeed, any pretext that keeps blame focused on Jews and away from classism. The analytic tool of oppression reveals the incompleteness of such studies, since they miss the intersecting structural dynamics that set Jews up as middle agents and divide them from other oppressed groups.

Holocaust historian Deborah E. Lipstadt's monograph *Antisemitism: Here and Now* does not break from this legacy of regarding antisemitism as hatred of Jews. Lipstadt recognizes "the historical and religious origins of Jew-hatred" and avers that antisemitism has a structure. But by structure she means simply that antisemitic beliefs have an "internal coherence" fueled simultaneously by "a heterogeneous passion," which can prompt "collective or state violence." She does not use the concept of structure, as I do in this chapter, to refer to dynamics such as how classism intersects with anti-Jewish oppression, how middle agency is formed, how Jews can be simultaneously oppressed and oppressor, and how all of these things combine to isolate Jews from other oppressed groups. Instead, Lipstadt remains focused on prejudice and hatred. "Antisemitism is not the hatred of people who *happen to be* Jews. It is hatred of them *because* they are Jews" (emphasis in original). She regards racism, too, as a "senseless hatred," and therefore she cannot examine how these oppressions might differ in their intersections with classism.[58]

We have seen the usefulness of studying anti-Jewish oppression in conjunction with classism. Let us now turn our attention to a study of the structural dynamics of the sandbar of racism and contrast it to anti-Jewish oppression. I suggest that although their justifying ideologies and forms of mistreatment may look similar on the surface, they are structured differently at the bottom of the bay. Once we have a good grasp of these similarities and differences, we can turn in the third section to see how these sandbars intersect to scuttle movements for change.



### The Sandbar of Racism Contrasted to Anti-Jewish Oppression

If white Jewish ethicists accept an analysis of their own oppression that ignores or minimizes structural dynamics, they are in a weak position to notice the structural realities of racism.[59] Jews would not be unique in studying racism as if it were only a social construct—prejudice, belief, discourse—without attention to material reality. Scholar of religion Jennifer Harvey argues that regarding race as a construct divorced from structural dynamics has at least two negative consequences. First, it has misled some whites into thinking that if they could disregard race—by becoming colorblind—they would cease participating in racism. This attitude is self-deceptive, Harvey argues, because not noticing race often reinforces the pattern of ignoring the material realities of structural white supremacy.[60]

Analyses of oppression that refer only to attitudes have a second consequence, Harvey adds, of diverting oppressors' attention to their interior life in ways that blind them to their complicity in racist policies and practices.[61] White Jews can deceive themselves that if they do not practice open bigotry, then they are not entangled in racism. Gentiles can deceive themselves that if they lack feelings of Jew-hatred or superiority, they cannot be complicit in anti-Jewish oppression.[62] White Jews might be lulled into thinking that ending racism requires individual solutions alone, without collective action to seek material change. Harvey proposes white reparations for slavery and genocide as one such material change.[63]

It can be confusing to differentiate antisemitism from racism because Jewish assimilation into whiteness can look similar to that of other European immigrants. Like the Irish and Italians, for instance, Ashkenazi Jews could evade the heavy racism aimed at people of color by giving up distinctive elements of their culture and becoming complicit in the demands of white supremacy.[64] Adoption of white habits of mind and conduct appeared preferable to solidarity with people targeted by racism. Activist Penny Rosenwasser quotes a Jewish woman: "White privilege was the *compromise*, the deal we struck as Jews in America: 'You'll allow us to become white, to be free, to live and get rich,' she laughed nervously. 'And in exchange, we won't talk about racism or anti-Semitism. So it's not just a choice of white privilege. It's also about agreeing to ignore injustice.'"[65] The term "ethnic" became reserved for non-Anglo-Saxon groups that escaped racial targeting by assimilating to norms and practices of whiteness (as modeled and driven by Anglo-Saxon cultural norms).[66]



This process for Jews in the United States has been detailed elsewhere.[67] Suffice it to say here that this process was different for Jews for several reasons. First, worldwide and in the United States, many Jews have been targeted, historically, by both racism and anti-Jewish oppression even though these two forms of persecution often have different dynamics. Ashkenazi Jews are those from northern, western, and eastern Europe, including Russia. Jews come in many colors and are members of groups targeted by racism—by being Jewish and African, Chinese, Korean, Indian, indigenous, Sephardic, or Arab (Mizrahi). These Jews of color are simultaneously targeted by anti-Jewish oppression and racism.[68] Nevertheless, the dynamics of racism and the visibility of prominent Jewish middle agents in the United States produced an image of the Jew as white. Whether in Orthodox attire or modern garb, the image of Jews over time in the United States became limited to Ashkenazim. This racism was internalized by white Jews who failed to see how Sephardic and Mizrahi Jews had been targeted by racism. Racism within the Jewish community thus became aimed at their own, not just at Gentiles of color. This pervasive racism has meant that Jews of color have found it difficult to be seen as "real" Jews, especially in predominantly Ashkenazi settings.

There is yet another difference from white Gentile ethnic groups. Ashkenazi Jews had the experience in twentieth-century Europe (and in the United States) of being barred from whiteness by being targeted as non-Aryan.[69] This history means that some older U.S. Ashkenazim have difficulty seeing themselves as white, especially if their extended families were murdered for not being Aryan. Thus, Ashkenazi Jews' relation to whiteness is different, historically, from that of white Gentiles who have not been targeted for genocide, with racism used as a pretext.

Jewish assimilation into whiteness differs from the experience of other European immigrants in a third way. Whiteness in America has been closely coded with being Christian, especially Protestant. As non-Christians, Jews had difficulty in being seen as white. Owing to the realities of anti-Jewish oppression in the United States, white supremacists such as the Ku Klux Klan targeted blacks and Jews as pernicious in ways that made Ashkenazi Jews targets of racism.[70] Today, this older kind of racial excuse for antisemitism is again raising its head.[71] Young Ashkenazi Jews with darker skin tones find themselves outsiders to the white Christian club. One of my students, a young woman with dark eyes and hair, was called "Anne Frank" for an entire year in middle school; at college, she found herself being called exotic. Ashkenazi Jews in the United States today have largely escaped racial stigma by becoming racialized as white, although they remain targeted as different.[72]

Similar cultural prejudices about color might cause us to overlook how the structural dynamics of racism and anti-Jewish oppression nevertheless differ. One difference is that racism results in class disadvantage, whereas anti-Jewish oppression results in visible class privilege (for the most prominent Jews). Another difference is that anti-Jewish oppression is cyclical; to return to our metaphor, at times with plenty of rainfall and glacier melt, the sandbar remains hidden. During these lulls, it is kept in place by processes that circulate underwater without much challenge. During good economic times, Jews can look hardly victimized at all. Yet the vulnerability to future isolation, blame, and exclusion remains, which feeds Jews' chronic terror about the cycle turning, as it now appears to be doing. In contrast, racism constantly crushes the bodies and souls of people of color. True, overt racial bigotry is more evident during difficult financial times, but the institutions that perpetuate racism, such as the criminal justice system, grind on daily.

Another difference is that Gentiles of color who achieve middle-class or even owning-class status are not blamed for being oppressors. They are not, as a group, scapegoated so as to divide them from other oppressed groups. Upwardly mobile Latinxs may fail to reach down to their brothers and sisters still struggling with poverty or lousy schools, but they are never maneuvered into complete isolation from their fellows of color. For all the ways in which African Americans are targeted—in education, housing, criminal justice, health care, and environmental injustice—the black middle class is not singled out for being too privileged, stereotyped as money-grubbing, or separated from other people of color. Racism in the United States has involved subjugation and deprivation of resources, whereas antisemitism grants some Jews enough economic assets to justify isolating them from other oppressed groups.

A different kind of complexity occurs when oppressions involve similar kinds of mistreatment even while their structural dynamics differ. For instance, both white Jews and people of African heritage have been mistreated similarly by being killed, threatened with violence, and pigeonholed into certain occupations, even while the structural dynamics of racism and anti-Jewish oppression differ. These and other similarities can make antisemitism look like a form of racism.

Not only is the precariousness of middle agency different from racist disadvantage, but enslavement and genocide also involve different structural dynamics.[73] The former exploits the enslaved as property, with economic profit paramount. Enslavement invokes the ideology that, as property, enslaved people have some economic value and therefore are disposable only when they threaten the master's dominance or profits. All oppressions eventually take on a life of their own, and their forms of mistreatment become less clearly justified in strictly economic terms. The wanton destruction of buffalo made little sense economically; neither did the callous destruction of an estimated two million Africans during the Middle Passage. Slavery requires the conditioning of the oppressor and oppressed to imagine the enslaved as less than fully human, primarily owing to their alleged inferior intelligence, as possessing no rights, and as not deserving more than what is needed for physical survival. Women are treated as breeders, valuable for the laborers they produce. In the academy, white internalized domination might be expressed by a white student as surprise that her African-heritage professor could use "big words."

In contrast, genocide treats the targeted group, such as Jews, as completely expendable, "as a pest to be destroyed."[74] In the case of Jews, they are useful economically only until the working class comes too close to exposing Gentile class exploitation or to overthrowing Gentile power structures. Then Jews are more useful as disposable scapegoats. Genocide invokes the ideology that there is something so terrible about the group that they need to be eliminated—that the dominant group's lives will go better without them. Their right to exist is not a given. Those in oppressor roles have to be conditioned to see the group to be eliminated as deservedly blameworthy and therefore meriting death; the oppressed need to feel that their existence is precariously dependent on the fickle goodwill of their oppressors. In contrast to slavery, women and children are especially targeted for extermination to ensure the group's extinction. In the academy, Gentile internalized domination might be expressed as: "If we just got rid of that difficult, overbearing [not acknowledged as Jewish] department chair, everything would be better."

These differences between antisemitism and racism are, like our sandbars, submerged from view. Ruling elites benefit if anti-Jewish oppression is neither recognized nor understood. Hence dominant white Gentile discourse suggests that the economic privilege of prominent Jews means that they are not oppressed. Weinstein and Mellen write, "The reality that groups like Jews can be oppressed even if they are not, per se, economically impoverished, has been understandably hard for many economically disadvantaged groups to fully grasp. Even more to the point, the existence of these antisemitic stereotypes keeps these other oppressed groups from identifying and challenging the real sources of exploitation."[75] From there it is easy to allege that only Jews' whiteness, not antisemitism too, has placed them in the role of middle agent.[76] This widespread obfuscation leaves only the term "racism" to describe acts of anti-Jewish bigotry or violence. The intersections between antisemitism and classism construct the denial: Jews have economic security—ergo, they are not oppressed. The existential vulnerability of this precarious class position—and its difference from racism—is obscured from view.



Racism is an inadequate and misleading way to frame anti-Jewish oppression.[77] A slippage between these two different kinds of structural oppression permits Gentiles to target white Jews as racist without recognizing antisemitism. Precision in Jewish ethicists' analyses will encourage further distinctions between racism and anti-Jewish oppression, even when they interlock and their forms of mistreatment are similar.

The sheer existence of Jews from many cultures and regions reveals the irrationality of the division that pits Jews against people of color. The binary that regards Jews as oppressors and people of color as oppressed places Jews of color in a no-man's-land. Jews of color have a difficult time, on one hand, being visible as Jews in settings populated mostly by Gentiles of color. On the other hand, they have a hard time being seen as "real" Jews in predominantly Ashkenazi settings, while their struggles with the white racism experienced there remain invisible. Binaries such as "Jews and blacks" or "Jews and Arabs" are believable solely because of the divide-and-conquer dynamic.

The elimination of racism can thus be seen as central to Jewish liberation, because racism prevents our own solidarity and isolates us from all people of color. White Jews will never form successful coalitions without learning from and backing the leadership of people of color—both Jews and Gentiles.[78]

Our tugboat captains have an urgent request. They want new coalitions entering the harbor to understand how so many previous social change movements have run aground on the sandbar of antisemitism. To expose this hazard, it behooves us to ask how, at the structural level, antisemitism intersects with racism.

### How Antisemitism Anchors White Supremacy

Once honed to include a more adequate grasp of anti-Jewish oppression, the tool of intersectionality can expose how antisemitism interconnects with white supremacy, creating hidden hazards.

Recall that the distinctive feature of anti-Jewish oppression propels Jews by external circumstance and internalized oppression into an exploitive role over the working class and poor, where a disproportionate number of Gentiles of color are confined. Many movements have failed when the anger of the oppressed is misdirected at Jews rather than at classism directly (especially when misdeeds of wealthy Jews make headlines). White supremacy needs antisemitism so that Gentile whites in power can remain untouched while blame is deflected onto Jews. The tool of intersectionality reveals something new: how anti-Jewish oppression functions in contemporary historical contexts to sabotage efforts to end racism.

Some examples.

Consider how Malcolm X failed to see the structural dynamics of middle agency. He saw Jews only as oppressors, rather than as simultaneously oppressed. Instead of exposing the manipulative hand of the white Gentile power structure, he was led to blaming Jews because of their exploitive role as landlords and shopkeepers in Harlem.[79] Although Malcolm X came to see his mistake in essentializing whites as the devil, to my knowledge he did not abandon his conditioning to blame Jews and to think mistakenly that targeting wealthy Jews was an adequate way to fight class exploitation and white supremacy.

In 1968, African-heritage Gentile teachers and white Jewish teachers were pitted against one another in the Ocean Hill–Brownsville school district in Brooklyn. Teaching jobs were open to Jews in predominantly African American areas; Jews were often willing to work in inner cities out of their commitment to racial justice. But when African American teachers became organized, they targeted Jews as visible agents of class exploitation as well as of racism rather than expose the role of white Gentiles in setting Jews up.[80] White Jewish teachers carried racist habits (as all whites do), were complicit in white systems of power, and failed to acknowledge and deal with these problems effectively. Meanwhile, African Americans were misled into attacking their potential Jewish allies rather than identifying the white Gentile power structure that set up Jews and African Americans to attack one another. Leaders of African heritage largely failed to see how their own anti-Jewish sentiments sidetracked them from the larger goal of eliminating racism. These dynamics kept any coalition from forming and kept white Gentiles safely in power. When two oppressed groups fight each other for the same jobs, we need to step back and ask, "Who is benefiting from this conflict?" Jewish ethicists, by studying such historical examples, can expose how efforts to combat racism have run aground on the sandbar of antisemitism.



After the 1960s, Jews as a group became increasingly isolated from people of African heritage, despite prior Jewish advocacy of civil rights. Jewish whiteness and middle agency brought Jews immunity to the daily onslaught of racism still targeted at Americans of color. In contrast, the structural dynamics of racism worked to continue depriving people of color of resources while subjecting them to mass incarceration, despite the entry of some people of African heritage into the professions. Prominent African Americans displayed antisemitic views.[81] Meanwhile, prominent Jews were visible in classic middle-agent roles that supported white supremacy, such as Henry Kissinger's implementation of President Nixon's Vietnam policies. Hopes for a black-Jewish coalition faded.[82]

The Occupy movement's criticisms of the banking industry sometimes slipped into anti-Jewish motifs—some protesters blamed "Zionist" Jewish bankers and repeated the antisemitic trope about "a conspiracy in this country where Jews control the media, finances," as if Jews were at fault, as Jews, for the exploitation of working people of color in ways that Christian, Muslim, Buddhist, or atheist bankers were not.[83] Some terrified Jews labeled the whole Occupy movement antisemitic, even after the Anti-Defamation League, while calling for condemnation of such bigotry, had judged that the few signs did not represent the movement as a whole. "When cars were torched and 'f**k the Jews' scrawled in a Brooklyn neighborhood, Occupy Wall Street (OWS) condemned the anti-Semitism and joined a protest rally."[84] Antisemitism nearly sabotaged the potential of this movement to form a united coalition against classism.

Effective efforts to eliminate racism can be derailed by unfairly singling out Israel or Zionism (legitimate criticism of Israel is not antisemitic).[85] Of course, Israeli Ashkenazi Jews are complicit in racism. Yet so deeply entrenched is the divisive habit of blaming Israelis (a.k.a. Jews) as *uniquely* racist that it prompted some African Americans to revise history by denying that any powerful Jewish-black alliances existed during the civil rights era. The otherwise excellent movie *Selma* deleted the prominent and outspoken rabbi Abraham Joshua Heschel on the arm of his personal friend Martin Luther King Jr. and substituted a Christian figure instead.

In the autumn of 2017, a white Jewish student told me how during her first year in college she had been active in a variety of student groups in helping form a coalition with broad goals, such as addressing environmental racism. When this coalition was joined by a group with an exclusive focus on Israel's destructive policies in the occupied territories, hostility toward Jewish members such as herself increased. This student comes from an economically well off white home and understood how students of color might view her as a white Jew linked to money and to Israel's racist treatment of Palestinians. If the Jews in the student coalition spoke up about the increasing hostility toward them, they were vulnerable to the charge that they supported "the racist state of Israel." By isolating the Jews, other students were undermined in their effort to challenge environmental racism through collective action. The coalition eventually split apart over the divisiveness of the Jewish question. The only group left standing was the one opposed to Israeli policy. When antisemitism prompts Jews to abandon social change movements (or forces them out),[86] coalitions have once again run aground.

These examples show how antisemitism intersects with racism to deflect the legitimate anger of Gentiles of color onto Jews rather than direct it at the oppressive conditions that harmfully constrain both groups.[87] Lerner has argued that "every class society needs to build this kind of racist safety valve for its ruling class"—that is, misdirecting legitimate anger onto a scapegoat.[88] Gentiles of color are vulnerable to being seduced into attacking the wrong target, which undermines their efforts to challenge white supremacy. Displacing legitimate racial and class resentment and anger onto Jews allows the Gentile owning class to remain in power and the interlocking structures of white supremacy, classism, and anti-Jewish oppression to remain intact. Thus are coalitions sabotaged and Jews isolated.

Such wreckages on the sandbars can also result from the intersections of different internalized oppressions. Jews, with their history of almost two thousand years of oppression, have often managed highly dangerous situations by outwitting Gentiles; their survival became internalized as a rigid need to win verbally. Meanwhile, African Americans, with their four-hundred-year history of being killed or brutally punished for speaking up, often internalized a rigid fear of being too verbally assertive. When scared, one group feels that its survival rests on showing its smarts, while the other group feels pulled to hide theirs.[89] These are generalizations, of course, but the larger point holds: the intersection of internalized oppressions can prevent alliances.

Coalitions also run aground owing to similarities in internalized oppressions, especially feelings of victimization. Victims do not feel in charge of their destiny but instead feel powerless in the face of external forces or internal emotions. When two groups have been hurt as deeply as African Americans and Jews have been, these feelings are understandable. Sometimes these feelings take the form of "competitive victimology," when in reality no oppression is worse than another. Every oppression is different; all are a scourge. However, when a group has been viciously mistreated, its unhealed wounds can make it difficult to take responsibility for its own internalized domination. White Jews often point to the Gentile foot on their neck that everyone else denies; this keeps them from seeing whose neck their foot might be resting on. These tensions are reflected in James Baldwin's observation that "it is galling to be told by a Jew whom you know to be exploiting you that he cannot possibly be doing what you know he is doing, because he is a Jew."[90] Meanwhile, African-heritage Gentiles fighting against police brutality might not be able to see their negative thoughts and feelings about Jews as oppressive. Indeed, one young African American activist asked a Jewish elder whether the term "Jew" itself was derogatory, because she had never heard it used positively. From within a habit of victimhood, taking responsibility for internalized domination can be difficult.

It is perhaps easiest to see how people enacting their internalized domination through oppression of one another would sabotage coalitions. One can deny responsibility for one's conduct on the basis of the mistaken idea that only ideologues and bigots harbor oppressive habits. For example, at a faculty meeting, a Gentile male colleague was arguing that differences were not a basis for discrimination, which prompted a female Jewish colleague to blurt out, "But that sounds like saying that Jews were never singled out; that the Holocaust never happened!" He immediately acted like a victim: "See, if one says the least little thing, one is accused of being a Holocaust denier." For the next two weeks, faculty emails were full of arguments about whether it ever made sense to raise the Holocaust in public because it had been used rhetorically so often to squelch debate. The Jewish colleague felt compelled to apologize. The consensus seemed to be that only two options were available: either one was a Holocaust denier (i.e., a neo-Nazi), or one was entirely free from oppressive habits. When only extreme acts are identified as antisemitic, it becomes difficult or impossible to say that the act of "blaming a Jew for making one feel bad" might fall on a continuum of antisemitic conduct.[91] Because of how anti-Jewish oppression is structured, Gentiles cannot help but participate in policies that benefit them, even if they intellectually reject the vilification of Jews. Whites are similarly enmeshed in racism; internalized domination distorts their conduct even if they never engage in or approve of overt bigotry. Failure to take charge of one's internalized domination sabotages coalitions.

A mix of internalized attitudes rooted in painful emotions combine to make building alliances challenging. A colleague of African heritage recounted how a cousin had lived for twenty-five years over the garage of a wealthy white Jewish family for whom she cleaned. When the cousin asked the white family for a small economic favor, they declined. The colleague explained how difficult it was to "get past this" in order to trust me. For my part, I could recall the thoughtless ways in which my panic and need for control had manifested themselves. Although white Jews and Gentiles of color want to work together, intersecting internalized domination and internalized oppression remain obstacles.



I have shown that anti-Jewish oppression functions today to do two things: it isolates Jews from fellow oppressed groups and it scuttles organized challenges to classism and racism. Without a good map of the "sandbars," we might miss how the history of antisemitism tempts Jews to fight anti-Jewish oppression at the expense of fighting all other forms of oppression. Or vice versa, Jews have a legacy of fighting on behalf of other groups without daring to challenge anti-Jewish oppression. If Jews are to maneuver past these interlocked sandbars, we need to join forces with other oppressed groups.

Intersectionality reveals that ending racism is as essential to Jewish liberation as it is to black, Asian, Latinx, and indigenous liberation, and vice versa. Jewish ethical analyses suffer if they leave unchallenged the ways in which anti-Jewish oppression anchors white supremacy. Reaching common ground requires that Jewish ethicists challenge all forms of oppression by refusing to be divided from other oppressed groups. White Jewish racism needs to end—as does Gentile exclusion and blame of Jews. Blame is not useful, because most oppressive behavior is neither intentional nor a personal fault (although it is a personal responsibility). With awareness, action, taking risks, apologizing for mistakes, and persistence, alliances can proceed. Ethicist Marc H. Ellis writes, "A Jewish theology of liberation is our oldest theology, our great gift to the world."[92] White Jews deserve to work alongside all oppressed peoples to dredge the harbors and rid them of these sandbars.

### Dredging the Harbors

The project of intersectionality, Collins argues, originally sought to join "holistic knowledge" with political engagement. Its original vision challenged scholars to think of themselves as offering programmatic platforms as well as analysis. As intersectionality remained in the academy, its project of analysis, Collins observes, became divorced from providing "a framework that might catalyze social justice projects."[93] This bifurcation has meant that much of the conversation has become a study of identity, which has proved useful for analyzing how it shapes and limits one's perspectives.



A singular focus on identity, however, can lure scholars away from studying the structural dynamics of oppression and from engaging in collective struggles. Identity studies can falsely imply that rejecting or changing one's identity is sufficient for liberation. As Harvey observes, the study of white identity has limits—claiming or rejecting a white identity does not actually change the material relations of white supremacy.[94] Jewish intellectual historians have presented Jewish identity as a central issue emerging from Jewish emancipation.[95] Ashkenazi Jews have puzzled over how to honor communal Jewish obligations while being citizens of democracies. Jewish identity is not irrelevant to Jewish ethics, but terror about the Holocaust—like any major trauma visited upon an oppressed group—makes debates over identity take on an urgency related to survival. The underlying fear is that settling on the wrong identity may have lethal consequences. Adding to this urgency, students of the Holocaust know full well that when essentialist, racialized forms of anti-Jewish oppression were operational, abandoning a Jewish identity did not guarantee survival. Jewish ethicists must steer a careful course when including analyses of identity in our ethical projects, because this can lead attention away from structural dynamics.

Collins has recommended pragmatism as a corrective to the departure from engaging in collective struggles. Pragmatists foreground the communal in ways that, she argues, might end the bifurcation of abstract analysis and practical engagement with power and politics.[96] Jewish ethicists might consider pragmatism's resources, but we have rich resources in our own tradition if we choose to engage with power and politics. The communal has never fallen far from Jews' frame of reference, given Jewish self-understanding as a covenanted people. Jewish ethicists have the opportunity to interrogate how a theory of social justice might respond to intersecting oppressions of classism, racism, and anti-Jewish oppression. But do we want to move from social justice theory to offering programmatic platforms for social justice projects? Should Jewish ethicists heed Collins's call to return to intersectionality's original role as a "catalyst" to social movements?

What new ethical questions would emerge if Jewish ethicists were to move from descriptive ethics to normative ethics? What would it take to forge alliances between white Jews, Jews of color, and Gentiles of color? On my own campus, I remain deeply involved in the Race and Pedagogy Institute, even while I have not been as successful as I would like in speaking up about antisemitism. I continue to learn about the intricacies of coalition building—for instance, how my Jewish internalized oppression (manifested in the form of interrupting African-heritage colleagues) comes across as racism ("whites know best"). I have learned to see how this habit links up with black internalized oppression.[97] I continue to make racist mistakes, but I repair the damage by walking steadfastly alongside my African American colleagues while backing their leadership. What can white Jewish ethicists contribute to a moral analysis of the duties, responsibilities, and virtues of our Gentile allies? Of ourselves as allies to people of color? Ethical questions to ask might include: How are allies similar to and different from friends?[98] What issues arise when we attempt to form alliances with a group that has been the victim of genocide, such as Native Americans?[99] What practices of solidarity might ethicists evaluate as needed to create "communities of subversive resistance," so as to work for everyone's liberation?[100]



How can we dismantle internalized oppression and domination? How might ethicists study how internalized oppressions interlock, and how they can sabotage efforts to sustain coalitions? White Jews have fought for the liberation of people of color and lost their lives in the process. We may not have done so consistently, or from the perspective that combatting anti-Jewish oppression was central to the elimination of racism. Nor may we have been aware of our white racist internalized domination. Barbara Love has argued that one's own liberation has to be brought into any struggle for another's group's liberation.[101] What do Jews need to face to be able to consistently stand against antisemitism and ask our allies to do the same?

What is the best moral response to oppressors who make mistakes—whether by Jews or Gentiles? Philosopher Nancy N. Potter offers a useful study of distrust and trustworthiness. She argues that distrust on the part of the oppressed is not a vice; indeed, suspicion of the oppressor may be a moral duty. But she proceeds beyond distrust to examine how allies can become trustworthy—for example, by making reparations after inevitable mistakes.[102] Genuine efforts to sustain relationships should invite reciprocity by the oppressed, such as accepting apologies and recognizing the growing trustworthiness of allies despite their many imperfections. How might Jewish ethicists build on studies such as Potter's so as to develop strategies to weather rough seas?

Might an awareness of how Jews are used as a wedge between the ruling elites and oppressed groups provide explanatory power elsewhere? Domestically, how might Jewish ethicists interrogate Jewish upward mobility with an eye to race, class, and internalized Jewish oppression? Jews in the oppressive role of middle agent can think about what it might mean to fight for our moral integrity by refraining from endorsing the status quo.



Internationally, how might Israeli leadership have been exploited as agents of Palestinian oppression by imperial powers? There is no doubt that Israel engages in racist practices toward Jews of color and Palestinians. Many Jews have condemned as antisemitic singling Israel out as the worst or only nation engaging in racism. Yet few Jewish ethicists have raised the question of how Israel may be operating as a middle agent between the Palestinians and imperial powers, such as the United States, and then been scapegoated in ways that keep the focus away from the role of the United States.[103] Would studying intersecting forms of oppression generate new responses to the politics of the Middle East on college campuses?

Whose voices have we not heard? Jewish ethicists have a rich opportunity to usher more Jews of color into the academy and into our research. Their experiences, voices, and leadership are vital to the future of Jewish ethics. Working-class Jews also need to be heard and brought into leadership. How can we give working-class Jews visibility and voice?

These are just a few of the questions that Jewish ethicists might address as we seek to join or form coalitions to free our harbors from interlocking sandbars of oppression.

## Conclusion

This chapter suggests that anti-Jewish oppression intersects with classism to isolate Jews from other oppressed groups, which leads to Jews' reliance on ruling powers for temporary protection. These interlocking sandbars and corresponding conditioned habits position Jews to occupy middle-agent roles that exploit other groups, while remaining vulnerable to mistreatment and isolation themselves. In turn, this sandbar intersects with white supremacy. When antisemitism surfaces, it can sabotage coalitions to end racism. Again, white Jews and people of color become divided.

To end Jews' isolation from other oppressed groups emerges as a central ethical task. Jewish ethicists can confidently assert that tackling white racism is not a distraction from fighting anti-Jewish oppression but a means to achieving liberation for all. Jewish ethicists can integrate antiracist and anticlassist work into their scholarship and practice while building mutually beneficial alliances. The liberation of white Jews and people of color ought to be seen as two facets of the same liberatory end rather than as competing or incompatible goals. By sustaining alliances, we can clear our harbors of dangerous interlocking shoals. With an improved understanding of white Jewish ethicists' complex social location, we can transform how we do ethics.



## Notes

My gratitude to Jonathan K. Crane, Donald H. Matthews, Gerald Saltzman, and Ann Holmes Redding for their colleagueship and comments on earlier drafts of this chapter.

1. I spell antisemitism with neither a hyphen nor a capital "S" because there is no such thing as "Semitism," and the term was always intended to apply solely to Jews. A preferable term is anti-Jewish oppression, although I use both terms in this chapter.

2. Weninger, "Dark History Whitewashed."

3. Drucker, *Adventures of a Bystander*, 162.

4. Evans, *Coming of the Third Reich*, 422–23.

5. Mishinsky, "Jewish Labor Movement," 290.

6. Lerner, *Socialism of Fools*, 60, 62.

7. See Cowen, "Socialist Roots of Modern Anti-Semitism," 9; Biale, Galchinsky, and Heschel, "Introduction," 11.

8. Sherover-Marcuse, *Emancipation and Consciousness*, 141.

9. Examples can be found in radical psychology, political economics, feminism, and antiracist reflection. When efforts to emancipate one's psyche become framed as "self-realization," that concept itself becomes "repressive" because it lacks a notion of "a self-in-solidarity." Ibid., 141, 142. Historian David Nirenberg's *Anti-Judaism* examines economists' use of negative "figures of Judaism" (445). Judaism becomes "a type of engagement with the world and one's neighbors, an excessive and misplaced attention on the accumulation of the signs, tokens, and objects of exchange" (436). This trope is evident when Marx writes that "*the* emancipation of the Jews, *in its ultimate meaning is the emancipation of mankind from Judaism*" (436). "In fact it is difficult," Nirenberg continues, "to think of a financial innovation, practice, or crisis that was not discussed in terms of Judaism in the nineteenth and the early twentieth century" (439), with the result that "the figures of Judaism" became translated "into tools of social science and economic thought" (445). Early feminism's analytic term "women and people of color," although intended to be inclusive, effaced the existence of women of color despite how "the early women's movement gained inspiration from the Black movement as well as an impetus to organize autonomously." Hull and Smith, "Introduction," xx. Professor of education Barbara Applebaum cautions that "even when white people act against the norm of whiteness, one does not become innocent and removed from power matrices because privilege is reproduced regardless of intent. Even when whiteness is disavowed, whiteness is reiterated." *Being White, Being Good*, 85.

10. Antisemitism's intersections with sexism are beyond the scope of this essay.

11. Patricia Hill Collins, "With My Mind Set on Freedom: Black Feminism, Intersectionality, and Social Justice," fifth annual Gittler Prize Lecture, Brandeis University, October 29, 2013, https://www.brandeis.edu/gittlerprize/videos/collinslecture.html.

12. Lebacqz, "Bio-Ethics," 84.

13. "If you are neutral in a situation of injustice, you have chosen the side of the oppressor." Desmond Tutu, quoted in Brown, *Unexpected News*, 19. "We must take

sides. Neutrality helps the oppressor, never the victim. Silence encourages the tormentors, not the tormented. . . . Wherever men and women are persecuted for their race, religion, or political views, that place must—at that moment—become the center of the universe." Eli Wiesel, "Nobel Prize Acceptance Speech" (1986), http://www.eliewieselfoundation.org/nobelprizespeech. *You Can't Be Neutral on a Moving Train* is the title of Howard Zinn's 1994 memoir.

14. Collins, "Social Inequality, Power, and Politics," 449.

15. Ibid., 449. Collins accidentally gives the date as 1982; the correct date is April 1977.

16. Collins, "Social Inequality, Power, and Politics," 451.

17. Barndt, *Dismantling Racism*, 28.

18. Collins, *Black Feminist Thought*, 287.

19. Young, *Justice and the Politics of Difference*, 39–40. Young presents a good analysis of five overlapping but different "faces of oppression": exploitation, marginalization, powerlessness, cultural imperialism, and violence (48–63). She notes that marginalization can lead to extermination (53). Kay, however, suggests that marginalization alone may miss the vulnerability of middle agents to genocide in her analysis of the Tutsis. Kay, "Middle Agents as Marginalized."

20. Delgado and Stefancic, *Critical Race Theory*, 6–9; Sherover-Marcuse, "Liberation Theory," 16–17; Tatum, *Black Kids in the Cafeteria*, 7–8; Harvey, *Whiteness and Morality*, 11, 21.

21. Bell, "Theoretical Foundations," 4.

22. Pat Griffin defines internalized domination in her "Introductory Module," 76.

23. Justifications for blaming Jews are legion. Prominent among them is Augustine's argument that Jews deserve to be persecuted because they reject Jesus as the Christ, but that because they are the predecessors of Christianity they do not deserve total annihilation. Because their misery is divinely ordained and a sign of God's divine plan, Christians are not to view the mistreatment of Jews as unjust. Carroll, *Constantine's Sword*, 218.

24. Among these material processes, Harvey mentions "the law, state violences, the machinations of capitalism, geographic expansionism, and more." *Whiteness and Morality*, 33.

25. Whether one feels victimized need not correlate directly with one's status as oppressed. Some white working-class males reported feeling victimized when people of African heritage appeared to advance economically while they did not. "Interview with C. P. Ellis," in Terkel, *American Dreams*, 200–211. Studies have focused on the indifference, psychic numbing, and lack of empathy evident in people who occupy oppressor roles. Baumeister, *Evil*, 220–25. Criminologists have studied how fear, frustration, and hatred can be sources of violent responses; see Athens, *Violent Criminal Acts*, 32–41. Others have focused on shame as a precursor to suicide and homicide. Gilligan, *Violence*, chap. 5.

26. Tatum, *Black Kids in the Cafeteria*, 10.

27. Smith, *Conquest*, chap. 1.

28. Ruth, "Middle-Class Oppression," 1–2. The United States has a capitalist class system, but there has been so much upward and downward mobility owing to repeated economic booms and busts that many people have complicated class backgrounds and experiences. For instance, working-class people might experience upward mobility as college education propels them into the middle class, only to work for wages again once divorced, incarcerated, or laid off. Ehrenreich, *Fear of Falling*, 49.

29. By "ruling elites" I mean members of the owning class, which in pre-capitalist societies may have meant royalty, nobility, the landed gentry, or all three.

30. Marx, *People in Between*, 5.

31. Kahan, "Early Modern Period," 71.

32. Holocaust historian Yehuda Bauer reminds us that of the 3.3 million Jews in Poland in 1935, only one-third were gainfully employed: "400,000 traders and their families were living in poverty. Of the laborers and employees, 60 percent were unemployed or working only part time." Bauer cites a 1937 report by the *London Jewish Chronicle* that "described the Jews of Poland as 'a helpless minority sunk in squalid poverty and misery.'" *History of the Holocaust*, 151.

33. Sociologists such as Fred L. Pincus differentiate three levels of discrimination. Individual discrimination involves "an intention to harm," whereas a second form, institutional oppression, has the same

intentionality but is mediated by people who implement unjust policies by virtue of their roles in institutions. By contrast, structural discrimination, the third form, is "neutral in intent," yet its outcomes have a differential, negative effect on oppressed groups. "Discrimination Comes in Many Forms," 187, 190. Critical race theorists differ from Pincus by arguing that individual complicity need not be intentional; see Applebaum, *Being White, Being Good*, 1, 82, 85. Delgado and Stefancic use the term "microaggression" to capture a "stunning small encounter with racism" that is not typically intentional yet is a feature of systemic mistreatment. *Critical Race Theory*, 2, 151.

34. Brown and Leos-Urbel, *Anti-Semitism*, 17.

35. McWilliams, *Mask for Privilege*, 142–61; Lerner, *Socialism of Fools*, 68.

36. Other disreputable occupations—such as operating (but not always owning) taverns—were open to Jews.

37. Lerner reminds us that many Jews in the United States continue to labor in working-class jobs. However, those with low incomes "are not economically oppressed *as Jews*—that is, their Jewishness is not a primary factor in preventing their economic mobility." *Socialism of Fools*, 79–80.

38. Ibid., 75.

39. Conditioning innocent humans into accepting oppressor roles does psychic and moral damage to them. Injustice does not promote anyone's genuine human interests or well-being. This reality in no way poses a false equivalency between the experiences of the oppressed and their oppressors. See Goodman, *Promoting Diversity and Social Justice*, chap. 6; Rose, "White Identity and Counseling," 42–47; Spanierman, Todd, and Anderson, "Psychosocial Costs of Racism"; Tessman, *Burdened Virtues*, esp. chap. 4.

40. Lipka, "How Many Jews Are There?"

41. After a bout of active persecution, Christians tend to retreat in guilt, while class exploitation remains intact. Christian guilt is not productive of social change; it often leads to blaming Jews for "making" Gentiles feel bad about themselves. "Jewish Liberation Policy Statement," 7. See also Grosser and Halperin, *Anti-Semitism*, 310; Yinger, *Anti-Semitism*, 74.

42. Lerner, *Socialism of Fools*, 65.

43. Weinstein and Mellen, "Antisemitism Curriculum Design," 190.

44. Sigmund Livingston, founder of B'nai B'rith Anti-Defamation League, locates antisemitism in the fringes of society or the lower classes—not in educated, Gentile elites. "It has been employed by the political charlatan, by the opportunist, by the witch hunter, and by the frustrated psychopath. . . . The masses did not—could not—know the real Jew. They could see only the false stereotype, the 'Shylock.' The technique for creating hatred of the Jew was perfect." *Must Men Hate*, xii.

45. Lewis, *Semites and Anti-Semites*, 22.

46. Ozick, "Afterword," 596, 606.

47. Quoted in ibid., 613. I sense that authors sometimes employ the term "hatred" because it captures the irrationality of anti-Jewish oppression. However, "hatred" associates irrationality with emotions, whereas many allegedly logical thoughts or premises can be equally irrational—that is, not an accurate picture of reality.

48. Marcus, "Defenses Against Antisemitism," 49. Marcus recognizes the structural dynamics that identify Jews with the "money economy," with the result that "responsible political and economic leaders have frequently diverted the hatred of the masses from themselves by directing it towards the Jews" (50); he argues that "there must be economic peace before there can be social peace" (52). Yet he does not imagine solidarity with the masses or their liberation, writing instead, "The only hope of the Jews, I believe, lies in an appeal to the masses whose rationality and educability we must assume" (56).

49. Sartre, *Anti-Semite and Jew*, 53–54.

50. Yinger, *Anti-Semitism*, 50.

51. Ibid., 77.

52. Grosser and Halperin, *Anti-Semitism*, 5.

53. Gutman, "Antisemitism," 1:55, 65, 70, 74.

54. Wistrich, *Lethal Obsession*, 5–6.

55. Ibid., 3, 9, 53, 67. Wistrich notes the limitations of surveys that may use outdated terms, fail to clarify what constitutes antisemitism, fail to "take into account the reluctance of many respondents today to

be identified as anti-Semites," or do not "attempt to go deeper into the motivations, influences, or agendas that animate anti-Semitic opinions" (38).

56. Ibid., 8, 53, 9, 12, 931.

57. Rosenbaum, "Introduction," in *Those Who Forget the Past*, xviii, lx.

58. Lipstadt, *Antisemitism*, 20, 17, 21, 17, 19, 99.

59. "In our liberation, our memory of slavery is in danger of being lost. This loss would allow us to forget what it means to be oppressed. Yet to forget one's own oppression is to open the possibility of becoming the oppressor." Ellis, *Jewish Theology of Liberation*, 26.

60. Harvey, *Whiteness and Morality*, 26–27.

61. Ibid., 41–43.

62. Gentiles can deceive themselves about their complicity in anti-Jewish oppression by denying that they feel any hatred. They might admit to a dislike of Jews, or even suggest that they like a few individual Jews, as if that rendered their passive or active complicity unoppressive. Adolf Eichmann may be the best-known and most striking example of the ability to deny responsibility based on a lack of negative emotion. He "'personally' never had anything whatever against Jews; on the contrary, he had plenty of 'private reasons' for not being a Jew hater," as Hannah Arendt tells us in her masterpiece *Eichmann in Jerusalem* (26). Eichmann's stepmother's family had married Jews and Jewesses; he once had a Jewish mistress, and a Jewish boyhood friend; he had also studied Jewish authors. "I myself had no hatred for Jews"; thus, he said, he should not be seen as antisemitic (30). See also "Eichmann Claims He Had 'Many' Jewish Relatives; Says He Is No 'Jew-Hater.'" Jewish Telegraphic Agency Archive, April 21, 1961, https://www.jta.org/1961/04/21/archive/eichmann-claims-he-had-many-jewish-relatives-says-he-is-no-jew-hater.

63. Harvey, *Whiteness and Morality*, chap. 4. Harvey's analysis raises an interesting question for Jewish ethicists. What material changes might be required to rectify anti-Jewish oppression?

64. "The truth is not, as some historians would have it, that slavery made it possible to extend to the Irish the privileges of citizenship, by providing another group for them to stand on, but the reverse, that the assimilation of the Irish into the white race made it possible to maintain slavery." Ignatiev, *How the Irish Became White*, 69.

65. Rosenwasser, *Hope into Practice*, 63.

66. Kay, "Middle Agents as Marginalized," 26.

67. See Goldstein, *Price of Whiteness*, chap. 8.

68. See Khazzoom, *Flying Camel*, xi–xiii; Kaye/Kantrowitz, *Colors of Jews*, chap. 1; Shohat, "Dislocated Identities." White Jews, of course, share with other whites the power to mistreat Jews and Gentiles of color as well as Native Americans. Like every other nation-state, Israel has engaged in racist practices toward its own inhabitants and neighbors.

69. Diane Tobin, Gary Tobin, and Scott Rubin "estimate at least 20% of the Jewish population [in the United States] is racially and ethnically diverse, including African, African American, Latino (Hispanic), Asian, Native American, Sephardic, Mizrahi and mixed-race Jews by heritage, adoption, and marriage." *In Every Tongue*, 21.

70. See Sundquist, *Strangers in the Land*, 26–28; Goldstein, *Price of Whiteness*, 165–68; Kay, "Exodus and Racism," 31.

71. See Green, "Are Jews White?"

72. Karen Brodkin treats antisemitism as a subset of racism, while I regard it primarily as a dynamic of classism. We both attribute the rise of Ashkenazi Jews into the postwar middle class less to personal merit than to privileges granted by ruling elites. We differ in that Brodkin attributes this economic rise to the granting of white privilege; I concur but argue that an essential factor was the granting of sufficient economic privilege to establish Jews as visible middle agents. *How Jews Became White Folks*, 168–74.

73. Enslavement and genocide are not mutually exclusive. Both Jews and African Americans have experienced both forms of mistreatment. Before extermination during the Holocaust, Jews were used as slave labor. African Americans have been under genocidal threat from practices such as forced sterilization, lynching, and killing by police. African Americans have argued that as their enslavement ended, their inherent worth has become questionable within the system of white supremacy. In

1951, William L. Patterson of the Civil Rights Congress petitioned the United Nations with his famous manifesto *We Charge Genocide*. The Black Lives Matter movement could be interpreted as resisting a new perception of African Americans as expendable.

74. Lewis, *Semites and Anti-Semites*, 22. See Duran's discussion of internalized genocide, *Healing the Soul Wound*, chap. 1.

75. Weinstein and Mellen, "Antisemitism Curriculum Design," 190.

76. Lerner, *Socialism of Fools*, 65.

77. Many will disagree with me. In his op-ed "Antisemitism Is Racism," English comedian David Baddiel writes, "Jews are, after all, the only entity, in terms of the racist stereotype that operates on two levels, low and high status—that can be imagined as vermin but also as moneyed and secretly in control. The moneyed and in-control thing undoubtedly still has some traction on the left (see France), and it's why Jews, at best, might not be considered to be really in need of the protections that anti-racism offers, and at worst might be the enemy." Shami Chakrabarti, a Labour MP in Britain, writes, "On 29 April 2016, and after considerable concern and controversy leading to high-profile and senior suspensions from the Labour Party, the Leader Jeremy Corbyn MP asked me to conduct this Inquiry into antisemitism and other forms of racism." Chakrabarti's report declares that "Islamophobia, antisemitism and Afriphobia are all equally vile forms of racism." "Shami Chakrabarti Inquiry," 2, 44.

78. There is no quid pro quo requirement here, as in "I'll interrupt your oppression only if you tend to mine."

79. Despite his good working relationship with the hustler "Hymie the Jew," Malcolm does not portray Hymie or other Jews as targeted by antisemitism. *Autobiography of Malcolm X*, 142–43, 184, 220–22, 279, 454.

80. For a good discussion of this conflict, see Kaufman, *Broken Alliance*, chap. 4.

81. As a white Jew in the United States, I found it difficult initially to listen to Louis Farrakhan's diatribes against wealthy Jews until I remembered that this is exactly how Gentiles of color have been manipulated into targeting Jews rather than joining forces to eliminate intertwining systems of classism, white supremacy, and anti-Jewish oppression. I made the decision that I would not let Farrakhan's internalized anti-Jewish domination force me away from African American liberation efforts.

82. Kaufman examines the complex reasons for this collapse in *Broken Alliance*, chap. 8.

83. Rubin, "Occupy Wall Street."

84. Rosenwasser, *Hope into Practice*, 47.

85. In July 2016, the New York University chapter of Students for Justice in Palestine posted this statement: "In the past 48 hours another two black men have been lynched by the police. The total number of black people lynched by cops in 2016 now totals 136. We must remember that many US police departments train with the #IsraeliDefenceForces. The same forces behind the genocide of black people in america are behind the genocide of palestinians." Rosenberg, "New York University's Students." By singling out Israel, these students fail to hold accountable white Gentiles whose expertise, since 1619, in brutally suppressing people of African heritage in what would later become the United States long predates the creation of Israel in 1948. If Israelis are regarded as the leading force behind U.S. racism, these students have failed to map accurately the sandbar of their own oppressions and their intersectionality.

86. Lerner, *Socialism of Fools*, 84–85.

87. Yinger notes that "anti-Semitism can obscure basic problems, can divert the hostility of the masses, can cloak an attack on democracy as 'necessary' for protection against the dangerous Jews. . . . A nation with a tradition of anti-Semitism can be led away from democracy and liberalism by manipulation of hostility toward the Jews." *Anti-Semitism*, 76.

88. Lerner, *Socialism of Fools*, 68.

89. For a description of "the hook" between these two internalized oppressions, see Brown and Leos-Urbel's succinct pamphlet *Anti-Semitism*, 16–17.

90. Baldwin, "Negroes Are Anti-Semitic."

91. As a white person, I used to bristle at the idea that I was infected with racist habits (see Metta, "I, Racist"). But as a white woman, I continued to be amazed by how men indulged in sexist behavior without the slightest awareness that they were doing so. They did not notice when

they interrupted me midsentence, took over a conversation, presented my ideas as their own, or ridiculed small grammatical mistakes. As I continued my participation in United to End Racism and the Race and Pedagogy Institute on my campus, I slowly began to understand that I was as unaware of my white racist habits as men were of their sexist ones. As an ethical stance, I made the commitment not to deny or defend my behavior, given the tenacity of such habits. As an ethicist, I think this is a defensible moral position and one that those who occupy oppressor roles ought to adopt. Arab Gentiles who deny that they have antisemitic habits of thought are being just as disingenuous as white Jews who deny that they harbor anti-Arab sentiments. Rather than a sign of an inherent moral failing, internalized domination is a sign of the pervasiveness of structural oppressions and the depth to which their supporting ideologies have become habituated in minds, hearts, and bodies.

92. Ellis, *Renewal of Palestine*, 23.

93. Collins, "Social Equality, Power, and Politics," 452.

94. Harvey, *Whiteness and Morality*, 36.

95. Hertzberg, "Introduction," 21.

96. Collins, "Social Inequality, Power, and Politics," 444.

97. Brown and Leos-Urbel, *Anti-Semitism*, 16–17.

98. See Austrian and Goldman, "Palestinian Solidarity Movement."

99. How might Jewish ethicists interrogate what it means when Jewish victims of the Holocaust can immigrate to the United States, a country made prosperous in part by the genocide of its indigenous peoples? Marcie Rendon, an enrolled member of the White Earth Anishinabek Nation, asked this question of U.S. Jews in her presentation "Dealing with Our Pasts to Approach the Present," given at the Conference for Allies to Indigenous Peoples, Camp Burton, Vashon Island, Washington, July 25–27, 2015.

100. Emilie Townes quoted by Harvey, *Whiteness and Morality*, 27.

101. Love, "Developing a Liberatory Consciousness."

102. Potter, *How Can I Be Trusted*, 12, 26–32.

103. Journalist Aliza Becker raises this question in "Don't Use Bibi as Cover."

## References

Anzaldúa, Gloria. *Borderlands/La Frontera: The New Mestiza*. San Francisco: Aunt Lute Books, 1987.

Applebaum, Barbara. *Being White, Being Good: White Complicity, White Moral Responsibility, and Social Justice Pedagogy*. Lanham, Md.: Lexington Books, 2010.

Arendt, Hannah. *Eichmann in Jerusalem: A Report on the Banality of Evil*. Rev. and enl. ed. New York: Penguin Classics, 1994.

Athens, Lonnie. *Violent Criminal Acts and Actors Revisited*. Urbana: University of Illinois Press, 1997.

Austrian, Guy Izhak, and Ella Goldman. "How to Strengthen the Palestinian Solidarity Movement by Making Friends with Jews." Colours of Resistance, January 2003. http://www.coloursofresistance.org/352/how-to-strengthen-the-palestine-solidarity-movement-by-making-friends-with-jews.

Baddiel, David. "Antisemitism Is Racism: We Need to Acknowledge That." *Guardian*, December 2, 2014. https://www.theguardian.com/commentisfree/2014/dec/02/antisemitism-is-racism-malky-mackay-david-whelan-mario-balotelli.

Baldwin, James. "Negroes Are Anti-Semitic Because They're Anti-White." *New York Times*, April 9, 1967.

Barndt, Joseph. *Dismantling Racism: The Continuing Challenge to White America*. Minneapolis: Augsburg, 1991.

Bauer, Yehuda. *A History of the Holocaust*. Rev. ed. New York: Franklin Watts, 2001.

Baumeister, Roy. *Evil: Inside Human Violence and Cruelty*. New York: W. H. Freeman, 1999.

Becker, Aliza. "Don't Use Bibi as Cover for Your War-Mongering." *Times of Israel*, February 5, 2015. http://blogs.timesofisrael.com/dont-use-bibi-as-cover-for-your-war-mongering-2/.

Bell, Lee Anne. "Theoretical Foundations for Social Justice Education." In *Teaching for Diversity and Social Justice: A Sourcebook*, edited by Maurianne Adams, Lee Anne Bell, and Pat Griffin, 3–15. New York: Routledge, 1997.

Biale, David, Michael Galchinsky, and Susannah Heschel. "Introduction: The Dialectic of Jewish Enlightenment." In *Insider/Outsider: American Jews and Multiculturalism*, edited by David Biale, Michael Galchinsky, and Susannah Heschel, 1–13. Berkeley: University of California Press, 1998.

Brodkin, Karen. *How Jews Became White Folks and What That Says About Race in America*. New Brunswick: Rutgers University Press, 1998.

Brown, Cherie R., and Amy Leos-Urbel. *Anti-Semitism: Why Is It Everyone's Concern?* Seattle: Jews and Allies United to End Anti-Semitism, 2018.

Brown, Robert McAfee. *Unexpected News: Reading the Bible with Third World Eyes*. Philadelphia: Westminster Press, 1984.

Carroll, James. *Constantine's Sword: The Church and the Jews*. New York: Houghton Mifflin, 2001.

Chakrabarti, Shami. "The Shami Chakrabarti Inquiry." June 30, 2016. http://labour.org.uk/wp-content/uploads/2017/10/Chakrabarti-Inquiry-Report-30June16.pdf.

Collins, Patricia Hill. *Black Feminist Thought: Knowledge, Consciousness, and the Politics of Empowerment*. 2nd ed. New York: Routledge, 2000.

———. "Social Inequality, Power, and Politics: Intersectionality and American Pragmatism in Dialogue." *Journal of Speculative Philosophy* 26, no. 2 (2012): 442–57.

Combahee River Collective. "A Black Feminist Statement." In *All the Women Are White, All the Blacks Are Men, But Some of Us Are Brave: Black Women's Studies*, edited by Gloria T. Hull, Patricia Bell Scott, and Barbara Smith, 13–22. Old Westbury, N.Y.: Feminist Press, 1982.

Cowen, Tyler. "The Socialist Roots of Modern Anti-Semitism." *Freeman: Ideas on Liberty* 47, no. 1 (1997): 8–11.

Delgado, Richard, and Jean Stefancic. *Critical Race Theory: An Introduction*. New York: New York University Press, 2001.

Drucker, Peter F. *Adventures of a Bystander*. New Brunswick, N.J.: Transaction, 1994.

Duran, Eduardo. *Healing the Soul Wound: Counseling with American Indians and Other Native Peoples*. New York: Teachers College Press, 2006.

Ehrenreich, Barbara. *Fear of Falling: The Inner Life of the Middle Class*. New York: Pantheon Books, 1989.

Ellis, Marc H. *The Renewal of Palestine in the Jewish Imagination*. Eugene, Ore.: Wipf and Stock, 1994.

———. *Toward a Jewish Theology of Liberation: The Uprising and the Future*. Maryknoll, N.Y.: Orbis Books, 1987.

Evans, Richard J. *The Coming of the Third Reich*. New York: Penguin, 2003.

Gilligan, James. *Violence: Our Deadly Epidemic and Its Causes*. New York: G. P. Putnam's Sons, 1996.

Goldstein, Eric L. *The Price of Whiteness: Jews, Race, and American Identity*. Princeton: Princeton University Press, 2006.

Goodman, Diane J. *Promoting Diversity and Social Justice: Educating People from Privileged Groups*. Thousand Oaks, Calif.: Sage Publications, 2001.

Green, Emma. "Are Jews White?" *Atlantic*, December 5, 2016. https://www.theatlantic.com/politics/archive/2016/12/are-jews-white/509453/.

Griffin, Pat. "Introductory Module for the Single Issue Courses." In *Teaching for Diversity and Social Justice: A Sourcebook*, edited by Maurianne Adams, Lee Anne Bell, and Pat Griffin, 61–81. New York: Routledge, 1997.

Grosser, Paul E., and Edwin G. Halperin. *Anti-Semitism: Causes and Effects; An Analysis and Chronology of 1900 Years of Anti-Semitic Attitudes and Practices*. New York: Philosophical Library, 1983.

Gutman, Israel. "Antisemitism." In *Encyclopedia of the Holocaust*, edited by Israel Gutman, 155–74. New York: Macmillan, 1990.

Harvey, Jennifer. *Whiteness and Morality: Pursuing Racial Justice Through Reparations and Sovereignty*. New York: Palgrave Macmillan, 2007.

Hertzberg, Arthur. "Introduction." In *The Zionist Idea: A Historical Analysis and Reader*, edited by Arthur Hertzberg, 15–100. Philadelphia: Jewish Publication Society, 1997.

Hull, Gloria T., and Barbara Smith. "Introduction: The Politics of Black Women's Studies." In *All the Women Are White, All the Blacks Are Men, But Some of Us Are Brave: Black Women's Studies*, edited by Gloria T. Hull, Patricia Bell Scott, and Barbara Smith, xvii–xxxi. Old Westbury, N.Y.: Feminist Press, 1982.

Ignatiev, Noel. *How the Irish Became White*. New York: Routledge, 1995.

Kahan, Arcadius. "The Early Modern Period." In *Economic History of the Jews*, edited by Nachum Gross, 55–78. New York: Schocken Books, 1975.

Kaufman, Jonathan. *Broken Alliance: The Turbulent Times Between Blacks and Jews in America*. New York: Scribner, 1988.

Kay, Judith W. "The Exodus and Racism: Paradoxes for Jewish Liberation." *Journal of the Society of Christian Ethics* 28, no. 2 (2008): 23–50.

———. "Middle Agents as Marginalized: How the Rwanda Genocide Challenges Ethics from the Margins." *Journal of the Society of Christian Ethics* 33, no. 2 (2013): 21–40.

Kaye/Kantrowitz, Melanie. *The Colors of Jews: Racial Politics and Radical Diasporism*. Bloomington: Indiana University Press, 2007.

Khazzoom, Loolwa, ed. *The Flying Camel: Essays on Identity by Women of North African and Middle Eastern Jewish Heritage*. New York: Seal Press, 2003.

Lebacqz, Karen. "Bio-Ethics: Some Challenges from a Liberation Perspective." In *On Moral Medicine*, 2nd ed., edited by Stephen E. Lammers and Allen Verhey, 83–89. Grand Rapids: William B. Eerdmans, 1998.

Lerner, Michael. *The Socialism of Fools: Anti-Semitism on the Left*. Oakland, Calif.: Tikkun Books, 1992.

Lewis, Bernard. *Semites and Anti-Semites: An Inquiry into Conflict and Prejudice*. New York: W. W. Norton, 1986.

Lipka, Michael. "How Many Jews Are There in the United States?" Pew Research Center, October 2, 2013. http://www.pewresearch.org/fact-tank/2013/10/02/how-many-jews-are-there-in-the-united-states.

Lipstadt, Deborah E. *Antisemitism: Here and Now*. New York: Schocken Books, 2019.

Livingston, Sigmund. *Must Men Hate?* Rev. ed. Cleveland: Crane Press, 1944.

Love, Barbara J. "Developing a Liberatory Consciousness." In *Readings for Diversity and Social Justice*, 4th ed., edited by Maurianne Adams, Warren J. Blumenfeld, D. Chase, J. Catalano, Keri "Safire" DeJong, Heather W. Hackman, Larissa E. Hopkins, et al., 610–15. New York: Taylor and Francis, 2018.

Marcus, Jacob R. "Defenses Against Antisemitism." In *Essays on Antisemitism*, edited by Koppel S. Pinson, 49–58. New York: Conference on Jewish Relations, 1946.

Marx, Robert J. *The People in Between: The Paradox of Jewish Interstitiality*. New York: C2C Publishing, 2014.

McWilliams, Carey. *A Mask for Privilege: Anti-Semitism in America*. Boston: Little, Brown, 1948.

Metta, John. "I, Racist." *Huffington Post*, July 10, 2015. https://www.huffpost.com/entry/i-racist_b_7770652.

Mishinsky, Moses. "The Jewish Labor Movement and European Socialism." In *Jewish Society Through the Ages*, edited by Haim Hillel Ben-Sasson and Samuel Ettinger, 284–96. New York: Schocken Books, 1971.

Nirenberg, David. *Anti-Judaism: The Western Tradition*. New York: W. W. Norton, 2013.

Ozick, Cynthia. "Afterword: The Modern *Hep! Hep! Hep!*" In *Those Who Forget the Past: The Question of Anti-Semitism*, edited by Ron Rosenbaum, 595–613. New York: Random House, 2004.

Patterson, William L. *We Charge Genocide: The Crime of Government Against the Negro People*. 1951. New York: International Publishers, 2017.

Pincus, Fred L. "Discrimination Comes in Many Forms: Individual, Institutional, and Structural." *American Behavioral Scientist* 40 (1996): 186–94.

Potter, Nancy Nyquist. *How Can I Be Trusted? A Virtue Theory of Trustworthiness*. Lanham, Md.: Rowman and Littlefield, 2002.

Re-Evaluation Counseling Community. "Jewish Liberation Policy Statement: Draft Policy No. 5." *Ruah Hadashah* 10 (2000): 4–11.

Rose, Lillian Roybal. "White Identity and Counseling White Allies About Racism." In *Impacts of Racism on White Americans*, 2nd ed., edited by Benjamin P. Bowser and Raymond G. Hunt, 24–47. Thousand Oaks, Calif.: Sage Publications, 1996.

Rosenbaum, Ron. "Introduction: Kidnapped by History." In *Those Who Forget the Past: The Question of Anti-Semitism*, edited by Ron Rosenbaum, xv–lxix. New York: Random House, 2004.

Rosenberg, Yair. "New York University's Students for Justice in Palestine Blames Police Shootings of Blacks on Israel." *Tablet*, July 8, 2016. http://www.tabletmag.com/scroll/207450/new-york-universitys-students-for-justice-in-palestine-blames-police-shootings-of-blacks-on-israel.

Rosenwasser, Penny. *Hope into Practice: Jewish Women Choosing Justice Despite Our Fears*. N.p.: June Jordan Literary Estate Trust, 2012.

Rubin, Jennifer. "Occupy Wall Street: Does Anyone Care About the Anti-Semitism?" *Washington Post*, October 17, 2011.

Ruth, Seán. "Middle-Class Oppression." *Our True Selves* 2 (1998): 1–6.

Sartre, Jean-Paul. *Anti-Semite and Jew*. Translated by George J. Becker. New York: Schocken Books, 1965.

Sherover-Marcuse, Erica. *Emancipation and Consciousness*. New York: Basil Blackwell, 1986.

———. "Liberation Theory: Axioms and Working Assumptions About the Perpetuation of Social Oppression." In *The Politics of Liberation: An American Studies Primer*, 4th ed., edited by Nicky González Yuen, 16–17. Dubuque, Iowa: Kendall Hunt, 1994.

Shohat, Ella H. "Dislocated Identities: Reflections of an Arab Jew." *Against the Current* 18, no. 2 (2003): 13.

Smith, Andrea. *Conquest: Sexual Violence and American Indian Genocide*. Durham: Duke University Press, 2015.

Spanierman, Lisa B., Nathan R. Todd, and Carolyn J. Anderson. "Psychosocial Costs of Racism to Whites: Understanding Patterns Among University Students." *Journal of Counseling Psychology* 56, no. 2 (2009): 239–52.

Sundquist, Eric J. *Strangers in the Land: Blacks, Jews, Post-Holocaust America*. Cambridge, Mass.: Harvard University Press, 2005.

Tatum, Beverly Daniel. *Why Are All the Black Kids in the Cafeteria Sitting Together? And Other Conversations About Race*. New York: Basic Books, 2003.

Terkel, Studs. *American Dreams: Lost and Found*. New York: New Press, 1980.

Tessman, Lisa. *Burdened Virtues: Virtue Ethics for Liberatory Struggles*. New York: Oxford University Press, 2005.

Tobin, Diane, Gary Tobin, and Scott Rubin. *In Every Tongue: The Racial and Ethnic Diversity of the Jewish People*. San Francisco: Institute for Jewish and Community Research, 2005.

Weinstein, Gerald, and Donna Mellen. "Antisemitism Curriculum Design." In *Teaching for Diversity and Social Justice: A Sourcebook*, edited by Maurianne Adams, Lee Anne Bell, and Pat Griffin, 170–97. New York: Routledge, 1997.

Weninger, Robert K. "A Dark History Whitewashed: The Heidelberg Myth." *New York Times*, Higher Education Special Section, September 5, 2003.

Wistrich, Robert S. *A Lethal Obsession: Anti-Semitism from Antiquity to the Global Jihad*. New York: Random House, 2010.

X, Malcolm. *The Autobiography of Malcolm X: As Told to Alex Haley*. New York: Ballantine Books, 1964.

Yinger, J. Milton. *Anti-Semitism: A Case Study in Prejudice and Discrimination*. New York: Freedom Books, 1964.

Young, Iris Marion. *Justice and the Politics of Difference*. Princeton: Princeton University Press, 1990.

Zinn, Howard. *You Can't Be Neutral on a Moving Train: A Personal History of Our Times*. Boston: Beacon Press, 1994.



## Classic Text and Questions to Ponder

The tool of intersectionality is used to "argue that power is relative to one's position within intersecting social group memberships." Acknowledging one's complex location in society is a vital first step to seeking a just world that works for everyone. The imperative to be self-aware and self-critical is not new. Consider, for example, how the prophet Isaiah rails against the Israelites in this famous passage, read annually on Yom Kippur:

> "Why, when we [Israelites] fasted, did You not see? When we starved our bodies, did You pay no heed?" [To which Isaiah replied:] Because on your fast day you see to your business and oppress all your laborers! Because you fast in strife and contention, and you strike with a wicked fist! Your fasting today is not such as to make your voice heard on high. Is such the fast I desire, a day for men to starve their bodies? Is it bowing the head like a bulrush and lying in sackcloth and ashes? Do you call that a fast, a day when the Lord is favorable? No, this is the fast I desire: to unlock fetters of wickedness, and untie the cords of the yoke, to let the oppressed go free; to break off every yoke. It is to share your bread with the hungry, and to take the wretched poor into your home; when you see the naked, to clothe him, and not to ignore your own kin. Then shall your light burst through like the dawn and your healing spring up quickly; your Vindicator shall march before you; the Presence of the Lord shall be your rear guard. Then, when you call, the Lord will answer; when you cry, He will say: Here I am. (Isaiah 58:3–9)

Isaiah implores Jews to acknowledge their social location and to see how a focus on religious observance in isolation from the commandment to pursue justice distorts both. When we fail to be aware of how the many dimensions of our lives are negatively affected by unjust social relations, we may fail to see how our well-intentioned and "good" actions sustain the status quo.

- Kay argues that a liberationist approach encourages "insight into how knowledge production [itself] is affected by social location." Do you agree? Why or why not?
- What prevents people—whether individually or communally—from acknowledging how we live at the intersections of multiple oppressions? From acknowledging our oppressor roles? From acknowledging that Jews can be simultaneously oppressed and oppressors?
- Kay insists that "intersectionality reveals that ending racism is as essential to Jewish liberation as it is to black, Asian, Latinx, and indigenous liberation, and vice versa." Further, she claims that this requires that "Jewish ethicists challenge all forms of oppression by refusing to be divided from other oppressed groups." Do you agree that cross-group solidarity is necessary for any and all liberation? Why or why not?

5

# Race and the Story of American Judaism

AARON S. GROSS

Most white-identified U.S. Jews, like most white-identified Americans, would be horrified to see themselves as participants in or supporters of racism, even unwittingly. Yet this chapter argues that we—for I count myself among their number—would do well to do precisely that. Further, I argue that this very aversion, among white Jews like myself, to seeing ourselves as agents perpetuating racism has been and remains a powerful factor in preventing an honest and productive confrontation with the enormous disparity between whites and people of color in America in terms of life chances.[1] Racism, as I define it here, is thriving in America and, almost as a corollary, we have good reason to suspect that it is thriving in large parts of American Judaism.

I hope it is obvious that I am not saying that white Jews are likely to be *bigots* who explicitly think of whites as superior to people of color, or anything so obviously hateful. Rather, I am suggesting that only a simplistic definition of racism could lead one to believe that American society, including American Jewish society, has ceased to be racist in important ways. When American Jews too confidently say, "we Jews are not racists"—as I might have said until recently—I fear that this sincere confession, in part precisely because it is sincere and thus feels true, has the effect of stopping critical thought. Overly confident that we white Jews know what racism is, and overly confident that we know ourselves, our country, and our history, we often prevent ourselves from asking questions that would illuminate how we do unwittingly participate in racism, even if only by virtue of an uncritical Jewish identification as white.

At the heart of the problem of white American Jewish racism is the fact that white American Jews, like other whites, have been hesitant to see *whiteness itself as a problem*—to see whiteness as a set of structures that continue to reproduce the vast inequities that constitute the very heart of racism in the United States. Whiteness is too often perceived as simply a biological fact, and the reproduction of whiteness—through policing practices, unfair housing markets, educational inequalities, unequal employment, and an enormous disparity in inherited wealth—is not even grasped as the kind of thing that can be both embraced *and resisted.*[2] Identifying racism solely with overtly hateful attitudes, and failing to see it as also support for the structures that reproduce inequalities, has allowed most white people, including white Jews, to sincerely believe themselves to be antiracist even as they play key roles in reproducing inequality.

What will be old hat to some readers but new to many is that the dominant view among academics is that racism in American can persist in full force without actively hateful conscious attitudes toward people of color. Eduardo Bonilla-Silva has eloquently written about "racism without racists" as one way of expressing this basic situation. While bigotry, arguably on the rise, remains pervasive in many communities, the racism that worries me most in American Jewish contexts is not bigotry but *systemic* racism.[3] And robust participation in and support for systemic racism is fully compatible with having no overtly racist thoughts or feelings and possessing a genuine commitment to "being color-blind."

Let me give an example of how racism works today that will be close to home for some students and professors. Let's imagine a professor at an elite college who strives to treat all her students equally. Let's assume that this professor manages to overcome the many documented ways in which professors may be biased against people of color (itself a big assumption). The professor genuinely treats everyone who comes into her classroom fairly. The professor even feels especially good that some of her students are first-generation college students, often people of color; if she and other professors do their job, these students will have better life chances than their parents, and their children will probably have even better life chances. Let's add that this professor actively teaches antiracism in her classes and does so more or less effectively.

Would these attitudes and actions free our professor from participation in racism? Can she be confident that she is part of the solution to racism, not a perpetuator of racism? Unfortunately, no; she would need to look more closely. It may be that if she takes that close look, she will realize that a combination of historical recruiting practices at her elite college and the relatively high cost of admission means that her students are disproportionately white and disproportionately privileged and wealthy (by no fault of their own), and that these advantages come at the expense of America's citizens of color. So, again through no fault of her own, her classroom replicates social inequalities—people of color are not entirely excluded, but they are fewer in number than their actual representation in the population would suggest. If she does her job, this professor will give her students a social advantage. In fact, her entire college is engaged in an ongoing, iterative process in which it continually strives not only to reach a particular standard but to do better than other educational institutions—it invests competitively in being better and better all the time. Let's say that the college succeeds; its high price of admission really does deliver on its promise, and its graduates, whatever their background, get a leg up in life. In this scenario, some forms of racism have been overcome, but inequality is nonetheless replicated indefinitely. This system may improve the lives of some people of color in important ways, but in other ways it perpetuates race-based inequality. "Whiteness" is the name for the structure that reproduces this inequality despite our imagined professor's best intentions. This is what critical race theory helps us see.



This chapter puts forth the proposition that American Jews in particular would do well to see whiteness as a problem and their investment in whiteness as racism. And, further, it argues that when white American Jews see their identity as white as a problem, they will also see their identity as *American* Jews as a problem. At least for white-identified Jews, Judaism and whiteness have become inextricably joined in the United States, and this chapter seeks to name the harm this has done to Judaism as a social and religious system animated in part by the idea of identifying oneself with former slaves. How might we tell the story of Judaism and America differently, in the service of more honestly wrestling with both American racism and the Jewish history of being slaves in Egypt?

### American Judaism and the Possessive Investment in Whiteness

At present, the overwhelming majority of white Jews, like most other progressive white-identified communities, do not challenge what George Lipsitz has described as a "possessive investment in whiteness," even as many white Jews use historical and ongoing support for greater civil rights as a marker of their antiracist identity. "Despite intense and frequent disavowal that whiteness means anything at all to those so designated, recent surveys have shown repeatedly that nearly every social choice that white people make about where they live, what schools their children attend, what careers they pursue, and what policies they endorse is shaped by considerations involving race."[4] Today, white-identified Jews in America are full participants, for better and worse, in white America and the perpetuation of white society.

There is nothing new in this assessment of how many Jews, especially of Ashkenazi descent, have fit into the U.S. racial landscape, except perhaps for the rhetorical emphasis on "whiteness as a problem"; it is substantially consistent with the assessment James Baldwin made some fifty years ago while writing about black anti-Semitism. "The Jew profits from his status [as white] in America, and he must expect Negroes to distrust him for it," Baldwin wrote in 1967. "The Jew does not realize that the credential he offers [to demonstrate his antiracism], the fact that he has been despised and slaughtered, does not increase the Negro's understanding. It increases the Negro's rage."[5] And it does so understandably, for past suffering does not necessarily make participation in oppression today less probable or less odious.

Unfortunately, many white-identified American Jews have more or less *internalized* white identity, weaving it into their Jewish identity. When white Jewish communities declare that "America has been good to the Jews," they also silently (and unintentionally?) say that becoming white has been good for the Jews. When Jews praise America for refusing to give anti-Semites the power over Jewish lives that they so long wielded in Europe, we forget that the price of this was becoming white. The price that American Jews paid for freeing themselves from anti-Semitism was accepting the view of white Gentile elites that Jews were more like them—those white, Christian elites—than they were like blacks. The psychological identification with whiteness, and thus with white Christian elites, even if incomplete and uncomfortable for many Jews, has, I submit, done violence to Jewish identity, at least insofar as Jewish identity has traditionally been bound up with identification with the oppressed. In making this argument, I follow historian Eric Goldstein, who has emphasized that becoming white in America was "slow and freighted with difficulty, not only because native-born whites had a particularly difficult time seeing Jews as part of a unified, homogenous white population, but also because whiteness sat uneasily with many central aspects of Jewish identity." Goldstein attempts to retell the usual history of American Jews less as one "of successful adaptation and transformation" and more as "a story of hard choices and conflicting emotions."[6] I wish to explore here what we might consider the *theological costs* for American Jews of becoming white—to examine the ways in which whiteness has obscured much of the visionary heart of the biblical narrative of Egyptian slavery: the

Jewish identity with slaves and the associated mandate to identify with other oppressed populations.

I call this cost "theological" for two reasons: first, because I take this Jewish origin story very seriously. I personally hold it dear, and as a scholar I recognize it as a "living" sacred narrative that, as a matter of sociological fact, has considerable influence on many contemporary Jews. And second, because I want to emphasize that my primary concern in this essay is not historical but existential and ethical. One the one hand, I am not at all concerned with the historical factuality of Jewish slavery in Egypt or other aspects of Jewish religious storytelling; on the other hand, I am not going to emphasize here the historically complex process that allowed most American Jews, especially Ashkenazi Jews, eventually to identify as white or, for that matter, the way in which the term "white" itself does violence to important differences among white-identified populations. To avoid confusion, let me stress again that white-identified Jews, like other immigrants now considered white, did not start out that way; a complex history of racialization means that depending on when and where in America we focus our gaze, the color of Jews will be different. For purposes of this chapter, however, I am interested in the existential and ethical position of the large number of American Jews who solidly participate in whiteness today. I focus here on white-identified contemporary American Jews not because they represent "the" American Jewish story in all times and places—they do not—but simply because, as a member of this population who is deeply dismayed by the ongoing harms of racism in America, I believe that this particular Jewish subgroup confronts a theological problem worthy of engagement.



## The Theological Price of Whiteness

In the process of empathetically interpreting but ultimately condemning black anti-Semitism, Baldwin describes what I mean by the "theological costs" of whiteness with remarkable precision: "In the American context, the most ironical thing about Negro anti-Semitism is that the Negro is really condemning the Jew for having become an American white man—for having become, in effect, a Christian."[7] Baldwin is suggesting here not that being a Christian is a bad thing in itself, but that Jews have assimilated into the bankrupt Christianity that he condemned for failing to be truly Christian. He is also alluding to the fact that for most Jews there is no mainstream religious identity as fully incompatible with Judaism as Christianity. To become a Christian in the sense Baldwin suggests here is symbolically to abandon

Judaism. And herein lies the force of Baldwin's critique: in becoming white, Jews may not only have joined (even if unwittingly and unwillingly) in black exploitation, but they may have abandoned Judaism itself. In critiquing black anti-Semitism, Baldwin does not wish to blunt the critical perspective on Jewish prosperity in America that a black lens can yield. Nor do I wish to blunt the force of this critique: for me, Baldwin argues convincingly that America has significantly menaced the very survival of Judaism, even as it has protected Jewish people. I am not stating this as a social scientific observation; I am not discussing statistical evidence that Jewish-identified Americans are about to cease identifying as Jewish. I am suggesting, though, that the compelling story I was told about what it means to be Jewish—the story told to me by grandparents, parents, rabbis, and countless Jewish leaders about the tradition of "remembering the stranger because you were a stranger"—is incompatible with an uncritical identification with whiteness.



Like many, perhaps most, American Jews, I am not interested in whether my biological ancestors were actually slaves in Egypt; whatever the historical facts, part of what being Jewish means to me is that the story of Jewish enslavement in ancient Egypt is theologically true even if not factually true. Standing *within* this religious construction of American Jewish identity, I ask how I can be a descendant of slaves, and thus sensitized to the suffering of society's most vulnerable members, when I identify less with the communities once legally classified as slaves and more with the community from which slave masters were drawn. Politically and economically speaking, becoming white in America has been good for Jewish people, good for the life chances of our children and the wealth of our communal institutions, but what Baldwin helps me see is that theologically this has created an existential threat to Judaism as an ethical system and a moral community. There has been a mass conversion out of Judaism by American Jews, but most Jews have not noticed this yet. Thankfully, we have spiritual friends, like Baldwin and, as we shall see, Rabbi Abraham Joshua Heschel, who have called our attention to this fact.

The threat posed to Judaism's ethical and moral health by whiteness is a particular version of a more general problem: how can the individual or minority community respond when the nation-state of which it is a part becomes a force of oppression? Rabbi Heschel spoke eloquently to this religious and civic question in his 1972 televised interview with Carl Stern. "How can I pray when I have on my conscience the awareness that I am co-responsible for the death of innocent people in Vietnam?" Heschel asked. "In a free society, some are guilty, all are responsible." I do not read this statement, as my students sometimes do, as meaning that Heschel could not or should not pray—prayer, for Heschel, was "to praise [God], to sing, to chant"—because of the awareness of his co-responsibility in the murder of Vietnamese people.[8] Rather, I take the question as precisely that, as a question meant to stalk us like a bad conscience: if prayer is praise, how can I praise God when I am so proximate to destroying the image of God that each Vietnamese person represents? How, Heschel asks, does the hope for redemption implicit in praising God survive alongside the reality that one finds oneself complicit in, co-responsible for, murder? How are we worthy to praise the Creator and how can we carry the weight of prophetic hope when we discover that the society we claim as our own is retarding rather than advancing the coming of the messiah? The more general form of the question that Heschel raises here in relation to Vietnam and to prayer is: *how can I be the kind of person Judaism demands that I be in the face of the responsibility for violence I bear as a member of American society?* Identifying whiteness as a problem and ceasing to "invest" in it, as George Lipsitz puts it, is one way to respond to this question.



Ultimately, any worthy response requires that we tell the story of Judaism in America differently. How might American Jews tell that story in a way that more directly confronts the centrality of racism to America's foundation? More specifically, how might white-identified American Jews tell the story of their becoming white Americans without eliding the violence that this involved both to Judaism and to people of color—some of whom were other Jews?

## Retelling the American Jewish Narrative

Outside the more nuanced historical accounts given by professional historians, the story of Judaism in America is often casually told as a story of triumph: in Europe, Jews were the primary *other*; they were politically disenfranchised and were regular victims of anti-Semitic violence. But in America, this changed. America, so this triumphal story goes, embraced Jews and allowed diverse forms of Judaism, and arguably a distinctly American kind of Judaism, to thrive. Jews, in this account, have vouched for America as a true land of opportunity. The question of how American Jews should retell this American Jewish narrative with a critical awareness of whiteness as a problem seems appropriate at a moment when white America has veered slightly closer to acknowledging the extent to which black lives don't matter here—that is, closer to acknowledging that the problem of American racism is as profound in "New York City as it is in Jackson, Mississippi,"[9] and that racism, rather than a cancerous growth, is a foundation of the American nation[10] and even a source of its wealth.[11] But my particular road to and through this question also matters, and I must review it here. This road is shaped, on the one hand, by my encounter with a founder of black theology, James Cone, and especially by his 2011 book *The Cross and the Lynching Tree*, and my subsequent reading of James Baldwin's fiery essay of 1967, "Negroes Are Anti-Semitic Because They're Anti-White," quoted above. On the other hand, it is also shaped by my reflection on the Shoah, specifically my reflection on Susannah Heschel's documentation of the relationship between German Protestant theologians and Nazi anti-Semitism during and after the Shoah.[12] Let me begin with Cone, revisiting Baldwin along the way, and then turn to Heschel.



### Religion in America and the Lynching Tree

James Cone's *The Cross and the Lynching Tree* is a moving call to fellow American Christians to tell the story of American Christianity in a new way by bringing together the central symbol of Christianity, the cross, and a central symbol of postslavery American racism, the lynching tree. Cone is speaking to Christians in particular, but he is also speaking to Americans of all religions or no religion and calling on them to remember lynching for the sake of avoiding a "fraudulent perspective" on the nature of American society.[13] His book convinced me that Jewish Americans, too, need to better remember the lynching tree. But just as Cone finds special reasons for Christian Americans to go beyond simply remembering lynching by calling them to connect the cross and the lynching tree, I find reason for Jewish Americans to go beyond simply remembering lynching by connecting central symbols of Judaism today—such as mythical slavery in Egypt and the historical event of the Shoah—with the lynching tree (in the specific sense in which Cone uses it).

Cone's argument is not so much that it is necessary to connect the cross and lynching tree to understand the wrongs of lynching and racism, but that a failure to connect them suggests a failure to know the cross in the first place. That is, a failure to connect them signals a failure to realize the basic "meaning of the Christian gospel for this nation," as Cone puts it. Lynching, he reminds us, was a systematic vehicle of terrorism used to control blacks after the end of slavery. As such, lynching was structurally similar to crucifixion, a means of terrorism used by the Romans to control conquered populations. Both cross and lynching tree were spectacles dramatizing the ultimate power of the oppressors over the oppressed. Despite these and other similarities between the crucifixion of Jesus and the lynching of black Americans, these two evils are not generally thought of together. Indeed, the extent, pervasiveness, and legacy of lynching, not to mention modern forms of lynching like the prison system (to which Cone alludes in a 2007 interview with Bill Moyers on PBS), are often forgotten entirely in public discourse.



For Cone, the tendency of Christian Americans to forget lynching is a symptom of a deeper malaise. Cone calls the cross "the great symbol of the Christian narrative of salvation" but laments that it "has been detached from any reference to the ongoing suffering and oppression of human beings. . . . The cross has been transformed into a harmless, non-offensive ornament that Christians wear around their necks." If Christian Americans are to recover the true cross, Cone insists, they must connect the cross with "the ongoing suffering and oppression of human beings" and that means connecting the cross with the lynching tree. At the core of Cone's argument is the belief that what it means to be a Christian is different in different historical moments, but that all legitimate forms of Christianity attend to the suffering of human beings and connect that suffering with the suffering of the cross.

The more fundamental theological idea that Cone defends here is that true religion is invariably concerned with the oppressed, especially the oppressed neighbor. He connects this theology of divine concern for the oppressed with a historical truth about the United States and its bountiful resources, which have accrued to so many white Americans: the riches of the United States were created in no small measure on the backs of black slaves and other exploited populations and continue to be generated on the backs of their descendants and newly exploited, often immigrant, populations. Cone is not saying that all Christians must respond to all forms of oppression by linking them with the cross, but that when the oppression of a particular people becomes as central to a nation as the enslavement and lynching of black Americans is to the United States, then that oppression must become a central concern of the Christians in that nation. For Cone, the evils symbolized by the lynching tree are simply too central to American life for an American Christian to fail to see the link between the cross and the lynching tree. "Until we can identify Christ with a 'recrucified' black body hanging from a lynching tree," Cone concludes, "there can be no genuine understanding of Christian identity in America, and no deliverance from the brutal legacy of slavery and white supremacy."

A similar argument becomes necessary in the Jewish American context, I would argue, at least for Jewish Americans who believe that Judaism carries within it an ethical responsibility for the stranger. Cone asks Christians to connect Jesus's crucifixion to past and contemporary violence to blacks in the United States. The Jewish parallel is to link violence to blacks in the United States with both Egyptian slavery and the Shoah. If the central narrative of Judaism is the exodus, and if a core act of Jewish identity is asking children to identify with Egyptian slaves, and to transform their own liberation from that slavery into a paradigm that foreshadows the liberation of all peoples, then it seems essential that Jews in particular confront the ongoing legacy of U.S. slavery by connecting the mythical enslavement in Egypt with the lynching tree. Yet this identification of American and Egyptian slavery would be insufficient for many Jews, because the central evil that must be remembered to preserve Jewish religious and ethical identity is not the mythical enslavement in Egypt but the living memory of the actual historical imprisonment and extermination perpetrated in the Shoah. To put it another way, the idea of being "descendants of Egyptian slaves" becomes an actual force in the identity of many Jews today through remembrance of the Shoah. If Cone is right to ask the Christian to recognize the cross in the lynching tree, then the theological correlate in the Jewish context is to make central narratives of Jewish identity—the exodus narrative *and* the remembrance of the Shoah at the very least—theologically relevant through an existential confrontation with the lynching tree. I am not proposing that we examine the parallels and differences among ancient slavery, U.S. slavery, and the Shoah, as valuable as that might be, but rather that we forge links between American Jewish "theological" identity as an oppressed people (something accomplished through remembering both Pharaoh and Hitler)[14] and our responsiveness to the ongoing oppression of people of color in the United States today.



At least, it seems to me, drawing together mythical slavery in Egypt with the historical evils of the lynching tree and the Shoah is one tangible way to tell the story of Judaism in America differently. For American Jews, connecting mythical slavery in Egypt not only with the Shoah—which is a theological given—but also with the lynching tree is made theologically essential by American Judaism's imbrication in whiteness. At the same time, it seems impossible to adequately bring together the Shoah and the lynching tree in this manner—impossible to hear the commanding voice that has issued from these distinct atrocities[15]—without confronting whiteness *as a problem*. Seeing the Shoah together with the lynching tree would require recognizing that becoming white was more than just a challenge to Jewish identity; it also distorted some of the most essential impulses of Judaism. It is a distortion insofar as Judaism is bound up with identifying with the stranger and the slave because we were, theologically if not in actual historical fact, strangers and slaves ourselves. Linking the Shoah with the lynching tree would require recognizing that the ongoing Jewish investment in whiteness, in terms of both identity and actual material resources, is potentially a perversion of Jewish ethical ideals. Above all, it would require looking at potential Jewish complicity in the historical specificity of the lynching tree. How did American Jewish identity as white become shaped by frequent Jewish silence in response to lynching? Above all, how does an ongoing identity as white replicate that silence in the face of contemporary lynching—the lynching perpetuated, as Cone and others have observed, by today's prison system and its massively disproportionate incarceration of people of color, to offer one example, or by the similarly disproportional police violence against people of color? How is it replicated as Jews respond to, do not respond to, or simply chose to live in a world that makes them radically unaware of the constant drumbeat of police killings of people of color—the deaths, for example, of Margaret LaVerne Mitchell, LaTanya Haggerty, Amadou Diallo, Kendra James, Ronald Madison, Sean Bell, Manuel Loggins Jr., Ramarley Graham, Shereese Francis, Rekia Boyd, Jamar Clark, Yvette Smith, Tamir Rice, Laquan McDonald, Akai Gurley, Eric Garner, Ezell Ford, Michael Brown, Christian Taylor, Walter Scott, Natasha McKenna, Freddie Gray, Brendon Glenn, Samuel DuBose, Greg Gunn, Akiel Denkins, and Sandra Bland?[16] These black men and women are just a few of the people of color who have died following encounters with the police that did not warrant deadly force—including some cases in which the victim literally did nothing to provoke suspicion of any crime whatsoever. How is Jewish identity reshaped today as Jewish communities both align with, ignore, and distance themselves from the largest social movement to respond to these deaths, Black Lives Matter?



Following Cone's argument that American Christianity is true to its spirit only when it draws together the cross and the lynching tree, I submit that American Judaism can similarly activate its best impulses only by drawing together slavery in Egypt, the Shoah, and the lynching tree, and, further, by connecting the lynching tree with its perhaps less visible contemporary incarnations. It is crucial here to understand that the lynching tree is not securely in the past. The continuity between lynching and the prison system—what Michelle Alexander calls the system of "mass incarceration in the age of colorblindness"—and between lynching and police killings is *historical*. In the foreword to Alexander's groundbreaking *New Jim Crow*, which exhaustively documents these injustices, Cornel West argues that once white Americans emerge from their sleepwalking, from their acceptance of incarceration rates for people of color that would be a national scandal if the prisoners were white, they will be "awakened to a dark and ugly reality that has been in place for decades and that is *continuous with the racist underside of American history from the advent of slavery onward*" (emphasis added).[17]

Telling the story of Judaism in America differently, so as to better remember past racism and its inheritance, would mean speaking about the American part of "American Jewish identity" as a problem as well as a source of pride. Many white-identified Jews have long seen the United States as a Promised Land, and as far as the material prosperity of some Jewish communities are concerned, the United States has indeed been a kind of salvation. But if the United States has allowed many white Jews to thrive materially, it has exacted a moral price: it has demanded Jewish participation in whiteness. It has "freed" many Jews to identify with a racial identity created for the very purpose of owning other human beings, and specifically *not* the racial identity created for the enslaved. Telling the story of Judaism in America differently will require confronting this darker part of the "success" of American Jewish life. It will require recognizing in a new way that America never became and *may never become* a nation of free people, and that the freedom and financial prosperity it bestowed on many white Jews and other white-identified immigrants was often purchased at the price of participation in (and expansion of) oppressive structures that have reproduced generations of racial inequality. To join the Shoah and the lynching tree in the service of following the central Jewish mandate to identify with former slaves is to see America as the house of bondage, whatever it might become in the future.

### America Is the House of Bondage

This is precisely what James Baldwin called American Jews to do: to know that America is the house of bondage, for if America is the house of bondage to any people, it is the house of bondage, full stop. As Heschel put it, "God is either the father of all men or of no man."[18] Recall Baldwin's statement: "The Jew does not realize that the credential he offers [to demonstrate his alleged antiracism], the fact that he has been despised and slaughtered, does not increase the Negro's understanding. It increases the Negro's rage." Baldwin continues, "For it is not here, and not now, that the Jew is being slaughtered, and he is never despised, here, as the Negro is, *because* he is an

American. The Jewish travail occurred across the sea and America rescued him from the house of bondage. But America *is* the house of bondage for the Negro, and no country can rescue him. What happens to the Negro here happens to him *because* he is an American."[19] How can white Jewish revelry in the American project be anything but an offense to those who have known this country only as the house of bondage? And how can it be anything but an offense to the understanding of Judaism that I am advocating here?



What, then, might the story of Judaism and America look like if we acknowledge that America remains a house of bondage? What would the central narratives of American Judaism look like when examined in the shadow cast by lynching trees in New York, Mississippi, California? Baldwin's essay presents one model: it would mean, among other things, recognizing the difference between how America remembers black suffering and black resistance and how it remembers Jewish suffering and Jewish resistance. "The Jew is a white man," writes Baldwin, "and when white men rise up against oppression, they are heroes: when black men rise, they have reverted to their native savagery. The uprising in the Warsaw ghetto was not described as a riot, nor were the participants maligned as hoodlums: the boys and girls in Watts and Harlem are thoroughly aware of this, and it certainly contributes to their attitude toward the Jews. . . . But, of course, my comparison of Watts and Harlem with the Warsaw ghetto will be immediately dismissed as outrageous." Such a dismissal was once the norm, which is precisely why we would now do well to view the Shoah in the shadow of the lynching tree. In remembering the evils that have been inflicted upon Jews, we are sensitized to the suffering of our neighbors. Again, I am not suggesting that we engage in a disciplined historical comparison, though that too would be valuable, and even less that "we have both known suffering," though this is also true. To bring the lynching tree and the Shoah together is to see the world with greater moral clarity: it shows us more honestly the moral stakes and pitfalls of being a white-identified American Jew. As Cone says, it is about the challenge of making the symbols of American religious life meaningful rather than ornamental. This entails the work of the historian but goes well beyond it; the histories that professional academic historians bequeath us must be made *our* history. And that act is always theological work, religious work, and it exceeds the task of the historian. It is the task of turning history into living sacred narrative (myth), into moral memory embodied in daily life, and ultimately into Jewish identity.

To the extent that Judaism has become a religion of white-identified Americans, it has become complicit in American racism. White Christians have their own particular challenges in confronting the disturbing ways in which their religion has become integral to American racism, and white Jews like me have ours. Christians have religious resources, what Cone calls "the cross," that can help them confront racism, and we Jews have our resources, among them the unique way in which Jews read history itself as the theater of divine action, and our ability to turn past wrongs into moral responsibilities.  When I speak of bringing together the exodus, the Shoah, and the lynching tree, I call upon the power of the Jewish imagination to read Jewish history in a manner that can be liberatory for all peoples and ultimately all creation.

### The Shoah and the Lynching Tree

Case in point: thinking about the Shoah and the lynching tree together means using the moral insights about the nature of evil, and resistance to it, learned from the Shoah to see more clearly the evils that beset us today. I have argued that much of American Judaism is ethically and theologically compromised by its relatively uncritical embrace of whiteness, and that Jews must recognize that Judaism and racism have sometimes been partners. This is a difficult and painful reckoning, one that most of us, being human, would prefer to avoid. Is it really essential to draw such vivid connections between American Judaism and American racism? Might we not better heal old wounds by emphasizing what Jews did right: Jewish support for civil rights and so on?

This is precisely the kind of question that can be positively transformed by allowing the exodus, the Shoah, and the lynching tree to interpret one another in exploring questions about racism and our contemporary response to it. Consider a problem that Susannah Heschel identifies in her book *The Aryan Jesus*. Heschel demonstrates that most German historians, theologians, church officials, and scholars of religion, in their approach to the Shoah, have attempted to exculpate Christianity and distance it from the evils of Nazi racism by disavowing affinities between Christian theology and racism. They have done this both generally and in the case of particular Christian political parties, institutions, and theologians. This impulse is understandable enough: if Christianity is to inspire its followers to live moral and ethical lives, it might seem necessary to say that Christianity *itself* (whatever that means) was not guilty of supporting Nazism. Such a theological move could be innocent enough if it were only a matter of finding an ideal, aspirational Christianity innocent of the crimes of anti-Semitism, but that is not what happened, as Heschel shows.

> The sharp division made by most historians, theologians, church officials, and scholars of religion between Christian theological anti-Judaism and modern racial antisemitism has fostered the postwar myth that theologians did not contribute to the Nazi murder of the Jews, and also the widespread notion, common among Jewish theologians as well, that Nazism represented an anti-Christian pagan revival movement. As the texts discussed in this book indicate, however, the boundary between theology and race was highly porous. . . . Theologians gravitated toward racism as a tool to modernize Christianity and to demonstrate that its principles were in accord with those of racial theory. In addition, they considered racial theory a tool to grant scientific legitimation to religion: racial claims of an inherent societal hierarchy reinforced religious beliefs in God's creation of a natural order and a hierarchy of plants, animals, and humans within it. . . . Racism itself can be seen as a form of incarnational theology, centrally concerned with moral and spiritual issues, but insisting that the spiritual is incarnate in the physical.[20]



In short, Christians' disavowal of the manner in which Christian institutions constructed, perpetuated, and enthusiastically supported racism, including its genocidal form of Nazi anti-Semitism, has gotten in the way both of recovering the historical facts and, more important, of the story those facts might tell—a story of a long, dark chapter in Christian history that must be addressed if it is to be moved past. From the perspective of most Jews, the necessary response to Christianity's imbrication in anti-Semitism (and racism more broadly), is, at a minimum, an owning of the problem. I believe that I speak for many Jews, probably most, when I say that few things seem more obvious from a Jewish perspective than the need for German Christians to acknowledge that Christian identity was often forged through anti-Semitism, and, specifically, that this played a large role in the Shoah. Jews know intimately that it is implausible to suggest that centuries of "Christian theological anti-Judaism" were largely irrelevant to the form of anti-Semitism that enabled and fueled the Shoah.

Heschel not only documents the infuriating failure of the postwar church in Germany "to come to grips with the responsibility of Christian theology for antisemitism and for the Nazis' disenfranchisement, deportation, and murder of the Jews." She also tells us about "a remarkable number of German theologians" who "have made concerted efforts not only to take responsibility for the church's role in the Holocaust, but to formulate new theologies and christologies that affirm Judaism. . . . The Holocaust, in this view, was a wound in the heart of Christian theology and a profound challenge to its moral authority."[21] Again, I will risk speaking for Jews more generally (which, of course, I have no authority to do) in saying that it is *these* theologians, the ones who admit the brokenness of Christianity and its contributions to anti-Semitism, that we Jews would prefer.



**Conclusion**

If I am right that Jews are more likely to admire Christian bravery in acknowledging Christianity's historical anti-Semitism than Christian denials of responsibility, then perhaps we have an answer to our query about whether white American Jews today should cling to the handful of acts of Jewish opposition to American racism or acknowledge that, in becoming white, American Judaism, like American Christianity, became complicit in American racism and remains so to this day. Just as Cone calls his fellow Christians to see not only the cross but also the lynching tree, I invite my fellow American Jews to hold together the meaning of being descendants of Egyptian slaves and the lynching tree as a symbol of an ongoing, distinctly American form of violence against people of color.

Joining mythical slavery, the Shoah, and the lynching tree means drawing upon the power of the Jewish moral imagination in the service of seeing America simultaneously *as it is*—as the house of bondage—and *as it should be*—as the Promised Land. As Langston Hughes paradoxically expresses it, "O, let America be America again—/ The land that never has been yet—/ And yet must be—the land where *every* man is free."[22] Jewish moral imagination has the potential to propel us beyond simply feeling concern for the other, so that we might identify ourselves as the other, as slave, *and thus walk in the world differently*. In the dominant streams of American Jewish thought, the culmination of the covenant is not an obligation of the heart alone but an obligation wound into the way one eats, talks, and walks—into *halakha*—into law and social action, into mercy and justice as dramas of deed. Concern for the other in contemporary culture can often devolve into a kind of hand-wringing "oh dearism," or hollow gestures at empowerment disconnected from actual efforts at change. But equally possible is an identification that circulates back and forth from heart to hands, and from aspirational hope to institutional change.[23]

Arguably, the central ritual act of Passover is to "relive" what the liturgy tells us is our own enslavement in Egypt, our own and not just our ancestors'.

At the climax of Passover, writes Jewish theologian Rabbi Irving Greenberg, "Pharaoh's tyranny and genocide stalk the land again. But the Jewish people rise up and set out for the Promised Land—slave again, free again, born again."[24] While I have not attempted to explain exactly how Jewish traditions can effect such a felt rebirth, I see evidence that they have done so and continue to, at least some of the time. Such transformation is, at minimum, a possibility offered by Jewish life, and it is precisely this precious possibility to awaken *rachamim*, compassion, that is imperiled by uncritical identification with whiteness.



## Notes

1. In one study, Joe Feagin reports, "70 percent of whites were found to hold one or more erroneous beliefs about important white-black differential in life conditions." *White Racial Frame*, 2.

2. Here and elsewhere, I am especially indebted to George Lipsitz and his book *The Possessive Investment in Whiteness*, and to Joe Feagin and his book *The White Racial Frame*, in defining "whiteness." I also wish to acknowledge the pivotal role played by conversations about race, religion, and whiteness with theologians Karen Teel and Christopher Carter, my departmental colleagues at the University of San Diego.

3. Race theorist Joe Feagin defines systemic racism as including "(1) the complex array of recurring exploitive, discriminatory, and other oppressive white practices targeting Americans of color; (2) the institutionalized economic and other social resource inequalities along racial lines (the racial hierarchy); and (3) the dominant white racial frame that was generated to rationalize and ensure white privilege and dominance over Americans of color." *White Racial Frame*, ix.

4. Lipsitz, *Possessive Investment in Whiteness*, vii.

5. Baldwin, "Negroes Are Anti-Semitic."

6. Goldstein, *Price of Whiteness*, 1, 4.

7. Baldwin, "Negroes Are Anti-Semitic."

8. Abraham Heschel, interview by Carl Stern, *The Eternal Light*, NBC, 1972, broadcast February 4, 1973, https://www.youtube.com/watch?v=FEXK9xcRCho.

9. James Cone, interview by Bill Moyers, *Bill Moyers Journal*, PBS, November 23, 2007, https://www.pbs.org/moyers/journal/11232007/watch.html.

10. Feagin, *White Racial Frame*, viii, 5.

11. See Baptist, *Half Has Never Been Told*.

12. See Heschel, *Aryan Jesus*.

13. This quotation and those in the following three paragraphs are from Cone, *Cross and the Lynching Tree*, xiv, xvi, xv.

14. I mean "remembering" as a moral act that is less about recalling past events than being mythically present at them in a way that allows the moral force of past events to speak to us today.

15. I allude here to Emil L. Fackenheim's notion of the "commanding voice of Auschwitz." See his essay by that title.

16. This list of black people "who died following police encounters" was published in Funke and Susman, "From Ferguson to Baton Rouge."

17. Cornel West, "Foreword," in Alexander, *New Jim Crow*, x.

18. Heschel, interview by Stern.

19. Baldwin, "Negroes Are Anti-Semitic." The quotation in the following paragraph is also from this essay.

20. Heschel, *Aryan Jesus*, 286.

21. Ibid., 287.

22. Hughes, "Let America Be America Again," in *Collected Poems*, 191.

23. I take the phrase "Oh dearism" from British documentary filmmaker Adam Curtis and his short films *Oh Dearism* (2009), available at https://www.youtube.com/watch?v=8moePxHpvok, and *Oh*

*Dearism II* (2014), available at https://www.youtube.com/watch?v=3UstNBrmJFc.

24. Greenberg, *Jewish Way*, 40.
25. Passover Haggadah.

## References


Alexander, Michelle. *The New Jim Crow: Mass Incarceration in the Age of Colorblindness*. New York: New Press, 2012.

Baldwin, James. "Negroes Are Anti-Semitic Because They're Anti-White." *New York Times*, April 9, 1967.

Baptist, Edward E. *The Half Has Never Been Told: Slavery and the Making of American Capitalism*. New York: Basic Books, 2014.

Bonilla-Silva, Eduardo. *Racism Without Racists: Color-Blind Racism and the Persistence of Racial Inequality in America*. Lanham, Md.: Rowman and Littlefield, 2006.

Cone, James H. *The Cross and the Lynching Tree*. Maryknoll, N.Y.: Orbis Books, 2011.

Fackenheim, Emil L. "The Commanding Voice of Auschwitz." In *God's Presence in History: Jewish Affirmations and Philosophical Reflections*, 67–104. New York: New York University Press, 1970.

Feagin, Joe R. *The White Racial Frame: Centuries of Racial Framing and Counter-Framing*. 2nd ed. New York: Routledge, 2013.

Funke, Daniel, and Tina Susman. "From Ferguson to Baton Rouge: Deaths of Black Men and Women at the Hands of Police." *Los Angeles Times*, July 12, 2016.

Goldstein, Eric L. *The Price of Whiteness: Jews, Race, and American Identity*. Princeton: Princeton University Press, 2006.

Greenberg, Irving. *The Jewish Way*. Northvale, N.J.: J. Aronson, 1998.

Heschel, Susannah. *The Aryan Jesus: Christian Theologians and the Bible in Nazi Germany*. Princeton: Princeton University Press, 2008.

Hughes, Langston. *The Collected Poems of Langston Hughes*. Edited by Arnold Rampersad and David E. Roessel. New York: Knopf, 1994.

Lipsitz, George. *The Possessive Investment in Whiteness: How White People Profit from Identity Politics*. Philadelphia: Temple University Press, 1998.




### Classic Text and Questions to Ponder

The contemporary Passover holiday emerges from the biblical story of Jews being emancipated from Egyptian slavery. This transition from enslavement to freedom, both literarily and historically, is hardly straightforward, however, as Gross indicates. In addition to the actual transitions' being complicated, the stories told about those transitions are also potentially problematic. Consider, for example, this classic text recited during the Passover seder meal: "In every generation, each individual is obligated to see himself as if he actually went out of Egypt, as it is said, *Because of this did God do wonders for me when I went out of Egypt* (Exodus 13:8). It was not our ancestors alone who were redeemed by the Holy Blessed One; we also were redeemed with them, as it is said, *And [God] took us out from there in order to bring us to the land that [God] swore to our ancestors and give it to us* (Deuteronomy 6:23)."[25]

This source acknowledges that there can be a difference between a person's actual experiences and the stories told about those experiences. The "as if" in the first sentence is critical: it empowers contemporary Jews to imagine that they were also redeemed from Egyptian slavery even though they themselves were not enslaved. That is, Jews are to tell the story of their own enslavement despite that story's not being factually true.

- For Gross and others, the American Jewish pattern of investing in whiteness is problematic. Do you agree? Why or why not?
- Whereas Cone labors within a Christian milieu to connect the cross and the lynching tree, Gross endeavors within a Jewish one to tie together Egyptian slavery, the Shoah, and contemporary forms of systemic and overt racism. How does this linkage challenge the core narratives of American Judaism?
- What do you make of this famous Passover source, by which Jews tell themselves a story about their relation to slavery and redemption? How is this a "reliving" of slavery and redemption, even though they were not experienced in the first place?

6

# The "Yiddish Gaze"

## American Yiddish Literary Representations of Black Bodies and Their Torture

JESSICA KIRZANE

Philosophers of race in America often focus on the black/white racial binary as a totalizing system that calcifies the ways in which black and white bodies are interpreted on an individual level and systemically throughout American culture. This perspective, though illuminating in many ways, can sometimes obscure the varieties of racialist thinking that appear throughout American history and culture. This chapter, which examines depictions of American Yiddish literature in the early twentieth century, aims to elucidate the range of expressions in racialist discourse. It offers an analysis of literary representations of American blackness from a marginal, Yiddish, Jewish immigrant position. Drawing upon the work of George Yancy and James Cone, it situates selections from American Yiddish literature within the broader American discourse of philosophy of race.

George Yancy, an existential philosopher, writes from his own experience as a black man living in a social reality in which white society places negative stereotypes onto his body that fundamentally shape the way he experiences the world. In his account of the black body's positioning under the "white gaze," *Black Bodies, White Gazes*, Yancy posits that the black body stands within a system of cultural semiotics that dictates the meanings placed upon it: "the Black body is not born free, but it is imprisoned by ideological frames of reference." He writes that the predetermined meanings of blackness in American culture are articulated from the perspective of whiteness, and that blackness is defined in relationship to whiteness "within a semiotic field of axiological difference, one that is structured vis-à-vis the construction of whiteness as the transcendental norm." Within this frame of reference, whiteness is the signifier of goodness, in contrast to the multiple stereotypes of the black body as hypersexual, criminal, lazy, and primitive. In Yancy's account, this system of meaning is calcified through history and is therefore essential and unchanging—"whites created/create fantasies regarding the Black body as sullen and immoral so as to stabilize dialectically their own fantasized identity as clean and moral." For Yancy, *every* "white gaze," regardless of circumstances, is filtered through these deep-seated and often unconscious meanings and values that determine the worth and significance of the black body within a modern social context.[1]



The power of cultural semiotics and the underlying exploitive system by which white-skinned Europeans established themselves as the norm through the interpretation of non-Europeans as "nonwhite, and of a different and inferior moral status," is undeniable, and the implications of this system of subjugation are deeply felt.[2] However, Yancy's analysis of the "white gaze" as a unified and invariable structure does injustice to the nuance of human experience, describing the entire experience of race through a black/white binary, and a homogeneous one at that. Moreover, in assuming that the "white gaze" always projects a singular meaning onto the black body, Yancy denies not only individuals' interpretation of the world but also the variety of histories that frame encounters between "white" and "black" people across time and space.

As a corrective to this totalizing analysis of the "white gaze," I have chosen to consider what I am calling a "Yiddish gaze"—the gaze of Yiddish-speaking Jewish writers in America in the early twentieth century who contemplate black bodies and blackness itself. While, to a certain extent, this "Yiddish" gaze might be considered part of the "white gaze" because of Ashkenazi Jews' physical similarities to other European Americans, the racial vantage point of these Jews is unique in American history. Ashkenazi Jews are what Charles Mills terms "white people with a question mark," forcing Mills to "fuzzify" the categories of white and nonwhite, since for much of their history, particularly in America, Ashkenazi Jews have been "ranked ontologically above genuine nonwhites" in terms of the way they were socially interpreted and the privileges they were allotted, but were not considered fully white.[3] As Eric Goldstein notes, from the nineteenth century until at least World War II, if not until the present moment, "Jews held an uncertain relationship to whiteness."[4] Their bodies were seen and interpreted as racially Jewish, and this had implications for others' and their own understandings of their character and position in American society.[5] As immigrants or children of immigrants from an anti-Semitic eastern European environment, Yiddish-speaking Jews in the early twentieth century largely resided in ethnically unified urban neighborhoods, were drawn to particular professions, and married endogenously. They spoke of themselves, and were spoken of, in a racialized discourse that referred to Jewish physiognomy or Jewish "blood," and race theorists debated whether Jews represented a distinct race and where they fit in the color scheme that defined racial discourse in the United States.[6] Indeed, Jews' indistinct position between blackness and whiteness threatened the very construction of race, as Jews could not easily be identified in terms of color or superficial features. Yiddish writers in particular, as cultural activists and producers within a language that marked them as outsiders to white Americanness, wrote with a sense of cultural distinctiveness, even as they wrote in a modern idiom and were influenced by American and European literatures from outside a specifically Jewish sphere. As Merle Bachman writes, Yiddish writers were "choosing to remain foreign in the United States by writing in Yiddish, despite their intense identification with America."[7] By nature of their writing in the Yiddish language, these writers declared that they were expressing themselves *as Jews*, even if their writing did not specifically relate to Jewish issues.[8] Therefore, because of Jews' own ambivalence regarding their status as a separate race and their potential whiteness, and because of the larger white society's indecisiveness in defining the nature of Jewishness, it is debatable to what extent a Jew's gaze in this period can be considered a "white gaze."

Moreover, when Yiddish writers employed themes of race in their writing, they often wrote from within European frames of reference rather than within, or in addition to, the binaries upon which race is mapped in the United States. The struggles of black Americans were thematized in Yiddish literature within and outside the United States as a way to draw parallels with and represent the position of Jews as a powerless, downtrodden people in Europe. Thus, in his introduction to his 1852 translation of Harriet Beecher Stowe's *Uncle Tom's Cabin*, Isaac Meir Dik (1807–1893), a widely popular author throughout the Yiddish-reading world, "translates the politics of racial difference into Yiddish terms," writing about the new politics of peasantry after the abolition of serfdom through his translation of Stowe's work.[9] Likewise, in his book-length poem *Der Fertsikyeriker Man* (The forty-year-old man), Soviet Yiddish writer Peretz Markish (1895–1952) describes the lynching of a black man in the American South as part of his critique of injustice in Europe and America, which is deployed to emphasize the urgent need for a new and more just world order. Both writers make use of racial injustice in America to elucidate and validate their political claims and investments in a European context. In the transnational landscape of Yiddish literature, Yiddish writers in America contributed to both American and European conversations about social ills through their writing about race in America, and this, in part, informs the way they gaze upon, sympathize with, and draw meaning from black bodies.



In general, when Yiddish writers in America depicted black people, as Adam Zachary Newton summarizes, they deployed "African Americanness as reflective Occasion or refracted Other alternately universalized or particularized, eroticized and exoticized—a mirror, a metaphor, a secret sharer and fellow traveler, a totem, an emblem, a vehicle for empathy or alienation . . . the gamut of identificatory possibilities."[10] In other words, Yiddish writers drew upon black figures and read into black bodies images of their own otherness, alienation, and subjugation, while also seeing them through the lens of racial hierarchies born in what Yancy calls the "white gaze." The long history and enduring scholarly and popular interest in "black-Jewish relations" bear witness to the intensity of Jews' identificatory feelings about black bodies, however contradictory these feelings may have been. Often, for Yiddish writers, representations of black bodies bore an ethical component; because of the symbolic weight of the black body as a signifier both of American racism and of mirrored Jewish suffering, to see a black body (in a literary text) was to think in ethical terms about social responsibility, about injustice, and about pain and sorrow.

In this chapter, I examine several examples from American Yiddish literature that depict the act of looking at blackness through Yiddish-inflected eyes.[11] These works narrate a process of looking and interpreting as an ethical act, in which the meaning of blackness is interpolated from and imposed upon imagined black bodies in the name of, and toward, a sympathetic political stance toward black men.[12] The Yiddish writers considered here were influenced by, aspired to, and participated in a European cultural system that imagines race within a binary logic in which whiteness is normative, good, and innocent over and against its strange, exotic opposite—blackness. This is in accord with the "white gaze" that Yancy describes. At the same time, European cultural systems position Jewish bodies as a central site for the construction of difference, and Jews are inheritors of the experience of being seen through myths and discursive practices that define and dehumanize them, in the way that Yancy describes the black experience.[13]

Examining the "Yiddish gaze" of these writers helps to add context and nuance to Yancy's vision of what a white person sees when faced with a black body. A reading of Yiddish writers' portrayal of the experience of looking at blackness helps elucidate how their positionality affects their application of the white gaze, and the extent to which it does not: whether, and to what extent, taking up the white gaze is a totalizing practice that does not change regardless of the language, experience, or position of the practitioner. It also elucidates a version of white gazing, which I am calling "Yiddish gazing," that resists itself, an ethics of gazing as a process of seeing difference, of interpreting it within existing frameworks, and then of attempting, in the name of universal or sacred morality, to see beyond the limitations of the "white gaze."

For Yiddish writers, looking at the black body was often indivisible from looking at and considering the violence of American racism, which was, for them, also a way of addressing the violence Jews were experiencing in Europe and the potential for that violence to emerge against Jews in America. In her historical treatment of Jewish-black relations in America, *In the Almost Promised Land*, Hasia Diner notes that for the Yiddish press, "the issue which crystallized all thinking on racist violence was that of lynching." Lynching was prominently featured in Yiddish newspapers, and "lynchings were always highlighted by their bloodiest and most tragic details."[14] Yiddish journalists were deeply concerned with the issue of physical violence against blacks, and through their reporting on this issue they took part in the larger American journalistic interest in lynching, which was "a media sensation" in English-language newspapers as well.[15] For Yiddish newspapers, which were the primary conveyors of Yiddish print culture, lynching was a topic of deep moral concern and fixation. Lynching made its way into Yiddish American literature, inspiring poetry and prose that variously focused on empathy for the lynching victim, concern for lynching victims as symbols of both black and Jewish suffering, and visions of what it meant to be American, Jewish, white, or black.

An examination of what it meant for Yiddish writers to look at black bodies therefore necessitates an examination of Yiddish literature about the spectacle of lynching—literature about looking at the black body as a victim of torture, as a martyr, as a symbol of universal suffering. These representations often brought into conjunction the notion of Jews and blacks as sharing the experience of being targets of a brutal and hypocritical application of Christianity in the service of hatred and bloodshed: the lynched black person, and by extension the persecuted Jew, were positioned in relation to the image of Jesus on the cross. This is consistent with what black liberation theologian James Cone describes as a central tenet of black Christian theology: "the crucified people in America were black—the enslaved, segregated, and lynched black victims," and a powerful religious imagination requires Christians in America to come to terms with the relationship between God and lynching by recognizing that "they can meet Jesus only in the crucified bodies in our midst." Cone himself notes that while many white artists and theologians failed to make the connection between the cross and the lynching tree, the two "most emotionally charged symbols in the African American community," some Jewish artists, such as Julius Bloch (1888–1966) and Abel Meeropol (1903–1986), drew these connections and portrayed Jesus as a victim of lynching, or they depicted black lynching victims' torture as a repetition of Christ's sacrifice, thereby voicing their own "existential solidarity" with those tortured black bodies as a result of their own people's "long history of suffering at the hands of white Christians."[16] In gazing on the black body in the context of the lynching tree, writers in Yiddish consistently noted that they were also gazing upon Jesus on the cross, that they had to wrestle with a theology and worldview that comes out of suffering—that of Jews and that of blacks—and to find hope or despair at the intersection of these powerful religious and political symbols of suffering.



But what is the position of a Yiddish poet vis-à-vis the symbol of the tortured black body as Jesus on the cross? Cone explains that black Christians in America had to search for new ways to express their understanding of Jesus as different from that of white Americans because "the Jesus they embraced was also, at least in name, embraced by whites who lynched black people" and who "defined the content of the Christian gospel."[17] Yiddish writers shared this project of recovery and reclamation of a Jesus separate from the violence that has been perpetrated in the name of white Christianity. Matthew Hoffman explains that in premodern Jewish culture, the figure of Jesus was often described and discussed with fear and contempt, a representative of "all that was other, alien, dangerous," and the primary symbol of Christian anti-Jewish hatred and persecution. European Jewish intellectuals participating in the Enlightenment reappropriated and reassessed Jesus as a part of Jewish history, separate from the Christianity that followed him. Modern Yiddish writers who employed the symbols of Jesus and the cross drew upon this nineteenth-century scholarship that separated a historical Jesus from the figure of Christ who has been employed by Christianity to enact violence against Jews.[18] Their move of separating Jesus from Christianity laid the essential groundwork for what Hoffman describes as the "landscape of the cross" in modernist Yiddish literature, or the widespread deployment of Christian iconography to articulate modern Jews' relationship to Western culture.[19] Yiddish writers who analogized black victims of lynching to Jesus and to Jewish victims of anti-Semitic violence were audaciously battling a Christianity of anti-Jewish hatred by remaking Jesus as an ally of the oppressed, a symbol of a Jewish theology and experience rooted in suffering and victimization, even as they asserted their worldliness and full participation in Western civilization and culture by using its most prominent and most foreign symbol. In looking at the cross and the lynching tree, Yiddish writers at once saw something absolutely foreign—the cross: a symbol of a religion and tradition that had persecuted Jews, and the lynching: the torture of strangers with histories and bodies they deemed exotic, and absolutely intimate—the cross and the lynching tree together forming a symbol of universal suffering and the torture of a hated group that could easily have been themselves. By positioning their narrators, Jewish characters, and readers in relation to the spectacle of lynching—that is, by looking at black bodies as they are tortured—these Yiddish writers could at once evaluate and discuss American Ashkenazi Jews' relationship to the violence and hypocrisy of American racism, their still uncertain position within American racial hierarchies, their relationship to Western culture and its symbols, and the ways in which American Ashkenazi Jews were implicated in, responsible for, and victims of suffering in a modern American context.



Through close attention to these artistic representations of the act of looking and interpreting, this chapter aims to elucidate the meaning of a Yiddish gaze, and to suggest what it might mean for Jewish ethics to engage with this gaze today.

## Yiddish Writers Seeing and Interpreting Black Bodies

Avraham Rayzin (1876–1953) was a prolific and beloved Yiddish poet in his native Poland as well as in America. He was known as a "poet of poverty" who used simple language and rhyme to convey complex, realistic, sympathetic portrayals of the downtrodden.[20] Inserting his own autobiography into his works, he created a sense of sympathy and shared experience between himself and his imaged readership.[21] In 1911, the year he arrived in America, Rayzin wrote "A Little Negro." In the poem, Rayzin positions his narrator as one who has never before seen a black body and lacks an interpretive system through which to understand it. The narrator gazes upon a black child and through a series of sensory observations and emotional responses searches for a way to understand and interpret the child's body from his vantage point as a spectator. Initially confused and chagrined by the blackness that he sees as utterly different from himself, the narrator overcomes this otherness by relating it to aspects of his own life and incorporating it into his sentimental, nostalgic longing for family and home. "A Little Negro" is a poem about the aesthetics of difference, and it insists upon seeing the black body as an Other and as familiar at the same time. It is also a poem about the process of constructing a "Yiddish gaze" from outside the interpretive framework of the "white gaze," weighing the possibilities for understanding racial difference and sameness:



| | |
|---|---|
| א. רייזען | A. Rayzin |
| **אַ נעגערל** | **A Little Negro** |
| אַ נעגערל, אַ קליינס, ווי סאַזשע שוואַרץ | It was a little Negro, black as soot |
| האב איך געזען זיך שפּילן בײַ אַ הויז, | that I saw playing by a house. |
| עס האט געטרויערט און געשראקן זיך מײַן האַרץ: | My heart was saddened and terrified: |
| מײַן גאט! ווי שוואַרץ דײַן באַשעפעניש זעט אויס! | My God! How black Your creature looks! |
| | |
| און פּלוצלינג האט דאס קינד דאס שוואַרצע זיך צעלאַכט, | Suddenly the black child burst into laughter, |
| זיך קויקלנדיק און שפּילנדיק אויף דער ערד: | rolling and playing on the ground: |
| מײַן גאט! וואס איז מיט מיר אַזוינס? האב איך געטראַכט, | My God! What's going on with me? I thought, |
| ווּ האב איך ערגעץ אַזאַ לאַכן שוין געהערט? | Haven't I heard laughter like that somewhere before? |
| | |
| איך האב דערמאנט זיך, אַז מײַן ברודער אַמאל, | I remembered that once my brother, |
| מײַן ווייס ברודערל, ווען ס'איז געווען קליין, | my little white brother, when he was small, |
| האט אויך געלאַכט אַזוי, עס איז דאס זעלבע קול— | also laughed like that, it was the same voice— |
| און גלײַך איז מיר דאס קינד געווארן ליב און שיין . . . | instantly the child seemed dear and beautiful to me . . .[22] |

As the poem begins, the narrator notices the black body only in its difference, its blackness. In the poem's very title and first line, the narrator labels the child he sees through the language of race, calling him a "little Negro" rather than simply a little boy, and therefore placing upon him a host of cultural assumptions and associations. In the first stanza, the narrator compares the color of the boy's skin to the discarded remains of a fire, implying its lack of value and its position as essentially and irrecoverably unclean. He betrays his own belief in his body as the unexamined norm through his shock at seeing blackness, and in an instantaneous moment of judgment, he articulates a version of the "white gaze" in accordance with Yancy's description—"[the black body] is constructed as a source of white despair and anguish, an anomaly of nature," and also a "fascinating" object to gaze upon.[23] The narrator is "saddened" and "terrified" by this difference, which is implicitly the opposite of his white self. The poem begins at once with the premise of the black body as a signifier of something negative in contrast to whiteness: the unfamiliar, for the narrator, is also the grotesque.[24]

The narrator is shocked by the mere presence of the black body, as though he had never before seen a person with dark skin.[25] His initial fear does not have to do with the threat of evil or criminality but with the shock of seeing difference, as if for the first time, and the experience of having the power to define it, and to differentiate himself from the otherness he sees. The narrator declares himself outside the interpretive community of the "white gaze," insisting that he does not know how he should understand the body before him, although he has already articulated his sense that the black body is shockingly different, exotic, interesting, and aberrant. Nevertheless, the narrator suggests that there is more to be understood, and that from his position as a newcomer, he has the freedom to construct a different kind of gaze from the typical "white gaze," to draw his own meanings from, and return these creatively and newly forged meanings onto, the black body before him.

The speaker's contemplation is interrupted as the child breaks into laughter and rolls on the ground. This sudden movement and voice are expressions of the child's agency, his transformation from a mere object to be studied into a living human being with whom interaction is possible. As Merle Bachman has noted in her reading of the poem, the child's movement forces the speaker's reaction to progress from consideration of skin color to a fuller reaction to the child's movements as an actor rather than as an object. This shakes the speaker, forcing him to rethink the body before him.

Initially, he does not know how to respond to the black child's laughter and movements, does not know whether to associate them with a "creature" or a human; he has no sense of what his own gaze should entail, or how best to interpret the spectacle before him. The description of the physicality and abandon of the child's movements suggests that the narrator may initially view the child as animalistic, primitive, less than human, an interpretation that would align with the normative stance of the "white gaze." Gradually, however, as though despite his best efforts, his perspective is transformed. The speaker asks, "What's going on with me?" as he struggles against his own impulse of sympathy toward the black child.[26]



Ultimately, the speaker recognizes that the black child's laughter is performed with the "same voice" as his own "little white brother, when he was small," and by associating the memory of his brother's laugh with the laugh of the black child he comes to recognize the child as human and worthy of love. It is only when the narrator can draw a connection between himself, his family, and his past and the black Other that he can see the beauty in the child. It is through this association that the narrator makes the strangeness of America, with its foreign bodies, part of the far away and familiar home he has left behind. Through this comparison, the narrator not only relinquishes the strangeness of the child's black skin and sees him as a lovable brother, but he also asserts his own belonging as an immigrant in a country that is not so different from his own, insofar as it is also home to children and their innocent laughter. The narrator thus "disarticulates" the white gaze through a new way of seeing, one enhanced by a sound that is beyond color and beyond words.[27] As Bachman notes, the narrator circumvents the prejudices of his gaze by interpreting the black body through sound—comparing the black child's laughter to that of his brother—and therefore "doing away with the problem of looking entirely," rejecting the meaning of the "white gaze" for a more generous and sympathetic white hearing.[28] The preverbal laughter these boys share is a sound beyond accent and language and apart from skin tone, and it at once reaches beyond the foreignness of the new immigrant and the color of the child to their shared and joyous humanity. This childlike bewilderment is a mark of ethnic difference through which the narrator expresses his identity and position as a new immigrant who is taken out of a context that he can interpret more easily. Insofar as he is an outsider to American racial binaries, the narrator offers a new and foreign version of the "white gaze" that is more sympathetic and more universalizing, and that resists itself, as it would rather depend less on sight than on sound (through which the narrator's own difference, via his foreign accent, is communicated). Foreignness and nostalgia become resources upon which to construct ethical ways of relating to difference.

Yet, at the moment of recognition, the narrator asserts that his brother was "white" and therefore pronounces his own whiteness in opposition to the blackness of the child before him.[29] The black child is innocent and good because he is similar to a white child, a child from the narrator's homeland, but he is marked as Other through the striking aesthetic of skin tone. This simultaneous rejection and articulation of the totalizing "white gaze" demonstrates how much, as Yancy argues, "disarticulating the white gaze involves a continuous effort," as the narrator denies and tries to shake his racialized assumptions about the body before him but is not entirely successful.[30] The sweet, tidy ending, in which the narrator understands the innocence and familiarity of the black boy through the sense of *hearing*, covers over his initial view of the black body as something bewilderingly different, and his confusion and lack of context, of cultural semiotics, through which to understand the difference that he *sees*.



More than a decade later, "introspectivist" poet A. Leyeles (Aaron Glanz, 1889–1966) wrote of the experience of looking at and interpreting a black body with a much greater consciousness and with reference to the cultural semiotics that Yancy describes as informing the "white gaze." Leyeles, who immigrated to the United States from Lodz in 1909, was an innovator and experimenter in form who wrote poetry that was modernist in sensibility and dedicated to urbanism, universalism, and linguistic eclecticism. He believed that art did not require a moral or social goal but should instead be the personal expression of the individual.[31] His "In Subway, 3," a segment of his famous series of free-verse subway poems that emphasized the jumbled, rushed, fragmented sensations of rush-hour travel on the New York subway, was published in his *Rondos un andere lider* (Rondeaux and other poems) (1926), a collection that celebrated the power and variety of life in New York City. The narrator of "In Subway, 3" watches as a black man and a white woman are pressed together in the transient, anonymous, crowded space of the subway, and imagines the desires and fears the black man might be experiencing in this fleeting moment of interracial contact. He interpolates from this scenario assumptions based upon the stereotype of the hypersexuality of the black male, filtered through a sympathetic stance:

| | |
|---|---|
| א. לעיעלעס | A. Leyeles |
| **אין סאבוויי, 3** | **In Subway, 3** |
| אין דעם גרויען, רירעוודיקן מויער | In the grey, quaking walls |
| אַרײַנגעמויערט | Walled in |
| איינס לעבן אַנדערן | One beside the other |
| אַ ווײַס מיידל און אַ נעגער. | A white girl and a Negro. |
| ריח פֿון שאַרפֿן מוסקאַט | Sharp musk scent |
| האַלדזט אַראמאַט פֿון אַנגסטיקן מיידלישן פֿלאַטער. | Clings to the perfume of nervous girlish flutter. |
| דער נעגער דריקט זיך שטאַרקער | The Negro presses more firmly |
| צום מיידל. | Against the girl. |
| שוואַרצע בענקשאַפֿט | Black longingness |
| בענטשט ווײַסע ענגשאַפֿט. | Blesses white crowdedness. |
| | |
| אַ ווײַס מיידל און אַ נעגער. | A white girl and a Negro |
| טרויער | Sadness |
| אין דעם רירעוודיקן גרויען מויער. | In the grey, quaking walls. |
| טרויער פֿון דעם יעגער, | The sadness of a hunter, |
| וואס ווייס, ער קאן זײַן געגראַטסטן פֿאַנג נישט קריגן. | Who knows he'll never get the finest prey. |
| נישט אונטן אויף די רעלסן רעדלען רעדער. | It's not down on the tracks that the wheels roll— |
| רעדער ווירבלען, שווינדלען, דרייען | Wheels whirl, swing, turn |
| אין אַ שוואַרצן, קרײַזלדיקן, אומגליקלעכן קאפּ. | On a black, curly, downtrodden head. |
| (לינטש-פֿײַערן—פֿלעקער, פֿלעקער, | (Lynching fires—flicker, flicker. |
| שלייף פֿון תּליה—שטײַפֿער, שטײַפֿער). | A gallows' noose—taut, taut). |
| דער נעגער דריקט זיך שטאַרקער | The Negro presses more firmly |
| צו דעם מיידל. | Against the girl.[32] |

As the third poem in a series of reflections about the space, anonymity, crowdedness, and concentration of human desire on the subway, this poem considers the liberation and dangers of the particular urban space of the subway car. Juxtaposing the emotionally fraught experience of desire with the cold, impersonal rigidity of the urban landscape, the poem displays a moment of intimate forbidden longing as the human heart of a seemingly utterly mechanized space.[33] It places the drama of American race relations, often understood as a southern, rural phenomenon—the feared and imagined sexual encounter between black male and white female and its extralegal punishment through violent murder—in the subway, a central symbol of the modern urban environment. In this way, the poem tersely offers a kaleidoscopic vision of America itself—southern and northern, black and white, rural and urban, all intersecting in one space as a kind of powder keg of emotional, physical, and mechanical tension that does not explode only because it is so hurried, so fleeting.



The narrator of the poem witnesses and interprets the crowded bodies before him and chooses to imagine the thoughts and desires of the black man, thus placing himself in the privileged position of interpreting the black body for his reading audience but ostensibly doing so from a sympathetic stance. He introduces the stereotypical menacing threat of the savage black man who lusts after white women: the black man pressing against the white woman poses a threat to her sexual purity—she is a frightened, fluttering girl, and he a man filled with longing who forces himself against the girl who cannot escape. In imagining the thoughts of the black man, the poet perhaps expresses his own hidden hunger for the white woman, projecting onto the black man his own desire to conquer and possess that which is forbidden.

For the narrator, the sadness of the situation comes not from the white girl's fear but from the black man's illicit desire, which cannot be fulfilled. Imagining that the black man is considering the violent consequences of interracial sexual contact, the narrator at once assumes the truth of the stereotype that black men desire white women and expresses pity for the tragedy that this desire is illegal and punishable by cruelty and violence.[34] In Leyeles's poem, the "Yiddish gaze" sees the same criminalized, sexualized body that is seen through the "white gaze" but interprets it with a sense of intimacy and alliance, a recognition that the fate of the black man is determined by the texture of his hair, and that this entrapment in the social restrictions of the body is tragic, even as it prevents the potential rape of the white woman (for whom little sympathy is expressed in the poem). In other words, the Jewish onlooker and the black man share in their maleness and in their outsider status an objectification of the white woman as object of desire, and although the consequences of acting on that desire would differ (this is the cause of the sorrow and sympathy), their mutual desire brings them together and equates their longing and their gratitude for a crowded white space, a setting that permits such illicit desires to be enacted.[35] In this poem the "Yiddish gaze" is shown to contain all of the pathology of whiteness, as Yancy describes it, but with the added component of sympathy and perhaps even a sense of a joined fate. It represents a Jew trying to understand the mind of a black person, but the framework established by white discourse is the starting point for his sympathy.

Moreover, by bringing the violence of lynching to bear on the black man's desire, the narrator calls into question the notion of the criminality and primitivism of that desire, in contrast to the violence of the lynching scene. While the black man in this poem is reduced to an object of spectacle and considered in terms of his stereotypically rapacious sexual desire, references to lynching suggest that the black man's desire is no less criminal than the white man's violence against that desire. By positioning the episode in a speeding subway car, the poem illustrates the ways in which the bodies of both the black man and the white woman are trapped within social systems that determine their encounter: the black man is pressed against the white woman unintentionally, and this creates the sexual tension that is forbidden by the society (those standing in the train) that forces the encounter upon him. It also suggests that underneath and within the efficient, mechanized, dehumanized structures of modern urban life, bodily desires and the threat of violence rage, so that even the newest and most sophisticated apparatuses of human life are only new containers for universally human, primitive desires: both those of the black man toward the white woman and those of white society toward the black man. This weighing and judgment of both the black man and the white society in which he is trapped are undertaken by the Yiddish/Jewish man through his position as an intimate outsider, privy to the nuances of the cultural semiotics of black and white but far enough outside the system that he has the ability to judge it.[36]

In each of these poems, the narrator seeks to establish a connection to and understanding of the black bodies he encounters, whether through appeals to common humanity or assumptions about shared desires and fears. H. Leyvik's poem "Negroes" more directly represents an imagined collective Jewish voice reaching out for alliance with an imagined black interlocutor, expressing a political and moral commitment for unity on the basis of shared suffering while recognizing the privileges and differences that keep the communities apart. "Negroes" reflects Leyvik's personal experience of suffering—he survived childhood impoverishment, political upheaval, and four years in a forced labor camp, and was exiled to Siberia for his socialist political activism, escaping to America in 1913. His personal story was imbued in his poetry, and he became a symbol of suffering and of "soft individual sensibilities in a harsh world."[37] He speaks to his imagined black audience as one who is representative of the Jewish experience of suffering, which held a central role in his own work. He also wrote out of his political convictions as a Communist writer who advocated a mass social movement that challenged social institutions, and he argued for allegiances across, and motivated by, issues of class rather than race. In "Negroes," the narrator proposes an alliance between Jews and blacks despite and because of differences and similarities in their experiences of suffering. He stands outside the black experience, considering the violent consequences of interracial desire and the injustices that black people face in American society, and he considers the position of Jews within this black/white dynamic of inequality. The poem demonstrates both the distance across which Jews consider black subjects and the closeness they imagine as a way of thinking about their own victimhood in dialogue with the most prevalent struggle in American discourse.



| ה. לייביק | H. Leyvik |
|---|---|
| **נעגערשעס** | **Negroes** |
| איך ווייס, נעגערס, כ׳וועל גארנישט ענדערן אין אײַך, | I know, Negroes, I will change nothing in you, |
| נישט פֿון דערנאענט און נישט פֿון דערווייטן; | Not from near or far; |
| מיר וועלן נישט ווערן איינס, נישט ווערן גלײַך, | We will not become one nor the same |
| און אונדזערע הויטן וועלן זיך נישט בייטן. | And our skins will not transform. |
| | |
| אײַערע ליפּן וועלן נישט ווערן דין, | Your lips will not grow thin, |
| און מײַנע וועלן נישט ווערן געשוואלן; | And mine will not swell; |
| און פֿאַר אַ רגע בענקשאַפֿט נאך ווײַסער זינד | And a moment of desire for white sin |
| וועט איר נאך אַלץ מיט גאַסן-טויט באַצאלן. | Will still cost you a horrible death. |
| | |
| א, איר וואלט באַדאַרפֿט מיט צער און שפּאט | Oh, if I came among you with curious steps, |
| מיך אַרומרינגלען און מיינע רייד פֿאַרקייכן,— | Like a man to his equal |
| ווען איך קום צווישן אייך מיט נייגעריקן טראט, | You would gather around me with pity and scorn |
| ווי כלומרשט אַ גלייכער צו אַ גלייכן. | And laugh at my speech |
| | |
| ווען איך קום מיט אפֿנקייט, מיט ווידוי-ליד | If I come with openness, singing confessions |
| אונטער אַ הימל, וואס קען זיך נישט פֿאַרשליסן; | Under a heaven that never closes its gates to prayer; |
| אַנטקעגן דעם געוויין פֿון אייער הויט און גליד— | Compared to the cries of your body and skin |
| איז לעכערלעך דאס געוויין פֿון מיין געוויסן. | The cry of my conscience is laughable. |

| | |
|---|---|
| אונטער אייערע פֿענצטער שטיי איך, צו אייער שוועל | Under your windows I stand, at your threshold |
| איך לאז זיך שטרויכלען איבער טרעפלעך דאַרע; | I come stumbling over wide stairs; |
| א, איך בעט רחמים פֿאַר דער שטאַרבנדיקער זעל | Oh, I beg for mercy for the dying soul |
| פֿון אייער נאַכטעקער איבערגעפייניקטער גיטאַרע. | Of your nightly long-suffering guitar. |
| | |
| דוכט זיך,—וואס?—איך בין אַן איבערגע־פייניקטער אַליין, | It seems—what?—I am long-suffering myself |
| אַן אויפֿגעהאַנגענער, ווי איר, אויף שטריק פֿון ראַסע; | Hanging, like you, from the rope of race; |
| מיין אויסזען אבער איז פֿאַר אייך נישט ווייניקער געמין, | But to you my face looks no less horrifying |
| ווי דאס אויסזען פֿון אַיעדן פֿון אַ לינטשער מאַסע. | Than the appearance of every face in a lynching mob. |
| | |
| זאל זיין דאס ווארט אונדזער אויסקויפֿדיקער פֿריינט | May these words make brothers of us: our recently emancipated friends |
| און אונדז פֿאַרברידערן, אונדז—לעצטע און באַהערשטע; | And us—the cursed and dominated |
| און באַזינגען חברשאַפֿט צווישן מחנות פיינט | And may they sing praises to our friendship |
| מיין יידיש ליד זאל איינס זיין פֿון די | amidst the throngs of our shared enemy |
| ערשטע. | My Yiddish song will be one of the first.[38] |

The speaker in this poem articulates his sense of a shared fate between the blacks whom he imaginatively addresses (the poem was written in Yiddish and therefore would not have been accessible to a real black audience) while recognizing the differences between the groups. A responsible and tenable alliance, the poem claims, would not overlook differences between the communities and hope for class-based unity that erases the particularities of racial features, history, and experiences. Instead, communication between these communities would require them to remain distinct, their physical features and their histories unique, with the narrator singing a song of alliance to, and not with, his black audience.

The speaker not only describes the physical differences between black and Jew/white (in which the Jewish face is so racially indistinguishable from the white face that it cannot be differentiated from "the appearance of every face in a lynching mob"), but he also acknowledges the social differences that shape black and Jewish experience—"a moment of desire for white sin / Will still cost you a horrible death"—and that this disparity in their treatment in America makes Leyvik's confessional potentially "laughable" in its inadequacy. The speaker nevertheless asks for brotherhood between black and Jew because both hang "from the rope of race," while acknowledging that the threat of hanging, of lynching, is unique to the black experience



in the American context. The speaker is humbled by the social differences experienced by black and Jew, and recognizes that he cannot approach his black "audience" with an equal claim for victimhood. Instead, he asks for racial alliance, as though wanting to latch onto the black experience as a way of expressing his own victimhood, which is invisible on American soil. His articulation of racial identity as "hanging" is evidence of his affiliation with the black experience in America as a representation of race-based suffering writ large, an experience that Jews can also identify with.

Indeed, as Colleen McCallum-Bonar notes, the narrator "suggests a joining in song and through word; he does not recommend political or social action. He encourages a relationship in which *he* is able to be productive" through writing and singing, rather than one that brings about social change.[39] This is consistent, to a certain extent, with Yancy's notion of the "white gaze"—Yiddish writers consider black people as objects in relation to their Jewish selves, creating blackness as a symbol for suffering (and perhaps for Jewish suffering that would otherwise be unseen in an American context). This is a demonstration of the "asymmetrical power relations between the gazer and the gazed upon" about which Yancy writes—Yiddish writers lay claim to the right to interpret the black body as an object, and to perpetuate that interpretation through writing and singing, taking agency away from the black people inside those bodies.[40] At the same time, the Yiddish poet begs to be heard by the black audience, placing himself in a vulnerable stance as someone whose interpretation of blackness needs approval and can only be made legitimate and worthwhile through conversation and in harmony with his imagined black audience. In this way, he invites his black audience to sing about his Yiddish readers, to interpret them as objects, and through that process to co-create an alliance. Without a Yiddish-reading black audience, though, this component of searching for an interlocutor is only an imaginary process, and the poem is ultimately about a Jewish desire to express solidarity with the downtrodden, about Jewish identity making as a group dedicated to social justice, and not about the actual work of building alliances between communities. The narrator in the poem gazes at black victimization and uses it as a mirror through which to reflect a vision of Jewish progressivism and righteousness, using black bodies without their consent to engage in the work of Jewish communal identity making.

However, as Sartre famously notes, Jews themselves are subject to the gaze of European white society, a gaze that defines them without their consent, indeed, without even their presence: "if the Jew did not exist, the anti-Semite would invent him."[41] Leyvik's desire for alliance with blacks draws upon his own objectification under the white gaze, through which his body, to use Yancy's language, is "returned" to him as an object of scorn. Leyvik sees himself as racially Other, even though he recognizes that the political and social consequences of this othering are different for him in America than they are for blacks in America, and it is through this sense of himself as an Other that he seeks to unite with blacks as fellow Others. In other words, Leyvik's "Yiddish gaze" objectifies blacks as symbols of suffering and otherness and uses them as a way to articulate how Leyvik's own body is "returned" to him as a symbol of suffering and otherness. Leyvik's interpretation of the black body as a suffering body corresponds to his understanding of the meaning of Jewishness as suffering, and his objectification of blackness follows from his essentialized understanding of his own Jewish identity.



In her account of Jewish authors who write about black subjects, Emily Budick notes that black and Jewish intellectuals have "tended to keep each other in mind, as if, indeed, there were a revelation for each of them in the existence of the other."[42] The works examined in this chapter demonstrate how Yiddish writers cast their gaze upon black bodies as a way to reveal something about their own Jewish identities. Through their "Yiddish gaze," poets acknowledged their own off-whiteness in contrast to the skin color and other physical features of the black bodies they describe, while expressing a sense of, or hope for, potential kinship. These writers accept prevalent racist stereotypes while offering a critique of the violence of racist perspectives. In accordance with the ambivalent Yiddish/Jewish racial positioning in the early twentieth century, the meanings placed on black bodies by Yiddish/Jewish eyes therefore seem both similar to and different from Yancy's assertion that the "white gaze" fixes moral inferiority onto blackness. These imaginings of blackness are constituted through a Yiddish/Jewish lens that seeks to articulate Yiddish writers' own sense of being outsiders in white American Christian society, while also recognizing their privileged position as white-skinned people in relation to the black people they address and consider.

Positioning the "Yiddish gaze" of these poets against Yancy's "white gaze" allows Yancy's insights to illuminate a reading of these works, to provide a language in which to discuss how Yiddish writers view and imagine black subjects from a distance, treating them as symbols rather than as full people. These Yiddish writers use their black objects as exemplars of difference and of race-based suffering through which to better understand their own identity and positioning in American society. In this way, their "Yiddish gaze," like Yancy's "white gaze," produces meanings independent of the black bodies themselves, and these meanings are forced onto the black bodies in a discursive act that erases the identity of the individual black person in favor of the beholder's interpretive stance.[43]



Conversely, reading Yancy's theory together with these Yiddish poems also forces Yancy's theory open, demonstrating that the "white gaze" comes in multiple forms and that while imposing meanings on black bodies may be a standard practice of the "white gaze," the meanings themselves differ depending on the historical and ethnic (as well as gendered, economic, etc.) context of the gazer. While Yancy is right to consider what it means for the black body to be interpreted, the meaning of blackness that is "returned" to the individual black person, it seems, differs depending on the eye of the beholder. Consideration of the Yiddish poems presented in this chapter adds texture and nuance to the broad strokes of Yancy's argument by demonstrating that American Jews have looked upon black people not only with Yancy's "white gaze" but with a gaze of their own, which was refracted through their own ethno-racial and historical circumstances.

## Yiddish Writers and the Spectacle of Lynching

When Leyeles, in "In Subway, 3," writes of the dangers that constrain and haunt black male desire, and when Leyvik, in "Negroes," offers a vision of shared Jewish and black victimhood as hanging "from the rope of race," these poets make use of the spectacle of lynching, a recurring theme in American Yiddish poetry as a symbol for the evils of American society.[44] In each case, the black body hanging from the lynching tree is a known image that can be alluded to, without need for description or explanation, as a terse and evocative reminder of black Americans' vulnerability and suffering. For these poets, who wish to express empathy with their black subjects and imagined interlocutors, to see a black (male) body is to see his potential torture. Their "Yiddish gaze" is one that turns each black body into a symbol of oppression and victimization, a symbol that can be used to advance their own political and aesthetic aims.

As the tortured black body became a symbol of injustice among Yiddish writers in America, many of these writers drew upon parallels between this image and that of the tortured, martyred body of Jesus. As several scholars have noted, the figure of Jesus played an important role in modern Jewish literature, at once expressing rebellion by defying Jewish taboos around the figure of Jesus and articulating identification with Jewish people through images of Jewish suffering at the hands of Christians, drawing upon Jesus as an emblem of that suffering.[45] Reclaiming the scene of the Passion, which has long been used to rationalize hostility and violence against Jews as "Christ killers," as one in which the venerated figure of Jesus stands in for Jews as victimized martyrs rather than as perpetrators, modern Jewish writers sought to expose the hypocrisy of white Christianity and its anti-Jewish violence. As Amelia Glaser notes, Yiddish poets' harnessing of the crucifixion in their writing about anti-Jewish violence "recirculates" in American Yiddish poetry as a metaphor for American race violence.[46] Yiddish writers saw in the lynching tree, as James Cone describes it, a "negation" of the message of hope and salvation of the cross, replacing religiously inspired loving kindness with an act of terror.[47] Because the use of the crucifixion to represent the hypocrisy of Christian-inspired anti-Jewish violence was already an established poetic trope, describing the tortured black body using the image of Jesus allowed Yiddish writers to make connections between Jewish and black suffering, between the evils of Russian anti-Jewish violence and the evils of American racism.



For Yiddish writers, the horrific spectacle of lynching was a locus for meditations on the process of looking and interpreting as a moral act. In the works discussed below, Yiddish writers and readers were encouraged through descriptions of lynching scenes as crucifixions to contemplate human suffering and achieve a heightened sense of moral outrage that would enable them to understand and rebel against the cruelties of their world.

In his poem "Lynching" (1919), Yehoash (the pen name of Solomon Bloomgarden, 1870–1927) depicts in graphic and racialized language the tortured body of a lynching victim as evidence for his religious indignation about American racial violence. Yehoash explicitly links the black body to Christ, claiming that the God who has "become flesh" has in the same moment become a victimized black body, and that the religious resonances of this human sacrifice expose the blasphemy of a white America that claims to be pious but fails to see lynching as contradictory to Christian values. In the poem, Yehoash rages against an individual who could call out to God and not see the sanctity of a murdered human life.

| יהואש | Yehoash |
|---|---|
| **לינטשען** | **Lynching** |
| ''פֿאָטער פֿון מיין זעל, | "Father of my soul, |
| וואו זאָל איך דיך געפֿינען?—" | Where shall I find You?—" |
| פֿאַרשוועכער! | Desecrator! |
| קוק אָן דיין ווערק: | Look at your work: |
| אַ שוואַרץ לייב מיט בלוט באַשטרייפט, | A black body striped with blood |
| אַ פּנים פעך מיט אויסגעקערטע ווייסלען, | A tar face with lolling eye whites, |
| אַ רויטער צונג געשוואָלען | A red tongue swollen |
| צווישן שימערדיקע ציין . . . | Between shimmering teeth . . . |
| | |
| ''פֿאָטער פֿון מיין זעל, | "Father of my soul, |
| און האַר פֿון אַלע לייבער, | And Lord of all flesh, |
| וואו זאָל איך דיך געפֿינען?—" | Where shall I find You?—" |
| לעסטערער! | Blasphemer! |
| דער, וואָס ציטערט אין בלויע וועבן | He who trembles in the blue webs |
| פֿון דײַנע הייליקע פֿאַרנאַכטן, | Of Your holy dusks, |
| דער, וואָס נעבלט זיך אין דיין געוויין | He who wafts in the fog of Your cries |
| ביינאַכט, | by night And songs by day, |
| און דײַן געזאַנג בייטאָג, | He who wriggles in the seeds |
| דער, וואָס צאָפּלט אין די רויגן | Of Your unborn desires, |
| פֿון דײַנע ניט-געבאָרענע באַגערן, | He who calls to You, tears You, elevates |
| דער,וואָסרופֿטדיך,רייסטדיך,גרייסטדיך— | You— |
| איז פֿלייש געוואָרן, | Has become flesh, |
| איז אַ שוואַרץ לייב געוואָרן | Has become a black body |
| מיט גראָבע ליפּן און מיט קרויזע קאָלטנס, | With thick lips and kinky hair, |
| און דײַנע נעגל האָסטו | And You buried Your nails |
| אין זין ריפּ געגראָבן, | Into his rib, |
| מעסערס אין זײַן ברוסט געשטאָבן, | Stabbed knives into his breast, |
| אים אַ גוססן באַשפּײַען, | Spat at him as he was dying, |
| אים געלאָזט זיך וויגן | Left him swinging |
| אויף אַ בוים . . . | From a tree . . .[48] |

Yehoash's poem is focused on the act of looking as a moral act. The narrator addresses a lynching perpetrator and seeks to refocus his gaze, calling on him to "look at your work" and to see his actions not only as a violent crime but also as a blasphemous, God-desecrating act: he accuses his interlocutor of being a Christ killer through his desecration of a black body. Through the act of looking, Yehoash insists, his interlocutor, and his reading audience, will experience disorientation, disgust, and wonder in relation to the object of the lynched black body—that this moment in secular time is also a moment of religious significance and that its moral weight is at the intersection of the sacred and the secular.

Although Yehoash employs language that emphasizes the physiognomic differences between his readers and the black body they view, he also asserts that the black body is ultimately a physical representation of something ephemeral that is intimately part of his interlocutor and his readership—that this body is God himself. Yehoash, who published widely in many newspapers and had an audience with a variety of political affiliations, does not indicate that his anti-lynching position comes out of class-based or other political platforms, but out of a Romantic stance that "rejects rationalism and embraces mystical experience as the heart of human life."[49] He calls on his interlocutor and his readers to view the tortured black body through the lens of religious tradition, trusting that this ancient, evocative cultural resource can lead to a poetic inspiration that would force the perpetrator of injustice into a revelation of his own wrongdoing. He calls upon them to see the tortured black body as a physical form of their deepest, innermost selves, the spiritual force that "wriggles in the seeds / Of Your unborn desires." In this way, while insisting on racial difference, Yehoash argues that there is a deeper spiritual reality beyond physical, aesthetic divisions between people, and that this unity is God. What makes the lynching act so shameful is not only that the perpetrator fails to see the black body as a victim of torture, but that he also fails to see the divine within the black body—that he is blinded by the visual component of the black body and cannot "see" his spiritual components, described in ephemeral terms as "webs," "fog," and "songs." For Yehoash, then, to gaze at the black lynching victim is to gaze upon the desecration of that which is most divine.

And yet the recognition of this divinity, Yehoash insists, must come together with the recognition of the body's humanity, and of the violence of the crime done to it that has stripped it of its dignity, turned it from a human being into a dead body on display. The narrator insists that his audience must look at the body in gruesome detail *as* a dead body hanging limp from a tree, bloodied, tongue lolling, eyes rolled back. The reader must bear witness to the spectacle of the lynched body in order to understand the religious act of desecration as also a physical act of torture—a bloody act of murdering, hanging, spitting on the defamed body, and walking away. Seeing the black body as Jesus means seeing lynching as an act of religious transgression and also, equally significantly, as a crime against an individual human body. It means drawing on religious faith to make moral claims about the terrors of the present world, or, as Cone has it, allowing the lynching tree to "liberate the cross [from false piety] and make it real in American history."[50]

The body that the narrator asks his interlocutor to see is not a human being who can speak for himself but flesh without soul, murdered and abandoned. The language Yehoash uses to describe the murdered body is grotesque: he accentuates the gleaming teeth against the backdrop of tar-colored skin, emphasizing the racial otherness of the lynching victim in stereotypical terms, and describes evidence of torture and death—blood, vacant eyes, swollen tongue—alongside his descriptors of the black body as though they were intrinsic to the body and not consequences of the murder. It is as though the black body only exists for Yehoash as evidence of torture, and it seems as though the black skin itself is as much a part of the torture as the swollen tongue—that God's making bodies black is evidence of God's injustice, even as the perpetrator's murdering of the black body is evidence of humankind's injustice. Here, then, Yehoash's "Yiddish gaze" interprets the black body as an emblem of torture and suffering by nature of its very blackness, and as a symbol of the spiritual and moral bankruptcy of racism. Through the poem he suggests that white perpetrators and Jewish readers can learn by gazing at, rather than in dialogue with, the black body's victimhood—as Yancy describes it, the "Black body in relation to the white gaze *appears* in the form of a sheer exteriority," viewed as a thing indivisible from and read entirely as its black surface, but in this case what is read onto the body is not its criminality but its victimhood, and through its victimhood its sanctity.[51]

Yosef Opatoshu's story "Lintsheray," first published in book form in Warsaw in 1923, offers a similarly grotesque, detailed act of gazing on a tortured black body that posits the possibility of moral witnessing by associating the lynching victim with the body of Christ.[52] Opatoshu (1886–1954), who immigrated to New York in 1907, wrote his story in the tradition of literary realism, offering a critique of the primitive violence underpinning modernity through his representation of mob violence and the torture of a victimized black man. In the story's climactic lynching scene, Opatoshu makes use of use of Christian imagery to turn the reader's gaze on the black body into a moral stance.

In the climactic scene in which Bukert, the black protagonist of "Lintsheray," is burned to death, as Marc Caplan explains, "Opatoshu invests Bukert's death with the mythic paradoxes of Christian salvation: he becomes both crucified deity and redeemed believer."[53] Bukert, described at the start of the story in racialized language that compares him to an animal in the jungle, becomes a sacred emblem of martyrdom as his death approaches.[54] The night before his lynching, when he has already been caught and tortured by an angry mob and knows that his public execution will take place the following day, he asks a preacher to "read to him about Jesus's crucifixion." Opatoshu writes, "And when the priest read to him the depression left his face and he glowed with such a full blackness that it seemed that if someone were to cut his skin, black blood would flow out."[55] Here, the victim's blackness is transformed from a symbol of his degradation into the essence of his holiness as a religious martyr. The blackness is described as "glowing" in a rejection of a light/dark dichotomy that, as Yancy observes, insists on darkness as a "signifier of negative values" in contrast to the morality, beauty, enlightenment, and purity of whiteness.[56] The blackness becomes more pronounced and gives off light as Bukert hears of the crucifixion, affirming the relationship between blackness and redemptive holy martyrdom. This, along with a description of a cemetery in which "a crucified God . . . calls out to the weak," guides the reader to see Bukert through a lens of religious parable and to read Bukert and his martyrdom as representative of all black people and the moral weight of their experiences.[57]



Bukert's execution is a public spectacle that valorizes the black victim, pushing against the "terrifying images of white power and black helplessness" circulated through photographs, songs, and news stories that affirmed racial hierarchy by celebrating the lynching act.[58] Opatoshu achieves this reversal of the lynching image (of black brutality punished by white justice) through his use of religious metaphor, which shifts the reader's practice of seeing from the perspective of the lynching crowd to moral witnessing, and to a "sacred gaze."[59]

Bukert is presented as a religious martyr who declares his faith before a crowd and is executed in spite of, and in mockery of, his piety. Before he is put to death, Bukert reads to the crowd from the Bible while the crowd is as "silent as a religious service," and Bukert's eyes turn "toward the sky like a saint. The first Christians must have looked like this when they stood at the stake." Then Bukert tears the pages of Revelations out of his Bible and scatters them over the crowd. Here, Opatoshu aligns Bukert with both Jewish and Christian practices and with the valorization of dying for God, taking part in martyrological discourses within both traditions: by reading from the Bible, Bukert engages in a speech act in which he declares his faith as the final act of his life, thus self-consciously declaring his death part of the tradition of the imitation of Christ, or of sanctifying God's name with his whole self.

Bukert then "knelt down again, prayed for a while, looked at a little worm that crawled by his knee, and raked it away as though he was afraid that he might step on it, and stood up calmly. . . . He walked to the chair, pulled himself up by his shoulders onto the iron bars, and silently looked at the crowd."[60] Bukert demonstrates his compassion and his respect for life in contrast to the bloodthirsty crowd, and with his calm and measured behavior he demonstrates his ability to subordinate himself to his fate, mastering his fear of dying in order to honor his death as one that sanctifies God.[61] The slow pace of the narration matches Bukert's measured self-control as he faces the brutality of his death, and his close attention to the details of his every action emphasizes the way in which his movements and his body are on display as a public performance to be consumed by the angry mob, who in their clamoring eagerness for violence fail to see the sanctity of Bukert's body and actions, and by the readers who have been given the interpretive tools to read Bukert's death and tortured body as a sacred symbol of spiritual transcendence over the violence and cruelty of the mob.



In his final moments, the rope around his shoulders and chest burns through and gives way, so that while "entirely aflame" Bukert lunges toward the crowd "with outspread arms," his body forming the symbol of the cross before he collapses in front of the assemblage.[62] This image of the flaming cross turns Bukert's body into the body of Christ, which falls toward the crowd, accusing them of toppling their own deity through their racism and bloodlust. Through his representation of the white Christian mob committing deicide, Opatoshu undermines the notion of white racial supremacy, reversing the idea of white civilization and black primitiveness by emphasizing the unbridled violence and barbarism of the lynch mob.[63] Opatoshu, like many other anti-lynching activists, insists that "to see an event was to understand its truth," and he pushes his readers to bear witness to the lynching while giving them a religiously inflected interpretive framework that will drive them to see that the truth of the lynching is not Bukert's vulnerability or the screaming tortured body to which he is reduced, but his strength of character and his valiant martyrdom in the face of white Christian mob violence.[64] He insists on the ethical illiteracy of the lynch mob, the members of which fail to read the Bible pages Bukert throws to them or to grasp the meaning of his body aflame, and he leads his readers to a moral way of seeing the tortured black body through his use of the religious framework of martyrdom, a practice held sacred by Jews and Christians alike.

Yet the lynching scene bears the excitement, the titillating and fascinating representation of cruelty and suffering, that so attracted audiences of written narratives, films, and photographs of lynching, who watched the spectacle "out of voyeuristic curiosity or for morbid thrills."[65] The reader is invited to read the scene through the moralizing lens of religious parable, gaining from it an assertion of the innocence and sanctity of the black body and the immorality of the white Christian mob (an act one might call "witnessing"), and at the same time is allowed the cathartic, pornographic pleasure of experiencing the details of intense and forbidden extremes of human experience (an act one might call "spectatorship"). As Elizabeth Dauphinee argues with reference to images of torture from Abu Ghraib, even within projects intended to politicize the immorality of suffering, the "drive to make visible what is essentially *unimaginable*" leads to a fetishization of suffering and an objectification of the tortured body.[66] Thus, in "Lintsheray," as in Yehoash's "Lynching," the act of looking at the tortured body is at once imbued with moral indignation and its opposite, a kind of immoral enjoyment at the expense of another's bodily horror. The reader becomes part of the lynch mob through the act of looking, even if that looking is ascribed moral and religious meaning.



Unlike the black body in Yehoash's poem, Opatoshu's black protagonist is a living being who speaks and can aid in others' interpretation of his death through his actions in life. And yet, from the very title of the story, and from the fatalistic, naturalistic account of his pursuit and murder, the reader knows at the outset that Bukert is bound to die: he is always already a tortured dead body, and his inevitable death is read with foreboding into his actions in life. In this way, Opatoshu's "Yiddish gaze" insists that to be black is to be a victim of torture, and that to be Jewish (to be a Yiddish reader of Opatoshu's work) is to have the ability to interpret black bodies as victims of torture, to stand apart from the lynch mob and understand the religious truth of lynching, a truth that the Christian lynch mob fails to see, even though it correlates so closely with their own religious tradition.[67] Yet as the narration of the story falls short of this ideal, depicting both the excitement of participation in the mob and repugnance at the mob's actions, Opatoshu's story asks whether the act of watching as an interested and sympathetic outsider can ever be an entirely moral act, and whether his readers can be expected to see the story as a call to action, or as a statement of religious or political belief, rather than as entertainment, however edifying.

For the American Christian reader, narratives and images linking the cross and the lynching tree work to expose the symbolic relationship between two familiar parts of the daily reality of American society, whereas for Yiddish writers, Glaser notes, works that "conflate Jesus's crucified body, already an exotic image for the Yiddish writer, with the exoticized Black body" may in fact have served to "defamiliarize" the "all too common occurrence of race violence."[68] That is to say, the moral valence of the comparison between the tortured body of Christ and the tortured body of the black victim is necessarily different in a Yiddish text than in, for instance, the writings of Harlem Renaissance poet Countee Cullen.[69] Yiddish writers and readers may distance themselves from and even disown American whiteness through their critique of white Christianity from the outside, denying their implication in systems of white supremacy by linking lynching with white Christian hypocrisy. They may also distance themselves from black victimhood by linking it to Christ's martyrdom rather than (or in addition to) Jewish suffering. To gaze upon the tortured black body as Jesus, for Yiddish writers and readers, is to gaze at otherness, even if this is a sympathetic gaze in recognition of shared suffering, or in moral outrage over the violence and suffering that they see.



And yet the comparison between the black tortured body and the body of Christ also makes these foreign entities—both black Americans and white Christians—related to the Yiddish audience: because the connection between Jews and the crucifixion had become an established trope in Yiddish writing, linking the suffering of Jesus (as a Jew) with contemporary Jewish martyrdom, the comparison between Christ and the black lynching victim is implicitly also a comparison of the lynching victim with the denigrated Jewish victim of anti-Semitic violence. And because the Yiddish reader witnesses rather than falls victim to the lynching, Yehoash's "Lynching" and Opatoshu's "Lintsheray" transform the Yiddish reader "from the persecuted to the empowered" beholder of the lynching scene.[70] Simultaneously positioned as potential victims and perpetrators, Yiddish readers, though distanced from the lynching scene in its foreignness, are called to do more than just gaze at the scene, but to find their (missing) place within the scene, to find a role that might be different from victim or perpetrator, black or white. As Leyvik's "Negroes" posits, this role could be that of ally, of activist, recognizing the differences between Jewish and black people in America while uniting under the banner of a shared knowledge of suffering, even while acknowledging the groups' different experiences of suffering.

## Conclusion

This chapter has attempted to elucidate a "Yiddish gaze" on black bodies that is implicated within a practice of white gazing that involuntarily assigns meanings to black bodies as objects but does so with a sympathetic stance. The Yiddish texts analyzed in this chapter, insofar as they are addressed to a Yiddish reading audience, are uniquely positioned in their act of interpreting black bodies in the intimacy of an imagined community separate from a potential black readership. They effectively translate American blackness, in its otherness and its victimhood, for a Yiddish-reading audience, attempting to make sense of American racism in terms that will be familiar to Yiddish readers in America and abroad. They also attempt to delineate the category of "Jew" in an American context as one who is able to read black bodies through a moral lens, thus inscribing the act of looking, of interpreting, of reading, as an essentially Yiddish/Jewish way of being. In this way, Yiddish writers claim authority to interpret the experiences of black people in their absence, gazing upon an individual who does not have the possibility of speaking (in Yiddish) and asserting their own practices of seeing as a moral stance that involves knowing the meaning and experiences of black bodies. Writing for Yiddish-reading communities also gave these Yiddish writers a space in which to fully express their outrage about white American racism and about a community (white America) to which its readers might actually aspire to belong, and might in other contexts be more hesitant to critique. In this private sphere of Yiddish writing, the foreignness of a Yiddish perspective could be emphasized without fear of compromising the possibilities for Jewish integration, both individual and communal, into white America. The particularities of the off-white positioning of the early twentieth-century Yiddish-speaking Jewish community in America, and the particularities of writing in Yiddish for a Yiddish-reading audience, created the circumstances for a separate sphere of "Yiddish gazing" practices that share in, but also depart from, the "white gaze."



The work performed by this "gaze" is manifold. A "Yiddish gaze" is one that both participates in the language and images of racism, seeing difference in skin color and placing moral value on it, and resists the totalizing power of that gaze by situating "the Jew" as neither black nor white but as off-white, decentering the racial dichotomy upon which the "white gaze" is predicated. This "gaze" makes use of foreignness and victimhood as lenses through which to aspire to a more ethical way of seeing racial difference. By relying on sound in addition to sight, by pointing at what is shared in divergent experiences of suffering, and by framing antiblack violence in religious terms that valorize suffering, the "Yiddish gaze" resists inclinations to view blackness as its own opposite, as evil or criminal, even though this resistance is incomplete, enmeshed in white gazing practices.

An analysis of the "Yiddish gaze" in dialogue with Yancy invites us not only to characterize the "gaze" in terms of the meanings placed on black bodies but also to see the narrators of Yiddish texts themselves in their off-whiteness, to look at the gazers and to question the positions of power and privilege that they claim by asserting their authority to gaze on and interpret black bodies. Yancy argues that the white gaze and its racial practices are "learned effortlessly, practices that are always already in progress," through which whiteness is made the invisible norm and black people are marked as different, deviant, dangerous. Fighting white power and privilege requires white allies to turn their gaze upon themselves, and to examine the ways in which their gaze upon black bodies "reveals whites to themselves." In other words, critical whiteness requires a "countergaze" that calls attention to whiteness itself as a site of privilege and power, and that observes "white discourse and white social performances that attempt to pass themselves off as racially neutral."[71] Therefore, any study of the "Yiddish gaze" must ask not only what the narrators are seeing (black bodies as different, hypersexual, dangerous, and so on, and as victims or martyrs) but what that act of interpolating blackness says about the narrators themselves as racialist thinkers who insist on their own invisibility through viewing the bodies of Others. What do these writers need from the black people they portray? An affirmation of the safety and security of their own invisibility as not the dominant Other in a racially divided society? A self-congratulatory confirmation of their position as those who are not performing a lynching, though, mercifully, who are also not the target of lynching? An assertion of their own superiority as a class of people with the authority to interpret black bodies in the absence of black voices? A representation of their own vulnerability? And how, we must further ask, do contemporary acts of "Jewish gazing" at black bodies and their torture continue to demand from others confirmation of the virtue and security of a Jewish position between American blackness and whiteness? The practice of asking these questions, of unpacking and interpreting a historical "Yiddish gaze" in all of its contradictions, in all of the ways in which it implicates the narrators in racist ways of being in the world, and as victims to those ways of being in the world, is an important step in determining the content of contemporary Jewish gazes and the Jewish community's responsibility for the ways we define ourselves (defensively, sympathetically, hierarchically, etc.) in seeing blackness.

The "Yiddish gaze" described in this chapter is by no means a singular "Jewish" way of gazing at black bodies. It is derived from a particular historical moment, drawing upon the experiences of Yiddish-writing and -reading

Jews who experienced their own marginality through their in-between racial status, their foreign language and accent, and their memories, experiences, and awareness of growing European and American anti-Semitism. So what are the stakes, in this volume on Judaism, race, and ethics, in writing about this particular vantage point of early twentieth-century Yiddish literature as a way of getting at the question of a Jewish ethics of race in America? As Aaron Hughes argues in his book about "rethinking" Jewish philosophy in a way that avoids apologetics and nationalistic claims, Jewish thought must be understood as speaking "with many voices to any given subject."[72] This requires expanding the perspectives and categories of texts that can be seen as evincing some version of Jewish thought as a set of ways of looking at the world reliant on their historical contexts. The set of texts presented in this chapter are one such "Jewish" perspective among many on the issue of race, a perspective that draws upon racial ideologies of its moment, on eastern European experiences of anti-Semitism, and on non-Jewish religious imagery, to present an ethical stance that urges readers to see the black objects of their gaze, despite their external otherness, as part of universal humanity and of the divine, and to see the specific threat of violence that they live under, and to feel outrage at this violence. Moreover, as literary examples, these texts offer readers an opportunity to step into and embody the position of the narrators, to look through their eyes, to adopt their gaze. They therefore translate a theoretical desire to interpret black bodies sympathetically into a lived experience of looking, through texts, at a black body and its torture, guided by narration that trains the eye to see sympathetically—translating ethics into a "more developed" text. A discussion of the ethics of gazing requires this more "discursively capacious" reading experience, which, by juxtaposing and interfacing with ethical literature, can help situate thought in the "human and the social domain."[73]



The works examined in this chapter demonstrate the ways in which Yiddish writers "absorbed the racism of the culture that surrounded them" and yet "did not feel the need to embrace a virulent racism to demonstrate or reinforce their whiteness," and so managed to find ways to resist racism from within established notions of racial hierarchy.[74] My reading of the "Yiddish gaze" itself thus resists the temptation to label a "Yiddish" version of the "white gaze" as entirely good or virtuous and instead suggests that good and evil, ethical and unethical ways of seeing and interpreting the world, are not so easily delineated, and that moral ways of looking can be attempted even from within, and even when they include elements of systemic inequity. The position of Yiddish writers engaged in acts of seeing within and against the dominant white gaze can serve as a reminder that even within and limited by positions and perspectives of power and privilege, even in our knowledge that any attempts at seeking justice may be incomplete, it is still incumbent upon us to try to witness oppression through moral eyes, and through creative efforts to see in new ways—by juxtaposing sight and sound, by reading ancient parables in contemporary contexts, by imagining the fears, desires, and vulnerabilities of the Other—to try to understand the world against the power structures we live in.

What would it mean for Jewish ethics today to advocate taking on the ways of seeing embedded in these works of literature? Is it possible, and should we try, to embody these practices of "Yiddish gazing"? Could we attempt to see black bodies as though we had recently arrived on American shores and lacked the cultural semiotics to interpolate from those bodies the same meanings enforced by the "white gaze"? Would it be desirable for us to take on practices of "gazing" that saw the black body as a symbol of suffering to the exclusion of seeing a black person as an individual with agency and power? Perhaps not, and yet the attempts in these works to see the unfamiliar Other as a reflection of the familiar through a universalizing stance and through analogy speak to the ethical potential of the "Yiddish gaze" in spite of its weaknesses. Perhaps in reading these texts we could seek to borrow and embody strategies of seeing with sympathy and out of shared experience, even as we would seek to reject gazing practices that reinforce the essentializing power of the "white gaze." In doing so, we would also have to ask ourselves what we are gaining and demanding from the black bodies we see, what we are asking them to reflect to us about ourselves, and how we can move from mere gazing to dialogue, exchange, to a mutual process of meaning making.

## Notes

1. Yancy, *Black Bodies, White Gazes*, xxi, 2, 49, 150, 12.

2. Mills, *Racial Contract*, 11.

3. Ibid., 79–80.

4. Goldstein, *Price of Whiteness*, 1.

5. Jacobson, *Whiteness of a Different Color*, 193.

6. Goldstein, *Price of Whiteness*, 2, 1, 40.

7. Bachman, *Recovering "Yiddishland,"* xxii.

8. In their poetic manifesto, the "introspectivists," a movement of American Yiddish modernist poets, emphasize this point, writing, "We are 'Jewish poets' simply because we are Jews and write in Yiddish. No matter what a Yiddish poet writes in Yiddish, it is ipso facto Jewish. One does not need any particular 'Jewish themes.' . . . It is not the poet's task to seek and show his Jewishness. Whoever is interested in this endeavor is welcome to it, and whoever looks for Jewishness in Yiddish poets will find it." Glatshteyn, Leyeles, and Minkov, "Introspectivism [Manifesto of 1919]," 780.

9. Rosenblatt, "Introduction."

10. Newton, "Jews on America's Racial Map," 506.

11. The poems discussed here represent only a small sampling of Yiddish literature written in America that thematizes race and race relations. For other discussions of the topic, see ibid.; Bachman, *Recovering "Yiddishland"*; McCallum-Bonar, "Black Ashkenaz"; Rontsh, "Neger in undzer literatur"; Krutikov, "Rase-inyen in der yidisher literatur," 12.

12. All of the authors and protagonists in this literary sampling are indeed men, interpreting race from their male-gendered perspectives. There are few representations of black female protagonists or of black Americans by female Yiddish authors in American Yiddish literature. Exceptions include Malka Lee's "Niger in sobvey" [Negro on the subway] and Roza Nevadovska's "Negershe kinderlekh" [Negro children] and "Tsu di shvartse froyen" [To the black women], both poems by women, and Alter Eselin's "Geburt" [Birth], which has as its subject a black woman.

13. Yancy, *Black Bodies, White Gazes*, xvi. For an account of the racializing meanings placed on the Jewish body, see Gilman, *Jew's Body*.

14. Diner, *Almost Promised Land*, 38.

15. Welch, "Tortured Shadows," 16.

16. Cone, *Cross and the Lynching Tree*, 73, 158, 3, 64, 101, 135.

17. Ibid., 118.

18. Hoffman, *From Rebel to Rabbi*, 4–6, 117.

19. Ibid., 3, 119. Several scholars have examined modern Jewish literature in relation to the crucifixion. Neta Stahl emphasizes that poets who represented Jesus did so because the "ambivalence itself was . . . attractive." Stahl, *Other and Brother*, 7. Jesus was both "other" as a signifier of the atrocities Christians perpetuated against Jews in his name and "brother" as a fellow Jew victimized by violence. Her primary interest is in Zionist writers of Hebrew literature who reclaimed Jesus for Jewish nationalism. In *Against the Apocalypse*, David Roskies discusses the use of the cross in twentieth-century Yiddish literature as a symbol of the redemptive quality of suffering. Melissa Weininger argues that one reason why Jesus was such an attractive symbol for modern writers was that he was born a Jew, in the East, but had become a symbol of Western Christian culture, "a kind of cultural displacement" with which modern Jewish writers identified. Weininger, "Imagining Jesus, Imagining Jews," 3. Amelia Glaser argues that Yiddish writers used the crucifixion in America "to conflate anti-Semitic and anti-Black violence" in order to "draw attention to the universality of Christian hypocrisy." She explains that "the transition from a Jewish to a Black Jesus figure reflects a transition, for many Jewish writers, from a nationally to an internationally oriented politics." Glaser, "From Jewish Jesus to Black Christ," 46.

20. Minkoff, *Avraham Reyzin*, 5; Sonntag, "Poet of Poverty."

21. Minkoff, *Avraham Reyzin*, 8.

22. Rayzin, "A Negerl." This is my own translation, with inspiration from the translation by Merle Bachman in *Recovering "Yiddishland,"* 159–60.

23. Yancy, *Black Bodies, White Gazes*, xvi.

24. Insofar as the black body is that of an innocent child, Rayzin's poem denies the possibility that the onlooker is afraid of the black body because of its associations with violence, and in this way this "Yiddish gaze" is different from the "white gaze" Yancy describes: the black body here is not interpreted as dangerous or violent, but it is nevertheless disturbingly disruptive to what the narrator considers the norm. The fear has to do with the shock of strangeness and the aesthetics of difference.

25. Merle Bachman notes that this is "entirely possible." *Recovering "Yiddishland,"* 160.

26. For Bachman's reading of the poem, see ibid., 161.

27. Yancy, *Black Bodies, White Gazes*, xxii.

28. Bachman, *Recovering "Yiddishland,"* 161.

29. Indeed, even in using the terms "neger" and "vays" to mean "Negro" and "white," the poet indicates his participation in a cultural semiotics specific to an American context, as these words have particular racial meanings in American Yiddish that correspond to American ways of thinking about race that lack exact equivalents in eastern European contexts. By labeling his brother "vays," in contrast to the "Negro" boy, the poet is accepting the premise of racial binaries between "neger" and "vays." In Merle Bachman's insightful reading of this

poem, the speaker articulates his own whiteness through seeing the child—his "dismay" in encountering the child causes "a shift in awareness" through which the speaker sees himself (and his brother) as white, even as he insists on their shared, universal humanity. The speaker's white identity is thereby solidified in the same moment that he acknowledges the humanity of the Other despite his black body. Ibid.



30. Yancy, *Black Bodies, White Gazes*, xxii.

31. See Zutra, "*In zikh* (1930–1940)," 5, 14.

32. My translation. For another version, see Harshav and Harshav, *American Yiddish Poetry*, 103.

33. See Stanciu, "Strangers in America."

34. The woman's desires and fears are rendered irrelevant in this poem, which is as much about the male gaze at the objectified female body as it is about the "Yiddish gaze" at the black man's body.

35. The Jewish onlooker's attention to the black man's sexual desire may also hint at the Jewish man's desire for the black man himself. In his consideration of the erotics of "black-Jewish relations," Jeffrey Melnick notes that Jews imagined that they could embody an idealized blackness in part as a way to co-opt black male sexual power. The intensity of the sexual discourse in Leyeles's poem may denote the speaker's illicit desire to embody or conquer the black man's sexuality, just as the black man desires the forbidden white girl. See Melnick, "Some Notes on the Erotics," 15.

36. The notion of sympathy for a hypersexualized black body can be further elucidated through Barukh Glozman's short story "Nakht in a dorem-shtot" (A night in a southern city) of 1927, in which Ora, a Jewish man, hears a "wild song" on the other side of town and crosses a bridge into the Negro quarter to dance in a primitive orgy of hypersexualized black bodies. In the morning, on hearing the sound of church bells, Ora retreats into white civilization. In writing this representation of blackness as a separate, debased sphere of sexual excess, Glozman accepts the terms of the American racial dichotomy, with its valuation of whiteness as moral goodness and intellectual ability, and its devaluation of darkness as the site of bodily desire. He places his Jewish character at the overlap of these spheres—he exists as the archetypical "wandering Jew" without a communal homeland, who can slip across the color line without creating or exposing fissures in the line itself. Ultimately, Ora's slippage between the racialized realms of sexual purity and impurity point to his foreignness in both spheres, his alienated position as a Jew in America. This, as in Leyeles's poem, demonstrates sympathy toward black bodies through a shared experience not only of racial otherness but also of a lack of white purity and innocence—a shared sinfulness—through accepting the terms of the "white gaze" that defines black, and sometimes Jewish, bodies as sexually sinful.

37. Harshav and Harshav, *American Yiddish Poetry*, 676.

38. This is my own translation. I am indebted to Colleen McCallum-Bonar's translation of this poem in her dissertation "Black Ashkenaz," 208.

39. Ibid., 136.

40. Yancy, *Black Bodies, White Gazes*, 149.

41. Sartre, *Anti-Semite and Jew*, 8.

42. Budick, *Blacks and Jews*, 1.

43. Yancy, *Black Bodies, White Gazes*, 112.

44. For a discussion of leftist Yiddish politics in poetry thematizing lynching, see Glaser, "Jewish Jesus to Black Christ." Marc Caplan, in "Yiddish Exceptionalism," includes a list of explicit references to lynching among American poets writing in Yiddish, most of which can be found in Harshav and Harshav, *American Yiddish Poetry*, or Glaser and Weintraub, *Proletpen*. See Caplan, "Yiddish Exceptionalism," 184.

45. See Hoffman, *From Rebel to Rabbi*; Stahl, *Other and Brother*; Weininger, "Imagining Jesus, Imagining Jews."

46. Glaser, "Jewish Jesus to Black Christ," 45.

47. Cone, *Cross and the Lynching Tree*, xiii.

48. My translation draws heavily on a translation by Benjamin Harshav and Barbara Harshav in *Sing, Stranger*, 107.

49. See Ponichtera, "Yiddish and the Avant-Garde," 22.

50. Cone, *Cross and the Lynching Tree*, 161.

51. Yancy, *Black Bodies, White Gazes*, 21.

52. The translations of "Lintsheray" are my own. For a full translation of the story, see Opatoshu, "A Lynching."

53. Caplan, "Yiddish Exceptionalism," 182.

54. Regarding the portrayal of the black man as a "wild animal," Caplan writes, "Because Opatoshu has inherited a discourse about Black people from white racism . . . it can only inhabit the limits set by that discourse in its imaginative poverty." Ibid., 177.

55. Opatoshu, "Lintsheray," 41.

56. Yancy, *Black Bodies, White Gazes*, 3.

57. Opatoshu, "Lintsheray," 51.

58. Wood, *Lynching and Spectacle*, 2.

59. David Morgan defines a "sacred gaze" as "the manner in which a way of seeing invests an image, a viewer, or an act of viewing with spiritual significance." *Sacred Gaze*, 3.

60. Opatoshu, "Lintsheray," 44, 47.

61. I have relied on Daniel Boyarin's description of elements of martyrology shared by Jewish and Christian traditions as a basis for my reading of Bukert's death as religious martyrdom. See Boyarin, *Dying for God*, 95–96.

62. Opatoshu, "Lintsheray," 50.

63. As Marc Caplan succinctly explains, "in Opatoshu's paradoxical realist parable, racism transforms the white Christian racist into his own imagined opposite." "Yiddish Exceptionalism," 183.

64. Wood, *Lynching and Spectacle*, 5.

65. Ibid., 12.

66. Dauphinee, "Politics of the Body in Pain," 140.

67. I have argued elsewhere that Opatoshu's story argues that Jews who maintain a Jewish identity characterized by Yiddish language and the memory of anti-Jewish violence have the ability to stand outside the lynch mob and maintain an ethical anti-lynching stance, but that Jews who integrate into American culture, losing their communal memory and language, participate in an "ethical assimilation" that ultimately makes them part of, rather than outside of, American racism in all its brutality. See Kirzane, "'This Is How a Generation Grows.'"



68. Glaser, "Jewish Jesus to Black Christ," 49.

69. James Cone uses Cullen as an exemplar of the "many black poets, novelists, painters, dramatists, and other artists [who] saw clearly what white theologians and clergy ignored and what black religious scholars and ministers merely alluded to: that in the United States, the clearest image of the crucified Christ was the figure of an innocent black victim, dangling from a lynching tree." *Cross and the Lynching Tree*, 93.

70. Glaser, "Jewish Jesus to Black Christ," 61.

71. Yancy, *Look, a White*, 3, 4, 5, 10, 11.

72. Hughes, *Rethinking Jewish Philosophy*, 111.

73. See Eskin, "On Literature and Ethics," 588.

74. Greenberg, "'I'm Not White—I'm Jewish,'" 40.

75. *Shemot Rabbah* 49:2; see also 23:10.

76. See Idelson-Shein, *Difference of a Different Kind*.

## References


Bachman, Merle L. *Recovering "Yiddishland": Threshold Moments in American Literature*. Syracuse: Syracuse University Press, 2008.

Boyarin, Daniel. *Dying for God: Martyrdom and the Making of Christianity and Judaism*. Stanford: Stanford University Press, 1999.

Budick, Emily Miller. *Blacks and Jews in Literary Conversation*. New York: Cambridge University Press, 1998.

Caplan, Marc. "Yiddish Exceptionalism: Lynching, Race, and Racism in Opatoshu's *Lintsheray*." In *Joseph Opatoshu: A Yiddish Writer Between Europe and America*, edited by Sabine

Koller, Gennady Estraikh, and Mikhail Krutikov, 173–87. London: Legenda, 2013.

Cone, James H. *The Cross and the Lynching Tree*. Maryknoll, N.Y.: Orbis Books, 2011.

Dauphinee, Elizabeth. "The Politics of the Body in Pain: Reading the Ethics of Imagery." *Security Dialogue* 38, no. 2 (2007): 139–55.

Diner, Hasia. *In the Almost Promised Land: American Jews and Blacks, 1915–1935*. Baltimore: Johns Hopkins University Press, 1977.

Eselin, Alter. "Geburt" [Birth]. In Mayzel, *Amerike in Yidishn vort*, 488–89.

Eskin, Michael. "On Literature and Ethics." *Poetics Today* 25, no. 4 (2004): 573–94.

Gilman, Sander. *The Jew's Body*. London: Routledge, 1991.

Glaser, Amelia. "From Jewish Jesus to Black Christ: Race Violence in Leftist Yiddish Poetry." *Studies in American Jewish Literature* 34, no. 1 (2015): 44–69.

Glaser, Amelia, and David Weintraub, eds. *Proletpen: America's Rebel Yiddish Poets*. Madison: University of Wisconsin Press, 2005.

Glatshteyn, Jacob, A. Leyeles, and N. Minkov. "Introspectivism [Manifesto of 1919]." Translated by Anita Norich. In Harshav and Harshav, *American Yiddish Poetry*, 774–84.

Glozman, Barukh. "Nakht in a dorem-shtot" [Night in a southern city]. In *Oyf di felder fun dzshordzshia* [In Georgia's fields], 135–40. Vilna: B. Kletskin, 1927.

Goldstein, Eric L. *The Price of Whiteness: Jews, Race, and American Identity*. Princeton: Princeton University Press, 2006.

Greenberg, Cheryl. "'I'm Not White—I'm Jewish': The Racial Politics of American Jews." In *Race, Color, Identity: Rethinking Discourses About "Jews" in the Twenty-First Century*, edited by Efraim Sicher, 35–55. London: Berghahn Books, 2013.

Harshav, Benjamin, and Barbara Harshav, eds. *American Yiddish Poetry: A Bilingual Anthology*. Berkeley: University of California Press, 1986.

———, eds. *Sing, Stranger: A Century of American Yiddish Poetry; A Historical Anthology*. Stanford: Stanford University Press, 2006.

Hoffman, Matthew. *From Rebel to Rabbi: Reclaiming Jesus and the Making of Modern Jewish Culture*. Stanford: Stanford University Press, 2007.

Hughes, Aaron W. *Rethinking Jewish Philosophy: Beyond Particularism and Universalism*. New York: Oxford University Press, 2014.

Idelson-Shein, Iris. *Difference of a Different Kind: Jewish Constructions of Race During the Long Eighteenth Century*. Philadelphia: University of Pennsylvania Press, 2014.

Jacobson, Matthew Frye. *Whiteness of a Different Color: European Immigrants and the Alchemy of Race*. Cambridge, Mass.: Harvard University Press, 1999.

Kirzane, Jessica. "'This Is How a Generation Grows': Lynching as a Site of Ethical Loss in Opatoshu's 'Lintsheray.'" *Zutot* 9 (2012): 59–71.

Krutikov, Mikhail. "Der rase-inyen in der yidisher literatur" [The subject of race in Yiddish literature]. *Der Forverts*, April 27–May 3, 2012. https://yiddish2.forward.com/node/4373/print/index.html.

Lee, Malka. "Der niger in sobvey." Translated as "The Negro on the Subway" in Glaser and Weintraub, *Proletpen*, 160–63.

Leyvik, H. "Negershes" [Negroes]. In *Ale verk fun H. Leyvik* [The complete works of H. Leyvik], 1:271–72. New York: H. Leyvik Yubiley Komitet, 1940.

Markish, Peretz. *The Forty-Year-Old Man* (excerpt). Translated by Rose Waldman. *In geveb: A Journal of Yiddish Studies* (May 2016). https://ingeveb.org/texts-and-translations/the-forty-year-old-man.

Mayzel, Nachman, ed. *Amerike in Yidishn vort* [America in Yiddish writing]. New York: Yidisher Kultur Farband, 1955.

McCallum-Bonar, Colleen. "Black Ashkenaz and the Almost Promised Land: Yiddish Literature and the Harlem Renaissance." PhD diss., Ohio State University, 2008.

Melnick, Jeffrey Paul. "Some Notes on the Erotics of 'Black-Jewish Relations.'" *Shofar: An Interdisciplinary Journal of Jewish Studies* 23, no. 4 (2005): 9–25.

Mills, Charles W. *The Racial Contract.* Ithaca: Cornell University Press, 1997.

Minkoff, N. B. *Avraham Reyzin der dikhter fun lid* [Avraham Reyzin: The poet and his poetry]. New York: Bodn, 1936.

Morgan, David. *The Sacred Gaze: Religious Visual Culture in Theory and Practice.* Berkeley: University of California Press, 2005.

Nevadovska, Roza. "Negershe kinderlekh" [Negro children]. In Mayzel, *Amerike in Yidishn Vort*, 755.

———. "Tsu di shvartse froyen" [To the black women]. In Mayzel, *Amerike in Yidishn vort*, 755–56.

Newton, Adam Zachary. "Jews on America's Racial Map." In *The Cambridge History of Jewish American Literature*, edited by Hana Wirth-Nesher, 503–24. New York: Cambridge University Press, 2016.

Opatoshu, Yosef. "Lintsheray" [A lynching]. In *Rase, lintsheray, un andere dertseylungen* [Race, A lynching, and other stories], 1–51. Warsaw: Perets-Bibliotek, 1923.

———. "A Lynching." Translated by Jessica Kirzane. *In geveb: A Journal of Yiddish Studies* (June 2016). https://ingeveb.org/texts-and-translations/a-lynching.

Ponichtera, Sarah. "Yiddish and the Avant-Garde in American Jewish Poetry." PhD diss., Columbia University, 2012.

Rayzin, Avraham. "A Negerl" [A little Negro]. In Mayzel, *Amerike in Yidishn vort*, 212.

Rontsh, Yitzchok. "Der neger in undzer literatur" [The Negro in our literature]. In *Amerike in der yiddisher literatur* [America in Yiddish literature], 203–50. New York: Y. E. Rontsh Bukh Komitet, 1945.

Rosenblatt, Eli. "Introduction." In Isaac Meir Dik, "Slavery or Serfdom," translated by Eli Rosenblatt. *In geveb: A Journal of Yiddish Studies* (November 2015). https://ingeveb.org/texts-and-translations/slavery-or-serfdom.

Roskies, David G. *Against the Apocalypse: Responses to Catastrophe in Modern Jewish Culture.* Cambridge, Mass.: Harvard University Press, 1984.

Sartre, Jean-Paul. *Anti-Semite and Jew: An Exploration of the Etiology of Hate.* 1944. Translated by George J. Becker. New York: Schocken Books, 1995.

Sonntag, Jacob. "The Poet of Poverty." *Jewish Quarterly* 1, no. 2 (1953): 43–52.

Stahl, Neta. *Other and Brother: Jesus in the Twentieth-Century Jewish Literary Landscape.* New York: Oxford University Press, 2012.

Stanciu, Cristina. "Strangers in America: Yiddish Poetry at the Turn of the Twentieth Century and the Demands of Americanization." *College English* 76, no. 1 (2013): 59–83.

Weininger, Melissa. "Imagining Jesus, Imagining Jews." PhD diss., University of Chicago, 2010.

Welch, Milton. "Tortured Shadows: Representations of Lynching in Modernist U.S. Poetry." PhD diss., University of Virginia, 2007.

Wood, Amy Louise. *Lynching and Spectacle: Witnessing Racial Violence in America, 1890–1940.* Chapel Hill: University of North Carolina Press, 2011.

Yancy, George. *Black Bodies, White Gazes: The Continuing Significance of Race.* Lanham, Md.: Rowman and Littlefield, 2008.

———. *Look, a White! Philosophical Essays on Whiteness.* Philadelphia: Temple University Press, 2012.

Yehoash. "Lintshn" [Lynching]. In Mayzel, *Amerike in Yidishn Vort*, 155.

Zutra, Itay Binyamin. "*In zikh* (1930–1940): Yiddish Modernism in Search of Jewish Self-Consciousness." PhD diss., Jewish Theological Seminary of America, 2011.



## Classic Text and Questions to Ponder

The "Yiddish gaze" Kirzane unpacks does several things simultaneously. It uses language and images of racism, acknowledges skin color and imposes moral value upon it, resists calling "the Jew" either black or white but describes him rather as off-white, and thus challenges the binaries that the more general "white gaze" produces and reinscribes. The impulse to resist the totalizing dichotomies of typical racialist seeing is also found in a rabbinic interpretation of the Song of Songs verse that proclaims, "I am black and beautiful, O daughters of Jerusalem" (1:6). A midrash wonders why scripture says, "I am black" and "beautiful." "This is what the community of Israel said: *I am black* refers to my own deeds; *and beautiful* refers to the deeds of my ancestors. *I was black* in Egypt, and *beautiful* when I said at Sinai, 'all that Adonai has spoken we will do and obey' (Exodus 24:7). *I was black* at the Red Sea, as it says, 'But we were rebellious at the sea, even at the Red Sea' (Psalm 106:7), *and beautiful* because I said, 'This is my God, and I will glorify [God]' (Exodus 15:2)."[75] The midrash opens the possibility that blackness and beauty can be connected; they need not be exclusive alternatives. By offering a temporal and performative relation between these classifications, this midrash, like Yiddish literature, promotes a countergaze that invites readers to see color and beauty not as mutually exclusive alternatives or distinct categories but as inherently malleable or permeable.

- Early twentieth-century Yiddish literature continues an already vibrant Jewish deliberation on race and racism that was occurring in folktales, philosophical literature, scientific writing, and children's books.[76] Why is it important to acknowledge that not all American Jews embraced a totalizing "white gaze" when contemplating real or fictional black bodies?
- Kirzane argues that Yiddish authors promote a sympathetic gaze through which to consider black bodies in particular and race generally. That this perspective resists binary vantage points is important for Jewish ethics. Do you agree? Why or why not?
- The midrash quoted above suggests that color and theological and moral aesthetics are performative in nature and thus need not be mutually exclusive. What is your perspective?

# 7

# Rituals of Commemoration

## Sites for Cultural Memories as Traumatic Silences and Memorial Cries for Social Change

NICHOLE RENÉE PHILLIPS

### Memory as "Homeland"

Cultural memory studies is a trans-, inter-, multidisciplinary field dedicated to studying the relationship between culture and memory. It demonstrates how social and cultural contexts shape memory, described as a dialogue between the past and present. Memory is not observable; it is a capacity. Remembering, however, is a process, observable in specific sociocultural contexts, that assists our understanding of the nature and function of memory. Three conceptual frameworks drive cultural memory studies: (1) lived experiences, (2) the selectivity and identity-related nature of group memory, and (3) the cultural transmission of memory through tradition.[1]

Social groups that experience devastating massacres exit the historical moment with fragile collective memories, described as "having holes in them."[2] Yet after such experiences, cultural memory endures.[3] Survivors revisit social traditions and exchange shared versions of the past in order to create cultural meaning in the present. This lays the foundation for a collective future. Collective memories assist group members in renegotiating group identity through the process of intentional remembering, which allows group members to focus on themselves and to reconstruct their social identities after an atrocity. Intentionally remembering a socially shared past through commemorations, celebrations, festivals, religious holidays, and intergenerational networks of communication facilitates healing and repair and reconciles families and communities to the concept of "home."[4]

Survivors of attempted mass destruction; those who experience displacement, forced migration, and expulsion; members of a community exiled from native lands who afterward live an uncertain existence in refugee camps—all anticipate and yearn for geographical places to call



home. Jewish feminist scholar Julia Epstein speaks to this longing: "It is the concept of home that is torn from victims of genocide and/or [mass atrocities]. . . . [Human rights violations] slice through the continuity of selfhood in a collective way. . . . Under catastrophic historical circumstances, memory becomes a homeland."[5] Forms of cultural remembering are then captured by the "mediality of memory"—books, monuments, statues, museums, television, radio, visual art, music, and other media—which serves collective interests through the group's interactions with a wider world.

In this chapter, I take the position that cultural memory is history as it is remembered, or, said another way, history as cultural remembering, and discuss how traumatic silences and memorial cries have served as raw material for the cultural memories of Jews and African Americans. The ritualization of these cultural memories translates into what cultural and political sociologist Fuyuki Kurasawa calls historic and contemporary rituals of commemoration,[6] which, I propose, signal the chronic subjugation of both ethnic and racial groups. Such rites of cultural memory are illustrated in Elie Wiesel's *Night*, Martin Luther King Jr.'s *Trumpet of Conscience*, and, today, by the Black Lives Matter and Say Her Name campaigns, twin American social and racial justice movements.

Nevertheless, by breaking traumatic silences—by "speaking out"—Jews have historically resisted genocidal violence as embodied in the religious traditions and cultural slogans "never forget" and "never again." For African Americans, memorial cries are also a form of "speaking out." They are social practices of protest that have become a medium for cultural memory and social change.

These ceremonial and transnational social practices serve two purposes. They are rites that humanize Jews and black Americans and have the potential to build stronger relationships between these two groups. Further, these rituals of commemoration are reconciliatory, with the power to enable moral discourse and solidarity with other persecuted and marginalized racial and ethnic groups.

## After Genocide, What Remains?

The term *genocide* was coined by the Polish Jewish lawyer and jurist Raphael Lemkin in *Axis Rule in Occupied Europe*, his 1944 book on Nazi atrocities. In creating the term, Lemkin's focus was on the Nazi campaign to exterminate European Jews, though not exclusively; his worldview was shaped at an early age by the account of the Roman emperor Nero's attempted annihilation of Christians. Leading up to his description of the Nazi campaign in Europe as genocide, Lemkin had studied the mistreatment of social and cultural groups over the centuries—"the Huguenots of France, the Catholics in Japan, Muslims in Spain."[7]



Lemkin concluded that "ethnic destruction was a universal and enduring problem," and he was inspired to become a defender of group rights. His intent was to define "genocide as the destruction of cultural symbols," and he based this definition on the premise that cultural symbols are the lifeline of groups because their function is to bond individuals and reinforce the cosmology, behaviors, and mindset (i.e., the cultural ethos) of the group.[8]

With the introduction of the Nuremberg trials at the end of World War II, Lemkin revised his understanding of genocide. The term was no longer limited to what had happened to the Jewish people; Lemkin broadened the term to include acts committed "with the purpose of destroying [a human group] in whole or in part, or of preventing group preservation or development," which can include murder, extermination, enslavement, deportation, and other inhumane acts against civilian populations.[9] After social groups and communities experience mass violence or attempted genocide, cultural memory is what remains.[10] Elie Wiesel's *Night* captures the beauty, persistence, and enduring nature of Jewish cultural memories in the aftermath of the Holocaust.

## Paradoxical Traumatic Silences in Jewish Cultural Memories

Written in Yiddish, Elie Wiesel's autobiographical account of the Nazi death camps was originally titled *And the World Remained Silent*. "It is obvious that the war which Hitler and his accomplices waged," Wiesel writes, "was a war not only against Jewish men, women, and children but also against Jewish religion, Jewish culture, Jewish tradition, therefore *Jewish memory*" (emphasis added).[11] Silence, secrecy, and shame are attributes of traumatic memory that eventually can undermine *both* victims' *and* perpetrators' responsibility for truth-telling and sharing their stories. All three, whether calculated or inadvertent, can deny social tragedy. Wiesel posits that the silence of God, the rest of the world, and, by implication, even European Jewry as it faced the threat of extinction contributed to the mass victimization of this sociocultural group.

Maurice Halbwachs's three-phase theory about collective (i.e., cultural) memory is applicable to Wiesel's memoir. Halbwachs connects individual and collective memories, proposing that (1) through interaction and communication with others in social settings, collectives shape individual memory, and "therefore through individual acts of memory the collective memory can be observed";[12] (2) family memory requires the oral transmission of stories from eyewitnesses to descendants within an eighty- to one-hundred-year period; these become exchanges of *living memory* even though not all family members have firsthand experience of the past event; (3) intergenerational memory uses the socially shared transmission of stories between generations to relate family members to a past beyond the eighty- to one-hundred-year time period (the stories are recounted from the perspective of the storyteller and supply the meaning he or she is attempting to create and convey); and (4) family and intergenerational memories establish the basis for cultural traditions, moving beyond the realm of *lived memory* and social sharing and into the sphere of *the cultural transmission of memory*.[13] The cultural transmission of memory reaches back thousands of years and is preserved through the development of culturally constructed knowledge and traditions. Wiesel's *Night* exemplifies Halbwachs's and other theories of cultural memory, writ large, because his individual memories function as collective memories that symbolize and communicate the cultural and historical dimensions of European Jewry. European Jews survived and outlived Nazism because of their resilience, acts of heroism, social relationships, and collective traditions, some of which are captured in the practice of religious liturgies and rites, despite their immense and unspeakable suffering under the Nazi death machine.

Throughout his memoir, Wiesel is deliberate about sharing cultural remembrances around traumatic silences. His individual memories and personal narratives about traumatic silences portray silence as one of the book's major themes and consequently promote traumatic silence as both precondition for and feature of social group annihilation. Silences often precede the persecution and mass killing of European Jews. Such silences can be interpreted contextually.

In certain places, traumatic silences serve as positive recall of memory, illustrating group strength against the odds of thriving and surviving under dreadful conditions. At other times, silences reflect group trauma, highlighting Jews' complicity in their fate and thus contributing to their near-genocidal experience. Associated with these silences is the prominence of father-son relationships, which become a pattern for introducing different genres of cultural memory while also capturing the immobility of an entire racial and ethnic group bound *by*, and at times *to*, traumatic silences.



To show the effect of traumatic silence on familial bonds, Wiesel draws upon intergenerational memories, a cross-generational history of immediately past memories that highlight the meaning of the memory for the storyteller. Intergenerational memories and the cultural transmission of memory via religious rites and traditions document the extent to which traumatic silences disrupt family relationships and Jewish communal bonds. Examples include both Wiesel's individual and collective and his father-son intergenerational memories. The father-son relationships in some cases illustrate the ominous nature of silence and how it works negatively on individuals and unravels social bonds in the Jewish community. In other cases, the father-son bond defies threat, elevating Jewish humanity, in spite of what might be a negative end result.

For instance, Wiesel introduces Moishe the Beadle in the first few pages of his text. Moishe is not Wiesel's actual father, of course, but their relationship typifies how father-son relationships sometimes function. Moishe is an oddity in the town of Sighet, Hungary, where Wiesel was born and spent his childhood. Wiesel describes him as utterly poor and awkward and as one "who had mastered the art of rendering himself insignificant, invisible."[14] Because Moishe spent his day in the *shtibl*, the Hasidic house of prayer, he subsequently became Wiesel's guide to Kabbalah, the ancient Jewish mystical study of the Bible. This is after his father had strictly forbidden Wiesel from venturing into such studies before mastering elementary religious subjects. Moishe is expelled from the city and deported alongside other Jews and "foreigners" by the Hungarian government and police.

Although the residents of Sighet quickly forget the deportees, Moishe eventually returns, and in his attempts at heroism he tells Wiesel, his trusted student, and other residents of Sighet about his adventures. In Poland, the cattle train into which the deportees were herded was taken over by the Gestapo, and Moishe was forced into hard labor. He witnessed the murder of fellow prisoners and babies and was left to die after being wounded by a machine gun that, unbeknownst to the Gestapo, only injured his leg. As Moishe and Wiesel participate in cultural remembering, Moishe, whose eyes lose their brilliance, weeps and pleads:

> "Jews, listen to me! That's all I ask of you. No money. No pity. Just listen to me!" he kept shouting in synagogue, between the prayer at dusk and the evening prayer. . . . "You don't understand," he said in despair. "You cannot understand. I was saved miraculously. I succeeded in coming back. Where did I get my strength? I wanted to return to Sighet to describe to you my death so that you might ready yourselves while there is still time. Life? I no longer care to live. I am alone. But I wanted to come back to warn you. Only no one is listening." (7)

In due course, Moishe falls "traumatically silent" because he tires of warning the townspeople, who do not listen. Wiesel concludes his memory of Moishe, describing him as one who "would drift through synagogue or through the streets, hunched over, eyes cast down, avoiding people's gaze" (8).

By the spring of 1944, German soldiers had entered the town of Sighet. The townsfolk had not only silenced Moishe but failed to heed his warning, I suggest, because they were in denial about an unavoidable and dismal future. The community's silencing of Moishe and denial of imminent events become a precondition for European Jewish annihilation. When the Hungarian police finally burst into the community at the command of the German soldiers, the Jewish people of Sighet are ordered to wear the yellow Star of David—the initial mark for extermination.

The next scenario in *Night* involves an actual father-son relationship. Rabbi Eliahu, a beloved rabbi from Poland, becomes separated from his son while they are forced to move in a line at the Buna concentration camp. In Wiesel's recollection, Rabbi Eliahu and his son had for three years in the camps "stayed close to one another. Side by side, they had endured the suffering, the blows; they had waited for their ration of bread and they had prayed. Three years, from camp to camp, from selection to selection. And now—when the end seemed near—fate had separated them" (91). Later, the reader learns that Rabbi Eliahu's son "had seen him losing ground, sliding back to the rear of the column. He had seen him. And he had continued to run in front, letting the distance between them become greater" (91). Rabbi Eliahu's case represents the incongruity—the paradox—of traumatic silences.

For father and son to brave extreme misery and suffering for three years suggests a silence characterized as "resistant." Social action and coordinated activities are not the sole measures of resistance when people and social groups face crises. Father and son worked as a team to resist unyielding adversity. Silently, father and son withstood death to embrace survival; silently, they rebuffed Nazism's inhumanity and maintained a semblance of dignity and self-respect; silently, for three years, they combatted harsh conditions and insults by exhibiting self-regard and self-worth. Three years of trauma endured together through daily acts of living produced a silent resistance.



However, there is a poignant irony behind the resistant yet "traumatic silence" shared by the father and son. Rabbi Eliahu whispers to the young Wiesel that he has lost sight of his son as he falls to the rear of the column of running men. In Wiesel's cultural memory, he realizes that Rabbi Eliahu's son *did* see his father falling behind the pack, but the son decides to "silently" run ahead, allowing the distance between him and his father to become greater. Surmising that Rabbi Eliahu's son left his father behind in order to preserve his own life, Wiesel prays, "Oh God, Master of the Universe, give me the strength never to do what Rabbi Eliahu's son has done" (91). Here, the incongruous nature of "traumatic silences" represents stoical resistance to human depravity and capitulation to the absolutism of Nazi tyranny, forcing Rabbi Eliahu's son to choose between life and death—to value his life over his father's. His silence and inaction as his father falls behind raise ethical questions about the value of human life: Whose life is more valuable? Those deemed weak or those deemed strong? On what grounds do we decide whose lives are more valuable? Choosing to save one's own life might cause others to die. In so doing, "traumatic silence" enables the mistreatment of others.

Wiesel also relates the story of Meir Katz and his son by recalling an intergenerational memory and showing the effect of traumatic silence on this father-son relationship. Katz's son was murdered during the first selection at Auschwitz. Burdened by the weight of this knowledge about his son, Katz held this information, closely and silently, guarding it until he was no longer able to advance in his duties at Buna. Katz buckles under the pressures of Nazism, unleashing a deluge of tears, knowing "he had reached the end" (102). In order to survive, Meir Katz is bound *to* traumatic silence; his actions are willful because any sign of weakness would have hastened his own death. Being bound *to* traumatic silence, however, does not obviate an encounter with death.

Rather than say Kaddish upon his son's death, Meir Katz embraces the "traumatic silence" forced on him by Nazi oppression; he is compelled to withhold the expressive outcry and lamentation of the Kaddish. The Kaddish is typically said at religious funerals; it is a mourning ritual that strengthens communal bonds, reinforces Jewish religious commitment, and cements the cultural traditions central to Jewish social identity. Genocide attempts to dismantle group culture, ethos, symbols. Meir Katz's silence—his inability to mourn his son by practicing an established cultural tradition—becomes one way in which the Holocaust succeeded in Jewish persecution. The deformation of Jewish cultural practices and traditions was a precursor to the group's demise.



In a twist of irony, Katz does finally break his silence, not conceding total control of his selfhood to his oppressor. His lamentations, under unyielding circumstances, translate into a reformation of a cultural practice. Wiesel writes that on the last day of their travels (to Buchenwald), "The lament spread from wagon to wagon. It was contagious. And now hundreds of cries rose at once. The death rattle of an entire convoy with the end approaching. All boundaries had been crossed. Nobody had any strength left. And the night seemed endless. Meir Katz was moaning" (103). Alongside his comrades, Meir Katz mourns. Such lamentations forcibly introduce a modicum of control over what has been, up to that point, a seemingly inexorable fate. Though a reconstructed religious and cultural tradition breaks the silence and foregrounds their fate, mourning nonetheless also ends in silence, by the ultimate silencer—death.

Like these father-son relationships, Wiesel's bond with his own father is tested by traumatic silence. In their last encounter, Wiesel remembers his father begging for water:

> "My, son, water . . . I'm burning up . . . my insides . . ."
>
> "Silence over there!" barked the officer.
>
> "Eliezer," continued my father, "water . . ."
>
> The officer came closer and shouted to him to be silent.
>
> But my father did not hear. He continued to call me. The officer wielded his club and dealt him a violent blow to the head.
>
> I didn't move. I was afraid, my body was afraid of another blow, this time to *my* head. My father groaned once more, I heard: "Eliezer . . ."
>
> His last word had been my name. He had called out to me and I had not answered. (111–12)

Wiesel implicates his own *traumatic silence* as the cause of his inhumanity toward his father, captured in an individual memory where he emphasizes his unresponsiveness to his ailing father's plea for water. The pleas of a dying father call for a reaction—even if that reaction is only to say goodbye.

The plea for water should have provoked a verbal exchange between father and son, but the only voice recorded is Wiesel's father's, begging his son to quench his thirst.

A few pages before this final encounter with his father, Wiesel remembers a verbal exchange in which he grudgingly gives his father his last morsels of bread and half a bowl of soup after learning that this sickly man has had nothing to eat in the five hours since his son, working in the labor camp, has seen him. Foreshadowing their final encounter, Wiesel declares, "Just like Rabbi Eliahu's son, I had not passed the test" (107). In describing both memories, Wiesel makes a truthful and lasting statement about human nature: that desperate times often call for desperate measures. He also points out the shortfall of human desperation as expressed through the behavior it may elicit—inhumanity toward other humans. That his traumatic silence is complicated by his despair at being subjected to Nazi cruelty does not excuse his inhumane treatment of his father; instead, it becomes a precondition for his father's death.



Wiesel also uses the silence of the father-son relationship to illustrate Jewish social memory, defined as how social groups and societies remember. One way in which social memory functions is by giving voice to the collective experience.[15] Wiesel addresses Jewish social memory in order to invoke a "sociology of moral responsibility," or principles and procedures that allow groups to deal with past crimes, including public acts of apology like repentance, forgiveness, and restitution, represented, for instance, by the Truth and Reconciliation Commission established after the abolition of apartheid in South Africa. A "sociology of moral responsibility" not only links social memory to past injustices and to attempts on the part of the injured to reconcile themselves with their pasts[16] but also ensures moral discourse that addresses how group pain and mass suffering are treated in public venues. Yet Wiesel's brief for a sociology of moral responsibility unfolds in unexpected ways. *Who* he ultimately blames for Jewish annihilation in the Holocaust is not only surprising but somewhat unsettling.

Readers of *Night* first encounter Eliezer Wiesel as a pious and observant Jewish boy. As a child, Wiesel is a Hasidic Jew who diligently studies the Torah and Talmud and wants to pursue Jewish mysticism through the study of Kabbalah. Jan Assmann describes "mnemohistory" as a subdiscipline of history that sees cultural memory through the lens of the past as it is remembered.[17] As Wiesel struggles with the notion of traumatic silence, he also participates in a form of cultural remembering that connects his family to the wider Jewish community by a history of mentalities and ideas. That is the thought behind mnemohistory.

This form of history as cultural remembering traces the Wiesel family's forced movement out of their home and into the ghettoes with other Jewish families. It catalogs the family's split and their unanticipated separation from one another, sees them herded into cattle cars alongside both competitors and comrades, and describes their deportation to Auschwitz, Buna, and Buchenwald.



These events strain not only the relationship between Wiesel and his father, but also between Wiesel and his heavenly father, God. Wiesel builds up such resentment and disdain for God, his seemingly impotent father, that he "no longer accepted God's silence" (69). He willfully resolves not to observe the High Holy Days that mark the beginning of the New Year, Rosh Hashanah and the Day of Atonement and repentance, Yom Kippur. "I was no longer able to lament," he writes. "On the contrary, I felt very strong. I was the accuser, God the accused. My eyes had opened and I was alone, terribly alone in a world without God, without man. Without love or mercy. I was nothing but ashes now, but I felt myself to be stronger than this Almighty to whom my life had been bound for so long. In the midst of these men assembled for prayer, I felt like an observer, a stranger" (68).

Reimagining the father-son relationship means having to reenvision the Jewish community's relationship with God during a trying historical period when Jewish lives are upended and burned to ashes because of their religion, cultural identity, and ethnicity. God's traumatic silence, which Wiesel portrays as social memory, not only reflects Wiesel's broken relationship with God but also symbolizes the distance that many others in the social collective had felt because of God's abandonment. In this place, God's desertion becomes a precondition and a feature of group annihilation.

Finally, the traumatic silences characteristic of the father-son relationships in Weisel's memoir capture a transcultural memory, pointing out the silence of governmental leaders throughout much of the world in the face of the Holocaust and other World War II social atrocities, which included the sexual enslavement of women in Japanese territories and the internment of Japanese Americans in the United States, to name just two. While transcultural memory is a type of global memory and illustrates how collective memory is affected by economic and cultural globalization, transcultural memory, unlike global memory, moves away from geographical sites and attends to the movement of memory across time and space.[18] Michael Rothberg, in a seminal text on the nature of "multidirectional memory," suggests that comparing collective memories does not have to elicit intergroup competition based on the extent and extremity of suffering.[19] Rather, multidirectional memory opens up public dialogical spaces in which oppressed groups can frame visions of justice.

Because multidirectional memory is "precisely that convoluted, sometimes historically unjustified [anachronistic], back-and-forth movement of seemingly distant collective memories in and out of public consciousness," it also qualifies as a distinctive aspect of transcultural memory.[20] By way of illustration, in the summer of 2015, one of my students, Tricia Hersey, joined a team of journalists, church leaders, and educators from Chicago called Abraham's Promise, which embarked on a listening and lecture tour that took them to fourteen cities in Israel and Palestine.[21]



Reflecting on her travels, Tricia wrote:

> I was in Palestine to study Palestinian liberation theology with a human rights group. I visited the Holocaust Museum for an entire day and wept with hundreds while experiencing each installation. In a very crowded space, I waited my turn behind a Jewish family to read a timeline of the extermination process. One of the steps was segregating Jews to live in ghettos as they awaited transport to concentration camps. The grandmother stared at the exhibit and began to cry silently. As she gathered herself to move away she looked at her daughter and said, "This is just like what has happened to blacks in America. It's the same story almost." I remember being so floored that I immediately pulled my journal from my purse and wrote down what I just witnessed. This is multidirectional, [transcultural] and borrowing. One choked cry brings up another choked cry in a different group. My place within a group that has experienced oppression and violence colors and drives my empathy for others who have experienced trauma. There is silent solidarity in our pains.[22]

Tricia simultaneously experienced transcultural and multidirectional memory in this cultural encounter in Israel. This Jewish grandmother's Holocaust memory, provoked by the exhibit, curiously and effectively became a portal back to sixteenth-to-nineteenth-century American slavery. Her cultural remembering immediately connected her to Tricia, a young African American woman who in that moment also juxtaposed cultural memories of black American enslavement with a Holocaust memory.[23] The scenario suggests transcultural memory because of the historical and geographical distance between American institutional slavery, the Holocaust, and modern-day Palestine and Israel, and the moment in which both women are viewing the exhibit's installations. The multidirectionality of cultural remembering forges a relationship between both groups' histories of victimization, based on the collective and historical remembrances of both women.

Wiesel adds multiple layers of complexity to his treatment of silence. He illustrates, through cultural memory, that "silence," especially when the result of trauma, is a socializing force that can humanize a subpopulation working to resist but on the brink of social group degradation. Nonetheless, silence, in containing a people's fear and anxiety, paradoxically has the potential to communicate complicity in a perpetrator's willful wrongdoing. Whether contestation or complicity, traumatic silence can lead to mass destruction. *Night* ends on a somber note, with Wiesel recognizing a grave reality, ever mindful that traumatic silence arrests social progress. Its transcultural nature is most evident in Wiesel's 1986 Nobel Peace Prize–winning speech, in which he asks, "How could the world remain silent?"[24] This question persists even today.

In posing this question, Wiesel, I am convinced, is remembering a younger self, the son, who over the course of years has repeatedly put this question to many, including his older self, the father. Confession becomes the only adequate response to such a question. When U.S. policymakers and allies remain silent in the face of social trauma caused by unjust killings and deadly violence, whether in the Bosnian genocide or the Kosovo War between Serbs and Albanians of the 1990s (both prompted by racial, ethnic, and religious animus); when an eight-year Syrian civil war claims the lives of hundreds of thousands because the government uses chemical weapons on civilians; when the rise in ultra-nationalistic forms of populism denigrates migrants, immigrants, and ethnic and racial minorities, narrowly defines social and national identity, and prompts violence toward religious and cultural groups, as in Europe and the United States; when neighbors remain silent as they witness the slaughter of fellow citizens and friends, stoked by language that creates political divisions between Christians and Muslims and divides an English-speaking minority from a French-speaking majority, as in Nigeria and Cameroon; when most international leaders remain silent as growing numbers of civil war refugees flee across borders to avoid proximate genocide, as in the present situation in Afghanistan, Syria, Myanmar, Venezuela, and the Sudan, what appears is "a dance of death." "Death . . . was settling in all around me, silently, gently," writes Wiesel. "One died because one had to" (89).

Silence, inaction, and nonintervention in social conflicts that amount to mass murder have largely characterized the global reaction to human and social atrocities; the initial international response during the Jewish Holocaust and immediately afterward was no different. The European Jewish experience of almost complete annihilation exposed the world's general tolerance of human depravity. The case is not exceptional—rather, it is the rule.

Wiesel wrestles in *Night* with the implications of silence—both good and bad. "Good" silence produces stalwart resisters and "bad" silence creates victims. European Jews' experience of the silence of the rest of the world, the perceived silence of God, and the immobility ensuing from their own traumatic silence threatened the identity and survival of this ethnic group. In addition, the Jewish diaspora was bound *by* silence in the shadow and aftermath of the Holocaust. Wiesel strives to convey the damage that can befall social groups if people remain silent and inactive when confronted by evil, thus pronouncing what can be considered the paradox of traumatic silence in Jewish cultural memories. While Wiesel ruminates on the "good" and "bad" of traumatic silences, it is striking that he also "speaks out," attesting to Jewish cultural memories of the Holocaust. But if traumatic silence is the hallmark of Jewish cultural memory, then so is the protest tradition of memorial cries, a reservoir of African American history and cultural memories.



## Memorial Cries: Reservoirs of African American Cultural Memories

History is pivotal to cultural memory studies because memory can "recast history," conferring new meanings on historical and past life events in the present.[25] With history foregrounded, cultural memory studies capably enlarge "ethnic group consciousness of the past." That is a critical exercise for interpreting and understanding present "ethnic, religious, and racial identities."[26] Before we consider the memorial cries of black America, modeled today by the Black Lives Matter and Say Her Name movements, let us turn to the past to anchor and to interpret the ways in which memorial cries are part of a tradition of African American social protest that has become one reservoir of black American cultural memory.

Gayraud Wilmore described Martin Luther King Jr. as "the high priest of the religion of the civil rights movement,"[27] a fitting characterization for a man born into the black experience of American segregation, birthed out of the black church tradition, a man whose coming of age catapulted him to the forefront of the American civil rights movement in the 1950s and 1960s. A civil rights activist, King was also a thought leader and a proponent of American democracy.[28] Three American founding documents, the

Declaration of Independence, the Constitution, and the Emancipation Proclamation, motivated King's articulation of the "American Dream" at the March on Washington in 1963.

Anchoring this "dream" were democratic notions of freedom, a tradition of inviolable (i.e., sacred) personal rights, and a belief in the worth of all human beings. By laying claim to the American Dream, King linked black America's lineage and heritage to America's settlement and founding. In doing so, he demonstrated what scholars of literature and cultural memory Aleida and Jan Assmann identify as foundational "cultural" memory. According to their theory, memory based on a distant past associated with origins and representing foundational history and collective knowledge also bonds and solidifies the identity of groups.[29] King's clever reversal of 1960s social thought and norms indirectly anticipates the Assmanns' theory, especially when he dismantled "blackness" as a construct—a racial designation—and replaced it with "Americanness," a nationality that white America equated with building the nation.

Nevertheless, the mistreatment of African Americans exposed the contradiction between their lived social realities and these three sacred documents, challenging King with a moral dilemma. American racial injustice (i.e., racism) was the crucible out of which King emerged as a social change agent, as the country witnessed and was compelled to listen to the memorial cries of African Americans as social protest and a sign of their subjugation. Memorial cries became the seedbed for public memories.

Civil rights activists fashioned a societal narrative about how the country and the rest of the world should view, interact with, and relate to blacks in America. Public memory dictated that society continuously relate to blacks in America as a marginalized and inferior group. Given de facto and de jure segregation, memorial cries begged for a "sociology of moral responsibility," while public memories negatively "related the memories of slavery to the development of black collective identity,"[30] reinforcing black people's lowly position in America's social hierarchy, and cementing the problem of a Du Boisian white-black color line that spurred an unresolvable double consciousness.

Though blacks confronted nationwide racial injustice in the 1950s and 1960s, the "democratization of the South" was King's primary project, a tool for improving black-white race relations and for precipitating systemic change.[31] Southern streets became the backdrop for campaigns coalescing around nonviolence, a term developed by Mohandas K. Gandhi, based on the Jain religious principle *ahimsa*, the "non-injury of created life." In the

South, crowds of blacks (and small groups of white allies) rallied, protested, marched, sat-in, waded-in, freedom-rode and demonstrated for the attainment of basic civil, constitutional, and political rights like the right to vote.

These African American memorial cries created a social memory that refused to ignore or dismiss America's prejudicial attitudes toward its darker-skinned citizens. Social memory, in this case, "identifies a group, giving it a sense of its past while defining its aspirations for the future," according to Astrid Erll.[32] America's portraiture and constructed social memory of blacks from emancipation into the 1960s can be aptly described as paradoxical. Economic, political, and social conditions in America forced blacks, as a people up from slavery, to continually hold dehumanizing experiences and deferred dreams in tension with hopes for equity, advancement, and a promising future.



King was keenly aware of an "agony of deprivation" that continued to stymie American progress and the advancement of people of color around the world.[33] This "agony of deprivation" produced memorial cries that triggered black rioting in northern U.S. cities in the late 1960s and threatened America's poor, prompting King and the Southern Christian Leadership Conference to organize the 1968 Poor People's Campaign for economic justice. "Agonies of deprivation" ignited memorial cries that heralded King's final statement about issues critical to him before he was assassinated in 1968.

*The Trumpet of Conscience* was King's final volume of essays written before he was murdered. These essays were critical social commentary on national and global issues pertinent to him. In the volume, he critiques American race relations, questions the morality of war, and analyzes society's indifference to poverty. The memorial cries of African Americans as an oppressed people amounted to a trumpet of conscience for King, who wrote, "developing a sense of black consciousness and peoplehood does not require that we scorn the white race as a whole. It is not the race per se that we fight but the policies and ideology that leaders of that race have formulated to perpetuate oppression."[34] King points out here that Anglo-Americans as a race are not the problem; the problem is the harmful social policies instituted by a white ruling class and white elites. Those policies were stunting the progress and development of people of color, especially blacks, and that was very problematic.

Although memorial cries called forth race consciousness, between 1955 and 1965 the social and political conditions of African Americans had only barely and superficially improved. Blacks in America received the right to vote, legal segregation of interstate bus travel and public restrooms was dismantled, and educational advancement and access to jobs were on the horizon, albeit nominally. Southerners were the primary beneficiaries of these legislative advances. King, however, faulted tokenism for the slow advancement of black people throughout the country. Inequality still reigned supreme across America, and it typified the black social experience.



During that period, northern blacks quickly became outraged by endless racial inequity, seen in high levels of poverty, low employment and job security, unequal education, housing discrimination, and the creation of black ghettoes. King blamed racist public and legislative policies and the refusal of white lawmakers to accept or promote radical structural change.[35] Oppressive living conditions precipitated black rebellion in northern inner cities. Blacks were blamed for the destruction of their communities, lawlessness, and disrupting social order. As is still the case today, many white Americans quickly came to see them as a menace to society intent upon destroying their own communities.

Instead of implicating an unyielding white power structure that maintained repressive policies, most white observers blamed the black and brown victims of an unjust and violent American sociopolitical system for the frustration that boiled over into open revolt. The protests and rebellion of the late 1960s hearkens back to W. E. B. Du Bois's question, posed in 1903: "How does it feel to be a problem?"[36] Despite some social and political gains, African Americans were still viewed as a "problem people," as Cornel West observes.[37] This is implied in King's assessment of the northern situation at the time, in which the social beliefs, policies, and racist structures in American society persisted, giving blacks, and especially poor black youths, no room to grow, move, breathe, or even exist.

### Choked Cries: Bearing With(ness) as a Transnational Social Practice of Empathy

The memorial cries of black youth in the 1960s have become the choked cries of early twenty-first-century millennial black youth culture. In the summer of 2014, the deaths of Michael Brown (by police shooting) and Eric Garner (by police chokehold) sparked nationwide demonstrations because of the failure of each grand jury to indict any of the white officers involved in the deaths. Social media users were instrumental in popularizing Garner's final words, "I can't breathe"—literal *choked cries* that have since become memorial cries for all black victims of overpolicing from the 1980s to the present, whose lives ended because of excessive and unwarranted police brutality. For participants in the Black Lives Matter movement, "I can't breathe" is a popular refrain bellowed at rallies to voice dissatisfaction with the excessive use of force by police in their encounters with ethnic and racial minorities, particularly young black men.

Police violence toward black women also became more widely acknowledged because of the publicity surrounding the death of Black Lives Matter campaigner Sandra Bland, who was pulled over by police for failure to signal a lane change.[38] Say Her Name has become the gender-inclusive racial justice movement partner of Black Lives Matter. Say Her Name coalesced around police use of lethal force against black women, whose stories are frequently left out of public discourses about the systemic police killings of black people.[39]



Choked cries of "We can't breathe" encapsulate much of what it means to be black in America, particularly for the poor. "We can't breathe" is shorthand that embraces the plight of diverse other subpopulations suffocating from social inequity and injustice, both in the United States and abroad. When these choked cries morph into memorial cries of social protest, they burgeon into transnational social practices that bear witness to the death of victims of state violence.

Sociologist Fuyuki Kurasawa writes about bearing witness as a "transnational mode of ethico-political labour" practiced by persons, social groups, and "communicative actors" (i.e., multilateral organizations, political networks, nongovernmental organizations, social movements, and overseas governments) that either have experienced extreme suffering or have become eyewitnesses to structural and systemic violence against others.[40] Bearing witness is not simply a historical exercise; it is social and religious practice as well as political and ethical behavior.

African Americans can offer Jewish people and other oppressed groups the "gift and power of the [choked] cry," memorial cries of protest testifying to the historical and cultural traditions of American blacks whose religiously rooted racial justice movements have assumed the form of outcries for social change. Out of this tradition and practice of memorial cries is born the current social activism of millennial and post–civil rights generations. These intergenerational groups empathize with the current pain and suffering of disenfranchised black Americans, disenfranchisement caused by unjust social, political, and economic conditions that result from structural racism.

Like the black youth of King's day, marginalized young blacks today rebel against a system ignorant of and inflexible regarding their economic deprivation, unemployment and underemployment, discrimination, undereducation, and police violence fueled by institutional and social inequities and eventually replicating generational social death.

With respect to social death,[41] young black men and women are disproportionately being incarcerated and killed at the hands of law enforcement officials who use excessive force as a form of social control. Social death is a consequence of their being dismissed and devalued. Though born on American soil, they are nevertheless alienated from birth, stripped of an identity that should brim with promise yet in fact offers limited future possibilities and little hope because of aggressive and inescapable forms of systemic violence. Revolts led by black youth in places like Ferguson, Missouri, Baltimore, Maryland, and Chicago, Illinois, have resulted in the destruction of businesses and properties in their own communities. And like the blacks King described in the 1960s, these young black people are implicated as both cause and effect of their own suffering, thus deflecting attention from the real source—an intransigent racialized social and political system that renders them invisible and thus of no value.

Demonstrators who become eyewitnesses to their pain respond to the social ferment by agitating for wide-ranging national and social changes, staging die-ins, rallies, and marches, and using social media platforms like Twitter and Facebook to spread their message. Accordingly, memorial cries of social protest bear witness to past distress that inflicts traumatic wounds. Theologian Shelly Rambo argues that trauma is the "wound" that remains after a life-altering encounter with death.[42]

Although the encounter might not result in literal death, the aftereffects and what remains constitute a fundamentally different view of life—a shattered perspective, inextricably linking life and death, making room for the possibility of future suffering.[43] Eyewitnesses are either themselves traumatized persons or those left behind who listen for the choked cries of survival from open wounds.[44] They testify to what survives—what remains—after the trauma; ergo, cultural remembrance is the debris removed from the wound.

Memorial cries also demand the supportive posture of a "witness," or what theologian Flora Keshgegian calls a "withness," who survives despite the pain, in defiance of far-reaching persecution, even when the victims are dead. Keshgegian describes the "withness" as a "witness [who] remembers." "When someone can look at wounds," she writes, "and want to tend to them, and when someone will express outrage and cries for justice and making right that gets forever caught in throats long tightened by silence and choked cries, the thread [i.e., the life connection] is strengthened."[45]

Black Lives Matter and Say Her Name campaigners bear with(ness), testifying to memories of torment and death caused by police brutality. They are a community of witnesses to the pain and suffering of victims of police violence and other systemic injustices, who testify in the following three ways. First, they acknowledge victims *and* survivors as they chant the mantras "Black Lives Matter" and "Say Her Name." Second, by translating choked cries from "a language of the unsayable"[46] into memorial cries, protesters create empathic connections to the outside world on behalf of black victims, recognizing that these lives are irreplaceable.



With respect to the cultivation of empathy through transnational testimonial practices, Kurasawa writes, "Although we should be wary of sentimentalizing limit-experiences, the phenomenologically thick descriptions of mass suffering contained in testimonial accounts expose audiences to the plight of distant strangers and can thereby awaken a sense of compassion (Alexander, 2002: 34–37; Rorty, 1989: 94). By reconstructing the socio-historical setting of a given catastrophe and the lifeworld of affected persons and groups, these accounts aim to draw audiences in, to provisionally dwell in the emotional, mental, physical and spiritual universes of survivors and victims."[47] Empathy, in this context, cannot be achieved without acknowledging the injustice of police brutality. Empathy is made apparent as a watching audience bears witness to this social havoc, not merely by paying lip service but by taking public, social, and political action.[48]

Toni Morrison's concept of "disremembering" can be applied here, because it cultivates empathy by using, in Julia Epstein's words, "a post-calamity language required to decipher the language of the scars left by collective, genocidal trauma."[49] Morrison addresses the paradox of traumatic cultural remembering articulated by the character Sethe in *Beloved.* The scars on the formerly enslaved Sethe's back are a physical reminder of the violence perpetrated on her body and its long-lasting aftereffects. The scars prevent her from ever forgetting, even though forgetting the trauma of the merciless whipping is necessary to her story if she is ever to move toward true liberation.

After a traumatic experience, disremembering is somaticized memory, in which the body registers collective trauma and remembers.[50] Disremembering (i.e., remembering forgetfully) nurtures empathy by remembering the trauma and giving witnesses the opportunity to mourn and to process the meaning of the scars. For Black Lives Matter and Say Her Name protesters, the scars left behind are dead black bodies that bear witness to the unconscionable acts of law enforcement authorities whose violence toward these bodies also leave marks on the community. The scars call forth an American history in which black bodies have been subjected to the race-based state violence of hunting, lynching, water hoses, and attack dogs.



Disremembering charges the American public with never forgetting this history, for as Epstein declares, "History is truly [a] way of saying Kaddish for the dead." Dead black bodies that remain in the aftermath of police violence are also a way for Black Lives Matter and Say Her Name demonstrators to disremember the victims in the absence of words. That happens by ironically "reinstating [the dead] as embodied selves because the [eyewitnesses] remember [i.e., the victim's] disremembering."[51] Protesters ultimately establish the atmosphere for empathy by grieving the numerous losses, disremembering and speaking life into a crowded void the names of once embodied selves, selves whose dead bodies initiated Black Lives Matter and Say Her Name.[52] Names and disremembered bodies are scattered throughout the nation. Here are some of their names.

2012: Trayvon Martin (Sanford, Florida)
2013: Renisha McBride (Dearborn Heights, Michigan)
2014: Tamir Rice (Cleveland, Ohio)
2014: Akai Gurley (Brooklyn, New York)
2014: Ramarley Graham (Bronx, New York)
2014: Michael Brown (Ferguson, Missouri)
2014: Eric Garner (Staten Island, New York)
2014: Yvette Smith (Bastrop, Texas)
2014: Jordan Baker (Houston, Texas)
2014: Laquan McDonald (Chicago, Illinois)
2015: Sandra Bland (Dallas, Texas)
2015: Freddie Gray (Baltimore, Maryland)
2016: Alton Sterling (Baton Rouge, Louisiana)
2016: Philando Castile (St. Paul, Minnesota)
2016: Terence Crutcher (Tulsa, Oklahoma)
2016: Jamarion Robinson (East Point, Georgia)
2018: Emantic "EJ" Fitzgerald Bradford Jr. (Hoover, Alabama)
2018: Jemel Roberson (Oak Lawn, Illinois)
2019: Eric Logan (South Bend, Indiana)
2019: JaQuavion Slaton (Fort Worth, Texas)
2019: Ryan Twyman (Los Angeles, California)
2019: Brandon Webber (Memphis, Tennessee)

Third, the memorial cries of protesters bear "withness" to black resiliency despite continuous and widespread discrimination in America. Such historical outcries for social change aim to shift the discussion from black death to the merits of preserving black life by demanding public policy changes that will demilitarize police and end the harassment and racial profiling of black and brown bodies. The millennial generation's memorial cries bring attention to grassroots activism bent on ending the school-to-prison pipeline, especially in a society where only 20 percent of African Americans get a four-year college degree, compared to more than 32 percent of white Americans.[53]

These memorial cries tackle negative stereotypes of black women by appreciating the ways in which race, gender, sexuality, and socioeconomic class reinforce negative perceptions that unleash deadly force against gendered, raced, sexed, and lower-classed black bodies. In all of these ways, memorial cries of social protest bear "withness" to large-scale black dehumanization. They are also social practices of empathy and communal healing that open the way to moral discourse in transnational public spaces about black America and other groups that have been subjected to genocidal, lethal, and unjust treatment.



Memorial cries are outcries of millennial black youths and other generations—a form of "speaking out" and breaking the silence around black pain, injustice, and suffering. Rooted in African American religious and cultural traditions of remembering and social protest, these memorial cries function in the same way that Jewish religious and cultural traditions of "never forgetting" do, as a transnational social practice of cultural remembering and bearing witness.

### "Never Forget"

"Remembering and forgetting are the two sides—or different processes—of the same coin, that is, memory," Erll writes.[54] As Wiesel puts it in *Night*:

> The topic of Auschwitz has become part of mainstream culture. . . . This may be because the public knows that the number of survivors is shrinking daily, and is fascinated by the idea of sharing memories that will soon be lost. For in the end, *it is all about memory*, its sources and its magnitude, and, of course, its consequences.
>
> For the survivor who chooses to testify, it is clear: his duty is to bear witness for the dead *and* for the living. He has no right to deprive future generations of a past that belongs to our collective memory. To forget would be not only dangerous but offensive; to forget the dead would be akin to killing them a second time. (15; emphasis added)

Wiesel defies the process of forgetting by remembering—breaking silences to recall a traumatic past—and by re-membering, selecting particular accounts of the past as it is remembered, in order to pay tribute to the living and the dead.

Forgetting is risky because it insulates groups from the unfathomable aspects of their group memories and histories. For Wiesel, forgetting is treacherous because it dishonors the dead. Though remembering binds survivors to the trauma, re-membering carves out a space for conversation between present and past generations and provides a place for the "circulation of testimonies about global injustices."[55]

Wiesel talks about "remembering" as a process "not meant to enshrine a memorial but to point to and affect present action," as Keshgegian puts it.[56] Kurasawa, as we have seen, interprets bearing witness (i.e., remembering) as a social and religious practice as well as a political and ethical action. As a "transnational mode of ethico-political labour," bearing witness demands that people and groups become eyewitnesses to structural violence toward others and that they remember such systemic violence.

Wiesel assumes that the duty of "never forgetting" is a global practice. As an eyewitness to the horrors of the Holocaust, he rejects the simplistic notions of traumatic silence that essentialize the father-son relationships in *Night*. Further, by participating in the transnational social practice of remembering in a public forum and in breaking his own silence, he lays a foundation for empathy for European (and diasporic) Jews in recognizing them and their social tragedy. He connects the Jewish experience, stories, and cultural memories to a wider network of groups who have faced similar horrors.

Moreover, Wiesel involves himself in the ethico-political labor of bearing witness by creating empathy for Jews in depicting the tenderness of the familial bond displayed by fathers and sons in extreme and harsh conditions. Wiesel also fosters empathy by writing about the raw emotions triggered as "sons abandoned their fathers to death" (92) and exposing their struggles with mortality and their desperate and uncommunicated pleas that they be allowed to live.

Empathy, in this context, cannot be achieved without acknowledging the catastrophic moments in the Holocaust-haunted cultural memories of European Jews, or without realizing the tenderness that marked family and community life *before* and *after* such mass suffering and social devastation. In this case, cultural remembering demands the transnational practice of breaking silence—of speaking out, of hearing victims and survivors. Both are forms of bearing witness that function to "never forget." Ultimately, the late Elie Wiesel, a renowned professor, writer, political activist, and Holocaust survivor, bears witness and establishes empathy for Jewish people by culturally remembering the traumatic silences.

Kurasawa advances a well-placed caution about the "constitutive paradox of bearing witness as a transnational form of ethico-political labour," one that easily applies to the traditions and social practices of "never forgetting" and "never again." Eyewitnesses to mass human destruction have often been met with "bystander apathy"—a lack of involvement by nations, governmental leaders, institutions, and citizens who fail to end the suffering, persecution, and genocide of targeted populations.[57] Nevertheless, "never again" as a social practice of bearing witness remains globally visible, prominent—and lasting.



Adopted by and adapted to the traditions of numerous cultural, social, and political groups, "never forget" articulates and elevates cultural memories, bearing witness to specific instances of social havoc. "Never forget" and "never again" are transnational global practices of bearing witness rooted in a distinct Jewish history, yet are reminiscent of universal histories of the attempted obliteration of racial, ethnic, and cultural groups. Jewish people can share "never forget" and "never again" with African Americans who are often pressed to forget their past of American slavery, segregation, and other social and political violations. Such violations continue to define, shape, and plague this social group and to influence their cultural representations around the world. By sharing the concept of "never forget," Jews participate with African Americans in establishing a "relationality" that can be advantageous to both groups.

### Traumatic Relationality: Forging New Relationships Through Rituals of Commemoration

Shelly Rambo proposes that while trauma is an encounter with death, cultural memories give evidence of the life that remains in the aftermath of a traumatic social affliction.[58] Survivors become witnesses even if they have not experienced but only carry knowledge about the event into the future. Witnesses' memorial cries and their tradition of "never forgetting" are social practices of empathy in transnational public spaces that possess the ability to forge new relationships (i.e., traumatic relationality). Those who survive and live in the aftermath of cultural trauma gain the opportunity to rewrite history, reconstruct memory, and live life anew.

The memorial cries of "we can't breathe," "black lives matter," and "say her name" emerged at the intersection of death and life; these cries that arise from an open wound are cries for sweeping social change. These cries derived from religiously rooted traditions hearken back to African American historical cries of social protest. These memorial cries demand public acknowledgment. They are gifts of lamentation, and they invite others to raise their voices in public and to cry alongside the victimized and the community.

The transnational practice of bearing witness to the Jews killed in the Holocaust also contributes to establishing traumatic relationality. As Epstein writes, "Remembering figures importantly in Jewish religious practice. . . . Once a year at Passover, Jews not only remember the exodus from Egypt but are also enjoined to reexperience the exodus as though each had been there personally."[59] Thus the message "never forget," derived from a rich Jewish cultural and religious heritage, testifies to breaking silence. Breaking silence resists and opposes genocidal violence and death, a ripping that empowers and connects the past to future diasporic generations of Jews.

"Never forget" links history to memory as collaborative and integrative partners.[60] Forgetting is as much a part of remembering as the selectivity of what is remembered is. The selectivity of memory requires history to balance memory, to ground cultural remembering in a social history meant to deter the distortion of the facts. What we know, therefore, is that the Holocaust is a historical fact. It did happen, although Wiesel recounts that fact as memoir.

"Never forget" also identifies survivors as responsible for keeping the stories and collective memories of a historical past aflame—so that the "dead are not murdered twice," and bearing witness as transnational social empathy and practice becomes the impetus for social change. The Jewish practice of "never forgetting" gives other groups a chance to fasten their history and memories of marginalization and violence to that of European and diasporic Jews.

African American memorial cries of "black lives matter" and "say her name" have the potential to forge new relationships between social and cultural groups when they morph into rituals of commemoration. Cultural memory is the substance of such rituals; these memories are ritualized to the point of becoming social patterns for culturally remembering peoples' histories of social atrocity and mass suffering. By creating and maintaining dialogue between groups via these rituals of cultural memory, groups can actively prevent structural and collective amnesia about state-sanctioned and genocidal violence.[61]

Explaining how rituals of commemoration avert forgetting, Kurasawa declares that groups become part of a process of regularly participating in public performances that illuminate collective memory of the social catastrophe; refusing to capitulate to the passage of time that will cause them to forget the traumatic event; and restaging the social cataclysm. By creating memorial days that denote the event and by circulating media memory in the form of films, photographs, art, literature, and museum displays, groups leave a legacy of education that explains the causes and consequences of mass extinction and social tragedy.[62] These are ritual performances that, because of social patterning, are likewise ritualizations of commemoration. By virtue of this process, rituals of cultural memory (i.e., commemoration) guard against forgetting and ensure interethnic and interracial dialogue, specifically as a result of the multidirectionality of memory.

I close this chapter by returning to Raphael Lemkin's efforts to end the mass murder of racial, ethnic, and cultural groups. Although Lemkin is often elided from the history of genocide studies and international law, his passion for the survival of social groups cannot be denied. A forerunner to Michael Rothberg and other modern-day scholars, he embraced a form of multidirectional memory that turned diverse victim groups into witnesses for other groups.



Lemkin's outrage at the near extermination of European Jews prompted him to act. He brought the world's attention to other grave ethnic and racial injustices and mass social horrors while crying out to save his own people. Twenty-first-century Jews and African Americans can follow in Lemkin's footsteps.

Memorial cries of "never forget" and "we can't breathe" are gifts of cultural memory. When ritualized, these ceremonial social practices can benefit *any* socially afflicted, subjugated, or persecuted group that, if it chooses to create and adopt rituals of commemoration, can precipitate social change. Dwelling within these rites of cultural memory is the power and potential for Jewish and black Americans to rebuild their relationship with one another, and for both groups to reach accord with others who have been persecuted, marginalized, or oppressed.

## Notes

1. Kurasawa, "Message in a Bottle," 104.
2. Erll, *Memory in Culture*, 110.
3. Stone, "Genocide and Memory," 102.
4. In her essay "Remember to Forget: The Problem of Traumatic Cultural Memory," Julia Epstein writes about the influence of the community in shaping the individual self and consequently individual and social identities. Memory is a crucial aspect of self-development that occurs in relationship to "other selves in community." When social selves experience a rupture of community because of a social threat, the interpretation of "home" is disrupted. "Under these conditions," says Epstein, "acts of remembering replace the mental geography of place and of home" (194).
5. Ibid.
6. Kurasawa, "Message in a Bottle," 96–99.
7. Lemkin quoted in Power, *"Problem from Hell,"* 20–21. Describing the Bosnian War of the early 1990s, which was fueled by centuries-old hatred between Bosnians, Croatians, and Serbs and which then secretary of state Christopher Warren called "a problem from hell," Power recounts how similar conflicts-turned-large-scale-massacres around the globe have exposed the inadequacy of the U.S. policy of

nonintervention and inaction, even if U.S. policymakers, political leaders, and the American public like to see themselves as good guy interventionists in world affairs, including those that involve the bloodletting of social, political, and cultural groups. She writes about the Holocaust as the most recognizable and salient study of U.S. inaction despite prominent avowals of "never forget" and "never again." Power spends a third of her book on Lemkin, whose prescience about the inevitability of repeated mass slaughter (absent international criminal law to "prohibit the destruction of nations, races, and religious groups" [19]) consumed three decades of his life. Upon that foundation Power builds a provocative conclusion about U.S. complacency in the face of incomprehensible social tragedy: "America's public awareness of the Holocaust often seemed to set the bar of concern so high that we were able to tell ourselves that contemporary genocides were not measuring up" (503). See also Moses, "Lemkin, Culture, and the Concept," 23.

8. Lemkin quoted in Moses, "Lemkin, Culture, and the Concept," 23, 25.

9. Lemkin quoted in ibid., 36.

10. Stone, "Genocide and Memory," 102.

11. Wiesel, *Night*, viii.

12. Halbwachs's theory is summarized in Erll, *Memory in Culture*; the quotation is at 16.

13. Ibid., 15–18.

14. Wiesel, *Night*, 3 (hereafter cited parenthetically in the text).

15. Erll, *Memory in Culture*, 58.

16. Ibid., 60.

17. In her introduction to memory studies, *Memory in Culture*, Erll explains that "mnemohistory" is a branch of historical studies focusing on the history of mentalities and ideas (41). Mnemohistory is the place where memory studies and history converge. Mnemohistory recognizes that memory cultures are shaped by history and context that significantly influence the selection and interpretation of past events (45).

18. Ibid., 61–62.

19. Rothberg, *Multidirectional Memory*, 5.

20. Ibid., 17.

21. Abraham's Promise, a group that originated in Chicago, was hosted by a U.S.-based ecumenical Christian group called Friends of Sabeel North America (FOSNA) that seeks justice and peace in the Holy Land. FOSNA also works against distortions of the Bible and other sacred texts, challenging anti-Semitism, Islamophobia, and theologies that lead to violence and racism, whether administered by states, individuals, or private groups. FOSNA partners with Sabeel, a group of Palestinian Christians in the Holy Land who founded a Palestinian liberation theology movement. Sabeel works with all faith groups that promote peace for Palestine/Israel on the basis of United Nations resolutions and international law. See FOSNA's website at http://www.fosna.org/about/who-are-friends-sabeel.

22. Tricia Hersey was a student in my course Memory, Culture, and Redemption. This passage is from her critical essay on Keshgegian's *Theology of Redeeming Memories*, November 29, 2015.

23. See Keshgegian, *Redeeming Memories*, 194. Keshgegian's scholarship proposes a theology of redeeming (traumatic) memories. Within this framework, she lays out the responsibilities of witnesses toward social groups whose "choked cries" signal that they have endured an atrocity. For Keshgegian, redemption begins when witnesses stand "with" (as in "withness") and in solidarity with victims. This shows their "ability to hold [together] the complex threads of remembering" that make up the victim's testimony/story, and their capacity to endure the survivor's wounds without turning away.

24. He asks the same rhetorical question in *Night*, 118.

25. Wiesel makes this point in *Night*, 1.

26. Julia Epstein and Lori Hope Lefkovitz, "Introduction: Shaping Losses, Cultural Memory, and the Holocaust," in Epstein and Lefkovitz, *Shaping Losses*, 1.

27. Quoted in Lincoln, *Race, Religion*, 108.

28. I refer to public intellectuals, cultural critics, and public theologians as thought leaders. Such people wield influence and authority over the collective. Regarding black America, thought leaders are informed by and shape the social, political, cultural, and moral thoughts emerging from the black experience in America. Thought leaders supply social commentary on and constructive criticism of American society and moral discourse on the meaning of blackness in America.

29. Erll summarizes the Assmanns' work in *Memory in Culture*, 29–30.

30. Ibid., 58.

31. Baldwin et al., *Legacy of Martin Luther King*, 139.

32. Erll, *Memory in Culture*, 58.

33. King, *Trumpet of Conscience*, 6.

34. Ibid., 9.

35. Ibid., 7–9.

36. Du Bois, *Souls of Black Folk*, 7.

37. West, *Race Matters*, 4–5.

38. Khaleeli, "#SayHerName." Kimberlé Crenshaw is a professor and an activist on the front lines of the Say Her Name racial justice movement for black women who have died because of police brutality. In this article, Crenshaw remembers the names of the seventy women who were killed by police in the three-year period 2014–16; their names tend to be less visible in the Black Lives Matter social movement, which traditionally focuses on the murder of black men by police. Say Her Name, according to Crenshaw, also shines a light on sundry forms of state violence against black women—from police sexual assault and abuse to racial profiling and killing. "More black people [in total] are killed [by police officers]—disproportionately to their rate in the population—and although the numbers are hard to assess, the reality is that black women are vulnerable to the same justifications used for killing black men," says Crenshaw.

39. The hashtag #SayHerName was developed by the African American Policy Forum at Columbia Law School's Center for Intersectionality and Social Policy Studies in February 2015 to raise awareness about the lethal force and other forms of state violence used against black girls and women. It has a large social media presence and is growing into a gender-inclusive racial justice movement that draws attention to black women's demand for justice, media representation in campaigns against police violence, and policy reform. See Crenshaw et al., "Say Her Name."

40. Kurasawa, "Message in a Bottle," 92–93. Transnationalizing the practice of bearing witness moves the responsibility of bearing witness beyond the borders of persons or cultural groups that have been victimized into the spaces of concerned citizens, institutions, and civil societies throughout the world. These global testimonial practices and the international community of witnesses formed around them emerged because national governments were either unable or unwilling to hold perpetrators of structural violence accountable. Transnational testimonial practices are a form of social action that publicly acknowledges victim groups and targeted populations; and they are used as a strategy to intervene in the affairs of global civil societies where near genocide, mass persecution, or social atrocities are occurring.

41. Patterson introduced this term in *Slavery and Social Death*, his groundbreaking 1985 study of sixty-six societies that practiced slavery. Social death is part of the process of institutional enslavement. Patterson describes the internal and external dynamics of slavery, stressing the enslaver's violent domination of the captive, which involves recruitment and incorporation into the new society. This social incorporation entails numerous losses, among them the loss of social bonds and family ties, the erasure of one's former identity, and the separation of people from their families and heritage. All of these losses contribute to the impotence and powerlessness of the enslaved. Though these social factors vary in their particulars depending on location and context, they all contribute to the alienation and social death that enslaved people suffer.

42. Rambo, *Spirit and Trauma*, 4. In *Trauma and Recovery*, Judith Herman explains how trauma disrupts normal psychological development by overwhelming the integrated systems we use to respond to danger and threat with a sufficient degree of care, control, and connection. Trauma causes psychic and emotional fragmentation; a consequence is maladaptation to everyday life. The symptomology of traumatized people emerges in the aftermath of the psychological trauma; the two symptoms I focus on here are *intrusion* and *constriction*. Long after the violence or other traumatic event is over, survivors are unable to forget it; the traumatic moment repeatedly intrudes into their daily lives, both waking and sleeping, in the form of flashbacks and nightmares, making memory abnormal. Constriction is the opposite of intrusion; during the traumatic moment, the traumatized person, feeling helpless and powerless, may dissociate—may

separate the painful event from the rest of consciousness. When this separation occurs after the event, it is called a "constriction" and can manifest as amnesia. See Herman, *Trauma and Recovery*, 37, 45.

43. Herman, *Trauma and Recovery*, 4.

44. Rambo, *Spirit and Trauma*, 4, 15, 22.

45. Keshgegian, *Redeeming Memories*, 194.

46. Rogers, *Unsayable*; Rambo, *Spirit and Trauma*, 21.

47. Kurasawa, "Message in a Bottle," 102–3.

48. Ibid., 96–97.

49. Epstein, "Remember to Forget," 198. Epstein interrogates the mantra "never forget" by examining the dialectic that inheres in traumatic cultural memory: remembering and forgetting. She explains the double bind of traumatic memory as expressed in the Israeli poet Dan Pagis's poem "Instructions for Crossing the Border": "You are not allowed to remember. / . . . You are not allowed to forget" (186). She introduces Toni Morrison's concept of disremembering as an imperfect yet plausible resolution to the double bind of traumatic cultural memory (197).

50. Rothschild, *Body Remembers*, xv.

51. Epstein, "Remember to Forget," 188, 197.

52. Khaleeli, "#SayHerName."

53. *Journal of Blacks in Higher Education*, "More Than 4.5 Million African Americans."

54. Erll, *Memory in Culture*, 8.

55. Kurasawa, "Message in a Bottle," 94.

56. Keshgegian, *Redeeming Memories*, 25.

57. Kurasawa, "Message in a Bottle," 95–96.

58. Rambo, *Spirit and Trauma*, 3, 6. In offering a theology of redemption, Rambo remarks that trauma changes the relationship between death and life; it reconfigures this relationship, challenging how we think about redemption.

59. Epstein, "Remember to Forget," 189.

60. In the field of cultural memory studies, there is ongoing debate about the relationship between history and memory. Scholars have suggested the following models for that relationship: conflictual, independent, dialogical, and integrated. In the present context, I am focused on the integrated model of history and memory that scholars like Bernard Lewis and Peter Burke write about as the "social history of remembering." Erll, *Memory in Culture*, 43.

61. Kurasawa, "Message in a Bottle," 104.

62. Ibid.

63. Babylonian Talmud *Niddah* 30b.

## References


Alexander, Jeffrey C. "On the Social Construction of Moral Universals: The 'Holocaust' from War Crime to Trauma Drama." *European Journal of Social Theory* 5 (January 2002): 5–85.

Alexander, Jeffrey C., Ron Eyerman, Bernard Giesen, Neil J. Smelser, and Piotr Sztompka. *Cultural Trauma and Collective Identity.* Berkeley: University of California Press, 2004.

Baldwin, Lewis V., Rufus Burrows Jr., Barbara A. Holmes, and Susan Holmes Winfield. *The Legacy of Martin Luther King Jr.: The Boundaries of Law, Politics, and Religion.* Notre Dame: University of Notre Dame Press, 2002.

Crenshaw, Kimberlé Williams, and Andrea J. Ritchie, with Rachel Anspach, Rachel Gilmer, and Luke Harris. "Say Her Name: Resisting Police Brutality Against Black Women." African American Policy Forum, Center for Intersectionality and Social Policy Studies, Columbia Law School, July 2015. http://static1.squarespace.com/static/53f20d90e4b0b80451158d8c/t/55a810d7e4b058f342f55873/1437077719984/AAPF_SMN_Brief_full_singles.compressed.pdf.

Du Bois, W. E. B. *The Souls of Black Folk.* New York: Signet, 1995.

Epstein, Julia. "Remember to Forget: The Problem of Traumatic Cultural Memory." In Epstein and Lefkovitz, *Shaping Losses*, 186–204.

Epstein, Julia, and Lori Hope Lefkovitz, eds. *Shaping Losses: Cultural Memory and the Holocaust*. Urbana: University of Illinois Press, 2001.

Erll, Astrid. *Memory in Culture*. Translated by Sara B. Young. New York: Palgrave Macmillan, 2011.

Herman, Judith. *Trauma and Recovery: The Aftermath of Violence—from Domestic Abuse to Political Terror*. New York: Basic Books, 1992.

*Journal of Blacks in Higher Education*. "More Than 4.5 Million African Americans Now Hold a Four-Year College Degree." June 24, 2016. http://www.jbhe.com/news_views/64_degrees.html.

Keshgegian, Flora A. *Redeeming Memories: A Theology of Healing and Transformation*. Nashville: Abingdon Press, 2000.

Khaleeli, Homa. "#SayHerName: Why Kimberlé Crenshaw Is Fighting for Forgotten Women." *Guardian*, May 20, 2016. http://www.theguardian.com/lifeandstyle/2016/may/30/sayhername-why-kimberle-crenshaw-is-fighting-for-forgotten-women.

King, Martin Luther, Jr. *The Trumpet of Conscience*. New York: HarperCollins, 1987.

Kurasawa, Fuyuki. "A Message in a Bottle: Bearing Witness as a Mode of Transnational Practice." *Theory, Culture, and Society* 26, no. 1 (2009): 92–111. http://doi.org/10.1177/0263276408099017.

Lincoln, C. Eric. *Race, Religion, and the Continuing American Dilemma*. New York: Hill and Wang, 1999.

Moses, A. Dirk. "Raphael Lemkin, Culture, and the Concept of Genocide." In *The Oxford Handbook of Genocide Studies*, edited by Donald Bloxham and A. Dirk Moses, 19–41. Oxford: Oxford University Press, 2013.

Patterson, Orlando. *Slavery and Social Death: A Comparative Study*. Cambridge, Mass.: Harvard University Press, 1985.

Power, Samantha. *"A Problem from Hell": America and the Age of Genocide*. New York: Harper Perennial, 2002.

Rambo, Shelly. *Spirit and Trauma: A Theology of Remaining*. Louisville: Westminster John Knox Press, 2010.

Rogers, Annie. *The Unsayable: The Hidden Language of Trauma*. New York: Random House, 2006.

Rorty, Richard. "Human Rights, Rationality, and Sentimentality." In *Truth and Progress: Philosophical Papers*, 3:167–85. Cambridge: Cambridge University Press, 1998.

Rothberg, Michael. *Multidirectional Memory: Remembering the Holocaust in the Age of Decolonization*. Stanford: Stanford University Press, 2009.

Rothschild, Babette. *The Body Remembers: The Psychophysiology of Trauma and Trauma Treatment*. New York: W. W. Norton, 2000.

Stone, Dan. "Genocide and Memory." In *The Oxford Handbook of Genocide Studies*, edited by Donald Bloxham and A. Dirk Moses, 102–19. Oxford: Oxford University Press, 2013.

West, Cornel. *Race Matters*. 2nd ed. New York: Vintage, 2001.

Wiesel, Elie. *Night*. Translated by Marion Wiesel. New York: Hill and Wang, 2006.



## Classic Text and Questions to Ponder

History eludes capture; memory can hardly hold in its grasp all that has happened. When memory concretizes history, what occurred becomes vivid and, in many instances, endures long after those directly involved are gone. Phillips identifies two particular expressions of cultural memory—traumatic silences and memorial cries—that serve as markers of Jewish and African American recollections of annihilation and subjugation. These expressions give shape and voice to histories that otherwise would go underappreciated in the larger society. History as it is remembered affects communities no less than individuals. The Talmud teaches that "as soon as [a fetus] sees the light [of the world,] an angel approaches, slaps it on its mouth and causes it to forget all the Torah completely."[63] Liberation, trauma, and wisdom intertwine here as much as deformation of the body, destruction of memory, and silence.

- Which, in your opinion, have greater durability in society: traumatic silences or memorial cries? Why?
- Which form better captures history? Why?
- The philtrum, or indentation between the lips and nose, signals the incompleteness of human memory. What else might it signify?

# 8

# Jewish Critical Race Theory and Jewish "Religionization" in *Shaare Tefila Congregation v. Cobb*

**ANNALISE E. GLAUZ-TODRANK**

You know, it might go to part of the Jewish psyche: you don't want to try to make yourself too known. Even though we're very safe and secure in America as Jews, there could be just that part. . . . I guess the people who were involved twenty years ago were more part of that generation, you know, don't make waves.

—RABBI JONAH LAYMAN, *SHAARE TEFILA CONGREGATION*

By the 1980s, Jewish Americans had fought a hard battle not to be seen as a "race" in the United States. They had married "out" in increasing numbers.[1] They had sought out professions—such as traveling salespeople in the South, or merchants journeying out west—where there was not a Jew to be found. In the United States, they strove to be a "religion." Yet Jews have been a "race" in Western societies since the Spanish *limpieza de sangre* (purity of blood) statutes in 1449.[2] In Europe, "Aryan" and "Semite" had become key terms by the nineteenth century. But in the United States, Jewish Americans were not forced to claim association with the discourse on racial theories, because the United States emphasized the histories of slavery, colonization, and westward expansion.[3]

In the American context, Jews have generally assimilated to the religious norms expressed by the white Protestant majority. For the most part, they have differentiated themselves into Reform, Conservative, Orthodox, and Haredi communities and other, smaller Jewish groups—certainly with some flow in between.[4] But this has come at a cost, for all but perhaps the Haredim. Scholars who have studied the need for Jewish Americans to conform to Protestant religious norms have noted that Jews have had to relinquish many components of Jewish culture, in particular many cultural and linguistic elements that do not fit within such norms.[5] What I call "religionization" means that people, in this case Jewish Americans, adopt the religious norms of the society while downplaying or even denying cultural attributes that do not fit with those norms.[6]



Similarly, many Jewish Americans currently pass as white or "mostly white." But Jewish Americans have generally passed or been "mostly white" *only* in the dominant discourse of the United States, which qualified them in these terms during the early part of the nineteenth century and again since around the end of World War II. Apart from these two historical periods, Jewish Americans have not been considered "white," but neither have they been, in most times and places, the *primary* object of racial hatred. With that in mind, most Jewish Americans who now can pass as white have, consciously or not, identified as such, often without thinking about the privileges that whiteness grants them—and yet those privileges erase components of Jewish American identification.

This chapter addresses the perception of Jews and the legal protection of Jews. I situate Jews within the American racial and religious infrastructure.[7] My aim is to explore the racial and religious dimensions of identity for Jewish Americans within the framework of critical race theory (CRT) and in most Jewish Americans' assimilation to religious norms, or what I call "religionization." Critical race theorists know that race is a multifaceted, multipurpose structure that changes over time, and that it serves the needs of the majority, whether those needs are economic, political, social, or all three. CRT also addresses the *ethical* problem of the American legal system, which values white Christian (Protestant) men more than it values other individuals.[8] For example, the legal system uses the benchmark of a "reasonable man" who might make decisions in various contexts; it is fairly obvious that this man is straight, white, Christian, able-bodied, and so on. With this in mind, I focus on Jewish Americans through the lens of racial formation and religionization, which allows us to better think through the challenges they encounter, the experiences that affect them, and the particular issues they face as Jews.[9] Furthermore, this approach provides an important perspective within CRT that allows us to interrogate sites or identifications where race is less apparent and even more abstracted from real life.

Throughout the chapter, I rely on one of Henry Goldschmidt's central arguments in *Race and Religion Among the Chosen People of Crown Heights*. Goldschmidt notes that "race and religion have helped define the very nature of the other." He argues that religion and race are "*co-constituted categories*, wholly dependent on each other for their social existence and symbolic meanings" (emphasis added). Goldschmidt points out that scholarship typically "has started from the assumption that race and religion are fundamentally distinct, clearly bounded categories, and only then traced the ways that these categories intersect. These intersections have typically been accorded a kind of secondary status—secondary, that is, to the presumed boundedness and integrity of the categories themselves." He emphasizes that "however fluidly they may interact in the course of social life, in the eyes of most scholars race and religion manage to retain their analytical clarity and autonomy."[10] Of course, people who are not scholars adopt this approach too, speaking of themselves and others in racial or religious terms.



With these concepts in mind, let us examine *Shaare Tefila Congregation v. Cobb* (1987) to consider more closely how Jewish Americans appeal to, and yet resist, the term "race" within the context of a civil rights lawsuit. *Shaare Tefila* was the first legal case to assert that Jews are *not* a race yet *are treated* as one. The case was brought by a synagogue in Silver Spring, Maryland, in response to Ku Klux Klan and Nazi-related vandalism on the surface of their building, playground equipment, and a car. The case ended up in the U.S. Supreme Court, after two lower courts dismissed the suit on the grounds that Jewish Americans were citing race-based protection, and the judges viewed Jews as white people.[11] So the synagogue's lawyers constructed the argument that although Jewish Americans are not "a racially distinct group," they have been *viewed* as one, and that the men who desecrated their synagogue were motivated by racial prejudice.

As noted above, Jewish Americans largely managed not to be caught up in the prevailing American racial theories that fueled colonization, slavery, and westward expansion, and they were generally governed by the dominant discourse that emphasizes the "color line," which divides peoples according to their apparent physiognomic differences.[12] Nevertheless, many Jews have called themselves and one another "Jews," and only very recently have Jewish Americans been associated with whiteness. This chapter examines how and why many Jewish Americans have tried to describe themselves for a non-Jewish public as a religious group, while (sometimes) thinking about themselves as a "race" among themselves. Before exploring the details of the case, let us look at how Jewish conceptions of race and perceptions of Jews as a race evolved, such that they emerged in the *Shaare Tefila* Supreme Court case.

### "Religionization": Assimilation to the Protestant American Conception of Religion



"Race" was something that many Jewish Americans prior to the Shoah wanted to preserve, because, ironically, it enabled them to ensure that Jews, who were not people of color, had a minority presence among other "white" people. For instance, a majority of them intended to marry within the community. Whereas other "white ethnics" could marry among Christians, whether Protestant or Catholic, it was undesirable for Jews to marry Christians. In public settings, however, "white" Jewish Americans often had to suppress what was explicitly "Jewish" about themselves to conform to the beliefs and expectations of the dominant majority of white people. "The ultimate loss of race as a term for self-description," Eric Goldstein writes, "rendered inarticulate some of their deepest feelings of group solidarity and difference." And "acceptance often came at a heavy price, belying the notion that whiteness conferred only privilege."[13] Thus it was a hardship to Jewish Americans—who had for so long been a persecuted minority in other places—to claim to be "white" in the United States.

Most Jewish Americans had only one option when they reached the United States, and that was to internalize *religious* norms.[14] The population of the northeastern segment of the original thirteen colonies[15] had fled Europe so that they could practice their religion openly, and they professed that viewpoint throughout the colonies. Even before their emigration, the Jews of western Europe had often conformed to the religious norms of the larger society. Owing in part to emancipation, Jews had begun to assimilate themselves to the Christian concept of religion.

In an exceptional book that examines this topic, Leora Batnitzky asserts that the German Jewish philosopher Moses Mendelssohn "invented" the modern idea that Judaism is a religion. "One can understand this Protestant notion," she writes, "simply as the view that religion denotes a sphere of life separate and distinct from all others, and that this sphere is largely private and not public, voluntary and not compulsory." She notes that Mendelssohn "had to defend Judaism without refuting Christianity," so he separated the secular laws of the state from laws pertaining to halakhah, and he claimed that Judaism was a "religion."[16] In 1791, Napoleon Bonaparte emancipated Jews, giving them citizenship, on the ground that Jews could be accepted into French society in the assumption that they would assimilate to Christian norms. A few years later, however, he forced a "Sanhedrin" of rabbis to accede to French law by making them answer a number of questions. He posed them with the "correct" answers in mind, the ones that conformed to French law—for example, do Jewish men take more than one wife? Do Jews follow biblical or French law?[17] As he advanced into the German regions east of France, he "liberated" the Jews there as well.[18] Emancipation had an important effect on the semi-autonomous Jewish communities, at once freeing them from the traditional Jewish life but also forcing them, as individual citizens, to obey Christian beliefs and values.



In the American context, Jews also had to adapt to religious norms. When the first major wave of Jewish immigrants came to the United States in the nineteenth century, the vast majority of them joined the Reform movement, begun in Germany and modeled on Mendelssohn's conception of a separation between church and state. It formed the most "Protestant-like" branch of Judaism. But when some two million eastern European Jews came to this country in the late nineteenth and early twentieth centuries, they struggled to make sense of the religiosity of Jewish American culture. For the most part, they had not experienced emancipation in their countries of origin. In eastern Europe, Jews were "Yiddishkeit," a people apart, and they brought this way of thinking about themselves to the United States, along with Yiddish theater, literature, and newspapers. These Jewish Americans brought their linguistic and cultural customs with them to this country, only for them to gradually dissipate due to religionization.

In her article "Other Moderns, Other Jews: Revisiting Jewish Secularism in America," Laura Levitt focuses on the fact that, in the United States, Jews are "supposed" to be a religious group. She writes about the Jewish students in her classroom who don't feel Jewish "enough" (because they are only "culturally Jewish") and about former U.S. senator Joe Lieberman, who is "too Jewish" to fit into the dominant Protestant paradigm. Reassessing the story of eastern European Jewish immigration to the United States, she writes, "Instead of seeing Jewish difference as necessarily a version of private faith, I resist this definition and look instead at many of the ways that Jewishness exceeds this definition. . . . At what cost have Jews been accepted into the dominant culture of the United States? What has it meant for Jews to conform to Protestant middle-class norms? What has it meant for Jews to refashion their Jewishness into a version of Protestant faith?"[19] Levitt then proceeds to demonstrate the stripping away of Yiddish eastern European identity and the effects of the argument that Judaism is a religion.[20]

Conservative and modern Orthodox Jewish Americans have taken separate stances in relation to U.S. Protestant norms, but they have acceded to them as well, in part by not discussing their halakhic practices with many non-Jews. As Batnitzky notes, "Nevertheless, notwithstanding these and other important differences and developments, Reform, Conservative, and Orthodox Judaism in the United States conform to the conceptual and political framework introduced by their German predecessors in understanding Judaism as a *religion*" (emphasis added).[21] Will Herberg's *Protestant, Catholic, Jew*, published in 1955, makes the case that these three religions exhibit similar behavior in that they all assume the significance of religiosity, and that it does not matter which one. Adopting American norms has always been the social ideal. As Shaul Magid asserts, "'Americanization' was not one of a variety of options for Jews in America. It was the default position."[22]

Not all Americans have attempted to fit into a religious role that assimilates them to Protestant norms. Haredim reject these categories by constructing their own, and they object to common perceptions that Americans hold about religion and race, for instance. They prefer not to associate with American ideals because they have their own.

Nevertheless, even Haredim are influenced by American norms when they tell their story to outsiders. These norms are based on their own court's lineage[23] via the Baal Shem Tov's examples.[24] For instance, as Henry Goldschmidt observes, "Lubavitchers have come to emphasize a vision of Jewishness as an inherent and inherited property of the soul." This understanding of Jewish identification, he notes, "tends to level distinctions between secular and orthodox Jews, while accentuating distinctions between Jews and non-Jews."[25] Goldschmidt remarks, "When he asked Lubavitchers how this Jewish soul was transmitted from the patriarchs to present-day Jews, many took pains to distinguish this theory of Jewish descent from racial biology (an understanding of Jewishness they tend to associate with Nazi antisemitism)." Goldschmidt emphasizes that we should examine how Lubavitch Jews think about "religion" and "race"—and how they are both shared and contested—in terms of, or in the place of, history and genealogy.[26]

In *Mitzvah Girls*, Ayala Fader writes, "This hierarchy of peoples, legitimated by a God-given soul and developed through the discipline of religious practice, engages with and inverts a particular narrative of modernity where a Protestant-inflected secularism represents the peak of civilization." Fader examines how Hasidic women and girls in Borough Park (Brooklyn) "strive to redefine what constitutes a moral society" by envisioning an "alternative religious modernity." This version of modernity specifically idealizes *Hasidic* qualities, like *tsnius* (modesty), or their control in switching back and forth between speaking Yiddish and English.[27] The American Hasidic Jews whom Fader discusses—as examples of the larger American Haredi community—make it a point to differentiate themselves from other, non-Haredi Americans in their values.



Most Jewish Americans, however, highlight the extent to which Jews occupy common ground with other Americans. They aim to follow the dominant tradition in American society rather than to differentiate themselves racially or in any other terms. Before the *Shaare Tefila* case, most Jewish Americans had painted over racist and antisemitic graffiti. When they did file lawsuits, they did so in terms that conformed to "religious" identification. But, guided by its executive director and its lawyers, Shaare Tefila Congregation did something different. Not only did it dare to show the graffiti to the neighborhood on the evening before an election day on which the synagogue would be a voting site; it also took the case to court as a race-based civil suit. In the following section, I discuss race-based rights according to critical race theorists, who analyze the experiences and legal difficulties faced by people of color.

### Critical Race Theory

Critical race theory aims to develop new ways of thinking about and enacting the relationships between race and the law. These new conceptualizations are necessary because the language of the law and the usual forms of legal interpretation do not sufficiently protect people who are categorized and then alienated on the basis of race. The fundamental flaw in the legal system that critical race theorists address is its ongoing inability to protect people of color from the marginalization that they experience by being racialized in American society.

"Marginalization" is a broad term that can include experiences ranging from economic inequality, to physical assault, to defacement of property with racist graffiti. Critical race theorists seek protections against such crimes that account for and match the *experiences* of the victims, who are targeted because of their socially assigned racial category or perceptions thereof. For example, after September 11, 2001, hate crimes against Muslim and Middle Eastern Americans proliferated, but many such crimes also "mistakenly" targeted Sikh Americans and other people who "looked Muslim."[28] Thus CRT can address the racism directed at the intended targets, but also the ways in which racism enables the marginalization and discrimination of those who are targets because of misperceptions.

Critical race theorists identify existing problems in the legal system with the objective of changing how laws are written and interpreted. In order to make sense of the relationship between racialization and marginalization, they write about specific situations and legal cases that highlight the distinctive experiences of particular groups of people. They often focus on the lack of fit between a legal decision and discourses or characteristics that define, or that are employed to define, a given group.



Central to the formulation of most such arguments is the primary role that mainstream conversations play in informing the unequal treatment that occurs. In other words, the problems in question do not pertain to qualities *inherent* in a particular group of people but rather to *conceptions* of that group that are also usually grounded in a long social and economic history of oppression. Because of these histories of oppression and because the conceptions at stake are often assumed to be inherent or factual, the discourses that undergird the discrimination are deeply rooted and difficult, if not impossible, to eradicate. As Eduardo Bonilla-Silva puts it, "although the racialization of peoples was socially invented and did not override previous forms of social distinction based on class or gender, it did not lead to imaginary relations but generated new forms of human association with definite status differences. After the process of attaching meaning to a 'people' is instituted, race becomes a *real* category of group association and identity" (emphasis added).[29] Thus racialization effectively "creates" social realities: it constrains groups of people on the basis of social perceptions that are seemingly ingrained.[30] The development of this process over time has functioned to give racial categories every appearance of being real and apparent.

Nevertheless, the prevailing contemporary "color-blind" approach to race pervades social discourse and predominates in legal rulings. As Neil Gotanda argues, "the U.S. Supreme Court's use of color-blind constitutionalism—a collection of legal themes functioning as a racial ideology—fosters white racial domination." Gotanda describes color-blind constitutionalism as beginning with the passage of the Thirteenth through Fifteenth Amendments and maturing with the passage of *Brown v. Board of Education* in 1954, the ruling that outlawed the "separate but equal" approach to racialized treatment that had characterized legal policy on race since the *Plessy v. Ferguson* decision in 1896. The underlying assumption of the color-blind approach is that we now live in a racially assimilated society in which race is irrelevant.[31] Critical race theorists point to much evidence that directly counters this assumption, such as the persistence of racial profiling, federal immigration policies, and the expectation that professionals must "act white."[32] But American courts and legislative bodies consistently implement "color-blind" laws, such as the U.S. Supreme Court's 2013 decision in *Shelby v. Holder*. This decision repealed two provisions of the landmark 1965 Voting Rights Act, lifting the requirement that states with a history of voting rights discrimination obtain federal approval before changing their voting laws or procedures, and thus enabling states to erect roadblocks to Black and other minority voting. The 5–4 majority held that the requirement, being more than forty years old, was no longer relevant or necessary.



Michael Omi and Howard Winant define "race" as a social category that is both structural and ideological, "racialization" as a process of instantiating race in social discourses, and "racism" as a "racial project" that "creates or reproduces structures of domination based on essentialist categories of race." Racism, in other words, is formed by and exists within the structural system of society. Omi and Winant emphasize, as well, the "fluid" and "contested" history of these social structures and discourses. Their definition of race also highlights fluidity and contestation. It is "a concept which signifies and symbolizes social conflicts and interests by referring to different types of human bodies." They further note that "although the concept of race invokes biologically based human characteristics (so-called 'phenotypes'), selection of these particular human features for purposes of racial signification is always and necessarily a social and historical process." Their summary of race as a fundamental characteristic of American society attests to the impossibility of eradicating it, particularly by means of the "color-blind" approach. "We should think of race as an element of social structure," they write, "rather than as an irregularity within it; we should see race as a dimension of human representation rather than as an illusion. These perspectives inform the theoretical approach we call racial formation."[33]

Omi and Winant note that conceptions of race and racial categories change over time. They also imply that because race is "an element of the social structure," Americans take it for granted—we often assume that race and racial distinctions are biological facts rather than socially constructed categories. They strongly suggest that this assumption means that we attribute a physical reality and factuality to race, such that we enable it to serve an *explanatory* role for social realities. Thus, race becomes "common sense" to us.

Lisa Tessman argues that Jews who experience the benefits of whiteness should acknowledge their racial assignment as white but should also understand that this racial assignment forms just one moment in a historical process of racialization. She aims to guard against the potential claim that because most Jewish Americans "became white," other racialized groups have that opportunity too. Rather, she notes the particularity of Jewish identities and the circumstances that facilitated their racial transformation, which involved a specific set of Jews at a particular historical moment. That transformation did not and does not apply to the many interracial, converted, and nonwhite adopted Jews. "Jewish identifications as contingently white highlight only contingency," she writes; "they do not suggest that the contingency will turn out in any particular way for other groups."[34]



Black, Latino, and Asian Americans, among others, should expect a legal system that protects them with respect to the particular ways in which that system racializes them, and Jewish Americans should do likewise. At the same time, because not all forms of racism look alike or act alike, Jewish Americans should not claim to experience *effects* of racism that do not pertain to how they have been racialized *as Jews*.

### The *Shaare Tefila* Case

The defacement of Shaare Tefila synagogue with Nazi and Ku Klux Klan–related images and phrases exemplifies the racist ideologies of those two organizations. On November 1, 1982, eight young men spray-painted the synagogue's exterior walls, a car, and playground equipment with swastikas, a six-foot-tall Nazi eagle, the words "Toten Kamf Raband" [*sic*], a burning cross in red and black, the words "Dead Jew" and "Death to the Jude," and a door on which they wrote "In, Take a Shower, Jew."[35] These are clear references to Nazi views of Jews as racially inferior and to the Nazis' attempt to eliminate Jews in extermination camps with "death's head units" and gas chambers, and to the Ku Klux Klan's history of terrorizing Jewish Americans.

As noted above, two lower courts dismissed the congregation's claim that the synagogue had been the victim of a racist attack, on the basis that Jews are "white." First, federal district court judge Norman Ramsey rejected the congregation's argument and dismissed the case, and then the three judges on the Fourth Circuit Court of Appeals determined that "no racial discrimination was present," in part because congregants did not identify themselves as members of a separate race.[36]

In the court of appeals, however, the judges were divided, with the majority claiming that to gain civil rights protections, Jewish Americans had to assert that they *were* members of a separate race. Outlier judge J. Harvie

Wilkinson III differentiated between the *embodiment* of race and the *discourses* that inform thinking on race. “Rather than allowing ignorance and misperception to provide their own defense,” he wrote in his dissenting opinion, “I would find the erroneous but all too sincere view of the defendants that Jews constitute a separate race worthy of humiliation and degradation sufficient to bring the claim.”[37] Nevertheless, the synagogue lost its appeal, and there the story would have ended had the U.S. Supreme Court not agreed to hear the case in conjunction with another case, argued on the same legal basis in another appeals court, which had resulted in a different ruling.



In the Supreme Court, the justices grappled with the question “can Jews claim race-based protection?” But instead of concluding immediately that Jews are white, as both of the lower courts had done, they considered Jewish American experiences of discrimination in historical context, noting that institutional restrictions on Jews in the past had significantly limited Jewish access to the social privileges held by whites. They also discussed the virulent racism against Jews in Nazi Germany and how vividly the graffiti evoked that history.

The lawyer for the defendants, Deborah Garren, argued that Jews are a “*religious* group,” and she still thinks that this is true.[38] Nevertheless, in an exchange with her, Justice Thurgood Marshall declared, “‘Death to the Jews.’ That’s what the swastika means.” Garren responded, “I appreciate what Nazis believed and I also think that that is not a belief that is common to society.” The justice replied, “I didn’t say Nazis. I said anybody that uses the swastika means, ‘Death to the Jews.’ German, American, or whoever he is, you don’t use the swastika.” Justice Marshall further stated, “It means that you should die.” “Pardon?” Garren asked. “It means that you should die.”[39] Justice Marshall focused here on the *message* of the graffiti, dramatizing its severity and recalling the grim history and consequences that it conveyed. In moments like this one, several of the justices seemed to identify with the perspective of the Jewish Americans who had experienced the attack along with the effects of the related historical events.

As part of the research for the book I am writing on the *Shaare Tefila* case, I conducted thirty in-depth interviews with people involved in the congregation or the civil suit, twenty-five of whom were members of the Shaare Tefila Congregation. I wanted to understand how the congregants used legal language to claim protection from the racist vandalism, and how they thought about the defacement as it related to their conceptions of themselves as Jewish Americans. My main question was how the legal language used to describe Jewish identification in the case diverged from the ways in which the synagogue members chose to describe themselves as Jewish Americans. I wanted to determine the extent to which the legal options available could adequately serve the needs of the congregants who had experienced the defacement.

What I found was that members of Shaare Tefila typically viewed themselves as part of a religious group. Here's one example: several congregants emphasized that the synagogue was the only Jewish member of the Colesville



Council of Community Congregations. The council consisted of churches and one synagogue that occupy locations along the Colesville corridor, a thoroughfare that runs through Silver Spring. Bill Harkaway, a member of the synagogue, commented:

> I was one of the synagogue's representatives for a long time. And we did a lot of good things at Colesville, "four C's" we referred to them [as]. . . . They have a clothes closet: people donate clothing and other people can come and take them without charge. . . . Barbara [his wife] and I work there usually in December before Christmas, so that the non-Jews can do the things they do at Christmas. . . . They have a board which meets regularly and they have an annual meeting, and they have a unit that delivers meals on wheels, and Barbara did that for almost thirty years, and once I retired, I joined her doing it once a week.

Congregants' involvement in this organization demonstrates that they value interfaith social action, and that their collaboration with local churches on issues of local poverty is meaningful to their own religious identities and values as Jewish Americans. Clearly, this was a point of pride for them.

Patricia Brannan, the congregation's lawyer, however, asked the Shaare Tefila board of trustees if they wanted to *identify* themselves as a race during the civil suit. Several members who were involved with the board at the time of the lawsuit recalled mixed responses to her proposal. Past president Bess Teller recalled:

> So the question came to us as to whether we should consider ourselves a race, and get protection as a race. That was one path we could have taken. And the discussion that was held about it was very interesting. And in some ways there is a part of me that says yes, we are a race, because we've interbred so much in a way, in some manner of speaking. You know, I mean Groucho Marx "looks Jewish." Racial features, there's something there that says that

> that's one way to go, but it isn't, it's a choice. It's an intellectual decision or an emotional decision to be Jewish. It was—it made me think about what it is to be Jewish, and Judaism, and Jews as a people, which was very interesting.

For Bess Teller, the question of which legal argument to pursue regarding Jewish identity provided an opportunity for reflection and consideration of different possibilities in describing Jewishness. Her statement reveals the impact of racial narratives about physical features described as "Jewish" and also of the dominant American discourse that views religious identity as a choice.



Former board member Jack Teller, Bess's husband, remembered:

> There was a lot of concern. I remember a couple of meetings in a row . . . and we were concerned about the definition of Jews, as people, as a race, as a community, as a religion. And what the courts would do with those, how we would be defined by law. And we decided that that was a risk we were willing to take, but there was a lot of debate about that. Because, you see, we're not a race. We are a religion, we are a culture. We are a people, and we are a community. . . . I do remember people worried about us getting pigeonholed. That if a new law were made, that we shouldn't be treated as a race because we're not. And you know, of course, the lawyers among us, and there were several on the board, really started setting forth all of these possibilities about [how] this could be good for us and this could be bad for us. What would be good for us as Jews as opposed to what's good for us as a synagogue. . . . I just remember that overwhelmingly we wanted to go after them, especially after we had had such a positive community response with the cleanup. So we went after them.

Jack Teller presented another perspective, one that sees Jews as a religion, a culture, a people, and a community—but decidedly not as a "race." In the 1980s, when, unlike Blacks or Asians, among others, Jewish Americans were not forced to be a "race," unless they were *identified* as Jews it was to some extent considered an intellectual or emotional decision, as Bess Teller noted. But many Jewish Americans often were and are identified in ways that could be interpreted as "racial": by their names, their "looks," or their ritual clothing, for example, because they didn't conform to Christian concepts of what a "religion" should be.[40]

Given that the case concerned racist graffiti that marred the walls of a synagogue, Brannan advised the legal necessity of associating Jews with the category of "race" to claim race-based protection, but she did not maintain that the synagogue members needed to claim to *be* a race. Here, CRT helps us understand that fixedness and "essential nature" do not form the basis of race. Rather, as Judge Wilkinson, Bonilla-Silva, and Omi and Winant point out, "race" (like "religion") is real, but it is also constructed from the collective beliefs of society.[41]



What surprised me was that most of the synagogue members were not terribly interested in the legal language of the case. Before I conducted the interviews, I had posited that a substantial gap would exist between the legal language pertaining to "race" used in the courtroom and the congregation members' depictions of their Jewish identities. Most congregation members, however, knew very little about the legal process or the arguments constructed on their behalf, although a few of them did go to the Supreme Court hearing and followed the case in the news. Their disengagement highlights the fact that the legal remedy did not completely address many synagogue members' need for social restitution.

Many of the congregants did, however, want to tell me how meaningful they found the cleanup day that the synagogue youths had organized under the direction of the executive director. On that day, hundreds of local community members of various backgrounds arrived to join Shaare Tefila members as they scrubbed the graffiti from the synagogue walls. In retrospect, the cleanup seems to have augmented the satisfaction of winning the case, but in a deeper, more emotional, more personal way. Jack Teller recalled,

> They came, and they helped and supported us. They brought kids, you know, volunteers, teenagers, and they helped to clean up, and some people who had little businesses to do painting . . . you know, cleaning supplies, they came and supported it. And that was, like, very warming, you know. . . . So it was really great. I mean, the whole community was involved. It was terrific. . . . I mean, that made me prouder of the community than anything. I mean, I really felt good about being a part of this community. . . . Thinking back on that time, I get a little misty-eyed about us.

The cleanup seemed to restore Shaare Tefila's faith in the goodwill of its neighbors. It seemed to fulfill a restorative function for them.[42]

In Jewish critical race theory, both legal and social remedies are significant and beneficial. The legal process highlights how the law initially failed to protect Jewish Americans from racist crimes and then finally, in 1987, delivered that protection with the unanimous Supreme Court decision, a landmark victory. In addition, the cleanup day bolstered the courage of the Shaare Tefila Congregation in the face of the vandalism. Arguably, both were necessary to support Shaare Tefila's relationship with the wider community.



But most non-Jewish Americans do not know that Jews continue to face *race*-based problems. In large part this is because non-Jewish Americans, like many Jewish Americans themselves, perceive the problem as an issue of "antisemitism." Liberal Americans in particular typically view race, over and above antisemitism, as a key problem in this country. Jewish Americans often complain about this division. If we understand anti-Judaism as a racial issue, however, we can perceive it with more breadth, provided that we are careful to acknowledge *only* those effects that pertain to Jewish Americans.

### The Conundrum of Jews and Race in America

Let us look at how two scholars have dealt with Jewish American difference. I chose these two scholars in part because they neglect a critical component of Jewish CRT: its significance in understanding Jewish American social location. Joe Feagin, a sociologist and race relations scholar, and Kenneth Marcus, a public affairs professor and former staff director at the U.S. Commission on Human Rights, comment on Jewish American identification.

In Feagin's 2009 book *The White Racial Frame*, a white student at a midwestern college reports on a scene that he witnessed among other white male students. "With the full group membership present," Feagin reports, "anti-Semitic statements abound, as do racial slurs and vastly derogatory statements. . . . Various jokes concerning stereotypes were also swapped around the gaming table, everything from 'How many Hebes fit in a VW Beetle?' to 'Why did Jews wander in the desert for forty years?' . . . The answers were 'One million in the ashtray and four in the seats' and 'because somebody dropped a quarter,' respectively." Feagin is confused by this narrative. He argues that these "jokes" suggest that those who tell them do not see their subjects as white: "Even *Jewish Americans* are included," he notes, "apparently as a people who are not authentically white" (emphasis added).[43] He expresses surprise when he encounters this fact throughout his research.

Kenneth Marcus, by contrast, asserts that the U.S. Department of Education's Office for Civil Rights (OCR) must confront the topic of Jewish identification so that Jewish Americans will be clearly defined at institutes of higher learning in order that the OCR can adjudicate claims of discrimination against them.[44] In *Jewish Identity and Civil Rights in America* (2010), he identifies a number of possible approaches to the topic. In none of them, however, does he adopt CRT examples of how Jewish Americans experience racialization. Rather, he treats CRT studies as antithetical to his purpose.



Jewish critical race theory must take these facts, and others like them, into account. Clearly, it would benefit from the theoretical arguments and examples of other CRT theorists. Unlike in the examples above, in which Feagin depicts Jews as racialized in the white student's account but not theorized as part of race theory, and in which Marcus dismisses CRT theorists, a more thorough coverage would acknowledge and address these incidents as *examples* of CRT.

To fully accommodate Jewish Americans—however they choose to identify—a Jewish CRT that also accounts for "religionization" must account for Jewish history. Whether Jewish Americans identify themselves as secular, Reform, Haredi, or something else, they must at least *consider* the Torah. Secular Jews, for instance, may acknowledge the Torah's existence or may be outright hostile toward it.[45] But *all* Jews look to the Torah for their origins. Whether they actually study the Torah, it forms the basis of Jewish existence. Many Jews think of themselves as a continuation of the lengthy history that Israelites, and then Jews, have experienced since biblical times.

Throughout Jewish history, from the rabbis onward, most Jews have turned to the narratives in the Torah as a means of informing their sense of self. A major focus entails God's bringing the Israelites to the land of Israel, God's exiling the Israelites (later the Jews) among the "nations," and God's redemption, which apparently will occur sometime in the future. Every year at Pesach (Passover), many Jews state that they *remember* coming to the land of Israel.

To adequately address Jewish history, Jewish critical race theory must not only take this history into account but also must consider how it affects Jewish American experience today. For instance, just as CRT draws on Black history in the United States to address how Blacks have responded to racism—and, more specifically, to Black narratives of slavery, theologies of liberation, "double consciousness," integrationism and nationalism, and the diasporic character of Black Americans[46]—Jewish CRT must emphasize not only the common history and traditions of Jews but the role of "religion" within them.[47]

Over time, the prevailing interpretation of "Jewishness" has been modified from simply "religiously alien," to "religiously alien" *and* "racially marginalized." In other words, a Jewish CRT must examine how religiosity is conditioned by, but not free from, the changing racial formulations that began in 1449 in Spain with the *limpieza de sangre* (blood purity) laws. Such laws were foundational for changing both Christian views of Jews and nationalistic discourses. By identifying Jewish converts to Christianity (*conversos*) as being of "Jewish lineage" and as "descending from the Jewish line," the *Sentencia-Estatuto* de Toledo marked the first time in history that conversion to Christianity did not eliminate Jewish identification.[48] In the *legal* language of the *Sentencia-Estatuto*, the identification of *conversos*, and by extension the identification of Jews, was reconfigured as embodied and determined by "lineage." The first use of *raza*, in Spanish, beginning in the fifteenth century, is translated as "race" in English.[49]



What was once a religion of the soul, according to Christian leaders, became a religion of the body. Augustine of Hippo charged in 426 in *The City of God* that Jews were both the "enemies" of and the "witnesses" to the church's superior Christianity. This doctrine governed the church's model for dealing with Jews from then until the thirteenth century.[50] In the late medieval era, Franciscan and Jesuit friars began reading the Talmud, which they determined was the "true" Jewish text, displacing the "Old Testament."[51] Thus, in June 1242 in Paris, Pope Gregory IX and the French king, Louis IX, ordered that all copies of the Talmud in France be burned, and the church decided that it no longer had to protect Jews. In light of this history, Jewish CRT should expressly address the "religious" reasons for which Jews were shunned, and, beginning in 1449, the "racial" reasons as well. Today, what people call "antisemitism" is a mixture of concepts that have targeted Jews in accordance with the dominant religious beliefs and racial trends throughout history, right down to the present day.

Like members of any minority community, most American Jews talk with one another about issues related to Jewishness. Many Jews tend to discuss with other Jews how they think about themselves as Jews, but they don't necessarily have such conversations with American non-Jews, the majority of whom are Christian. A Jewish CRT must consider how this behavior affects the "whiteness" considered applicable to most Jewish Americans.

Unlike most other "races," however, many Jews have hailed the wonders of being American. In fact, Beth Wenger asserts that Jewish Americans have even correlated Jewish biblical ideals with American democracy.[52] While the dominant white culture grappled with Black Americans' slave heritage, with Native Americans' land rights, and with Latinxs' pursuit of immigration claims, Jewish Americans, for the most part, could go unnoticed, as long as they asserted that they were a "religious" group. A Jewish CRT should examine this claim as well.

Most Americans expressed horror at Adolf Hitler's demonization of Jews and the Nazi murder of over six million Jews in Europe. As a result of this horror at the Shoah, a shift in the dominant thinking occurred in the United States, such that it was no longer socially acceptable to refer to Jews as a "race." Specifically, judges could not identify Jewish Americans as a race. Eric Goldstein writes, however, that many Jewish Americans expressed an emotional attachment to race as a way that they were set apart. But after World War II, "ethnicity" largely replaced "race" as "a linguistic strategy designed to recast their continued attachment to a racial self-understanding in terms more acceptable to the non-Jewish world." In the 1950s, Goldstein writes, "at bottom it was still the basic commitment to Jewish social identity and peoplehood—once articulated in the language of 'race'—that animated most Jews."[53] A Jewish CRT must consider this linguistic shift from "race" to "ethnicity" from the end of World War II to the present.

This decision, on the part of most Jewish Americans, finally to deny their categorization as a race had a number of results. In the postwar period, the assumption became that Jewish Americans are "white," which increasingly they are not, nor have they ever been exclusively so. Nevertheless, according to this assumption, *no* Jewish Americans are of color. Owing to the prevailing acceptance of Jewish Americans within the white and Christian American norm, most Jewish Americans are likely to conform to this norm. As a consequence, few scholars of racism and few people of color recognize that some Jewish Americans desire to be considered a "race" *despite* their supposed whiteness. A Jewish critical race theory must recognize that being accepted as white by the white majority becomes a roadblock, for many Jewish Americans, to feeling accepted by people of color, an acceptance for which many of them may yearn. This acceptance as "white" also has implications for Jews of color, who can be marginalized by their own communities because these assumptions do not account for multiple identifications among Jews.

For most Jewish Americans, being situated squarely within "whiteness" means that they may be mocked behind their backs by white American non-Jews.[54] It means that, depending on where one is in the United States, Jewish Americans may choose to display more or less of their Jewish identification.[55] It means that however nice Christian Americans may appear to be to Jewish Americans on the surface, quite a number of them still believe that Jews killed Jesus.[56] Many non-Jewish Americans think that they can identify Jews by their pointed noses, their hair, or even . . . their horns.[57] Jewish Americans continue to conceal their synagogues architecturally, so that they do not attract attention, not wanting to expose them to vandalism or other forms of destruction and attack.[58] A Jewish CRT must examine the fact that many Christians, and other non-Jews, have passed down religious dogma to their children that paints a negative picture of Jews, must look at how that dogma has been structurally reinforced, and must take account of how both things have, to some degree, incorporated Jewish racialization along the way.



In addition, some Jewish Americans identify as "ethnically" or "culturally" but not as "religiously" Jewish. Rabbis lament that most of them do not come to their synagogues, except maybe on Yamim Noraim (the High Holy Days). Perhaps they grapple with some problem that they have with Judaism, some memory of Jewish day school or even Yiddish camp.[59] Maybe their parents were secular Jews, imbuing them with socialist and labor union values. A Jewish CRT must account for these Jewish Americans as well, who insist that they are not "religious."[60]

Jewish Americans have never been defined by U.S. law. Whereas Black Americans were counted as only three-fifths of a person until 1865, and Native Americans were not citizens until 1924, Jewish American citizenship has not been codified by law. Early U.S. court documents mentioned "Hebrews" in cases where immigrants were trying to become "white" in order to be American, but never did Jews themselves file lawsuits demanding such treatment.[61] A Jewish CRT needs to account for Jewish Americans, who, until 1987, with *Shaare Tefila v. Cobb*, have hovered just below the surface of racially identified legal matters.

In the 1980s, the Jewish Advocacy Center, which sponsored Shaare Tefila's civil suit, aimed to replicate, in part, the Southern Poverty Law Center, one of whose main goals was to bankrupt the Ku Klux Klan. At the time, most Jewish Americans were still quietly repairing the damage that anti-Jewish vandals did to their buildings or synagogues, some of which probably occurred owing to the prevalence of Ku Klux Klan members nearby. In other words, Jewish Americans tended to hide whatever racialized damage the Ku Klux Klan and other vandals did. For the most part, Jewish Americans did not even begin to articulate a legal claim to a "racial designation" until 1982. And in this case, Irvin Shapell, one of the two members of the Jewish Advocacy Center, had to persuade Shaare Tefila Congregation to file a case against the vandals who had defaced their synagogue. In the context of the civil suit, Patricia Brannan followed the lead of the synagogue: she argued that the particular actions against the synagogue were racist, regardless of whether Jewish Americans themselves were a "race." A Jewish CRT must examine this distancing from, and yet identifying with, a racialized category in order to make sense of how Shaare Tefila members and, more broadly, Jewish Americans situate themselves in regard to race.



Investigating the concept of how Jewish Americans *experience* race allows Jewish studies scholars and critical race theorists to examine their complicated history outside the boundaries of the typical ways in which Americans think about race. Certainly, Jews were a considered a "race" in many contexts before they came to the United States. But even in the United States, Jews have dealt with racial forms of discrimination. Many Jewish Americans encounter, to varying degrees, injustice in a long history of past harms.

Thinking about how Jewish Americans identify and are identified racially as an ethical issue provides an entry point into discussion about the ways in which race, religion, gender, and ability, among other factors, affect their standing under the law. Relative privilege and marginalization accompany these and other categories, such that American norms have urged Jewish Americans to identify Judaism predominantly as a "religion" rather than as a "race." Considering this type of problem as an *ethical* one enables us to identify it as a social justice issue: CRT aims to correct the problem of racialized discord in the law, in which people's experiences do not match the legal arguments that are made for them, or in which no legal arguments account for those experiences. This is where we are now, perhaps: we have a race-based ruling in *Shaare Tefila Congregation v. Cobb* but very little legal theory—or little theory that accounts for legal issues—that can help us situate Jewish identification according to ideas about "racialization." We need future writings, discussions, and conferences in which Jewish studies scholars further develop what I have begun to address here.

## Notes

I want to thank, most of all, the members of Shaare Tefila Congregation who allowed me to interview them and who welcomed me to their synagogue. Many thanks also to Aaron Gross, who encouraged me to present a paper at the Society of Jewish Ethics in the first place, inspiring an earlier version of this chapter. And much gratitude to Jonathan K. Crane, who convened our panel, "Race with Jewish Ethics: A Symposium," at Emory University, and was very kind in presenting my paper for me in my absence; without him, this volume would not exist. Thanks to Stephen Glauz-Todrank, Aaron Gross, Shana Sippy, and to the reviewers who read earlier drafts of this chapter and gave me such helpful feedback, and to Tanisha Ramachandran, who commented on a later version. And thank you to the Law and Society Program, which sadly no longer exists at the University of California, Santa Barbara, and to the marvelous professors who informed my thinking there and here, specifically

Eve Darian-Smith and Lisa Hajjar. And I am most grateful to the wonderful Rudy V. Busto in the Department of Religious Studies, whom I always have in my head when I write about race.

1. But Keren McGinity makes it a point in her book *Still Jewish* that Jewish Americans remain Jewish even after they marry Protestants or Catholics.

2. Wolf, "*Sentencia-Estatuto* de Toledo."

3. Nevertheless, immigrants fought to "become white" in the cities.

4. A Pew Research Center Forum on Religion and Public Life survey finds that many Jewish Americans have shifted between movements, tending to become less observant as they age. See Pew Research Center, "Portrait of Jewish Americans."

5. See Levitt, "Other Moderns, Other Jews."

6. Khyati Joshi briefly discusses "religionization" in her article "Racialization of Hinduism, Islam, and Sikhism."

7. I also wrote about the Shaare Tefila case in "Judging and Protecting Jewish Identity"; see in particular p. 44 for my discussion of religion and race.

8. For a historical perspective on this issue, see Maldonado-Torres, "Race, Religion, and Ethics," esp. 706–7.

9. "Racial formation" is Omi and Winant's term, but whereas they employ it to discuss only the American context, I apply it with a wider geographical context and a longer historical period in mind. I adopt Irene Silverblatt's conception of "race thinking," in which she uses Hannah Arendt's term to examine the development of the idea of race by Spanish imperialists in the fifteenth to seventeenth centuries. I agree with Silverblatt's argument that the concept of race begins in the time and place that she indicates, as long as we acknowledge that it evolves and shifts depending on context. See *Modern Inquisitions*, 1–27.

10. Goldschmidt, *Race and Religion*, 26–28. On the concept of co-constituted categories, see also Maldonado-Torres, "Race, Religion, and Ethics."

11. The Supreme Court heard the case in tandem with *Al-Khazraji v. Saint Francis College*, 784 F.2d 505 (1985), in which a professor, Al-Khazraji, filed a suit against his college, which he claimed had denied him tenure on the basis of his "Arabian race."

12. See Du Bois, *Souls of Black Folk*, 34; Omi and Winant, *Racial Formation*, 66.

13. Goldstein, *Price of Whiteness*, 6.

14. Herberg, *Protestant, Catholic, Jew*, 23.

15. What Colin Woodard deems "Yankeeland" in his *American Nations*, 5–6, 57–64.



16. See Batnitzky, *How Judaism Became a Religion*, 13–14. For another perspective, see Boyarin, *Border Lines*. Boyarin asserts that early Jewish rabbis formulated their tradition in relation to and in opposition to Christian leaders, with the claim—although they did not say it in quite this way—that to be Jewish is *not* to be a member of a religion. In fact, he argues that both Christian and Jewish leaders defined themselves in opposition to one another, with Christian leaders growing in strength and overpowering Jewish ones.

17. Mendes-Flohr and Reinharz, *Jew in the Modern World*, 128–33.

18. I've put "liberated" in quotation marks because Jews were forced to give up many features of their daily lives and were expected to be Jewish only at home.

19. Levitt, "Other Moderns, Other Jews," 111.

20. Most Jewish Americans have conformed to the idea that Judaism is a religion, although there are some "secular" and "cultural" Jewish holdovers, which is a conundrum that many non-Jewish Americans cannot seem to fathom.

21. Batnitzky, *How Judaism Became a Religion*, 169.

22. Magid, *American Post-Judaism*, 5.

23. The names of courts, or lineages, such as Lubavitch or Satmar, are usually taken from the town in eastern Europe where the community began.

24. The Baal Shem Tov, or "Master of the Good Name," was a mystical Polish rabbi who is regarded as the founder of Hasidic Judaism.

25. Goldschmidt, *Race and Religion*, 21.

26. Note that Goldschmidt uses the terms "shared" and "contested" as well as "history" and "genealogy." Ibid., 202.

27. Fader, *Mitzvah Girls*, 14, 3, 32, 138–42. For another source on Jewish and

non-Jewish souls, see Wolfson, *Open Secret*.

28. *Express Tribune*, "9/11 Attacks."

29. Bonilla-Silva, *White Supremacy and Racism*, 40.

30. Hall, "Work of Representation," 28.

31. Gotanda, "Critique of 'Our Constitution,'" 257, 268.

32. See, respectively, Tehranian, *Whitewashed*; Ngai, *Impossible Subjects*; Carbado and Gulati, *Acting White?*

33. Omi and Winant, *Racial Formation*, 71, 55.

34. Tessman, "Jewish Racializations," 141–42.

35. Kurland and Casper, *Landmark Briefs and Arguments*, 417.

36. *Shaare Tefila Congregation v. Cobb*, 785 F.2d 523 (4th Cir. 1986).

37. Ibid., 538.

38. Deborah Garren, phone interview by author, September 22, 2009.

39. *Shaare Tefila Congregation v. Cobb*, 481 U.S. 615 (1987), 697.

40. It's important to note that ritual clothing is *logically* associated with "religion." In this context, however, it may seem quite odd to the dominant Christian majority in the United States, and here it might fall into the category that Levitt describes as "too religious." See Levitt, "Other Moderns, Other Jews," 111. I posit that what is meant by "too religious" could shift so much that it refers to "race"—as Omi and Winant define it ("a concept which signifies and symbolizes social conflicts and interests by referring to different types of human bodies")—in that people who wear these items *cannot do without them*. See Omi and Winant, *Racial Formation*, 55. If we can "tell" that people are different, there is some leeway between "religion" and "race," particularly from the perspective of people who wear ritual clothing, or have beards for religious reasons, etc. Goldschmidt remarks, "most Hasidim do not view their observance of religious laws and customs that shape their distinctive dress as negotiable or disposable aspects of their selves. Indeed, one Lubavitch leader told a journalist that he could 'identify with the Black plight' precisely because, 'What they say is we, the Blacks, can never assimilate here in America, and that's just the way I feel. The bottom line is, you can't change your color, and I can't take my yarmulke off. I can't take my beard off.'" Goldschmidt, *Race and Religion*, 163.

41. Silverblatt, *Modern Inquisitions*, 17; Bonilla-Silva, *White Supremacy and Racism*, 40; Omi and Winant, *Racial Formation*, 55.

42. Much later, the apparent ringleader of the vandals, Michael D. Remer, wrote a letter of apology to the congregation and then met with the rabbi, the synagogue's lawyer, and congregation president Shirley Altman to express his regrets in person.

43. Feagin, *White Racial Frame*, 11, 12.

44. Marcus, *Jewish Identity and Civil Rights*, 5.

45. Biale, *Not in the Heavens*, 1.

46. On Black narratives of slavery, see Douglass, *Life of Frederick Douglass*; on theologies of liberation, see West, *Prophesy Deliverance*, 69–91; on "double consciousness," see Du Bois, *Souls of Black Folk*; on integrationism and nationalism, see Peller, "Race Consciousness"; and on the Black diaspora, see Gilroy, *Black Atlantic*.

47. I put "religion" in quotation marks because, like "race," its meaning changes over time, and because religion was not a separate component of identification in ancient Israelite times. See Dubuisson, *Western Construction of Religion*; Masuzawa, *Invention of World Religions*; Batnitzky, *How Judaism Became a Religion*.

48. See Glauz-Todrank, "'Race Thinking' and Rights Making."

49. Nirenberg, *Anti-Judaism*, 238–39.

50. Steinberg, *Jews and Judaism*, 59.

51. Cohen, *Friars and the Jews*, 14–16.

52. Wenger, *History Lessons*, 2.

53. Goldstein, *Price of Whiteness*, 115, 206, 207.

54. See Martire and Clark, *Anti-Semitism in the United States*, 15–30.

55. See Goldstein's *Price of Whiteness* on "tribalism" and the observation that Jewish Americans are "choosing certain spaces and times to express it" (224).

56. Starr, "Millions Still Believe."

57. Kaye/Kantrowitz, *Colors of Jews*, 12, 29–30; Helmreich, *Things They Say Behind Your Back*, 16.

58. I have noted this in my observations of Shaare Tefila Congregation in Silver Spring, Maryland, Temple Emanuel in Winston-Salem, North Carolina, and Ohavay Zion in Lexington, Kentucky,

among other places. See also Stiefel, *Jewish Sanctuary*.

59. See, for instance, Goodheart, *Confessions of a Secular Jew*.

60. See Eisner et al., *Who Are We Now?* See also Levitt, "Other Moderns, Other Jews"; Glauz-Todrank, "Race, Religion, or Ethnicity?"

61. Between 1790 and 1952, potential Americans had to show that they were "white" or "black," although the clear majority tried to demonstrate whiteness. In his article "Performing Whiteness," John Tehranian argues that Ian Haney Lopez states that the Supreme Court's rulings in *Ozawa v. United States* and *United States v. Thind* mark the end of the courts' competing doctrines, between the "scientific model" and the "common-knowledge test," with the "common-knowledge" test ultimately winning out. In this reversion to "common knowledge," the courts assert the processes of social construction at work in race (see Lopez, *White by Law*). Tehranian rightly asserts that an additional factor is at work: racial performance. "Performance" is the ability to demonstrate "evidence of whiteness in their character, religious practices and beliefs, class orientation, language, ability to intermarry, and a host of other traits that had nothing to do with intrinsic racial grouping." "Performing Whiteness," 820–21.



## References


Batnitzky, Leora. *How Judaism Became a Religion: An Introduction to Modern Jewish Thought*. Princeton: Princeton University Press, 2011.

Biale, David. *Not in the Heavens: The Tradition of Jewish Secular Thought*. Princeton: Princeton University Press, 2011.

Bonilla-Silva, Eduardo. *White Supremacy and Racism in the Post–Civil Rights Era*. Boulder: Lynne Rienner, 2001.

Boyarin, Daniel. *Border Lines: The Partition of Judaeo-Christianity*. Philadelphia: University of Pennsylvania Press, 2006.

Brodkin, Karen. *How Jews Became White Folks and What That Says About Race in America*. New Brunswick: Rutgers University Press, 1998.

Carbado, Devon W., and Mitu Gulati. *Acting White? Rethinking Race in "Post-Racial" America*. New York: Oxford University Press, 2013.

Cohen, Jeremy. *The Friars and the Jews: The Evolution of Medieval Anti-Judaism*. Ithaca: Cornell University Press, 1984.

Douglass, Frederick. *Narrative of the Life of Frederick Douglass, an American Slave, Written by Himself*. 1845. Reprint, Mineola, N.Y.: Dover, 1995.

Du Bois, W. E. B. *The Souls of Black Folk*. 1903. Reprint, Mineola, N.Y.: Dover, 1994.

Dubuisson, Daniel. *The Western Construction of Religion: Myths, Knowledge, and Ideology*. Translated by William Sayers. Baltimore: Johns Hopkins University Press, 2003.

Eisner, Jane, Josh Nathan-Kazis, Dan Friedman, J. J. Goldberg, Steven M. Cohen, Elissa Strauss, Alan Wolfe, Sergio DellaPergola, Bethamie Horowitz, and Leonard Saxe. *Who Are We Now? Interpreting the Pew Study on Jewish Identity in America Today*. New York: Forward Association, 2013.

*Express Tribune* (Pakistan). "9/11 Attacks: How Turbans Instigate Hate Crime in America." September 11, 2013.

Fader, Ayala. *Mitzvah Girls: Bringing Up the Next Generation of Hasidic Jews in Brooklyn*. Princeton: Princeton University Press, 2009.

Feagin, Joe R. *The White Racial Frame: Centuries of Racial Framing and Counter-Framing*. New York: Routledge, 2010.

Gilroy, Paul. *The Black Atlantic: Modernity and Double-Consciousness*. Cambridge, Mass.: Harvard University Press, 1993.

Glauz-Todrank, Annalise E. "Judging and Protecting Jewish Identity in *Shaare Tefila Congregation v. Cobb*." In *Who Is a Jew? Reflections on History, Religion, and Culture*, edited by Leonard Greenspoon, 43–60. West Lafayette: Purdue University Press, 2014.

———. "Race, Religion, or Ethnicity? Situating Jews in the American

Scene." *Religion Compass* 8, no. 10 (2014): 303–16.

———. "'Race Thinking' and Rights Making." *Critical Research on Religion* 2, no. 2 (2014): 191–94.

Goldschmidt, Henry. *Race and Religion Among the Chosen People of Crown Heights*. New Brunswick: Rutgers University Press, 2006.

Goldstein, Eric L. *The Price of Whiteness: Jews, Race, and American Identity*. Princeton: Princeton University Press, 2006.

Goodheart, Eugene. *Confessions of a Secular Jew: A Memoir*. New York: Overlook Books, 2001.

Gotanda, Neil. "A Critique of 'Our Constitution Is Color-Blind.'" In *Critical Race Theory: The Key Writings That Formed the Movement*, edited by Kimberlé Crenshaw, Neil Gotanda, Gary Peller, and Kendall Thomas, 257–75. New York: New Press, 1995.

Hall, Stuart. "The Work of Representation." In *Representation: Cultural Representations and Signifying Practices*, edited by Stuart Hall, Jessica Evans, and Sean Nixon, 13–74. 2nd ed. Los Angeles: Sage Publications, 2013.

Helmreich, William B. *The Things They Say Behind Your Back: Stereotypes and the Myths Behind Them*. Piscataway, N.J.: Transaction, 1983.

Herberg, Will. *Protestant, Catholic, Jew: An Essay in American Religious Sociology*. Garden City, N.Y.: Anchor Books, 1960.

Joshi, Khyati. "The Racialization of Hinduism, Islam, and Sikhism." *Equity and Excellence in Education* 39, no. 3 (2006): 211–26.

Kaye/Kantrowitz, Melanie. *The Colors of Jews: Racial Politics and Radical Diasporism*. Bloomington: Indiana University Press, 2007.

Kurland, Philip B., and Gerhard Casper, eds. *Landmark Briefs and Arguments of the Supreme Court of the United States: Constitutional Law, 1986 Term Supplement*. Frederick, Md.: University Publications of America, 1988.

Levitt, Laura. "Other Moderns, Other Jews: Revisiting Jewish Secularism in America." In *Secularisms*, edited by Janet R. Jakobsen and Ann Pellegrini, 107–38. Durham: Duke University Press, 2008.

Lopez, Ian Haney. *White by Law: The Legal Construction of Race*. 2nd ed. New York: New York University Press, 2006.

Magid, Shaul. *American Post-Judaism: Identity and Renewal in a Postethnic Society*. Bloomington: Indiana University Press, 2013.

Maldonado-Torres, Nelson. "Race, Religion, and Ethics in the Modern/Colonial World." *Journal of Religious Ethics* 42, no. 4 (2014): 691–711.

Marcus, Kenneth L. *Jewish Identity and Civil Rights in America*. New York: Cambridge University Press, 2010.

Martire, Gregory, and Ruth Clark. *Anti-Semitism in the United States: A Study of Prejudice in the 1980s*. New York: Praeger, 1982.

Masuzawa, Tomoko. *The Invention of World Religions: Or, How European Universalism Was Preserved in the Language of Pluralism*. Chicago: University of Chicago Press, 2005.

McGinity, Keren R. *Still Jewish: A History of Women and Intermarriage in America*. New York: New York University Press, 2009.

Mendes-Flohr, Paul, and Jehuda Reinharz. *The Jew in the Modern World: A Documentary History*. New York: Oxford University Press, 1995.

Ngai, Mae M. *Impossible Subjects: Illegal Aliens and the Making of Modern America*. Princeton: Princeton University Press, 2004.

Nirenberg, David. *Anti-Judaism: The Western Tradition*. New York: W. W. Norton, 2013.

Omi, Michael, and Howard Winant. *Racial Formation in the United States from the 1960s to the 1990s*. 2nd ed. New York: Routledge, 1994.

Peller, Gary. "Race Consciousness." In *Critical Race Theory: The Key Writings That Formed the Movement*, edited by Kimberlé Crenshaw, Neil Gotanda, Gary Peller, and Kendall Thomas, 127–58. New York: New Press, 1995.

Pew Research Center Forum on Religion and Public Life. "A Portrait of Jewish

Americans: Connection with and Attitudes Toward Israel." October 1, 2013. https://www.pewforum.org/2013/10/01/chapter-5-connection-with-and-attitudes-towards-israel.

Silverblatt, Irene. *Modern Inquisitions: Peru and the Colonial Origins of the Civilized World*. Durham: Duke University Press, 2004.

Starr, Bernard. "Millions Still Believe 'the Jews' Killed Jesus." *Algemeiner*, December 16, 2013. http://www.algemeiner.com/2013/12/16/millions-still-believe-the-jews-killed-jesus/#.

Steinberg, Theodore L. *Jews and Judaism in the Middle Ages*. Santa Barbara: Praeger, 2008.

Stiefel, Barry L. *Jewish Sanctuary in the Atlantic World: A Social and Architectural History*. Columbia: University of South Carolina Press, 2014.

Tehranian, John. "Performing Whiteness: Naturalization Litigation and the Construction of Racial Identity in America." *Yale Law Journal* 109, no. 4 (2000): 817–48.

———. *Whitewashed: America's Invisible Middle Eastern Minority*. New York: New York University Press, 2009.

Tessman, Lisa. "Jewish Racializations: Revealing the Contingency of Whiteness." In Tessman and Bar On, *Jewish Locations*, 131–48.

Tessman, Lisa, and Bat-Ami Bar On, eds. *Jewish Locations: Traversing Racialized Landscapes*. Lanham, Md.: Rowman and Littlefield, 2001.

Wenger, Beth S. *History Lessons: The Creation of American Jewish Heritage*. Philadelphia: University of Pennsylvania Press, 2010.

West, Cornel. *Prophesy Deliverance*. Louisville: Westminster John Knox Press, 1982.

Wolf, Kenneth Baxter, trans. "*Sentencia-Estatuto* de Toledo, 1449." Medieval Texts in Translation. http://sites.google.com/site/canilup/toledo1449.

Wolfson, Elliot R. *Open Secret: Postmessianic Messianism and the Mystical Revision of Menahem Mendel Schneerson*. New York: Columbia University Press, 2009.

Woodard, Colin. *American Nations: A History of the Eleven Rival Regional Cultures of North America*. New York: Penguin Books, 2011.



## Classic Text and Questions to Ponder

This chapter explores how American Jews have related with the socially constructed concepts of religion and race. They assimilated to the American category of "religion" and now, for the first time, they protected themselves as a race. Glauz-Todrank says that American Jews generally have taken the public position that they are a religious community among others in American society, yet have privately, among themselves, sometimes thought of themselves as a race. This is due in part to the ways in which race has been color-coded within the American context, because "blackness," referring to Black slaves from Africa and to people of African descent, was differentiated from "whiteness," as Black slaves attempted to convert to Christianity to try to escape enslavement.

Put differently, color becomes most apparent when juxtaposed with contrasting shades; otherwise it is relatively difficult to "see" a color as such. The Mishnah, the earliest layer of rabbinic law (ca. 200 C.E.), discusses the relativity of color, and skin color in particular, in the following ruling. "At times a white patch of skin (baḥeret) will appear dull on a white person (*germani*) yet bright on a black person (*kushi*). The children of Israel are [at this time] like boxwood, neither black nor white but intermediate. Rabbi Akiva says that, like portrait painters with paints with which to portray figures in black, white, and intermediate, one should put intermediate paint around a baḥeret to evaluate it. Rabbi Judah disagrees, saying that it is better to evaluate a skin patch vis-à-vis the person's own skin color" (Mishnah Negaʿim 2:1). Either way, assessing the severity of a baḥeret requires that it be juxtaposed with a different skin complexion, whether natural (the person's own skin) or manufactured (painted on by the evaluator).

- The rabbis develop a law that discusses different ways to assess baḥeret depending on the skin color of the afflicted person. What are the merits and drawbacks of this instruction?
- Glauz-Todrank explores the curious situation of Shaare Tefila Congregation's seeking protection, on the advice of its lawyers, under race-based civil rights, because this was the best way for them to receive coverage. Consider that racialization is set by the ruling class, and that Jewish Americans did not really fit into the category of "religion" or "race." How is this effort a natural or a manufactured fit?
- Critical race theory highlights *experience* as critical to appreciating race and racism, and Glauz-Todrank demonstrates how Jews, at least in this one congregation, experienced themselves as "white" but simultaneously as victims of racism. Why might it be ethically important for the law to acknowledge racialized experience?

# 9

## Racial Standing

### How American Jews Imagine Community, and Why That Matters

SARAH IMHOFF

In this chapter, I take a rather unorthodox path to analyzing Jews and race: I begin with internet advertisements and end at Mount Sinai. The route that connects the ads to the Israelites at the mountain is an epistemology of Jewishness, and the questions that propel the journey are: How do we know who is Jewish? How should we know? And what are the consequences of these ways of knowing? In particular, I look at how ideas about race can structure Jewishness—often invisibly, always with consequences. After the devastating effects of the racist constructions of the Third Reich and the Shoah, "race" talk as it related to the Jewish community receded.[1] In U.S. American contexts, talk about "Jews and race" came to refer to how Jews interacted with Blacks, or, more recently, how Jews inhabited their whiteness.[2] But just because Jews today rarely explicitly invoke the idea of a "Jewish race," this doesn't mean that race-based conceptions of Jewishness have also disappeared. Even though the language of "race" has fallen out of cultural favor, many of the ideas connected with it persist.[3] I thus begin by discussing this racialist construction of Jewishness, then suggest its liabilities, and finally pose a categorically different means of answering the question "Who is a Jew?"

I began this project after a few chance encounters with internet ads. When internet-based DNA-testing companies pay for splashy ads that ask "Are You Jewish?" and market "Jewish DNA kits" and "Jewish DNA tests," they imply a genetic basis for Jewishness.[4] These services, sometimes implicitly and sometimes explicitly, claim that a gene sequence can determine Jewishness. This is, both biologically and halakhically speaking, nonsense. There is no gene that all Jews and only Jews have. There are gene sequences that are common in those who identify as Ashkenazi, some for Sephardim, and several across both Ashkenazim and Sephardim.[5] But the statistical likelihood of finding these gene sequences is helpful only at the level of population and probability. The presence or absence of particular gene sequences in an individual person's DNA cannot determine whether or not that person is Jewish.



Yet over the past decade or so, this gene-based mode of defining who is a Jew has become widespread in popular discourse.[6] Thus these personal DNA tests—a new scientific tool for understanding oneself—actually represent an instance of a much broader set of assumptions about Jewishness and who is a Jew. I am just one of a great many people interested in the question of who is a Jew, but I am less interested in the answer than in investigating how people construct that answer.

In this chapter, I am interested in the expansive category of identification called Jewishness, rather than in more narrowly defined conceptions, such as halakhic definitions of who is a Jew for religious purposes, or Israeli determinations of who is eligible for the right of return. The more expansive category I am calling *Jewishness* is a far better match for the social realities of contemporary life. (This chapter generally focuses on the United States, though some of the discussion applies to Jews throughout the world today.) In 2013, the Pew Forum on Religion and Public Life polled American Jews. In order to determine whether the person who answered the phone was eligible for the survey, they didn't just ask, "Are you Jewish?" A peek at the results suggests why that question would have yielded unreliable, and perhaps unrepresentative, results. While 78 percent of Jews surveyed said that they were "Jewish by religion," 22 percent of American Jews identified themselves as having no religion.[7] In addition to religious and nonreligious Jews, the poll also interviewed people it categorized as "non-Jewish people of Jewish background" and those with "Jewish affinity." It defined "non-Jewish people of Jewish background" as those who were raised Jewish or had at least one Jewish parent and no longer considered themselves Jewish. Those with "Jewish affinity" included people who were not raised Jewish, had no Jewish parents, and did not identify themselves as practitioners of Judaism, yet claimed some affinity for Judaism and/or Jewishness. The survey wanted to catch all manner of Jewish identification—the religious Jews, the "just Jewish," the "half-Jewish,"[8] and those with "Jewish affinity."

Jewish identifications are complex and various, and many defy the norms of halakhah. As author Sadie Stein writes, "'Half-Jew,' said the more religious, was not an identity. But, as any of us can tell you, it most certainly is."[9] As Stein and the Pew survey suggest, halakhah cannot tell the whole story of Jewish identification. Scholarly literature on intermarriage is now moving toward asking *how* families with one Jewish parent are Jewish, rather than *whether* they are.[10] Shaul Magid has recently argued that these kinds of shifting and partial identifications are in fact a central characteristic of American Jewish life.[11] "Jewishness," then, is an expansive category of identification that includes some combination of having Jewish ancestors, having Jewish family members, and participating in cultural or religious practices conceived as Jewish.



## Racialist Logics of Jewishness

Critical race theory provides useful vocabulary for understanding how individuals and groups identify themselves, and it offers particular insight into ways of "knowing" Jewishness. Kwame Anthony Appiah uses the term "racialism" to describe a way of thinking that posits "heritable characteristics, possessed by members of our species, which allow us to divide them into a small set of races, in such a way that all the members of these races share certain traits and tendencies with each other that they do not share with members of any other race."[12] Racialism is not inherently unethical, Appiah explains; one might assume that each race had distinctive traits and tendencies without assuming that some races are better than others. Racialist thinking need not be racist thinking. Nevertheless, like all cultural modes of knowing, it is not innocent of power.

People have used explicitly racial definitions of Jewishness for almost as long as there have been conceptions of race. Although racialist definitions often posit essentialist or transhistorical constructions of the identity in question, the constructions themselves are not transhistorical but are differentiated products of their own cultural context. The racialist definitions of Jewishness used by the Catholic Church during the Crusades assumed that some measure of Jewishness lingered even after a person converted to Christianity.[13] Jews' physical and spiritual traits were ontologically related to their status as rejecters of Jesus as messiah. When, in 1909, the rabbi Judah Magnes talked of the potential of the "Jewish race," he imagined a shared biological, cultural, and even spiritual heritage that didn't require religious belonging or practice.[14] He imagined something like a Lamarckian heritage, wherein both intellectual and physical traits—even if they were acquired rather than innate—passed down from parents to children. These racialist constructions and their contemporary counterparts are different from the ones we see today, though a family resemblance remains.



Although few Americans today describe Jewishness in the language of race, many nevertheless use racialist ideas about Jewishness when they talk about who is a Jew. These conversations often include heritable traits and tendencies—including physical appearance, intellectual capacity, physical aptitude, and psychological disposition. Racialism lurks in the implicit definitions of Jewishness when Madeleine Albright is "discovered" to be Jewish because her maternal grandmother was Jewish, when Jews of color are treated as outsiders in their own synagogues, and even when Jews cite the number of Jewish Nobel Prize winners as evidence of the superior Jewish intellect.

Racialist logics of Jewishness underwrite each of these examples, but there are different species of the genus "racialist conception of Jewishness." Though there are many, I will explore two of these species here: the genetic body and the apparent body. The genetic body encompasses discourses about DNA, "Jewish diseases," and other kinds of gene talk, while the apparent body relies on visual cues on the surface of the body, such as skin color, hair texture, stature, and eye color. The two modes of conceptualizing Jewishness are by no means identical, but they do similar work: they create boundaries that seem clear but are in fact incoherent when applied to the social world in which we live. I have argued elsewhere that conversations about personal DNA testing and recently increased interest in claiming *anusim* (or "crypto-Jewish") heritage demonstrate how racialist ideas undergird many cultural constructions of Jewishness.[15] Whether they discuss the genetic body or the apparent body, it becomes clear that people use biological and geographical discourses—both components of the social construction of race—to claim Jewish identity. DNA studies and American crypto-Jews are only two manifestations of this biologized thinking about Jewish identity. "Gene talk" runs through discussions of Jewish genealogy, in both professional and amateur settings.[16] And in political ones too: in 2013, Birthright Israel refused to accept nineteen-year-old (light-skinned, Russian) Masha Yakerson without a DNA test "proving" that she was Jewish.[17]

This racialist logic of Jewishness is perhaps most clear in discussions of genetics, yet it also subtly pervades dominant popular contemporary understandings of Jewishness. While some racialist ideas of physical traits—such as comic celebrations of big noses or "Jewfros"—seem innocuous and superficial, others are more deeply embedded in the notion of what it means to be a Jew and have a Jewish body. The normative Jewish body, to take a nonexhaustive list, has light skin, hair that may be curly, and a certain sort of nose (not aquiline). Persons who do not conform to these norms are often perceived by others as non-Jews, regardless of whether they actually identify as Jewish. Blonde-haired, blue-eyed Jews are often told they "don't look Jewish." And so are many Jews of color.



Personal narratives from Judith Weisenfeld, Julie Iny, Erika Davis, and dozens of others show how assumptions about skin color can shape—and even structure—experiences for Jews of color.[18] Reacting to Hasidic outreach efforts on the streets of New York, Weisenfeld reflects on how she is perceived: "Dark and curly hair, yes, but also brown skin that makes it easy for the Hasidic man to allow me to recede into the background as he surveys the crowd. That I have never been taken to be a candidate for reincorporation into Jewish observance has been the source of some irritation to me and I have been known, on occasion, to loiter nearby such an evangelizing event trying to be both conspicuous and inconspicuous at once, resentment brewing inside me. Why won't he ask me?"[19]

These two species of racialist conceptions of Jewishness, those of the genetic and the apparent body, are not always separate, and they frequently intersect with each other. For instance, the reluctant inclusion of the Lemba as "real Jews,"[20] Israeli attitudes toward Ethiopian Jews[21] and Bene Israel (Indian Jews),[22] and even to some extent ethnic inequality among Ashkenazim, Sephardim, and Mizrahim[23]—all demonstrate the complicated relationships among Jewishness, race, and DNA. Racialist constructions of Jewishness, then, are not merely vestiges of Nazism or antisemitism, and we see their subtle workings far beyond contemporary racist discourse.

In short, racialist thinking does not have neutral effects. So if implicitly racialist definitions of Jewishness exclude or devalue many people who identify as Jews, and if Jewish communities generally want to include and value Jews, then why do they persist? Part of the answer to why Jews of color in particular experience exclusion is the continuing racism across all strata of American culture. But American racism is not a sufficient explanation for all of the species of racialist conceptions of Jewishness. Even beyond skin color and other visible traits that seem to make race knowable, racialist logics structure ideas about Jewishness. Elsewhere, I have suggested that racialist discourse about Jewishness has gained such popularity and explanatory power because of its appeal to biomedical criteria for Jewishness: these criteria may be so attractive precisely because they seem to provide objective criteria for "who is a Jew" at a time when Jewish identity has become increasingly fluid and contested. For instance, a discourse in which genetic language and scientific authority produce Jewish bodies can seem to provide certainty instead of complexity or ambiguity when it comes to defining Jewish identity.  Racialist definitions seem to offer fixity and predictability, which can be both calming and alluring.

In the end, of course, they cannot: genes for Tay-Sachs disease or linked to Cohen ancestors cannot make a person Jewish, nor can their absence make someone non-Jewish.[24] These genetic markers, and other racialized traits such as skin color, do not always align with other norms of Jewishness, such as Passover observance, eating lox, or even having a Jewish mother. Tying Jewishness to genetics, for instance, might be done to ensure the certainty of who is a Jew on a case-by-case basis, but the resulting collection of people deemed Jewish would bear little relationship to the boundaries of any current community or theological ideas of the Jewish people. Nevertheless, the appearance of certainty holds appeal for many Jews and non-Jews who find the increasingly porous boundaries of Jewish identity destabilizing.

In the following sections, I explore the process of identification, suggest the costs of leaving these racialist constructions unacknowledged and unchanged, and offer one alternative epistemology for theorizing Jewishness. This focus on racialist discourse helps us explore questions about what is lost and what is gained, and about who and what is excluded, when it constructs Jewishness. Judith Butler's account of identity and subject positions serves as a jumping-off point for thinking about the racialist picture of Jewishness, the kinds of bodies it excludes, and the people it does or does not interpellate as Jewish. When we read racialist discourse with an eye to the construction of subjectivity and communal identity, we encounter the paradox that a seemingly coherent racialist identity position for the individual Jew may come only at the expense of a recognizable communal Jewishness. In the end, I hope to displace the preoccupation with a "standing" that would unequivocally establish one's Jewishness with the performative question "With whom do you stand?"

## Identification

To understand what happens if we leave a racialist conception of Jewishness unchanged, we must first ask how the process of identification works. I have intentionally avoided the common phrase "Jewish identity" here because, in my view, it misleads: it suggests that there is a singular, stable, definable thing we can call "Jewish identity." It obscures differences in historical and cultural context. Jewishness was not the same in fifth-century Babylonia as it was in medieval Spain or the twenty-first-century United States. It also obscures the differences among people. The norms for women identifying as Jewish, for instance, differ from the norms to which men would conform to be Jewish.[25]



Most important, the phrase "Jewish identity" suggests that identity is fixed, complete, and stable, though it is actually always in flux, always in a state of becoming, always partial and incomplete. In this way Jewish identification is similar to all identifications. At the simplest level, we can recognize moments when a person identifies as more Jewish or less Jewish. At Christmas, or at a dinner party where pork chops are served, or on Passover, one might find Jewishness to be a prominent part of one's self-conception. At other times, perhaps in the presence of Jews who are far more religiously observant, or in conversation with those who identify a particular political view with which one disagrees as Jewish, or when talking about non-Jewish relatives or ancestors, one might see Jewishness as a less prominent part of one's self-conception.

Even beyond these examples, the very process of identification itself is shot through with instability. Judith Butler and other poststructuralists who write about identification remind us that identity is never a given. It is a process that takes place through complex interaction between a subject and the social norms of her cultural world. It involves her own subjectivity as well as recognition by others, both of which are structured by social norms. This interaction is not merely one in which a preexisting subject comes to confront social norms that are exterior to her. Rather, those social norms structure the very possibility of her existence as a subject.[26]

Identification, then, is not merely an act of individual will. The phenomenon known as "passing"—in which someone who is "really" one (typically) race, religion, or sex "passes" as a person of a different race, religion, or sex—makes visible the presence of these norms and the process of conforming to them. To take a recent example that received national attention, Rachel Dolezal conformed to many of the norms of blackness—her hair, clothing, and political activism all suggested that she was Black. And she saw herself as Black. But when it came out that she was born to two white parents, others did not see her as Black.[27] When she did not conform to the norm of having Black parents or grandparents, she was no longer recognized as Black. As the cultural conversation about Rachel Dolezal starkly demonstrates, because of the strength and ubiquity of social norms, a person cannot identify as something and expect to be treated as such unless others also recognize her as such. This process of identification, therefore, is subject not only to one's own sense of self but also to one's ability to convince others that one has conformed to social norms.



Thus identification, whether as Jewish, as a woman, as a person of color, or as something else, is performative. That is, a person behaves, speaks, or appears in a certain way that either conforms (what Butler calls "citing") or does not conform to norms associated with an identity. A woman might wear makeup, or bear a child, or defer to someone else in a conversation. A Jew might eat matzah ball soup, use self-deprecating humor, or go to a synagogue. These performatives are always a process of interaction between the subject herself and a set of social norms. This process is ongoing and sometimes fragile. If one stops citing norms, then one risks no longer being recognized as that identity. A man who wore only dresses and makeup would risk his identification as a man, even if he'd worn a suit every day for the previous ten years. A Jew who converted to Christianity or regularly participated in Christian practices would risk her identification as Jewish. Identification, then, is not a fixed or irrevocable achievement or possession. Some identifications are more fragile than others, but all are results of the ongoing process of interaction between performances and cultural norms.

### The Costs of Racialist Conceptions of Jewishness

Racialist conceptions of Jewishness reinforce the sense that identity is fixed and stable, rather than acknowledging that identification is an ongoing process subject to missteps. Rejecting the scholarly insistence that race is socially constructed, racialist ideas hold that there is something essential—often biological—and therefore immutable about how people identify themselves and are identified by others. When Jewishness is underwritten by racialist conceptions, then the idea of Jewishness seems more stable. But there are costs to such stability. Many of these costs are exacted from those who do not clearly conform to the norms of racialist senses of Jewishness, such as Jews of color, converts, and others who do not "look Jewish."

Erika Davis reflects on the difference between her own experiences and those of a Jewish woman who has lighter skin: "With her dark curly hair and olive skin she can walk into most any shul on any Shabbat or holiday without an upward glance. When it's time to enroll her children in Jewish schools, if that's what she chooses, she'll most likely not have her Jewishness questioned. She can shop in a kosher grocery store or peruse the wares in a Judaica shop and no one will follow her around. No one will ask how she reads Hebrew so well, no one will ask her to share her story, no one will ask how she came to Judaism."[28] Jennifer Sartori's study of Jewish adoptive couples shows how other Jews frequently assume that Asian, Black, and Hispanic Jews are never "really Jewish."[29] The Jewish Multiracial Network publishes a "privilege checklist" that lists privileges "that many people take for granted today, but which are not available to most Jews of color in the United States." Some items on the list: "I do not worry about access to housing or apartments in predominately Jewish neighborhoods." "My rabbi never questions that I am Jewish." "I do not worry about being seen or treated as a member of the janitorial staff at a synagogue or when attending a Jewish event." "I am never asked 'how' I am Jewish at dating events or on Jewish dating websites." And "I have not been asked to leave a shul or a class or have been barred from entering a shul or a class due to my skin color."[30]



But there are also costs to every person who identifies as Jewish, whether or not they "look Jewish." Butler explains that in order to inhabit a coherent, seemingly stable identity, a person must exclude or conceal parts of herself that are at odds with the norms of that identity.[31] This is not merely about conformity to norms of appearance or taste. It is more expansively about a person's conformity to deeply embedded social norms, and it is especially true for minority groups that often define themselves over and against majority groups. Butler often uses the example of gays and lesbians, and we might see similar dynamics in the ways U.S. Jews define themselves as *not* Christian.

Yet any attempt to conform to all of the norms associated with a given identity will necessarily fail, because these norms are not always or in every way compatible with one another. For most identities, it is impossible to conform to all the associated norms. If one wanted to conform to all the norms of American womanhood, for instance, one would have to be both a sexual being and a virgin, a stay-at-home mother and a working mother, a sinner and a saint. Since one cannot conform to both the norms of feminine purity and the norms of feminine sexuality at once, it is impossible to be a perfect American woman. To be a Jew, one might have to be both funny and tragic, religious and atheistic, a socialist and a capitalist. In this sense, no one can perform all of the norms associated with being a Jew—yet another reason to question the notion of a single and coherent thing labeled "Jewish identity."

We cannot create genetic or bodily categories in a way that would include only self-identified Jews and not others, or in a way that would match any existing Jewish community. If we created a category of all people with the "Cohen gene," we would have a group with many Jewish men—but it would have no women at all, and it would likewise exclude the vast majority of Jewish men. If we created a category with people in the J haplogroup, it would have many Jews—but it would also have many non-Jewish Middle Easterners, and it would exclude converts, adoptees, and many of their descendants. If we looked only at people who have certain nose shapes and certain hair textures (and what, precisely, would they be?), we would exclude some people who consider themselves Jews and include others who do not consider themselves Jews. Any definition of Jewishness based on genetics or physical features would be exclusionary, falsely inclusionary, or both. And none would map neatly onto the way that Jewish communities define themselves.



The individual process of identification mirrors the construction of a group identity: certain physical types, traits, appearances, and behaviors are seen as central, whereas others are excluded. Both Jews and non-Jews might recognize Jewishness in eating matzah, using Yiddish expressions, having a worrying or meddling mother, using self-deprecating humor, having brown eyes and curly brown hair, being bookish or nonathletic, possessing expertise in financial matters, having light skin, preferring rye bread to white, finding mayonnaise vastly inferior to mustard, or even having certain DNA sequences. Although this list is somewhat whimsical, it is probably recognizable to most American readers. That is because some of its features actually do work to regulate who is recognized as a Jew. People are unlikely to doubt a person's Jewishness solely because she admits to disliking rye bread or preferring athletics to reading, for instance, but if she has dark skin, their doubt becomes far more likely.

Butler also calls attention to the ways in which such exclusionary definitions can impose a cost on individuals who espouse them. She expresses concern about "the cost of articulating a coherent identity position by producing, excluding, and repudiating a domain of abjected specters that threatens the arbitrarily closed domain of subject positions."[32] That is, the creation of a fixed and coherent identity, especially a minority identity, requires not only the inclusion of some traits and persons but the exclusion of other traits and persons. Those other people "out there" are necessary for us "in here" to be distinctive; we need a "them" to enable the fixed and rigid boundaries of an "us." Here we might think of how some Jewish community members discuss "the goyim," or Lenny Bruce's famous routine poking fun at the division of the world into things that are Jewish and things that are goyish. The concept of the non-Jewish buttresses the seeming coherence of the identity position "Jew," but it also forecloses possibilities for people who take up that identity position. The whole process reifies what it means to be a Jew and also what it means to be a non-Jew.

Butler is concerned about the regulation of identity because it closes off certain traits and people. But without the regulation of identity, how can people define a community? If we don't define our group on the basis of "us vs. them," how can we feel connection and togetherness? "Perhaps only by risking the *incoherence* of identity is connection possible," Butler suggests.[33] Paradoxically, by the very act of *giving up* certainty, clear answers, and bright boundary lines, people can create community. Holding fast to the markers of coherent and certain identity—for instance, specific DNA sequences to mark Jewishness—would create a clearly defined community. But such boundaries exclude many of the very people who both see themselves and are seen by others as part of that community.

Identification always makes reference to a community, relationships, or a collection of individuals. The idea of being "Jewish" only makes sense if there are others who are also identifiable as Jewish, and then others who are identifiable as not-Jewish. Butler's critique of identity does not go so far as to say that all boundaries are bad and should be done away with. Indeed, if we had no social categories, we would have trouble creating communities. Butler's concern, which I share, is not that the existence of communities itself is exclusionary, but that assumptions about the fixedness of identity can make communities exclusionary. Jewishness, like other communal markers, still needs to be associated with identifiable characteristics. But assuming the certainty and coherence of criteria for belonging is damaging.

The costs of this certainty—and of its social practices of community gatekeeping—reverberate beyond the exclusion of potential and current community members. There are also costs to how Jews could understand Jewishness religiously. Reliance on DNA, for instance, would exclude some Jews who are recognized by halakhah, the Reform movement, or other Jews. Converts, adopted children, and their descendants would find themselves written out of Jewishness. And there is also a cost for those who would be deemed Jewish by genetic criteria or racialist conceptions more broadly. One cost of a certainty based on racialist definitions of Jewishness is the weakening of the meaning of communal ties and religious practice. The power exercised through biomedical discourse would displace some of the power of religious discourse to produce and regulate Jewish bodies and the Jewishness of bodies.

When we fully recognize and articulate these racialist notions of Jewishness (that one can "discover" Jewish identity through DNA tests, that Black Jews must be converts, that Asian children adopted into Jewish families will never "really" be Jewish), we see that they operate in exclusionary ways. If racialist definitions of Jewishness exclude many self-identified Jews and work at cross purposes with communally stated practices of inclusion, then we need an alternative way of theorizing Jewishness.



One might suggest that there is already a system for clearly determining Jewishness, and that system is halakhah. However, as I have argued, Jewishness as a lived identification exceeds the bounds of halakhah and therefore needs to be theorized as such. I am not suggesting that halakhah is not religiously authoritative, that it should lose its religious authority, or even that it should change. Instead, I am claiming that Jewish identifications as they appear today cannot be meaningfully explained within the bounds of halakhah. In the most obvious instance, many Reform and Reconstructionist Jews are not halakhically Jewish, because they have a Jewish father but not a Jewish mother. In other instances, when Black Jews are halakhically Jewish, through descent or conversion, they are frequently still interpellated as non-Jews. Halakhah makes religious determinations and categorizations, but the social norms associated with Jewishness far exceed its parameters. This critique of racialist definitions of Jewishness, and the proposal to move toward a performative definition, then, does not require that we replace halakhah, or undermine it. This proposal concerns Jewish identifications, which relate to, but are not reducible to, halakhic ways of knowing.

## A Performative Alternative

Once articulated, the racialist logics of Jewishness raise a theological issue related to the social process of identification: they profoundly confuse the concept of the people of Israel. Peoplehood remains a central theological concept in Judaism, but it begs the question of who, precisely, is included in that people. Racialist logics suggest that the contours of peoplehood are fixed and knowable, that there is a clear "us" and a clear "them." But there are textual resources in Jewish tradition that suggest otherwise and conceive of Jewishness in a more open, perhaps even performative, fashion.

Let me clarify that the goal of this performative picture of Jewishness is not to collect a more moral group of people under the term "Jewish." People can and do perform Jewishness in abhorrent ways—American Jews who used the Bible to support slavery in the early nineteenth century and Baruch

Goldstein's murder of Muslim worshippers at the Cave of the Patriarchs in 1994 are just two examples. This performative definition of Jewishness would still include these people as Jews. It is not meant to distinguish between good expressions of Jewishness and bad ones. That is the task of other kinds of ethical distinctions. The goal of this performative notion of Jewishness is to reflect more accurately the ways people identify Jewishly in the world, which includes the normative dimension of greater inclusiveness for Jews of color, converts, and other Jews who experience marginalization.



In Jewish textual tradition, the revelation at Mount Sinai marks the moment when the people of Israel accept God's offer of the Torah.[34] In interpretations of the event, both inner-biblical and rabbinic, the event becomes one of critical importance for all Israelites (and then Jews) at all times throughout history. The inner-biblical interpretation in Deuteronomy 29:9–14 at first glance appears to be about a new covenant that God commanded Moses to make with the Israelites when they were in Moab. But it is also a clear reference to—and a reminder to the Israelites of—the revelation and covenant with their God at Sinai: "You stand this day, all of you, before the Lord your God—your tribal heads, your elders, and your officials, all the men of Israel, your children, your wives, and even the stranger within your camp, from the woodchopper to the water drawer—to enter into the covenant of the Lord your God, which the Lord your God is concluding with you this day, with its sanctions; . . . I make this covenant, with its sanctions, not with you alone, but both with those who are standing here with us this day before the Lord our God and with those who are not with us here this day." This covenant affirms both communal identity (a community that *includes* the "strangers" who were not officially recognized as Israelites) and that community's relationship with God. In its biblical context, Deuteronomy 29 is a recapitulation of the Sinai revelation in Exodus 19. It textually and ritually recalls the revelation at Sinai, though its setting is the land of Moab.

Ancient Jewish interpreters returned to Deuteronomy 29 to think about communal identification. Two rabbinic texts, Midrash Tanhuma and Babylonian Talmud Shevuʿot, both read the Deuteronomy passage to say something not only about events in Moab but also about Sinai: they interpret it to say that all Israelites throughout time were actually present at Sinai. These texts read the event at Sinai as a moment that not only defines the historical community that was physically present but also the transhistorical community of the people of Israel throughout history. They draw the warrant for this reading from the ambiguity of the text: if Moses began Deuteronomy 29 by calling "all Israel" (29:1) together—and even reiterated that everyone, from the infants, to the workers, to the leaders, was present—then every Israelite was "standing with us." Who, then, could Deuteronomy 29:14 mean when it referred to those who were "not with us here this day"? Rabbinic readers of the biblical text interpreted this to mean all members of the community throughout history. They read themselves, and all future Jews, into the event at Sinai.



Midrash Tanhuma-Yelamdenu, a rabbinic compilation from sixth- or seventh-century Palestine, attributes the tradition to R Isaac.[35]

> R Isaac said: "All the prophets received the inspiration for their future prophecies at Mount Sinai. How do we know? It is written: 'But with him who stands here with us this day before the Lord our God, and also with him that is not here with us this day' (Deut 29:14). 'Who stands here with us this day' refers to those who were already born, and 'with him that is not here' alludes to those who were to be born in the future. Hence they are '*not with us this day.*' 'Not standing here with us this day' is not written in this verse, but rather 'is not here with us this day.' This alludes to the souls who were to be born in the future since 'standing here' could not be said of them."[36]

Bodily presence at Sinai was not a necessity for being "with us" at Sinai. Both the "standing" and those for whom standing was not yet possible were together as one audience, one community before God. Even those who had no bodies yet were nevertheless present. The midrash includes these not yet embodied members of the community in the story and places them alongside the historical community members. In this way, the text defines belonging not by genetics, bodily attributes, ancestry, or even tribe. It defines belonging performatively: those who stand together form the community.

The Babylonian Talmud, often considered the central text of postbiblical Judaism, contains a similar (but here unattributed) tradition about all of Israel's presence at Sinai. "As it is written: 'Neither with you only' [Deuteronomy 29]. 'But with him who stands here with us.' From this we know only those who were standing by Mount Sinai. But the coming generations, and proselytes who were later to be proselytized, how do we know? Because it is said, and 'also with him who is not here with us this day.'"[37] The Talmud suggests a widening circle: God's covenant is and will be not only with Moses, or with only each person who stands "here with us," which means everyone gathered at Sinai. The rabbis read the subsequent text to expand the covenant to include all the future generations of born Jews and converts. Again, the mode of belonging is one not of descent but of performance: those who "stand with us" are, by their presence, part of that "us." Those who could not stand at the Sinai event nevertheless also participated in the covenantal act. They, like those who physically stood at Sinai, performed belonging in the community by affirming the covenant with God.



The idea of the Jewish people is a theological one, and it cannot be reduced to the apparent body, to genetics, or to biological relation. Ancestry and progeny do feature prominently in biblical, Talmudic, and midrashic texts; in fact, this Talmudic passage from Shevuʿot explains the "oath of judges," which has implications for past and future generations if one breaks it. And yet even with this emphasis on descent, the revelation at Sinai—the seminal event of the Jewish people—defines Jewishness not by descent but by "with"-ness. The deciding factor is who is "with" the community at Sinai. The text specifically includes converts, both present and future. Presence and connection, not descent, signal communal belonging.

These Jewish texts do not, of course, fully espouse a theory of performativity. But they open the door for it. First, they emphasize the idea of "standing with" rather than an essentialized and predetermined idea of who was (and is) Jewish. Second, they do not locate all Jewish bodies at the defining moment of Jewishness. At first, the absence of bodies seems like it cannot fit with the performative notion of identification, because bodies and materiality are a crucial part of how people engage in the process of identification.[38] However, because the bodies are not all predefined through the Sinai event, the text allows individual people to go through the process of identification in whichever cultural context their bodies come to inhabit. By *not* locating all Jewish bodies at Sinai, the text opens up the possibility for each person's body to inhabit his or her own historical and cultural space in the context of "local" norms, one of the fundamental aspects of identification.

These are, of course, not the only texts that think about how to define Jewishness. I am offering them as a model, not as the univocal judgment of the tradition. Especially because they are not meant to displace halakhah, but rather to help us think through Jewishness in all its everyday messiness of identification, they need not do the same work as halakhah. Performativity allows for the instability of identification. Unlike racialist conceptions, it admits the precariousness and ongoing nature of identification for all subjects.

I am not merely saying that Jewish communities need to do a better job of recognizing and including Jews of color. That is absolutely necessary but not sufficient. What I am suggesting here is a broader recognition, and then refusal, of racialist conceptions of Jewishness where we find them. When journalists announce that scientists have proved that "Jews are a race," or when a DNA lab informs a practicing Catholic priest that he "is Jewish,"[39] and when at the same time Jewish communities suggest that adoptees, converts, and their children are not quite real Jews, the Jewish community has an epistemological mess on its hands. But better to embrace the epistemological anxiety of Jewishness with borders drawn in the sand than the clarity of a Jewishness with impenetrable walls.



## Notes

1. But it never receded completely. See, for instance, Entine, "Jews Are a 'Race.'" For one sophisticated conceptualization of the idea of the "Jewish race" and its relationship to the body in western European Jewish history, see Gilman, *Jew's Body*.

2. The very phrase "how Jews inhabited their whiteness," of course, writes Jews of color out of the narrative of Jewishness.

3. For a psychoanalytic reading of this phenomenon, see Slavet, *Racial Fever*.

4. See, for example, "Are You Jewish?" at https://www.igenea.com/en/jews.

5. For a brief and lucid description of these genetics for a nonspecialist audience, see Sutton, "'Jewish Genes.'"

6. For scholarly resources about the cultural meaning of "Jewish DNA," see Kahn, "Multiple Meanings of Jewish Genes"; Kahn, "Are Genes Jewish?"; Hirschman and Panther-Yates, "Peering Inward for Ethnic Identity."

7. Pew Research Center, "Portrait of Jewish Americans."

8. There are communities of people who specifically identify as "half-Jewish"—see, for instance, the Half-Jewish Network, http://halfjewishnetwork.wordpress.com.

9. Stein, "Half-Jew's Complaint."

10. See, for example, McGinity, *Marrying Out*; Thompson, *Jewish on Their Own Terms*.

11. Magid, *American Post-Judaism*, 16–34.

12. Appiah, *My Father's House*, 13.

13. For some of the most sophisticated scholarship about Jewishness in this context, see Silverblatt, "Black Legend and Global Conspiracies."

14. See, for example, Magnes, "No Positive Principles," 7. For in-depth historical discussions of Jews, race, and whiteness, see Jacobson, *Whiteness of a Different Color*; Goldstein, *Price of Whiteness*; Efron, *Defenders of the Race*.

15. Imhoff, "Traces of Race" and "Problem of Jewish Embodiment."

16. I have borrowed the phrase "gene talk" from Tallbear, *Native American DNA*.

17. *Times of Israel*, "Teen Told She Can't Join Birthright"; Zeiger, "Russian-Speakers Who Want to Make Aliyah."

18. Weisenfeld, "On Not Being Jewish"; Iny, "Ashkenazi Eyes"; Davis, "Problem with Jewish Media." In addition to writing for popular Jewish media—Jewcy, Sh'ma, etc.—Davis writes an eloquent blog at blackgayjewish.com.

19. Weisenfeld, "On Not Being Jewish," 9.

20. Thomas et al., "Y Chromosomes Traveling South"; Parfitt, "Constructing Black Jews"; Parfitt and Egorova, *Genetics, Mass Media, and Identity*; Tamarkin, "Religion as Race"; Zoloth, "Yearning for the Long Lost Home."

21. Ben-Eliezer, "Multicultural Society"; Mizrachi and Herzog, "Participatory Destigmatization Strategies."

22. Parfitt and Egorova, *Genetics, Mass Media, and Identity*.

23. Khazzoom, *Shifting Ethnic Boundaries*.

24. For more on Tay-Sachs disease, see Imhoff, "Traces of Race." For a reflection on the cultural meanings of scientific claims

about Jews, intelligence, and hereditary disease, see Gilman, "Are the Jews Smarter?"

25. In making this point, Susannah Heschel asks provocatively, "Can women be Jews?" "Gender and Agency," 580.

26. For a longer description of this account of identification, see Butler, *Giving an Account of Oneself*, esp. 1–20.

27. See, for example, Samuels, "Rachel Dolezal's True Lies."

28. Davis, "Problem with Jewish Media."

29. See Sartori, "Modern Families."

30. Jewish Multiracial Network, "Privilege Checklist," https://www.jewishmultiracialnetwork.org/privilege-checklist.

31. Butler, *Psychic Life of Power*, 147–50. A gesture toward this argument appears in Imhoff, "Problem of Jewish Embodiment."

32. Butler, *Psychic Life of Power*, 149.

33. Ibid.

34. For feminist Jewish scholarship in particular, this is a familiar moment for thinking about who is included in the Jewish people. Judith Plaskow's classic *Standing Again at Sinai* takes this textual moment as the place to critique the invisibility of women in the tradition. That feminist critique remains an important one, and my discussion here is not meant to suggest a supersession of that critique.



35. More information about the manuscript variations, history, and text are available in Bregman, *Tanhuma-Yelammedenu Literature*.

36. Translation adapted from Berman, *Midrash Tanhuma-Yelammedenu*, 465.

37. Babylonian Talmud Shevu'ot 39a.

38. Butler, *Bodies That Matter*.

39. Kelly, "DNA Clears the Fog." For discussion of this event, see Imhoff, "Traces of Race," 10–13.

40. Rosenzweig, *Star of Redemption*, 317–18.

## References


Appiah, Kwame Anthony. *My Father's House: Africa in the Philosophy of Culture*. Oxford: Oxford University Press, 1992.

Ben-Eliezer, Uri. "Multicultural Society and Everyday Cultural Racism: Second Generation of Ethiopian Jews in Israel's 'Crisis of Modernization.'" *Ethnic and Racial Studies* 31, no. 5 (2008): 935–61.

Berman, Samuel, ed. *Midrash Tanhuma-Yelammedenu*. Hoboken: KTAV, 1996.

Bregman, Marc. *The Tanhuma-Yelammedenu Literature: Studies in the Evolution of the Versions*. [In Hebrew.] Piscataway, N.J.: Gorgias Press, 2003.

Butler, Judith. *Bodies That Matter: On the Discursive Limits of Sex*. New York: Routledge, 1993.

———. *Giving an Account of Oneself*. New York: Fordham University Press, 2005.

———. *The Psychic Life of Power: Theories in Subjection*. Stanford: Stanford University Press, 1997.

Davis, Erika. "The Problem with Jewish Media." *Black, Gay, and Jewish*, August 8, 2015. http://www.blackgayjewish.com/the-problem-with-jewish-media-2/#more-1810.

Efron, John M. *Defenders of the Race: Jewish Doctors and Race Science in Fin-de-Siècle Europe*. New Haven: Yale University Press, 1994.

Entine, Jon. "DNA Links Prove Jews Are a 'Race,' Says Genetics Expert." *Haaretz*, May 7, 2012. http://www.haaretz.com/jewish-world/jewish-world-news/dna-links-prove-jews-are-a-race-says-genetics-expert-1.428664.

———. "Jews Are a 'Race,' Genes Reveal." *Forward*, May 4, 2012. https://forward.com/culture/155742/jews-are-a-race-genes-reveal.

Gilman, Sander L. "Are the Jews Smarter Than Everyone Else?" *Mens Sana Monographs* 6, no. 1 (2008): 41–47.

———. *The Jew's Body*. New York: Routledge, 1991.

Goldstein, Eric L. *The Price of Whiteness: Jews, Race, and American Identity.* Princeton: Princeton University Press, 2006.

Heschel, Susannah. "Gender and Agency in the Feminist Historiography of Jewish Identity." *Journal of Religion* 84, no. 4 (2004): 580–91.

Hirschman, Elizabeth C., and Donald Panther-Yates. "Peering Inward for Ethnic Identity: Consumer Interpretation of DNA Test Results." *Identity: An International Journal of Theory and Research* 8, no. 47 (2008): 47–66.

Imhoff, Sarah. "DNA and the Problem of Jewish Embodiment." *Critical Research in Religion* 2, no. 2 (2014): 181–84.

———. "Traces of Race: American Jewish Identity." In *Who Is a Jew? Reflections on History, Religion, and Culture*, edited by Leonard J. Greenspoon, 1–20. West Lafayette: Purdue University Press, 2014.

Iny, Julie. "Ashkenazi Eyes." In *The Flying Camel: Essays on Identity by Women of North African and Middle Eastern Jewish Heritage*, edited by Loolwa Khazzoom, 81–100. New York: Seal Press, 2003.

Jacobson, Matthew Frye. *Whiteness of a Different Color: European Immigrants and the Alchemy of Race.* Cambridge, Mass.: Harvard University Press, 1999.

Kahn, Susan Martha. "Are Genes Jewish? Conceptual Ambiguities in the New Genetic Age." In *Boundaries of Jewish Identity*, edited by Susan A. Glenn and Naomi B. Sokoloff, 12–26. Seattle: University of Washington Press, 2010.

———. "The Multiple Meanings of Jewish Genes." *Culture, Medicine, and Psychiatry* 29 (2005): 179–92.

Kelly, David. "DNA Clears the Fog over Latino Links to Judaism in New Mexico." *Los Angeles Times*, December 5, 2004.

Khazzoom, Aziza. *Shifting Ethnic Boundaries and Inequality in Israel; or, How the Polish Peddler Became a German Intellectual.* Stanford: Stanford University Press, 2008.

Magid, Shaul. *American Post-Judaism: Identity and Renewal in a Postethnic Society.* Bloomington: Indiana University Press, 2013.

Magnes, Judah. "No Positive Principles." *Jewish Record* (Philadelphia, Pa.), November 28, 1909.

McGinity, Keren R. *Marrying Out: Jewish Men, Intermarriage, and Fatherhood.* Bloomington: Indiana University Press, 2014.

Mizrachi, Nissim, and Hanna Herzog. "Participatory Destigmatization Strategies Among Palestinian Citizens, Ethiopian Jews, and Mizrahi Jews in Israel." *Ethnic and Racial Studies* 35, no. 3 (2012): 418–35.

Parfitt, Tudor. "Constructing Black Jews: Genetic Tests and the Lemba—the 'Black Jews' of South Africa." *Developing World Bioethics* 3, no. 2 (2003): 112–18.

Parfitt, Tudor, and Yulia Egorova. *Genetics, Mass Media, and Identity: A Case Study of the Genetic Research of the Lemba and Bene Israel.* New York: Routledge, 2006.

Pew Research Center Forum on Religion and Public Life. "A Portrait of Jewish Americans: Connection with and Attitudes Toward Israel." October 1, 2013. https://www.pewforum.org/2013/10/01/chapter-5-connection-with-and-attitudes-towards-israel.

Plaskow, Judith. *Standing Again at Sinai: Judaism from a Feminist Perspective.* San Francisco: HarperSanFrancisco, 1991.

Rosenzweig, Franz. *The Star of Redemption.* Translated by Barbara E. Galli. Madison: University of Wisconsin Press, 2005.

Samuels, Allison. "Rachel Dolezal's True Lies." *Vanity Fair*, July 19, 2015. http://www.vanityfair.com/news/2015/07/rachel-dolezal-new-interview-pictures-exclusive.

Sartori, Jennifer. "Modern Families: Multifaceted Identities in the Jewish Adoptive Family." In *Mishpachah: The Jewish Family in Tradition and in Transition*, edited by Leonard J. Greenspoon, 197–218. West Lafayette: Purdue University Press, 2016.

Silverblatt, Irene. "The Black Legend and Global Conspiracies: Spain, the Inquisition, and the Emerging Modern World." In *Rereading the Black Legend: The Discourses of Religious and Racial Difference in the Renaissance Empires*, edited by Margaret R. Greer, Walter D. Mignolo, and Maureen Quilligan, 99–116. Chicago: University of Chicago Press, 2007.

Slavet, Eliza. *Racial Fever: Freud and the Jewish Question*. New York: Fordham University Press, 2009.

Stein, Sadie. "The Half-Jew's Complaint." Jezebel: A Supposedly Feminist Website, July 9, 2009. http://jezebel.com/5311118/the-half-jews-complaint.

Sutton, Wesley K. "'Jewish Genes': Ancient Priests and Modern Jewish Identity." In *Who Is a Jew? Reflections on History, Religion, and Culture*, edited by Leonard J. Greenspoon, 105–16. West Lafayette: Purdue University Press, 2014.

Tallbear, Kim. *Native American DNA: Tribal Belonging and the False Promise of Genetic Science*. Minneapolis: University of Minnesota Press, 2013.

Tamarkin, Noah. "Religion as Race, Recognition as Democracy: Lemba 'Black Jews' in South Africa." *Annals of the American Academy of Political and Social Science* 637, no. 1 (2011): 148–64.

Thomas, Mark G., Tudor Parfitt, Deborah A. Weiss, Karl Skorecki, James F. Wilson, Magdel le Roux, Neil Bradman, and David B. Goldstein. "Y Chromosomes Traveling South: The Cohen Modal Haplotype and the Origins of the Lemba—the 'Black Jews of Southern Africa.'" *American Journal of Human Genetics* 66, no. 2 (2000): 674–86.

Thompson, Jennifer A. *Jewish on Their Own Terms: How Intermarried Couples Are Changing American Judaism*. New Brunswick: Rutgers University Press, 2013.

*Times of Israel*. "Teen Told She Can't Join Birthright Without DNA Test." July 28, 2013. http://www.timesofisrael.com/teen-told-she-cant-join-birthright-without-dna-test.

Weisenfeld, Judith. "On Not Being Jewish—And Other Lies." *Soundings* 1 (2003): 3–11.

Zeiger, Asher. "Russian-Speakers Who Want to Make Aliyah Could Need DNA Test." *Times of Israel*, July 29, 2013. http://www.timesofisrael.com/russian-speakers-who-want-to-immigrate-could-need-dna-test.

Zoloth, Laurie. "Yearning for the Long Lost Home: The Lemba and the Jewish Narrative of Genetic Return." *Developing World Bioethics* 3, no. 2 (2003): 127–32.



## Classic Text and Questions to Ponder

Imhoff rejects racialist ways of knowing who is or is not Jewish in favor of performance. It is what people *do* that matters, not who or what they *are*. The early twentieth-century Jewish philosopher Franz Rosenzweig held a different position, perhaps inspired by the popular eugenics movements raging in his native Germany and throughout Europe and the United States. For Rosenzweig, Jews are connected by blood, and this biology promises Jewishness eternal life. Jews ("the community of the same blood") only need to propagate to ensure their durability, whereas all other communities must rely upon hope and will (that is, performance) to make "arrangements in order to pass the torch of the present on to the future."

> There is only one community in which such a relationship of eternal life reaches from the grandfather to the grandson, only one that cannot express the "We" of its unity without hearing as well within its core "are eternal" as its complement. It must be a community of the same blood, for only the blood gives to hope for the future a guarantee in the present. Every other one [community not based

on blood], every community can be propagated differently than by blood if it wants to establish its We for eternity, and it can do so only by safeguarding a place for itself in the future; all bloodless eternity is founded on the will and on hope. The community of the same blood alone feels even today the guarantee of its eternity running warmly through its veins. For it alone time is not an enemy to be restrained, over which, perhaps, perhaps even not—but it hopes that—it will be triumphant, but child and grandchild. That which for other communities is future and therefore in any case that which is still on the other side of the present—is for it alone already present; for it alone, that which is future is nothing foreign, but something that is its own, something that it carries in its womb, and it can give birth to it every day. Whereas every other community that lays claim to eternity must make arrangements in order to pass the torch of the present on to the future, only the community of the same blood does not have need of making such arrangements for the tradition; it does not need to trouble its mind; in the natural propagation of the body it has the guarantee of its eternity.[40]

The biological basis of eternal Jewish life relieves the mind, says Rosenzweig; there is no need to worry about how to transmit Jewish identity or tradition.

- Rosenzweig offers a biological, heritable foundation for how Jews embody and transmit Judaism. How does this racialist perspective help us know who is (and is not) Jewish?
- Imhoff rejects biology and champions performativity as the basis for group membership and identity, because it "allows for the instability of identification. Unlike racialist conceptions, it admits the precariousness and ongoing nature of identification for all subjects." She would have everyone refuse "racialist conceptions of Jewishness." What are the respective merits of racialist or performative paradigms for Jewish identity? What other paradigms might we use?
- Could a synthesis between racialist and performative paradigms be possible? What arguments could be made that both biology and performance are justifiable ways to identify who is Jewish and what Jewishness is? What arguments could be made that they fundamentally conflict?

10

# Race, Racism, and Psychopathology

## From Anti-Semitic Vienna to the Post-Civil Rights Era in the United States

SANDER L. GILMAN

### Toward a Statement of the Problem

In 2012, an interdisciplinary team of scientists at the University of Oxford reported that a clinical experiment had shown that the beta-blocker drug Propranolol could reduce implicit racial bias among its users. Whites were given a single oral dose of the drug and then asked to complete the "implicit association test," a reliable measure of racial prejudice. Relative to the placebo control group, those who were given Propranolol demonstrated no indicators of implicit racial bias. Though the researchers warned of the danger of biological research being used to make a "more moral society," they also asserted that "such research raises the tantalizing possibility that our unconscious racial attitudes could be modulated using drugs."[1] Shortly after the experiment, an article in *Time* magazine citing the study asked the question, *Is racism a mental illness?* In light of studies like the one of Propranolol, and the interest they generate within the mainstream press and academic circles, this chapter sketches the genealogies of race and racism as psychopathological categories from mid-nineteenth-century Europe and the United States up to the clinical experiment at the University of Oxford, addressing a question slightly different from the one posed by *Time* magazine. To wit, how did racism become a mental illness? Using historical, archival, and content analysis, it is possible to sketch how the nineteenth-century "sciences of man," among them anthropology, medicine, and biology, used race as a means of defining psychopathology at the very beginning of modern clinical psychiatry, and to see how these claims about race and madness became embedded within the claims of disciplines that deal with mental health and illness. I also analyze the contemporary shift that occurred after World War II in explaining racism—from a social, political, and cultural consequence to a pathological by-product.



From their birth in the late nineteenth century, the social sciences, along with clinical practice, have been haunted by biology.[2] That the psychological sciences have increasingly turned to pathological explanations to account for racism underscores the urgency of understanding the origin of this claim in the global study of race and racism. First, we need to explain the historical and cultural processes through which race and racism become tethered together as *psychopathological* conditions. We also need to develop a paradigm for the study of race and racism that does not stand in radical opposition to the life and psychological sciences, but instead properly contextualizes their role in modern-day racialization, including racism.

The question of how race was made into a pathological condition has been explored in numerous academic articles and books. Martin Summers, Dennis Doyle, and Jonathan Metzl have written about the history of race and mental illness in U.S. psychiatry (as perhaps, has some of the literature on mid-twentieth-century psychiatry in colonial settings); Natalia Molina, Samuel Roberts, and Keith Wailoo have studied race and the foundations of modern public health; and Jonathan Holloway, Darryl Scott, and others have examined the history of race and urban social science.[3] However, the shift toward pathologizing *racism,* and demonstrating the relationship between this shift and the previous pathologization of *race*, has not been documented.

Since the nineteenth century, the concept of race and racial difference has shifted from one of biological consequence to one of social structure. This is in part due to the early work of W. E. B. Du Bois and to the Chicago school of sociology prior to and during World War II, and to the rejection of biological notions of racial superiority in the aftermath of the Nazi regime's defeat. Yet, though the origins of the concept of race have been reframed as effects of complex social processes, racism has been increasingly pathologized within academic and clinical circles, including the social sciences. That is, race is explained predominantly in sociological terms, whereas racism is explained within a medicalized (specifically a psychological) framework.

### The Madness of the Victims

The first documented occurrence of the pathologization of racism is found in the subsequently important but at the time little recognized work of the proto-Zionist physician Leon Pinsker (1821–1891), *Mahnruf an seine Stammgenossen* (*Auto-Emancipation*) (1882). Before Pinsker, although some had labeled anti-Semitism a "phobia," such claims remained a metaphor, not a diagnosis. Pinsker undertook the first systematic attempt to analyze "Judeophobia" as a true mass mental illness of late nineteenth-century Europe that could never be cured:



> Judeophobia, together with other symbols, superstitions and idiosyncrasies, has acquired legitimacy as a phobia among all the peoples of the earth with whom the Jews had intercourse. Judeophobia is a variety of demonopathy with the distinction that it is not peculiar to particular races but is common to the whole of mankind, and that this ghost is not disembodied like other ghosts but partakes of flesh and blood, must endure pain inflicted by the fearful mob that imagines itself endangered. Judeophobia is a psychic aberration. As a psychic aberration it is hereditary, and as a disease transmitted for two thousand years it is incurable.[4]

Pinsker saw racism as an "inherited predisposition" that amounted to madness![5] He may have been employing a German version of the term Hebrewphobia, first used by the Irish reformer Richard Lalor Sheil in his speech "On the Disabilities of the Jews," given on February 7, 1848, before the House of Commons on the occasion of the reelection of Lionel de Rothschild, the first Jewish member of Parliament. But Sheil used the term only to signify an aversion to Jews. Pinsker was the first to provide a clinical definition of the term. He also isolated the etiology of this particular form of madness in the inherent racism of "Judeophobes." In his view, the cause of Judeophobia was the Enlightenment demand that Jews become "like everyone else" in a national society—become Germans, French, English—while repressing their own Jewish identity. Enlightenment philosophes saw this mandate as one based on "toleration" and as the most politically opportune way of integrating Jews into the nation-states that were taking shape in Europe. Pinsker's objective here was to create a new category, the double consciousness or self-hatred created by the internalization of this external image of the Jew. The Jew, Pinsker argued, was driven mad by trying to appease the anti-Semite's Judeophobia, and he saw this desire to appease as a result of the modern status of the Jew in the age of nationalism. The statelessness of the Jew in the age of nationalism condemned him to be an outlier, and this, Pinsker said, was the genesis of "the madness of the Jews." For Judaism, he argued,



> produces in accordance with its nature, vagrant nomads; so long as it cannot give a satisfactory account of whence it comes and whither it goes; so long as the Jews themselves prefer not to speak in Aryan society of their Semitic descent and prefer not to be reminded of it; so long as they are persecuted, tolerated, protected or emancipated, the stigma attached to this people, which forces it into an undesirable isolation from all nations, cannot be removed by any sort of legal emancipation. . . . Intelligent and rich in experience . . . we have never asked whether this mad race . . . will come to an end.[6]

This represented a radical break from the claim of nineteenth-century biological psychiatry that madness lay in the biological predisposition of racial groups.[7] The biology of race stood at the center of the nineteenth-century "sciences of man" (which included biology, medicine, and anthropology). But this was also the age of biological psychiatry; as the German neurologist and psychiatrist Wilhelm Griesinger wrote in 1868, "The so-called mental illnesses are found in individuals suffering from brain and nerve illness."[8] Race was seen as a precipitating factor in the etiology of mental illness, but only in "inferior races," such as Black Africans in the United States, the Irish in Great Britain, and the Jews in western and central Europe. Those born into such communities, according to this view, were already predisposed to mental illnesses of most every sort.

The civil emancipation of European Jews beginning in the late eighteenth century was paralleled by the growth of scientific racism. The nineteenth century was for Europeans, especially for German Jews, the best of times and the worst of times. European Jews slowly gained civil emancipation, increased economic and social mobility, and access to secular education, but all of these developments were resisted by the rise of political anti-Semitism (which wanted to reverse civil emancipation) and the reappearance in altered form of older forms of anti-Semitism like the "blood libel." Political realities in the Russian Empire led to massive pogroms and the flight of millions of eastern and mainly unacculturated Jews to the cities of western Europe and beyond. Political anti-Semitism also met with a range of Jewish responses, from assimilation and conversion, to the rise of political and cultural Zionism, to the establishment of secular Jewish political parties (at least in the Austro-Hungarian Empire). This brief summary does not attempt to do justice to a complex situation, but it provides a snapshot of large movements of people and thought, especially of the marginalized.

Throughout western Europe, the gradual integration of Jews into the body politic was seen both as the cause of Jewish psychopathology and as a source of danger to the nation-state. It is therefore unsurprising that Georg Burgl's  handbook of forensic medicine of 1912 said that "the Jewish race has a special predisposition for hysteria," a condition that would endanger society if left unchecked. This was a result of the degenerative nature of the Jew, wrote Burgl, and was marked by "physical signs of degeneration such as asymmetry and malocclusion of the skull, malocclusion of the teeth, etc."[9] The visibility of the Jew was hardly different from the visibility of the degenerate, their signs and symptoms pointing to their susceptibility to hysteria and other forms of mental instability. In Paris, the most important French neurologist of the late nineteenth century, Jean-Martin Charcot, averred that "nervous illnesses of all types are innumerably more frequent among Jews than among other groups." Charcot saw "the Jews as being the best source of material for [studying] nervous illness."[10] Charcot diagnosed the Jewish predisposition to mental illness as the result of religious practice, not of race per se. In particular, the Jews were mad because of their intermarriage. The dean of fin-de-siècle German psychiatrists, Emil Kraepelin, the founder of the Institute for Psychiatric Research in Munich, wrote with authority about the "domestication" of Jews, and claimed that their isolation from nature and their exposure to the stresses of modern life were the source of their predisposition to mental illness.[11]

Given the centrality of biology to race theory in the nineteenth-century sciences, it is extraordinary that anyone who thought of himself as a scientist could have avoided exploring the possibility that mental illness had a biological dimension. And scientists who were labeled different within this science (for example, Jews) had to come to terms with the fact that the field that gave them their status as scientists also demanded that they acknowledge (or refute) their inherent biological difference. Even acculturated Jewish doctors had to accept the consensus that they were predisposed to mental illness, for this supposition was part of what defined clinical medicine. The Italian forensic psychiatrist Cesare Lombroso, who helped establish the concept of "degeneration," was a Jew. In response to the charge that Jews were a degenerate subclass of human beings, a class determined by their biology, Lombroso wrote *Anti-Semitism and the Jews in the Light of Modern Science* (1893), in which he accepted the basic view that Jews were more prone than others to specific forms of mental illness.[12] He quoted Charcot to this effect and saw the reason for this tendency not in the physical nature of the Jew but in the "residual effect of persecution." In his account, racist persecution caused madness. But was racism itself also a form of madness?



Such diagnoses were not limited to the racial biology of Jews. In the United States, analogous diagnoses of mental illness aided in constructing African Americans as psychically weak and inferior, and the categories of mental illness were employed to present the nature of African American character and will as part of the justification for slavery throughout the nineteenth century. The former U.S. vice president John C. Calhoun used the 1840 census to argue that freed slaves suffered from mental illness at higher rates than slaves did. In 1851, the southern physician Samuel A. Cartwright invented a mental disorder he called drapetomania, or a slave's desire to escape his master, writing that if a slave was kept "in the position that we learn from the Scriptures he was intended to occupy, that is, the position of submission; and if his master or overseer be kind and gracious in his bearing toward him, without condescension, and at the same time ministers to his physical wants, and protects him from abuses, the negro is spell-bound, and cannot run away."[13] American abolitionists viewed such notions with a certain amusement, as when the architect Frederick Law Olmsted, in his *Journey in the Seaboard Slave States* (1856), observed that white indentured servants had often been known to flee as well, and satirically hypothesized that the supposed disease was actually of white European origin and had been introduced to Africa by traders.[14]

One difference between the responses of nineteenth-century European Jews and African Americans to such pronouncements was that the former were gradually integrated into the world of medicine and science, where they were required to accept such arguments concerning race as part of their certification as physicians and scientists. As I have argued elsewhere, such men had an obvious incentive to accept such concepts of biological race that was understandably lacking among those, like African American slaves, who were perpetually marginalized.[15]

The assumption that race was a biological reality informed the "science" of eugenics in the nineteenth century. Physical characteristics were seen as markers of racial pathology among European Jews in nineteenth-century Europe, and the physical and biological inferiority of Jews was equated with psychopathology in late nineteenth- and early twentieth-century Europe and America. No longer easily identified by external markers such as clothing, occupation, or address, assimilated Jews came to be identified by specific biological and physical characteristics. Perceived physical signs of mental and moral degeneration (the so-called Jewish nose, eyes, hair, etc.) were linked to diagnoses of mental illness. There was also anxiety about race mixing, which was "scientifically" relabeled "miscegenation," and its corollary, the potential invisibility of the Black, as one of the central themes of American and European society. Mark Twain's novel *Pudd'nhead Wilson* (1894) depicted the implications of such invisibility and the associated anxiety.[16] Both Jews and Blacks had to be seen if they were to be controlled; their potential invisibility through the act of passing as white gave rise to insurmountable anxiety about the source of this fear.



Newer theories of race science, such as Francis Galton's notion of eugenics, advocated the improvement of the white race by selective breeding for positive traits and the elimination of defective ones, especially mental illness. In an interview with a Jewish newspaper in England at the end of his life, Galton remarked, "It is one part of eugenics to encourage the idea of parental responsibility: the other part is to see that the children born are well born. It is a praiseworthy feature of the Jewish religion that, as a religion, it enjoins the multiplication of the human species. But it is still more important to determine that the children shall be born from the fit and not the unfit."[17] Eugenics sought to increase positive traits, but eliminating negative ones was even more important.

Thus, by the late nineteenth century, there was a growing trend among academics to locate the foundations of mental illness, including both racial formation and structural racism, in social relations. Epidemiological findings in Europe about the excessive number of mentally ill Jews, and in the United States about the equivalent problem among former slaves and their descendants, came at the beginning of the expansion of statistical evidence in the mental health field. The new science of measurement became one of the tools of contemporary clinical psychiatry among public health figures like John Shaw Billings, one of the first librarians at the National Library of Medicine.[18] Madness became linked to notions of degeneracy in race science, and rates of mental illness among African Americans and Jews were frequently invoked as empirical evidence of their inability to deal with "modern life." Such views drove the development of new tools for the evaluation of mental status that later became linked to both immigration policies at Ellis and Angel Islands and the civil rights movement of the 1950s and '60s, with its emphasis on the psychological impact of segregation on the psyche of the oppressed.

### The Crowd as the Source of Racism



The foundations on which race was pathologized were firmly established in psychiatry by the early twentieth century. Once these foundations were laid, the mental state of the racist became a question for study. Theories on crowds and collective behavior provided a category of analysis missing in earlier works, including those that sought to define prejudice as a response to the attitudes of collectives, such as Pinsker's. Racism came to be seen not only as a mental illness but as one that manifested itself among crowds and in the behavior of crowds. Thus "the crowd" became the twentieth-century equivalent of "race" in psychiatric literature. As Gustave Le Bon wrote in his *Psychologie des foules*:

> Whoever be the individuals that compose it, however like or unlike be their mode of life, their occupations, their character, or their intelligence, the fact that they have been transformed into a group puts them in possession of a sort of collective mind which makes them feel, think, and act in a manner quite different from that in which each individual of them would feel, think, and act were he in a state of isolation. There are certain ideas and feelings, which do not come into being, or do not transform themselves into acts except in the case of individuals forming a group.[19]

In the increasingly industrialized spaces of Europe and the United States, racism was construed not only as a psychopathological product of modernity but as a pathology that was encouraged and took on new contours in the crowd. In *Group Psychology and the Analysis of the Ego* (1921), Sigmund Freud rejected Le Bon's biological view of race while accepting his idea that collective mass behavior encouraged neuroses such as racial prejudice. Writing after World War I, Freud saw social proximity as the source of group prejudice.[20] Differences between groups, according to Freud, combined with close physical proximity, produced "insuperable repugnance."

> Every time two families become connected by a marriage, each of them thinks itself superior to or of better birth than the other. Of two neighbouring towns each is the other's most jealous rival; every little canton looks down upon the others with contempt. Closely related races keep one another at arm's length; the South German cannot endure the North German, the Englishman casts every kind of aspersion upon the Scot, the Spaniard despises the

> Portuguese. We are no longer astonished that greater differences should lead to an almost insuperable repugnance, such as the Gallic people feel for the German, the Aryan for the Semite, and the white races for the coloured.[21]

Ironically, Freud's early views were echoed by the Third Reich to explain the danger of miscegenation between the Aryan and "lesser" races. The consequences of close contact between Germans and Jews, and between whites and nonwhites in the United States, were viewed as potentially pathological. The predisposition of Jews and Blacks to mental illness was understood as the internalization of anti-Semitic or racist prejudice, manifested as self-hatred. The formulation of a complex theory of the psychopathology of racism accompanied the rise of political anti-Semitism in the 1890s and, especially, its realization in Austrian and German politics in the early twentieth century. Thus, after the rise of the Nazis in Germany and of Austrofascism in Vienna in the early 1930s, Freud developed a specific theory of the origins of a German racial madness defined by anti-Semitism:



> We must not forget that all those peoples who excel today in their hatred of Jews became Christians only in late historic times, often driven to it by bloody coercion. It might be said that they are all "mis-baptized." They have been left, under a thin veneer of Christianity, where their ancestors were, who worshipped a barbarous polytheism. They have not got over a grudge against the new religion which was imposed on them; but they have displaced the grudge on to the source from which Christianity reached them. The fact that the Gospels tell a story which is set among Jews, and in fact deals only with Jews, has made this displacement easy for them. Their hatred of Jews is at bottom a hatred of Christians, and we need not be surprised that in the German Nationalist-Socialist revolution this intimate relation between the two monotheist religions finds such a clear expression in the hostile treatment of both of them.[22]

The academic acceptance of theories of racial inferiority and degeneracy was the source of the racism that self-hatred seemed to internalize. After 1933, in works by Wilhelm Reich and others, the image of the mentally ill racist became the focus of much of the interest in the psychology of race. Reich's *Mass Psychology of Fascism* (1933) was the first truly systematic investigation of the psychology of racism.

Reich described racism in terms that he took from Freud but that incorporated the Nazi rhetoric of race: "There is a direct connection between the 'dominion' over animals and racial 'dominion' over the 'black man, the Jew, the Frenchman, etc.' It is clear that one prefers to be a gentleman than an animal. To disassociate himself from the animal kingdom, the human animal denied and finally ceased to perceive the sensations of his organs; in the process he became biologically rigid." It was Reich who described a "Hitler psychosis": "The race theory proceeds from the presupposition that the exclusive mating of every animal with its own species is an 'iron law' in nature. The National Socialist went on to apply this supposed law in nature to peoples. Their line of reasoning was something as follows: Historical experience teaches that the 'intermixing of Aryan blood' with 'inferior' peoples always results in the degeneration of the founders of civilization. The level of the superior race is lowered, followed by physical and mental retrogression; this marks the beginning of a progressive 'decline.'"[23] Yet Reich wrote of a predisposition for madness among racists in a world in which the internalization of racism as a form of mental illness remained a commonplace. In Anna Freud's *The Ego and the Mechanisms of Defense* (1936), the ego's defense mechanisms that her father had described (repression, displacement, denial, projection, reaction formation, intellectualization, rationalization, undoing, sublimation) were augmented by a new category very much in keeping with the spirit of the times: identification with the aggressor. This defense mechanism had been addressed in earlier German Jewish writings about the internalization of anti-Semitism. In his widely read and translated *My Life as German and Jew* (1921), the German Jewish novelist Jacob Wassermann wrote:

> I have known many Jews who have languished with longing for the fair-haired and blue-eyed individual. They knelt before him, burned incense before him, believed his every word; every blink of his eye was heroic; and when he spoke of his native soil, when he beat his Aryan breast, they broke into a hysterical shriek of triumph. . . .
>
> I was once greatly diverted by a young Viennese Jew, elegant, full of suppressed ambition, rather melancholy, something of an artist, and something of a charlatan. Providence itself had given him fair hair and blue eyes; but lo, he had no confidence in his fair hair and blue eyes: in his heart of hearts he felt that they were spurious.[24]

In exile in London after the war, Anna Freud encountered such views in her own clinical practice. In her Hampstead Clinic for Children there were boys and girls who had escaped on the *Kindertransport* from Germany and Austria who were observed playing "Nazis and Jews." Everyone wanted to be a Nazi!

The antecedents of identification with the aggressor were already present in discussions of the responses to prejudice in the United States. By the early twentieth century, there had emerged a sociological explanation of race and racism that centered on their social and structural causes, but these factors were largely marginalized. Clinical research trumped sociological work. In *The Philadelphia Negro* (1899), for example, W. E. B. Du Bois had provided strong empirical evidence of the historical and social nature of social problems that plagued the Black community. Du Bois saw the status of Jews in Germany as a model for the "talented tenth" of African Americans, who internalized their inferiority in the form of "double consciousness." His early twentieth-century Atlanta papers provided further grounds for rejecting psychopathological explanations of race and racism, but among his contemporaries, Du Bois was simply not widely read. Du Bois had absorbed theories of racial science concerning the mental status of Jews during his education in Berlin. How these theories were transmuted into the theory of the social causation of self-hatred is central to this story. But during this same period, a similar, less marginalized development was occurring within the American academy. At the University of Chicago, a new "clinical" sociology was focused intently on studying the conditions of intergroup conflict in its "natural" setting. In the 1930s, the role of self-hatred in the "social pathology of African American culture" became a source of great interest.[25] Yet these years were in many ways still haunted by the specter of nineteenth-century biological science, which saw the African American as predisposed to mental illness by his race but did not see racism as anything more than a response to the status of the African American. There were exceptions, but they too assumed that there was a psychological explanation for racism. Bruno Lasker's *Race Attitudes in Children* (1929) argued that there was no inborn hostility to other races, only "acquired habits." Anthropological accounts of race in the early twentieth century continued to view racial differences as innate, and cultural variations as linked to different evolutionary processes between "varieties of men." By the late 1930s, anthropologists saw racism as a result of "caste and class" in the work of African American scholars such as Allison Davis, and understood racism as a problem of psychological development within economic castes.[26]

Yet it is striking how many of the researchers working in the social sciences in the 1920s and 1930s were American Jews, often second-generation immigrants. In psychology, young scholars such as Eugene Horowitz saw race patterns as determined by external attitudes toward the group; his spouse, Ruth Horowitz, was interested in self-awareness as a means of exploring the impact of segregation on African Americans. The tension between the African American experience of racism and social science work on racism by American Jewish scholars whose own experience of anti-Semitism shaped their research agenda added to the impact of this period.



## The Post-Holocaust Worldview

The modern movement to pathologize racism coincided with two related phenomena: the rise of the civil rights movement in the United States, and the collapse of the Nazi regime following World War II. Regarding racism, two branches of concern emerged. The first concerned itself with the pathological *consequences* of racism and was typified by academic analyses of the mental, physical, and emotional illnesses caused by structural and systemic racism. Many studies were undertaken by Jewish refugees, among them scholars as radically diverse as the Frankfurt school sociologist Theodor Adorno and the Austrian novelist and philosopher Hermann Broch, who studied both Nazi racism and what they saw as its American parallel, racism against African Americans. In Great Britain, the future Nobelist Elias Canetti was working on a parallel project, which appeared in 1960 as the book *Crowds and Power*. Much of this work was funded by the Rockefeller, the Rosenwald, and other foundations, which had their own research agendas regarding racism and its impact. Adorno collaborated with the Freudian psychoanalyst Else Frenkel-Brunswik and the social psychologist R. Nevitt Sanford at the University of California at Berkeley, together with Frenkel-Brunswik's student Daniel J. Levinson, in the most influential of these studies, *The Authoritarian Personality* (1950). Funded by the American Jewish Committee as a study of the sources of anti-Semitism, this book defined racist personality traits and then ranked these traits and their intensity in any given person on what it called the "F scale" (F for fascist). The book identified the authoritarian personality type as defined by nine traits that were believed to cluster together as the result of childhood experiences: conventionalism, authoritarian submission, authoritarian aggression, anti-intellectualism, anti-intraception, superstition and stereotypy, power and "toughness," destructiveness and cynicism, projectivity, and exaggerated concern with sex. These categories curiously mirror those in Wilhelm Reich's study of 1933. But unlike Reich, the authors of *The Authoritarian Personality* were more interested in questions of statistical measurement than in the social etiology of anti-Semitic psychosis. They found a high correlation between scores on the F scale and anti-Semitism and anti-Negro prejudice. And they concluded that family dynamics explained the psychic conflict that led to surface personality traits, social beliefs, and behavior. Much of the data on which they based this conclusion was collected by the use of projective tests (also psychoanalytic) like the Thematic Apperception Test (TAT), which are notoriously unreliable.[27] Another serious criticism is that because it analyzes individuals rather than collective social factors, the F scale fails to explain prejudice in societies where racial prejudice is the norm (e.g., South Africa, the American South).



Other scholars did address these social factors. The anti-Nazi Swedish economist Gunnar Myrdal's *An American Dilemma: The Negro Problem and Modern Democracy* (1944), funded by the Carnegie Corporation in 1938, looked at the contrast between the idealized American notion of equality and the racism of Jim Crow America. In *The Origins of Totalitarianism* (1951), Hannah Arendt argued that South African racism and European anti-Semitism were not only linked but were the result of Britain's "colonial imperialism" and Germany's "continental imperialism," rather than of individual or mass psychopathology. Arendt denied that the underlying assumptions of racism stem from the irrationality of the "mob" and therefore present a collective form of psychopathology. In 1963, Arendt published *Eichmann in Jerusalem: A Report on the Banality of Evil*, arguing that the racism and anti-Semitism of psychologically average, "normal" people undermined the view that Nazis were insane and had infected the populace with their racist madness.[28]

The psychological explanation for racism and its effects extended to other groups in North America. Consider the Indian Personality Project, created in 1940 by John Collier, head of the Bureau of Indian Affairs, which set out to investigate the formation of Native American personalities on several reservations in the United States.[29] The Indian Personality Project was cast as something that would help the Bureau of Indian Affairs better administer the reservations, but it was also supposed to help Native American groups maintain their languages and cultures in the face of institutionalized prejudice. Many of the ideas for Collier's reconstruction of Indian affairs during the New Deal arose from contact with Mexican educational specialists who were trying to refurbish Native American village life in Mexico. The Indian Personality Project was thus also extended to Mexico with the approval of

Manuél Gámio, an anthropologist trained by Franz Boas at Columbia, and Moises Saenz, an educational specialist trained by John Dewey at the same institution.



The second branch of social anthropology was concerned with diagnosing *racism itself* as a pathological illness. Academic arguments aimed to specify the specific mental, physical, and emotional disorders associated with *being* racist, or *harboring* racism. The general argument was that racism made people crazy, and it followed the dominant psychoanalytic models after World War II in the West. For example, in *Black Skin, White Masks* (1952), the Algerian psychiatrist Frantz Fanon used psychoanalytic theory to explain the feelings of dependency and inadequacy that Black people experience in a white world. Fanon wrote of the divided self-perception of the Black subject who has lost his native cultural originality and embraced the culture of the white mother country (France). Language facilitated this divided self-perception. "To speak," said Fanon, "means above all to assume a culture, to support the weight of a civilization."[30] As a result, the Black subject will try to appropriate and imitate the cultural code of the colonizer. This behavior, Fanon argued, was even more evident in upwardly mobile and educated Black people who could afford to acquire status symbols. The result was invariably self-hatred:

> I recommend the following experiment to those who are unconvinced: Attend showings of a Tarzan film in the Antilles and in Europe. In the Antilles, the young Negro identifies himself *de facto* with Tarzan against the Negroes. This is much more difficult for him in a European theater, for the rest of the audience, which is white, automatically identifies him with the savages on the screen.
>
> . . . I will go farther and say that Bushmen and Zulus arouse even more laughter among the young Antilleans. It would be interesting to show how in this instance the reactional exaggeration betrays a hint of recognition. In France a Negro who sees this documentary is virtually petrified. There he has no more hope of flight: He is at once Antillean, Bushman, and Zulu.[31]

Fanon was only tangentially concerned with the origin of racism in white society:

> The Negro is a phobogenic object, a stimulus to anxiety. . . . One discovers all the stages of what I shall call the Negro-phobogenesis. There has been much talk of psychoanalysis in connection with the

> Negro. Distrusting the ways in which it might be applied, I have preferred to call this chapter "The Negro and Psychopathology," well aware that Freud and Adler and even the cosmic Jung did not think of the Negro in all their investigations. And they were quite right not to have. It is too often forgotten that neurosis is not a basic element of human reality.[32]



Fanon's argument mirrors that of Freud in the 1920s, in denying any historical specificity to the French situation but rather seeing it as part of a universal anti-Black feeling on the part of white colonial society.

The politics of such a position is clearest in the United States in the 1940s and 1950s. One of Gunnar Myrdal's research assistants at Columbia University, Kenneth Bancroft Clark, and his wife, Mamie Phipps Clark, had begun in 1939 extrapolating from the work of Ruth E. Horowitz on the etiology of Black self-hatred. The Clarks began with Horowitz's study of "the beginnings of race consciousness as a function of ego-development." Horowitz had tested children in a "WPA nursery school, 2 to 5 years in age, of both sexes. . . . Several negroes were in the group. . . . A choice test was used: a page with two pictures relevant to the test item was shown the child, and the question 'Which one is you?' was asked. A portrait series was also used. Ten portrait pictures were exposed one at a time, and the child was asked, 'Is this you?' . . . The white boys were more confused than were the negro boys about race identification, but the girls showed no clear difference."[33] Horowitz was much more interested in the identification of the young "negro boys" with whiteness than either the gender differences or the confusion of the white children about their racial identity.

The Clarks substituted dolls for portraits. They used four plastic, diaper-clad dolls, identical except for color. Almost all of the Black children from age three to age seven readily identified the race of the dolls. When asked which they preferred, however, the majority selected the white doll and attributed positive characteristics to it. The Clarks also gave the children outline drawings of a boy and girl and asked them to color the figures the same color as themselves. Many of the children with dark complexions colored the figures with a white or yellow crayon. The Clarks concluded that "prejudice, discrimination, and segregation" caused Black children to develop a sense of inferiority and self-hatred.

> Skin color differentials also seem to break down with a change in the environment of the subjects. In the segregated group racial

> identifications were made for the most part upon the basis of the skin color of the subjects. This same trend was found to be operative in the semi-segregated group. However, there was no tendency whatsoever toward this trend in the mixed group. This suggests the possibility that the racial identifications of children in the mixed group were to a large extent determined by the physical characteristics of those in their immediate environment. It is a question, to be settled by further work, whether this social factor has not gained priority over the factor of their own skin color as a determinant of the racial identifications of these Negro children.[34]



The Clarks' exclusive focus on the Black children's response, rather than on the comparative question of how other children responded in other environments, led them to assume the universal origin of self-hatred within racially segregated society.[35] What about the white kids? Is liking white dolls a sign of psychopathology or health? The Clarks' view that there could be no ambiguity, and their failure to consider the possibility that such identification could lead to sublimation rather than repression of identity, echoes Anna Freud's findings in the Hampstead Clinic during the late 1940s and early 1950s. But more important were the political implications of such a finding, for the Clarks testified as expert witnesses in *Briggs v. Elliot*—part of *Brown v. Board of Education*, 347 U.S. 483, in 1954. The Clarks' work contributed to the Supreme Court ruling that de jure racial segregation in public education was unconstitutional.

For the first time in a court case not concerned with questions of competence, an American court had recognized the psychological evidence of the impact of racism on African Americans, while not commenting at all on the question of whether the racism was itself a form of mental illness: "Whatever may have been the extent of psychological knowledge at the time of Plessy v. Ferguson, this finding is amply supported by modern authority. Any language in Plessy v. Ferguson, 163 U.S. 537 (1896), contrary to this finding is rejected," Chief Justice Earl Warren wrote in the *Brown* opinion.

> To separate [Black children] from others of similar age and qualifications solely because of their race generates a feeling of inferiority as to their status in the community that may affect their hearts and minds in a way unlikely ever to be undone.
>
> Segregation of white and colored children in public schools has a detrimental effect upon the colored children. The impact is greater when it has the sanction of the law, for the policy of

separating the races is usually interpreted as denoting the inferiority of the negro group. A sense of inferiority affects the motivation of a child to learn. Segregation with the sanction of law, therefore, has a tendency to [retard] the educational and mental development of negro children and to deprive them of some of the benefits they would receive in a racial[ly] integrated school system.[36]



The vocabulary is Adlerian (inferiority complex), but the core of the statement reflects Anna Freud's view in the 1950s that society must always ask what is in the "best interest of the child," not what causes societal deformation. The focus was on the child's welfare, not on ridding society of the psychopathology of racism.

### Conclusions

Since the 1960s, a number of scholars have made claims about the mental health consequences for Blacks of structural and systemic racism, including alien-self disorder, anti-self disorder, self-destructive disorders, and organic disorders.[37] While the rise of the mental health model in the 1950s and 1960s in the United States gave way to an emphasis on the negative consequences of racism on its victims, the same mental health model also worked to subsume racist practices. This reflected a more general trend in health and medicine, where new ground being broken in biology and genetics was co-opted to develop treatment models for what had previously been considered a social and cultural problem.

The relationship between biology, psychology, and racism is creating a new language for treatment and disorders today. New language redirects not just the psychological disciplines but also the social ones toward treating social problems as clinical ones. This trend in turn is producing new modalities of subjectification. The expansion of the U.S. mental health industry has transformed our understanding of personhood, changing social and cultural conceptions of what persons are, how we should behave toward them, and also our individual shortcomings and how to properly address them. Since the 1970s, the increasing involvement of the government in mental health diagnosis and treatment has expanded the scope and reach of mental health services, virtually eliminating the distinction between spaces previously considered public or private. Individuals can now do work on themselves, guided by specific services meant to alleviate "brand new" personal troubles, including the problem of individual racism.

The characterization of racism as an individual pathology, I fear, will shift society's focus toward individualized treatment models rather than systemic ones. For example, if racism is a mental illness, should a racist murderer be able to plead insanity rather than assume responsibility for his actions? If we treat racism as a disease, does this provide an incentive to search for an individual cure, rather than dealing with the social roots of racism? Finally, who stands to benefit from this movement to pathologize racism? The global pharmaceutical industry? Clinical practitioners? Racists themselves?



## Notes

1. Terbeck et al., "Propranolol Reduces Implicit Negative Racial Bias," 419.
2. Rose, "Human Sciences in a Biological Age."
3. Summers, "'Suitable Care of the African'"; Metzl, *Protest Psychosis*; Doyle, "'Fine New Child'"; Doyle, "'Where the Need Is Greatest'"; Grob, *Mental Illness and American Society*; Keller, *Colonial Madness*; Anderson, Jenson, and Keller, *Unconscious Dominions*; Wailoo, *Dying in the City*; Molina, *Fit to Be Citizens?*; Roberts, *Infectious Fear*; Scott, *Contempt and Pity*; Holloway, *Confronting the Veil*; McKee, *Sociology and the Race Problem*.
4. Pinsker, *Auto-Emancipation*, 3.
5. Ibid., 4.
6. Ibid., 7, 12.
7. See Gilman, "Jews and Mental Illness."
8. Griesinger, "Vorwort," iii.
9. Burgl, *Hysterie und die strafrechtliche Verantwortlichkeit*, 19.
10. Charcot, *Leçons du Mardi a la Salpêtrière*, 2:11–12. See the translation in *Poliklinische Vorträge*, 2:11.
11. Kraepelin, "Zur Entartungsfrage," 748.
12. Lombroso, *Antisemitismo e la scienze moderne*, 83.
13. Cartwright, "Report on the Diseases," 620. Calhoun argued that freeing slaves who could not function in a state of freedom was cruel, as it exposed their inherent inability to function in more complex societies, which he said was proved by their higher rate of mental illness. This was a standard racist trope used in support of slavery, which argued that slavery preserved the health and sanity of the slave.
14. Olmsted, *Journey in the Seaboard Slave States*, 1:226.
15. Gilman, with Stepan, "Appropriating the Idioms of Science."
16. See Gubar, *Racechanges*.
17. Galton, "Eugenics and the Jew," 16.
18. Billings, "Vital Statistics of the Jews," 70.
19. Le Bon, *Crowd*, 148. See also 39.
20. Freud, *Group Psychology and the Analysis of the Ego*, in vol. 18 of *Complete Psychological Works*, 74.
21. Ibid., 100.
22. Freud, *Moses and Monotheism*, in vol. 23 of ibid., 91.
23. Reich, *Mass Psychology of Fascism*, 64, x.
24. Wassermann, *My Life as German and Jew*, 156.
25. Jackson, *Social Scientists for Social Justice*, 34.
26. See the discussion of these approaches summarized in Davis and Dollard, *Children of Bondage*.
27. On the question of the reliability of the TAT, see Cramer, "Future Directions." For a recent argument that abandoning visual testing increases reliability, see Gruber and Kreuzpointner, "Measuring the Reliability." See also Bergmann, *Error Without Trial*, 85.
28. See Pick, *Pursuit of the Nazi Mind*.
29. Blanchette, "Citizens and Savages," 289–302.
30. Fanon, *Black Skin, White Masks*, 17–18.
31. Ibid., 152–53.
32. Ibid., 151.
33. Horowitz, "Racial Aspects of Self-Identification," 92.
34. Clark and Clark, "Segregation as a Factor," 162.

35. Cross, *Shades of Black.*

36. See https://www.law.cornell.edu/supremecourt/text/347/483.

37. See the discussion in Wellman, "From Evil to Illness."

38. Babylonian Talmud Ḥagigah 3b.

39. Rashi, at Babylonian Talmud Ḥagigah 3b; see also Midrash Tanhuma ʿEdut 9:9 and 9:10.

## References




Anderson, Warwick, Deborah Jenson, and Richard C. Keller. *Unconscious Dominions: Psychoanalysis, Colonial Trauma, and Global Sovereignties.* Durham: Duke University Press, 2011.

Bergmann, Werner, ed. *Error Without Trial: Psychological Research on Antisemitism.* Berlin: De Gruyter, 1988.

Billings, John Shaw. "Vital Statistics of the Jews." *North American Review* 152, no. 4 (1891): 70–84.

Blanchette, Thad. "Citizens and Savages—Applied Anthropology and Indian Administration in the United States, 1880–1940." PhD diss., Universidade Federal do Rio de Janeiro, 2006.

Burgl, Georg. *Die Hysterie und die strafrechtliche Verantwortlichkeit der Hysterischen: Ein praktisches Handbuch für Ärzte und Juristen.* Stuttgart: Ferdinand Enke, 1912.

Cartwright, Samuel A. "Report on the Diseases and Physical Peculiarities of the Negro Race." *New Orleans Medical and Surgical Journal* 7 (May 1851): 691–715.

Charcot, J.-M. *Leçons du Mardi a la Salpêtrière.* 2 vols. Paris: Progrés Medical, 1889.

———. *Poliklinische Vorträge von Prof. J. M. Charcot.* Vol. 1, translated by Sigmund Freud. Vol. 2, translated by Max Kahane. Leipzig: Deuticke, 1892–95.

Clark, Kenneth B., and Mamie K. Clark. "Segregation as a Factor in the Racial Identification of Negro Pre-School Children: A Preliminary Report." *Journal of Experimental Education* 8, no. 2 (1939): 161–63.

Cramer, Phebe. "Future Directions for the Thematic Apperception Test." *Journal of Personality Assessment* 72 (1999): 74–92.

Cross, William. *Shades of Black: Diversity in African American Identity.* Philadelphia: Temple University Press, 1991.

Davis, Allison, and John Dollard. *Children of Bondage: The Personality Development of Negro Youth in the Urban South.* New York: Harper and Row, 1964.

Doyle, Dennis. "'A Fine New Child': The Lafargue Mental Hygiene Clinic and Harlem's African American Communities, 1946–1958." *Journal of the History of Medicine and Allied Sciences* 64, no. 2 (2009): 173–212.

———. "'Where the Need Is Greatest': Social Psychiatry and Race-Blind Universalism in Harlem's Lafargue Clinic, 1946–1958." *Bulletin of the History of Medicine* 83, no. 4 (2009): 746–74.

Du Bois, W. E. B. *The Philadelphia Negro.* 1899. Reprint, Philadelphia: University of Pennsylvania Press, 1996.

Fanon, Frantz. *White Skin, Black Masks.* Translated by Charles Lam Markmann. New York: Grove Press, 1967.

Freud, Sigmund. *Standard Edition of the Complete Psychological Works of Sigmund Freud.* Edited and translated by James Strachey, Anna Freud, Alix Strachey, and Alan Tyson. 24 vols. London: Hogarth, 1955–74.

Galton, Francis. "Eugenics and the Jew." *Jewish Chronicle* (London), July 29, 1910.

Gilman, Sander L. "Jews and Mental Illness: Medical Metaphors, Anti-Semitism, and the Jewish Response." *Journal of the History of the Behavioral Sciences* 20 (1984): 150–59.

Gilman, Sander L., with Nancy Stepan. "Appropriating the Idioms of Science: Some Strategies of Resistance to

Biological Determinism." In *The Bounds of Race: Perspectives on Hegemony and Resistance*, edited by Dominick LaCapra, 72–103. Ithaca: Cornell University Press, 1991.
Griesinger, Wilhelm. "Vorwort." *Archiv für Psychiatrie und Nervenkrankheiten* 1 (1868): iii–viii.
Grob, Gerald N. *Mental Illness and American Society, 1875–1940*. Princeton: Princeton University Press, 1983.
Gruber, Nicole, and Ludwig Kreuzpointner. "Measuring the Reliability of Picture Story Exercises Like the TAT." *PLOS One* 8, no. 11 (2013). https://doi.org/10.1371/journal.pone.0079450.
Gubar, Susan. *Racechanges: White Skin, Black Face in American Culture*. New York: Oxford University Press, 2000.
Holloway, Jonathan Scott. *Confronting the Veil: Abram Harris, Jr., E. Franklin Frazier, and Ralph Bunche, 1919–1941*. Chapel Hill: University of North Carolina Press, 2002.
Horowitz, Ruth E. "Racial Aspects of Self-Identification in Nursery School Children." *Journal of Psychology* 7 (1939): 91–99.
Jackson, John P., Jr. *Social Scientists for Social Justice: Making the Case Against Segregation*. New York: New York University Press, 2005.
Keller, Richard C. *Colonial Madness: Psychiatry in French North Africa*. Chicago: University of Chicago Press, 2007.
Kraepelin, Emil. "Zur Entartungsfrage." *Zentralblatt für Nervenheilkunde und Psychiatrie* 19 (1908): 745–51.
Le Bon, Gustave. *The Crowd: A Study of the Popular Mind*. New York: Macmillan, 1896.
Lombroso, Cesare. *L'antisemitismo e la scienze moderne*. Turin: L. Roux, 1894.
McKee, James B. *Sociology and the Race Problem: The Failure of a Perspective*. Urbana: University of Illinois Press, 1993.
Metzl, Jonathan M. *The Protest Psychosis: How Schizophrenia Became a Black Disease*. Boston: Beacon Press, 2009.
Molina, Natalia. *Fit to Be Citizens? Public Health and Race in Los Angeles, 1879–1939*. Berkeley: University of California Press, 2006.
Olmsted, Frederick Law. *A Journey in the Seaboard Slave States: With Remarks on Their Economy*. 2 vols. New York: Dix and Edwards, 1856.
Pick, Daniel. *The Pursuit of the Nazi Mind: Hitler, Hess, and the Analysts*. Oxford: Oxford University Press, 2012.
Pinsker, Leon. *Auto-Emancipation*. Translated by D. S. Blondheim. New York: Maccabean, 1906.
Reich, Wilhelm. *The Mass Psychology of Fascism*. Translated by Theodore P. Wolf. 3rd rev. ed. New York: Orgone Press, 1946.
Rigdon, Susan M. *The Culture Facade: Art, Science, and Politics in the Work of Oscar Lewis*. Urbana: University of Illinois Press, 1988.
Roberts, Samuel Kelton. *Infectious Fear: Politics, Disease, and the Health Effects of Segregation*. Chapel Hill: University of North Carolina Press, 2009.
Rooks, Noliwe M. "Is Racism an Illness?" *Time*, May 4, 2012. http://ideas.time.com/2012/05/04/is-racism-an-illness.
Rose, Nikolas. "The Human Sciences in a Biological Age." *Theory, Culture, and Society* 30, no. 1 (2013): 3–34.
Scott, Daryl Michael. *Contempt and Pity: Social Policy and the Image of the Damaged Black Psyche, 1880–1996*. Chapel Hill: University of North Carolina Press, 1997.
Summers, Martin. "'Suitable Care of the African When Afflicted with Insanity': Race, Madness, and Social Order in Comparative Perspective." *Bulletin of the History of Medicine* 84, no. 1 (2010): 58–91.
Terbeck, Sylvia, Guy Kahane, Sarah McTavish, Julian Savulescu, Philip J. Cowen, and Miles Hewstone. "Propranolol Reduces Implicit Negative Racial Bias." Psychopharmacology 222, no. 3 (2012): 419–24.
Wailoo, Keith. *Dying in the City of the Blues: Sickle Cell Anemia and the Politics of Race and Health*. Chapel Hill: University of North Carolina Press, 2001.
Wassermann, Jacob. *My Life as German and Jew*. London: George Allen and Unwin, 1933.
Wellman, David. "From Evil to Illness: Medicalizing Racism." *Journal of American Orthopsychiatry* 70 (2000): 28–32.

## Classic Text and Questions to Ponder

Drawing from nineteenth- and twentieth-century anthropology, medicine, and biology, Gilman aims to document the relationship between the pathologizing of racism and the earlier pathologizing of race itself. One of the dangers of pathologizing racism is that the remedies are often individualized, tailored to unique cases and circumstances, instead of systemic. And determining what constitutes (the illness of) racism or race is no less problematic, for how should it be diagnosed? Such questions have serious ramifications, for they influence who is empowered with legal agency. Demarcating the boundaries of who does and does not have legal agency through a medical lens is not new. The Talmudic rabbis, for example, wrestled with the definition of mental incompetence. In their view, someone is incompetent if he "goes out alone at night, spends the night in a cemetery, and tears his garments."[38] They disagree about whether all three behaviors must be performed or just some, and they disagree about the manner in which a person does these things: "if he does them in an insane manner, even one is sufficient" to judge someone mentally incompetent. The significance of how we answer this question is huge. Those who are mentally incompetent are universally exempt from responsibility (may not enter into contracts) and from punishment (for breach of contract, for example), and their testimony is legally vacuous.[39]

- How is pathologizing racism any less or more problematic than pathologizing mental illness?
- In *Brown v. Board of Education*, Chief Justice Warren noted that segregation has detrimental impacts on Negro children by generating "a feeling of inferiority as to their status in the community." To protect their feelings and not negatively affect their educational and mental development, Warren ruled in favor of integrating schools. How does this ruling deal with a symptom of racism (segregated schools) and not its underlying systemic causes?
- Do you think racists can claim they are afflicted with a disease? Why or why not?

11

# Whiteness as Anti-Theological

## An Ethics of No Edges

**GEORGE YANCY**

When Jonathan Crane asked me to participate in this exciting and important project, I thought that there wasn't much for me to say given that my scholarship isn't within the philosophical area of ethics, and certainly not within the area of Jewish ethics. And while I'm certainly interested in philosophy of religion, I initially failed to see what sort of contribution I could make to a project on race, ethics, specifically Jewish ethics, and religion. In fact, I began to worry about disciplinary intrusion, historical inaccuracies, and issues of epistemic distortion. However, the more I thought about the complex conceptual layers of this book—its contemporary urgency, especially within our current historical moment of so much untruth, outright disrespect for the truth, mass distraction, the rise of unabashed white nativism and xenophobia, and what I perceived as the lack of powerful religious prophetic voices—the more I thought, yes, I have something to say.

My aim in this closing chapter is to tarry with various manifestations of our social, historical, and existential suffering. My sense is that given the gravity of so much suffering in our world, especially the kind of suffering caused by race, though, more specifically, by racism, I might find the words that enable processes of healing, of repair. The theme of repair, it seems to me, must be central to a Jewish ethics, one predicated upon a certain understanding of our collective brokenness. My work in the areas of critical whiteness studies, critical philosophy of race, critical phenomenology, and philosophy of the Black experience, speaks directly to the theme of social, political, spiritual, and phenomenological damage, wreckage, and brokenness. I am thus profoundly engaged with such issues as white supremacy, white embodiment, white identity formation, white obfuscation, white privilege, white power, and white complicity. I am specifically concerned with the hegemonic dimensions of whiteness vis-à-vis Black bodies and bodies of color. Furthermore, my work intersects with the work produced by white religious studies scholars, theologians, and ethicists who attempt to grapple with dimensions of whiteness. Hence, the place where religion, ethics, and racism meet is more than an intellectual curiosity; indeed, for me, it is a deeply existential site that is fraught with confusion, perplexity, and risk. This risk, needless to say, comes with the territory when one dares to speak out, perhaps *prophetically*, against so much hypocrisy when it comes to that triumvirate mix. I would like to think of this last chapter or epilogue, which is by no means a *conclusion*, despite its etymology, as "a scream in the night."[1]



What does it mean to be *haunted* by the sadness of death and dying, to tremble with affective intensity in the face of the current reality and historical legacy of so much racism, oppression, suffering, abuse, terror, violence, injustice, divisiveness, brutality, poverty, sexism, homophobia, hatred? As early as 1999, Cornel West noted that "we live at the end of a century of unprecedented brutality and barbarity, a period when more than two hundred million fellow human beings have been murdered in the name of some pernicious ideology." West locates such horror within the context of Nazism, Stalinism, European colonial desire, imperialist usurpation, and degradation of people from Africa, South America, and Asia. Furthermore, the horror of patriarchal domination "of sisters of all colors and all regions and all countries is evident. The devaluation and degradation of gay brothers and lesbian sisters across race, region, and class, as well as the marginalization of the disabled and physically challenged," cannot be denied.[2] Etymologically, to be "haunted" suggests *returning* to a place, a site, a space.

As a young boy, through my teenage years, and at the moment of this writing, I have continued to be haunted by, and have *returned* to, a space of deep sadness. I seem to have embodied, and certainly now embody, the weight of a certain existential pathos. When I face the magnitude of human suffering, I can't be philosophical about it, that is, I can't remain dispassionate and detached. I am a philosopher who weeps. As a young boy, I was haunted by our collective finitude and the irreducibility of *my death*. Because of my pathos, the world showed up for me as a site of meaninglessness, weighed down by the reality that we are here (our birth) for no apparent reason and will leave and disappear (our death) with no clear and definitive answer. Along with these two poles of absurdity, there was also the fact that between birth and the grave, there is so much pain and sorrow. While steeped in this pathos, I was preoccupied (perhaps obsessed) with what it meant to be ethical, to be redeemable. Perhaps this is why, as a young boy, I prayed for the devil. One night I asked my mother if I could and she said yes. It was certainly a shocking question to ask my mother, a Christian fundamentalist. To this day, I don't know why she said yes and I doubt that she recalls the event, but there I was on my knees: "And God bless the devil."



We partly make sense of who we are through a backward look, a retrospective questioning. Through such a retrospective process, we come to have new relationships with our former interpreted selves; through the hermeneutic horizon of the present, the past can and does take on new meaning. The extent of God's grace is now for me a rich philosophical and theological problem, though as a young boy I was more than likely motivated to pray for the devil out of a sense of compassion, a desire to believe in forgiveness, where redemption is always possible. I no longer pray for the devil, but I continue to endure the weight of pathos. This is why, for me, practicing philosophy has never simply been about Platonic wonder, but about *suffering*; practicing philosophy, loving wisdom, places me in the very midst of what it means to grapple with and strive to be human in an inhuman world, what it means to be finite and move ever closer to the grave, the precipice of what feels like an abyss. It is also about looking pain and suffering in the face, *tarrying* with its reality, losing sleep over so much human wreckage. As embodied as Black vis-à-vis white supremacy/whiteness, this raises another dimension of suffering. The suffering is not just about the looming cloud of cosmic existential absurdity or about the absurd *in* America and the absurd *in* the world, but, as West writes, "the absurd *as* America."[3]

After hearing the 911 audio tape of the killing of seventeen-year-old Black male Trayvon Martin on February 26, 2012, *I wept*. When I hear the "I can't breathe" cries of forty-three-year-old Black male Eric Garner on July 17, 2014, who eventually died of what the coroner described as a chokehold from a white police officer, I constrict my body. His cries were existential entreaties that fell on opaque ears and hearts. When I think about the racial profiling of twenty-eight-year-old Sandra Bland on July 10, 2015, and the subsequent treatment of her by a white police officer as if she was a "criminal," I'm angered by the violence of the white state. When I see past photos of lynched Black bodies as white men, women, and children look with curious and excited white gazes, there is that distinct feeling of disgust, physical and moral. I was overcome by an unspeakable horror as I looked at the photo of the little body of three-year-old Alan Kurdi, who, in 2015, lay dead and face-down on a Turkish beach after his family attempted to flee violence in

Syria. Not seduced by our collective desire for hyperreality or the latest in "newsworthy" photojournalism, I wanted to save Alan. I wanted to hold his dead body to mine and cry, weep for and over him, literally scream on his behalf and on behalf of his father, the only surviving member of the family who fled. When I look at that photo, it is not just a dead child that I see. I see my sons and painfully comprehend their vulnerability. I see the deaths of hundreds of thousands of innocent children who are suffering, who are being murdered, who are starving and living in poverty around the world. I see the piling up of deaths of unarmed young Black bodies in America killed by white police officers and proxies of the state. I see the horrible deaths of Palestinian and Jewish children in which both sides suffer in agony as a result, though the military power is imbalanced. I see the brutal murders of transgender people, the banning of refugees, the ostracizing of our neighbors from Mexico, the dehumanization of those subjected to sex trafficking around the world, those suffering from American's racist incarceration rates, those suffering from patriarchal domestic violence, especially in the form of femicide, those suffering from the inequalities of classism, and those rendered "monstrous"—the disabled.



Catastrophe surrounds us. Its longevity and pervasiveness is evident in the transatlantic slave trade (or *Maafa*, a Swahili term meaning "great disaster"), the Trail of Tears, the Holocaust, the gratuitous violence of European colonialism, and so many other horrendous acts of unethical barbarity throughout history. I try as best I can, though always falling short, to give voice to such horrible suffering. Hence, philosophy is not simply about conceptual clarity, rigorous argumentation, and asking the "big" questions, but it is also about bearing witness to forms of quotidian suffering, actively carrying out the role of the parrhesiastes, the one who speaks, at personal risk, parrhesia, or courageous speech in the face of so much obfuscation vis-à-vis the harsh realities of our social, political, and existential condition. I try to avoid being mesmerized by a respectability politics steeped in ethical simulacra. I try to face the reality of brutal injustice and death. As Abraham Joshua Heschel writes, "We live in an age when most of us have ceased to be shocked by the increasing breakdown in moral inhibitions. The decay of conscience fills the air with a pungent smell."[4] Ceasing to be shocked raises the problem of the many ways in which our vision is blocked and blinders limit our ethicality, which are important themes raised in Jonathan Crane's introduction to this book. I confess that there have been times when just smiling, seeing a movie at my leisure, having plenty of food to eat and clean running water to drink, weighs heavily upon my conscience in the face of so much pain, suffering, and deprivation. And yet, even here, there is a certain perk of privilege in having my conscience pricked, in being *reminded*. What of those who, *right now*, cannot forget, who are, in this moment, experiencing a living hell? Heschel writes, "One's integrity must constantly be examined." My aim is not to deny life its beauty and existence its ecstasy, but there is something to be said about our "self-assurance [and] smug certainty of our honesty" (176).



In the face of all of this moral foulness, terror, turmoil, pain, and suffering, many of us are compelled to ask: God, where are You? Yet perhaps there is another question that we must ask: Where are *we* in all of this? Where are *you* in all of this? Where am *I* in all of this? Not that the problem of theodicy is irrelevant. It is indeed a theological aporia. As a *hopeful theist*, though, I'm driven by a certain "orphaned" sorrow that is shot through with hope. In short, in the face of sorrow, evil, and dread, I persist, I endure in my hope for the existence of the divine. Such hope is not an act that I engage in alone, but is a collective and communal act that is grounded upon years of shared familial and nonfamilial hope in the "Not-Yet-Become—the refusal to accept the present as final."[5] Yet there is that silence; there is the divine as *Deus absconditus*. However, there is something hermeneutically profound in that silence. Perhaps within the internal logic of that silence is a normative ethics that is necessary and expressible precisely through a radical awareness of our *nearness* to one another, our interdependency upon each other—the fact that our corporeal existence is always already one that is haptic, already touching through a broadly construed social integument/skin. On this score, partly what is needed is an ontology that puts to rest a conceptually and ethically bankrupt neoliberalism, a neoliberalism that obfuscates the ways in which we are mutually interconnected. It is out of this radical sense of being neighbors (etymologically, "to dwell near") that a robust, universal and consistent, historically grounded and focused, horizontally expressed love and compassion that speak to and act toward the *least of these* can grow. What we do on the road from Jerusalem to Jericho, or what we do in the overwhelming presence of those who suffer (the oppressed, the precariat, the refugee), speaks to our ethical commitments on the proverbial ground, within the context of the quotidian, especially as we are always already linked. To walk by the "unclean" stranger leaves its mark; to turn away *impacts* the stranger. It is in the turning away that the embodied stranger remains unhealed, bruised; indeed, violated yet again. To walk away doesn't create a clear-cut distance that frees one from imparting violence. Walking away creates an accretion of violence; increasing the possible imminence of death through the *effect* of one's absence. One's absence is like a vector; it has its force and influence. Like the death of a mother during childbirth, the reverberations of that absence affect the child.

In stream with my conceptualization of our mutual interconnectedness, what I have called in the title an ethics of no edges, Heschel writes, "The situation of the poor in America is our plight, our sickness. To be deaf to their cry is to condemn ourselves" (84). It is this moral "deafness," whether motivated by indifference or by hatred, that I would argue is anti-theological. Heschel writes, "The prophets' great contribution to humanity was the discovery of the evil of indifference. One may be decent and sinister, pious and sinful" (68). Within a similar prophetic register, Cornel West is critical of "the widespread accommodation of American religion to the political and cultural status quo," which he sees as a form of idolatry that "worships the gods created by American society and kneels before the altars created by American culture." For West, this raises the question: just how will Christians, Jews, and others of different religious faiths and traditions "think about and act on enhancing the plight of the poor, the predicament of the powerless, and the quality of life for all in a prophetic manner?"[6] After all, "Whosoever claims to love God yet hates a brother or sister is a liar. For whoever does not love their brother and sister, whom they have seen, cannot love God, whom they have not seen" (1 John 4:20).



Martin Luther King Jr., during the Montgomery bus boycott, was painfully aware of the failure of some religious leaders' ethical and religious praxis vis-à-vis white racism. He writes, "I felt that the white ministers, priests and rabbis of the South would be some of our strongest allies. Instead, some have been outright opponents, refusing to understand the freedom movement and misrepresenting its leaders." He continues, "All too many others have been more cautious than courageous and have remained silent behind the anesthetizing security of the stained-glass windows."[7] Behind those stained-glass windows is a religiosity that is truncated by a lack of fierce religious praxis prepared to confront injustice directly. Heschel writes that "the prophet is [one] who feels fiercely" (62); the prophet is one who is stunned at our collective cruelty. Indeed, like Amos, the prophet is one who would see to it that "justice roll on like a river, righteousness like a never-failing stream" (Amos 5:24). Long before King, Heschel, and West, Frederick Douglass understood the hypocrisy embedded within forms of white "Christianity." "I love the pure, peaceable, and impartial Christianity of Christ," he writes. "I therefore hate the corrupt, slaveholding, women-whipping, cradle-plundering, partial and hypocritical Christianity of this land."[8]

In our contemporary moment of Trumpism, with its unabashed neo-fascism, white nativism, xenophobia, divisiveness, and "alternative facts," and within a Trump America where nuclear weapons are seriously considered an option, we are desperately in need of prophetic voices, of those who feel fiercely. In the light of spray-painted signs, just days after Trump's election, that read, "Black Lives Don't Matter and Neither Does Your Votes," "#FuckNiggers, #FuckAllPorchMonkeys," "Heil Trump," and "Make America White Again," and spray-painted swastikas on buildings, along with American Islamophobia where women were threatened for wearing their hijabs, racism, which has never ceased to exist within the institutions and psyches of white Americans, requires a powerful response that functions like "a scream in the night." Given that race is a central theme of this text, I ask: where are the screams in the night against white racism, white power, white privilege, and white hegemony? Given the reality and persistence of whiteness as a site of oppression and injustice in America, Heschel's question—"Where does moral religious leadership in America come from today?" (83)—is an urgent one. I argue that if moral religious leadership is to emerge within an America that continues to be plagued by whiteness, then it must begin with a conception of religion that is unafraid to critique whiteness, unafraid to trouble its privilege and its sites of institutional embeddedness and psychic opacity. Referring to chattel slavery in America, Heschel writes, "You cannot worship God and at the same time look at man as if he were a horse" (66). Indeed, how can one worship the divine and simultaneously see a Black man or woman as a "coon," as a "nigger"? How can one worship God and refuse or fail to engage critically the ways in which one's whiteness functions as a site that perpetuates racial injustice? Heschel writes, "As a standard of values and behavior, race operates as a comprehensive doctrine, as racism" (66). Racism is the basis upon which "our" country was founded. And within our contemporary context, it is *white racism* that consists of conscious and unconscious white standards of values, behaviors, performances, sites of racist interpellation, racist microaggressions and macroaggressions. Heschel's prophetic voice against white anti-Black racism did scream in the night. Courageously laying bare the reality of white racism, he writes, "Pigmentation is what counts. The Negro is a stranger to many souls" (67).

The Black body qua "stranger" is partly constituted through the white gaze, where the Black body is rendered invisible and yet hypervisible. Through the white gaze, the Black body is paradoxically both a site of ontological nullification and a site of the hyperbolic "criminal," the rabid "rapist," the site of racial "dysfunctionality." In short, to be Black within contemporary

America is to be marked on a racial cartography as the damned of the earth. In 2020, the Black body continues to suffer under the yoke of whiteness. In stream with Heschel, "the exodus began but is far from having been completed" (65). Emphasizing the sheer social, political, and ideological weight of white supremacy on the backs of Black Americans, Heschel writes, "In fact, it was easier for the children of Israel to cross the Red Sea than for a Negro to cross certain university campuses" (65). Within the context of America, where whiteness functions as the transcendental norm, a norm that leaves whiteness (white bodies) unmarked as human, persons as such, unraced, as a site of racial neutrality, the Black body is racially stigmatized like an indelibly fixed stain. The white gaze is the site of "an eye disease" (66), in the words of Heschel. As Frantz Fanon notes, the "movements, the attitudes, the glances of [whites] fixed me there, in the sense in which a chemical solution is fixed by a dye."[9] And while it is true that Heschel believes that thinking of human beings "in terms of white, black, or yellow is more than an error," and further argues that such a distinction is "a cancer of the soul" (66), in this chapter my focus is on whiteness. As Kalpana Seshadri-Crooks makes clear, "The system of race as differences among black, brown, red, yellow, and white makes sense only in its unconscious reference to Whiteness, which subtends the binary opposition between 'people of color' and 'white.'"[10]



I know the phenomenological fixity of this dye all too well. After the publication of "Dear White America," a letter that I referred to as a gift to white America, I underwent the phenomenological return of my Black body as a "nigger" through a process of white racist ontological truncation, a form of truncation undergirded by the logics of a racialized Manichaean divide. Being inundated with so much white racist vitriol left its corporeal mark—fatigue, depression, irritability.

Here are two voice messages left on my university answering machine:

> Dear Nigger Professor. You are a fucking racist. You are a piece of shit destroying the youth of this country. You are neither African nor American. You are pure, 100 percent Nigger. You would never marry outside of your Nigger race. That's a fact. You're a fucking smug Nigger. You are uneducated with education. You are a fucking animal. Just like all Black people in the United States of America. Including that Nigger Kenyan that was born in fucking Kenya that has usurped the white house. Yes. It is called the white house for a reason because white people made this country great you fucking Nigger.

> Hey Georgie boy. You're the fucking racist, asshole. You wouldn't have a job if it wasn't for affirmative action. Somebody needs to put a boot up your ass and knock your fucking head off your shoulders you stupid fucking goddamn racist son of a bitch.



Embodied in those two messages, and many more, is the white America that I face; it is, in spirit, Trump's America, an America where some wrote to tell me to "go back to Africa." It is the America that needs to be made "great" again, which is a lamentable nostalgia for all things white.

We must bear in mind that Trump, just last year (2019), targeted four congresswomen of color (Alexandria Ocasio-Cortez, Ilhan Omar, Ayanna Pressley, and Rashida Tlaib) with the remark, "Why don't they go back and help fix the totally broken and crime infested places from which they came."[11] Trump's desire for their ostracization is indicative of a form of racial cleansing. For me, then, from the perspective of my own racialized *Erlebnis*, to raise the question of ethics, religion, and race within our contemporary moment is to raise the theme of the Black/white binary, a binary for which Black Americans are not responsible. As Joe Feagin writes, "White-on-black racism is thus a—if not *the*—crucial paradigmatic case of racism historically and in the present."[12] Whiteness is structurally binary. Its social ontology or social metaphysics is predicated upon parasitism; its structure produces processes of othering, of marking the "other" as "different" and "deviant." In short, the "other" is a necessary feature of whiteness, yet the other is disposable, perhaps infinitely so. At the core of whiteness is a *lie*. Whiteness is empty; it needs an "other" to sustain itself. To live its lie, it requires other lies. Hence the lie regarding the "supremacy" of whiteness requires the lie of "Black inferiority."

Heschel asks, "What is a sin?" His answer: "The abuse of freedom" (85). In Sartrean terms, bad faith can be seen as an "abuse" of freedom. Freedom, for Sartre, is the fundamental reality of what it means to be human. Bad faith is a form of lying to oneself, where human beings flee the truth of their freedom as both transcendence and facticity. Robert Birt argues that "whiteness is to embrace the bad faith of privilege. Whiteness is the privilege of *exclusive transcendence*. But it can live as such only through the denial of the transcendence of an Other, the reduction of that Other to an object, to pure facticity."[13] As an instance of "abusing" freedom through an act of bad faith, whiteness places responsibility under erasure. On this score, bad faith involves the subordination of freedom to the lie of whiteness, where whiteness is valorized as an idol. Heschel understood the monstrous implications of lies. He writes, "Indeed, when human beings establish a modus vivendi on the basis of mendacity, the world can turn into a nightmare" (177). He locates that lie within the context of the Holocaust. He writes, "It had its origin in a lie: that the Jew was responsible for all social ills, for all personal frustrations. Decimate the Jews and all problems would be solved" (177).

Concerning sin, Heschel writes, "The root of sin is callousness, hardness of heart, lack of understanding what is at stake in being alive" (85). Part of what it means to be alive is coming to terms with the profound ways in which we are interconnected, not atomic and exclusively transcendent but mutually implicative. King writes, "We are caught in an inescapable network of mutuality," which I see as pointing to an ethics of no edges.[14] There is something, then, about separateness, an ontology of embodied imperviousness, that bespeaks sin. According to Heschel, sin is also "a failure of depth" (85). Depth implies complexity, not the surface, as in the uppermost layer or epidermis. Whiteness, then, functions as a structural sin. It is structurally an abuse of freedom and makes a fetish of surfaces. Whiteness is also a site of abstraction, an ethical solipsism (where only whites matter), and an epistemology of ignorance,[15] where ignorance is *actively* maintained. Hence whiteness as sin is not simply a failure of depth but resistance to depth.



Whiteness masquerades as a site of the sovereign, the discontinuous, of absolute self-preservation. Judith Butler writes, "One of the problems with insisting on self-preservation as the basis of ethics is that it becomes a pure ethics of the self, if not a form of moral narcissism."[16] Heschel wonders, "Religion and race. How can the two be uttered together?" (65). Lillian Smith, growing up in the South, understood that the two operated in "harmony." She was raised to understand that God was love and that she "was better than a Negro." Smith adds that she "learned that God so loved the world that He gave His only begotten Son so that we might have segregated churches in which it was my duty to worship each Sunday and on Wednesday at evening prayers."[17] Religion, ethics, and whiteness. How can the three be uttered together? In stream with Heschel, to engage the world through a prophetic form of religious praxis is to "unite what lies apart" (65); it is to challenge the ontology of whiteness, along with its moral narcissism, which functions "to sunder, to slash, to dismember the flesh of living humanity" (65). Within this context, whiteness is anti-theological.

*Tikkun olam* means to repair the world. Whiteness, however, attempts to disarticulate the enfleshed ontological seams that bind us. A prophetic religion, grounded upon an ethics of repair, one that is unafraid to speak parrhesiastically, valorizes the pregnancy of our corporeal porosity and nurtures the affective intensity and practice of love, which functions as a healing, mending power. Insightfully, James Cone writes, "Love is a refusal to accept whiteness. To love is to make a decision against white racism."[18] Love, then, presupposes an ethics that is deeply aware of how we are ontologically contiguous (etymologically, "to touch upon"). Within the context of whiteness, where whiteness is a site of closure, "purity," segregation, redlining, building walls, neighborhood covenants, love is a species of death. On this score, whites must die to white forms of embodiment conceived as monadic, where an outside limit is presumed. My point here is that white embodiment is always already a site that is "given over from the start."[19] The embodied white self, then, if it is to adopt an ethically relational ontology that troubles a white monadic identity with presumptive discrete edges, must undergo a species of death. Butler writes, "But this death, if it is a death, is only the death of a certain kind of subject, one that was never possible to begin with, the death of a fantasy of impossible mastery [and separateness], and so a loss of what one never had."[20]



An ethics of no edges that I have in mind rethinks or, better, lays bare a dynamic (not atomized) ontology of connectedness and thereby calls for a robust sense of ethical responsibility, indeed, white responsibility. King writes, "Injustice anywhere is a threat to justice everywhere."[21] One way of thinking about this is that injustice is not an isolated phenomenon, but bleeds into the body politic. Heschel writes, "Whenever one person is offended, we are all hurt" (69). Within this context, affectivity is not a node, but something more akin to an expressive wave. He also writes, "Few are guilty, but all are responsible" (62). This last point, along with the other two, is difficult to explain to my white students. They see themselves not only as living in a "post-racial America" where acts of white racism, if they exist at all, are "incidental" and "infrequent," but as bodies ontologically bound by edges, as autonomous (laws unto themselves), as ahistorical subjects, as unconditionally self-possessed, and as freed from the "past" of white supremacy. My objective is to get them to see how they are constituted relationally and preconfigured in the lives of Black people and people of color, especially in the ways in which they perpetuate white racist oppression. So I try to get them to tarry within the space of the heteronomous, to see how they are not "laws unto themselves" but how they undergo processes of white racist interpellation and how that process of interpellation negatively affects Black bodies and people of color. Within this context, it follows from the concept of an ethics and an ontology of no edges that "all whites are responsible for white dominance since their 'very being depends on it.'"[22] For example, according to Cynthia Kaufman, "The image of the black thief helps stabilize the image of the average good citizen (who of course is coded as white). When I walk into a store and the clerks look at me with respect and assume that I am not going to steal anything, the trust that I receive is at least partially built upon the foundation of my distance from the image of the savage. When an African American walks into the store that unconscious material comes into play in the opposite way."[23]



I provide examples like this one in order to challenge my white students to think about how whiteness, *their* whiteness, is inseparable from the racist profiling that the Black body and bodies of color have to bear. So when the white security guard follows me and leaves white people alone to shop, their white bodies are able to move through the space of the store with effortless grace; they are able to shop without having their bodies stopped or even watched. Their not being profiled or stopped, though, is contingent upon my Black body's being profiled or stopped. After all, according to white racist logic, I am the "thief," the "savage." It is as if the white security guard and the white shopper are signatories of an invisible contract, written in invisible ink, that agrees that I am "the problem." Beyond this triadic racialized and racist predicament, though, is the weight of white history and how it structures these events. My being stopped is part and parcel of the sedimentation of historically embedded racist images, stereotypes, narratives, and emotions, and epistemological, though distorted, frames of reference regarding the Black body and the white body. And while it is true that what has counted as "the white body" (or who is white) has waxed and waned throughout American history, whiteness continues to exist as the site of racist and racialized hegemony, and the stabilization of the Black body as "the problem body" is rarely, if ever, unclear. Of course, this raises the important question of how Italians, Irish, Jews, and others "became white."

My objective, in the context of the classroom, is to draw out the deeper ethical and ontological issues embedded within Kaufman's example. I want my students to grasp Heschel's point that while they might not be as "guilty" as the white security guard who follows me, they are, nevertheless, responsible. Hence the white bodies that get to shop are doing so at my expense, to my detriment, and thus they are all responsible for my predicament. That is the ethical quagmire. Their white bodies are not immune, as it were, to affecting my pain and suffering. The history of white supremacy saturates those presumed "innocent" spaces of shopping, while whiteness gets performed, reenacted, within the space of that store. Being able to shop without being stopped discloses the reality of white racist lived history, ever present, ever constitutive. And while shopping is such a benign activity, it is my objective to enlarge the frame of reference that my white students have come to adopt, one that has shaped them into an "atomized and passive citizenry."[24] I want them to understand that their "passivity" implicates them in the phenomenologically lived Black embodied turmoil that I undergo. In short, they are complicit. My aim is to get them to rethink the distinction between "spectacular" racist events (say, a lynching) and the "mundane" types; both are destructive. Heschel writes, "What we face is a human emergency" (72). In that store, I want my white students to face the urgency of my pain, to realize that my suffering and their sense of "innocence" constitute a human emergency. I want them "to feel ashamed of [their] peace of mind" (176) while shopping, reading about themselves as the creators of civilization in history books, or reading about how they gave birth to reason itself.



According to Heschel, "Daily we should take account and ask: What have I done today *to alleviate the anguish, to mitigate the evil, to prevent humiliation*?" (74). That is the question that my white students seem afraid to ask with respect to Black bodies and bodies of color. The question is prophetic, for it asks that my white students tarry with, face head-on, the issue of their own ethical complicity in the perpetuation of racial injustice. Heschel's question also raises what I am calling an ethics and an ontology of no edges. Their white bodies are always already haptic vis-à-vis Black bodies and bodies of color. There is no edge to their white bodies. Contiguous within a racialized and racist social integument, my white students' modes of being, or what Barbara Applebaum calls their "white ways of being,"[25] constitute sites of ontological relationality that are indivisible; hence, whether "passive" or active with respect to the perpetuation of racialized injustice, whiteness sunders, as Heschel puts it, "the flesh of living [Black] humanity" (65).

Unafraid to speak courageously, King says, "I am sorry to have to say that the vast majority of white Americans are racists, either consciously or unconsciously."[26] "Dear White America" said as much. My contention was that to be white in America is to be racist. It was not meant to encourage unproductive guilt but to encourage white people to undo the masks of "innocence" they live behind. And isn't this, after all, a species of love? James Baldwin was right: "Love takes off the masks that we fear we cannot live without and know that we cannot live with." Baldwin sees this love not as infantile or consisting of that which simply makes us happy, but he understands love as a "universal sense of quest and daring and growth."[27] And so, in "Dear White America," I dared to look beneath the mask of my sexist "innocence," I dared to grow, laying bare the ways in which, consciously or unconsciously, I am sexist.

It wasn't about confession, especially as we often expect redemption after confessing. I didn't seek redemption. My aim was to complicate my "peace of mind," to interrogate my "integrity," to trouble my smug certainty regarding my "honesty." Without conflating the Holocaust with the oppression of women under patriarchy and sexism, perhaps we should also critically ask in reference to the latter what Heschel asked in relationship to the former: "Has mankind become less cruel, less callous?" (177). My response: By no stretch of the imagination.



Heschel raises the stakes. In 1968, he writes, "Martin Luther King is a voice, a vision, and a way. I call upon every Jew to harken to his voice, to share his vision, to follow in his way. The whole future of America will depend upon the impact and influence of Dr. King" (84). West says that those words by Heschel "still haunt us." West elaborates, "The fundamental question is: Does America have the capacity to hear and heed the radical King or must America sanitize King in order to evade and avoid his challenge?" It seems to me that it is and has been the latter. And while King, like all of us, was a broken vessel, his prophetic voice continues to seriously challenge us in 2020. Given the stark material and political inequalities in our contemporary moment, the reality of those who are suffering from starvation, oppression, and brutalization, what is to be done? King spoke out against the seductions of materialism, the brutalities of militarism, and the unequivocal malaise of those who live in poverty. The earth itself is under our collective oppression. It, too, suffers. It, too, needs to be repaired. And yet most of us remain silent, callous, afraid. As West says, "Clever gimmicks of mass distraction yield a cheap soulcraft of addicted and self-medicated narcissists."[28] Of the "prophets," Heschel writes, "There are so many pretenders" (63). As guided drones kill civilians in Yemen and Somalia, and as air strikes kill civilians in Mosul, and as white supremacists kill innocent people in Charleston, South Carolina, Pittsburgh, Pennsylvania, Gilroy, California, and El Paso, Texas, King's voice has been muted. What is lacking is a sense of the "*monstrosity of inequality*" (69), but also lacking is the sense of the monstrosity of global suffering, the suffering of those whom *we* share the earth with or walk by each day. Not seeing such suffering is also a disease of the eye, a cancer of the soul. We are, for the most part, a people who prefer to sleep. Socrates knew this during his own time. An ethics of no edges, and a radical rethinking of a relational ontology where the body does not terminate at some fictive corporeal edge, encourages a different response from each of us. The connections are already there, both local and global. We are already touching. Yet we remain callous, milquetoast, spineless, silent, and often brutally indifferent. I'm still listening for the scream in the night.

Heschel asks, "Where does moral religious leadership in America come from today?" (83). In 2019, I don't have the answer. But it must come from those voices that refuse to allow the world to remain as it is. It must come from those who emphasize "the speciousness of tranquility" (178). It must come from those who find it hard to sleep, "a person who suffers the harm done to others" (86). We need a religiosity that is discontented with so much suffering, one that is emboldened by parrhesia and an ethical rage that refuses to be silent or silenced. If religious faith is to become a living and transformative reality, then it must be prepared to reject those idols to which we cling even as our brothers and sisters suffer under the weight of such idolatry. If racism divides and murders, then what are forms of religious idolatry that render the human heart indifferent to another's pain? A robust ethics, a Jewish ethics, a Christian ethics, must dispense with idols. I end (or perhaps it's a beginning) with Heschel. "What is an idol? *Any god who is mine but not yours*, any god concerned with me but not with you, *is an idol*" (66). That, it seems to me, is the *scream* in the night with which we must begin.



### Notes

1. Heschel, *Essential Writings*, 63.
2. West, "Moral Obligations," 5.
3. Ibid., 6.
4. Heschel, *Essential Writings*, 90 (hereafter cited parenthetically in the text).
5. Young, "Who Belongs to Christ," 134.
6. West, with Ritz, *Brother West*, 147, 148.
7. King, *Testament of Hope*, 299.
8. Douglass, *Life of Frederick Douglass*, 105.
9. Fanon, *Black Skin, White Masks*, 109.
10. Seshadri-Crooks, *Desiring Whiteness*, 20.
11. Katie Rogers and Nicholas Fandos, "Trump Tells Congresswomen to 'Go Back' to the Countries They Came From," *New York Times*, July 14, 2019.
12. Feagin, Vera, and Batur, *White Racism*, xii.
13. Birt, "Bad Faith of Whiteness," 58.
14. King, *Testament of Hope*, 290.
15. Charles Mills coined the term "epistemology of ignorance." See *Racial Contract*.
16. Butler, *Giving an Account of Oneself*, 103.
17. Smith, *Killers of the Dream*, 28.
18. Cone, *Black Theology of Liberation*, 74.
19. Butler, *Precarious Life*, 26.
20. Butler, *Giving an Account of Oneself*, 65.
21. King, *Testament of Hope*, 290.
22. Applebaum, *Being White, Being Good*, 5. The statement that whites' "very being depends on it" is from Leonardo, "Flipping the Script."
23. Kaufman, "User's Guide to White Privilege," 32.
24. Protevi, *Political Affect*, 163.
25. Applebaum, *Being White, Being Good*, 29.
26. See https://drewdellinger.org/58-tweetable-mlk-quotes-to-reclaim-kings-legacy.
27. Baldwin, *Fire Next Time*, 94.
28. Cornel West, "Introduction: The Radical King We Don't Know," in King, *Radical King*, x, xi.
29. Mishnah *Yoma* 8:9.

## References


Applebaum, Barbara. *Being White, Being Good: White Complicity, White Moral Responsibility, and Social Justice Pedagogy*. Lanham, Md.: Lexington Books, 2010.

Baldwin, James. *The Fire Next Time*. New York: Modern Library, 1995.

Birt, Robert. "The Bad Faith of Whiteness." In *What White Looks Like: African-American Philosophers on the Whiteness Question*, edited by George Yancy, 55–64. New York: Routledge, 2004.

Butler, Judith. *Giving an Account of Oneself*. New York: Fordham University Press, 2005.

———. *Precarious Life: The Powers of Mourning and Violence*. New York: Verso, 2006.

Cone, James H. *A Black Theology of Liberation*. Maryknoll, N.Y.: Orbis Books, 2005.

Douglass, Frederick. *Narrative of the Life of Frederick Douglass, an American Slave, Written by Himself*. Edited by David W. Blight. New York: Bedford / St. Martin's Press, 1993.

Fanon, Frantz. *Black Skin, White Masks*. Translated by Charles Lam Markmann. New York: Grove Press, 1967.

Feagin, Joe R., Hernán Vera, and Pinar Batur. *White Racism: The Basics*. New York: Routledge, 1995.

Heschel, Abraham Joshua. *Abraham Joshua Heschel: Essential Writings*. Edited by Susannah Heschel. Maryknoll, N.Y.: Orbis Books, 2011.

Kaufman, Cynthia. "A User's Guide to White Privilege." *Radical Philosophy Review* 4, nos. 1–2 (2002): 30–38.

King, Martin Luther, Jr. *The Radical King*. Edited by Cornel West. Boston: Beacon Press, 2015.

———. *A Testament of Hope: The Essential Writings and Speeches of Martin Luther King, Jr.* Edited by James M. Washington. New York: HarperCollins, 1991.

Leonardo, Zeus. "Flipping the Script . . . and Still a Problem: Staying in the Anxiety of Being a Problem." In *White Self-Criticality Beyond Anti-Racism: How Does It Feel to Be a White Problem?*, edited by George Yancy, 1–19. Lanham, Md.: Rowman and Littlefield, 2015.

Mills, Charles W. *The Racial Contract*. Ithaca: Cornell University Press, 1999.

Protevi, John. *Political Affect: Connecting the Social and the Somatic*. Minneapolis: University of Minnesota Press, 2009.

Seshadri-Crooks, Kalpana. *Desiring Whiteness: A Lacanian Analysis of Race*. New York: Routledge, 2000.

Smith, Lillian. *Killers of the Dream*. New York: W. W. Norton, 1994.

West, Cornel. "The Moral Obligations of Living in a Democratic Society." In *The Good Citizen*, edited by David Batstone and Eduardo Mendieta, 5–12. New York: Routledge, 1999.

West, Cornel, with David Ritz. *Brother West: Living and Loving Out Loud; A Memoir*. New York: SmileyBooks, 2009.

Young, Josiah U., III. "Who Belongs to Christ?" In *Christology and Whiteness: What Would Jesus Do?*, edited by George Yancy, 128–35. New York: Routledge, 2012.




### Classic Text and Questions to Ponder

Yancy bemoans the insidious nature of white racism and how it pervades nearly every crevice of society. He considers it his duty to awaken others, especially white students and fellow citizens, to the fact that they hold within themselves racist ideologies and practices, even if only unwittingly. He proposes an ethics without edges that disturbs people's racist slumber and rouses them to question their impulses to differentiate, divide, denigrate, damage, and damn others. Following Abraham Joshua Heschel, he calls for a religion "unafraid to critique whiteness, unafraid to trouble its privilege and its sites of institutional embeddedness and psychic opacity." His is a call for self-critical interruption. On Yom Kippur, the holiest of holy days, Judaism requires that its members interrupt themselves with searing self-criticism. People are to investigate their patterns and passions, behaviors and intentions, so to acknowledge waywardness and unrighteousness and to commit to doing better. A Mishnah rules: "If a person says, 'I will sin and I will repent, I will sin and I will repent'—he will be given no opportunity to repent. [If he says,] 'I will sin and Yom Kippur will effect atonement'—Yom Kippur does not effect atonement. For transgressions between man and God, Yom Kippur effects atonement. For transgressions between man and his fellow—Yom Kippur does not effect atonement, until he appeases his fellow."[29] Sinners expecting future repentance to atone for the wrongs habitually done will come to think their transgressions permitted. The one who thinks the holiness of Yom Kippur will fix the wrongs done is also mistaken. Yom Kippur atones for wrongs done toward God. The vast majority of human waywardness, however, is social, and the only way to ensure that one's repentance is efficacious is to seek out the victims' forgiveness. Laziness is no virtue here. One must conscientiously interrupt one's assumptions and habits and deliberately seek the forgiveness of those whom one has harmed. Heschel pushes this task beyond the confines of Yom Kippur when he says, "Daily we should take account and ask: What have I done today *to alleviate the anguish, to mitigate the evil, to prevent humiliation*?"

- Heschel considers callousness and indifference a sin, something for which one can atone. Do you agree? Why or why not?
- Yancy's ethics without edges rests on an observation that human bodies don't interact at some abstract benign distance but physically touch and bump into each other (e.g., haptic, contiguous, integument), branding some as Black and denigrated and others as white and privileged. If this borderless ethic is to succeed, it requires the death of "white monadic identity with presumptive discrete edges." Might this challenge be given to Jewish ethics as well—to acknowledge that Jewish identity does not have untouched discrete edges?
- Yancy invokes Applebaum to claim that all whites, even if not personally guilty of racist attitudes and behaviors, are responsible for them. Could something similar be said about all non-Jews—that even if not personally guilty of anti-Semitic attitudes and behaviors, they are responsible for them? Why or why not?

# Contributors

**Jonathan K. Crane** is the author of *Eating Ethically: Religion and Science for a Better Diet* and *Narratives and Jewish Bioethics*, the editor of *Beastly Morality: Animals as Ethical Agents*, co-editor of *The Oxford Handbook of Jewish Ethics and Morality* (with Elliot N. Dorff), co-author of *Ahimsa: The Way to Peace*, and founder and co-editor of the *Journal of Jewish Ethics*. He is a past president of the Society of Jewish Ethics, a former Wexner Graduate Fellow, and the recipient of an honorary degree from Wheaton College in Massachusetts. As the Raymond F. Schinazi Scholar in Bioethics and Jewish Thought at the Emory University Center for Ethics, he is an associate professor of medicine and of religion.

**Sander L. Gilman** is a distinguished professor of the liberal arts and sciences and professor of psychiatry at Emory University. A cultural and literary historian, he is the author or editor of well over ninety books, including recently *Stand Up Straight! A History of Posture*, and *The Oxford Handbook of Music and the Body*. His earlier works *Seeing the Insane* and *Jewish Self-Hatred* are considered classics in their fields. He has taught in distinguished positions at Cornell University, the University of Chicago, and the University of Illinois at Chicago, and has been a visiting scholar at the National Library of Medicine in Maryland, the Center for Advanced Study in the Behavioral Sciences at Stanford, the American Academy in Berlin, Oxford University, the Institute for the Humanities at Birkbeck College, the University of Hong Kong, and many other universities in North America, South Africa, the United Kingdom, Germany, Israel, China, and New Zealand. He was president of the Modern Language Association in 1995. He was awarded an honorary Doctor of Laws degree at the University of Toronto in 1997, elected an honorary professor of the Free University of Berlin (2000) and an honorary member of the American Psychoanalytic Association (2007), and made a Fellow of the American Academy of Arts and Sciences (2016).

**Annalise E. Glauz-Todrank** focuses on the intersections of religion, race, and law in the configuration of Jewish identification, particularly in the modern period. She investigates how these socially constructed categories become normalized, instantiate institutional inequalities, and shape conceptions of the self and the other. Currently, she is completing a book titled *Judging Jewish Identity in the United States: A Critical Race Theory*, in which she examines the 1987 U.S. Supreme Court case that provided race-based civil rights protection to Jewish Americans for the first time. Her recent publications include articles in *Religion Compass*, *Critical Research on Religion*, and *Who Is a Jew? Reflections on History, Religion, and Culture*, edited by Leonard Greenspoon. She has served as an assistant professor in the Department for the Study of Religions at Wake Forest University since 2012. Previously, she taught at Wesleyan University and at the University of California, Santa Barbara, where she earned her MA and PhD in religious studies. Her BA is from Hampshire College.



**Aaron S. Gross** is an associate professor at the University of San Diego, where he serves as the Jewish studies specialist in the Department of Theology and Religious Studies. Gross is a historian of religions who focuses on modern and contemporary Jewish thought and ethics. He is a past president of the Society of Jewish Ethics and the founder and CEO of the nonprofit advocacy organization Farm Forward. He is the author of numerous articles and two books, including *The Question of the Animal and Religion: Theoretical Stakes, Practical Implications*.

**Susannah Heschel** is the Eli Black Professor and chair of the Jewish Studies Program at Dartmouth College. She is the author of *Abraham Geiger and the Jewish Jesus* and *The Aryan Jesus: Christian Theologians and the Bible in Nazi Germany*, and of numerous articles and edited volumes, including *Insider/Outsider: American Jews and Multiculturalism* (with David Biale and Michael Galchinsky). She has held research grants from the Carnegie Foundation and the Ford Foundation, a Rockefeller fellowship at the National Humanities Center, and a yearlong fellowship at the Wissenschaftskolleg in Berlin. Currently a Guggenheim Fellow, she recently completed a book on European Jewish scholarship on Islam titled *Jüdischer Islam: Islam und jüdisch-deutsche Selbstbestimmung*, published by Matthes und Seitz as part of the Fröhliche Wissenschaft series.

**Sarah Imhoff** is an assistant professor in the Department of Religious Studies and the Borns Jewish Studies Program at Indiana University. She writes about religion and the body, with a particular interest in gender, sexuality, and American Judaism. She is also interested in the role of DNA and genetic discourse in constructions of Jewishness, race and Jewishness in the American context, and the history of the field of religious studies, especially in its relation to U.S. law. Her first book, *Masculinity and the Making of American Judaism* (2017), explored the ways in which the categories of gender and "good" religion shaped each other in the early twentieth-century United States. Her current book project considers what it means when our embodied lives do not match our religious and political ideals, largely by considering the life of a queer disabled American Zionist woman named Jessie Sampter.

**Willa M. Johnson** earned her doctoral degree in Hebrew Bible at Vanderbilt University. She is an associate professor in the Department of Sociology and Anthropology at the University of Mississippi. Since completing her first book, *The Holy Seed Has Been Defiled: The Interethnic Marriage Dilemma in Ezra 9–10*, she has published a variety of journal articles. At present, she is finishing a book manuscript that analyzes Karl Schwesig's artworks created from 1933 to 1945. The book investigates National Socialism's torture, violence, and ill treatment of avant-garde artists, Communists, and Düsseldorf's Jewish community, and it examines these artworks for empirical evidence about the social conditions affecting Jewish refugees in three French concentration camps from May 1940 until June 1943.

**Judith W. Kay**, professor emerita of religious and social ethics and African American studies at the University of Puget Sound, earned her PhD jointly from the Graduate Theological Union and the University of California, Berkeley. Her essays relevant to this volume include "Middle Agents as Marginalized: How the Rwanda Genocide Challenges Ethics from the Margins"; "The Exodus and Racism: Paradoxes for Jewish Liberation"; "Is Restitution Possible for Murder? Surviving Family Members Speak," in *Wounds That Do Not Bind: Victim-Based Perspectives on the Death Penalty*; and "Murder Victims' Families for Reconciliation: Story-Telling for Healing, as Witness, and in Public Policy," in *Handbook of Restorative Justice: A Global Perspective*. In *Murdering Myths: The Story Behind the Death Penalty*, she argues that bystanders, wrongdoers, and punishers tell a retributive story that recycles violence. Twice selected for study at the Center for Advanced Holocaust Studies at the U.S. Holocaust Memorial Museum, Kay developed and taught for two decades the only Holocaust course at the University of Puget Sound. She is a Roothbert Fellow and has held many roles with the Justice Studies Association and the Society of Christian Ethics. She has also been a leader in Puget Sound's Race and Pedagogy Institute since its inception in 2004.

**Jessica Kirzane** is the Assistant Instructional Professor of Yiddish at the University of Chicago. She holds a PhD in Yiddish studies from Columbia University, where her dissertation focused on inter-ethnic romance in Jewish American fiction in Yiddish and English in the early twentieth century. Kirzane is the editor-in-chief of *In geveb: A Journal of Yiddish Studies*. She was a 2017 Translation Fellow and a 2018 Pedagogy Fellow at the Yiddish Book Center. Kirzane is the translator of *Diary of a Lonely Girl, or the Battle against Free Love* by Miriam Karpilove.

**Nichole Renée Phillips** is a sociologist of religion and the Associate Professor in the Practice of Sociology of Religion and Culture as well as the Director of the Black Church Studies program at Candler School of Theology, a Senior Faculty Fellow at the Center for Ethics, an Associate Faculty member of Emory's Sociology Department, and a university-wide Andrew W. Mellon Foundation Humanistic Inquiry Fellow. Her areas of research and teaching interest include community and congregational studies at the intersection of religion and American public life; religion, culture, and society; race, ethnicity, and gender; and the use of the sociology and anthropology of religion to explore the moral commitments of individuals in institutional settings. An ordained itinerant elder in the African Methodist Episcopal Church, Phillips first monograph, *Patriotism Black and White: The Color of American Exceptionalism* was published in 2018.

**George Yancy** is the Samuel Candler Dobbs professor of philosophy at Emory University. His work focuses primarily on the critical philosophy of race, critical whiteness studies, critical phenomenology, and philosophy of the black experience. His books include *Black Bodies, White Gazes*; *Exploring Race in Predominantly White Classrooms: Scholars of Color Reflect*; *Pursuing Trayvon Martin: Historical Contexts and Contemporary Manifestations of Racial Dynamics*; *Look, a White! Philosophical Essays on Whiteness*; and *Critical Perspectives on bell hooks*, many of which have received national critical awards. His latest books are *Our Black Sons Matter*, coedited by Maria Davidson and Susan Hanley and selected as a *Booklist* Top 10 Diverse Nonfiction book of 2017; *On Race: 34 Conversations in a Time of Crisis*; and the second edition of *Black Bodies, White Gazes*; *Buddhism and Whiteness: Critical Reflections*; *Educating for Critical Consciousness*; and, *Across Black Spaces: Essays and Interviews by an American Philosopher*. His book *Backlash: What Happens When We Talk Honestly About Racism in America* is based upon his controversial article "Dear White America," which was published in the *New York Times* in 2015. Yancy is the editor of the Philosophy of Race book series at Lexington Books, and is known for his influential interviews and controversial articles on the subject of race at the *New York Times* online philosophy series The Stone.

# Index